PLANNING, IMPLEMENTING, AND EVALUATING HEALTH PROMOTION PROGRAMS

A Primer

Second Edition

James F. McKenzie
Ball State University

Jan L. Smeltzer
Lake Hospital System, Painesville, Ohio

Allyn and Bacon
Boston • London • Toronto • Sydney • Tokyo • Singapore

This book is dedicated to four special people—
Bonnie, Anne, Hilary, and Mike—
and to our teachers and mentors—
Marshall H. Becker (deceased), Mary K. Beyrer,
Noreen M. Clark, Nancy Kinney, Terry W. Parsons,
Irwin M. Rosenstock, and Yuzuru J. Takeshita

Senior Editor: Suzy Spivey
Editorial Assistant: Lisa Davidson
Marketing Manager: Quinn Perkson
Production Administrator: Annette Joseph
Production Coordinator: Susan Freese
Editorial-Production Service: Karen Mason
Manufacturing Buyer: Megan Cochran
Cover Administrator: Suzanne Harbison

A Viacom Company
160 Gould Street
Needham Heights, MA 02194-2310

Library of Congress Cataloging-in-Publication Data

McKenzie, James F.
Planning, implementing, and evaluating health promotion programs : a primer / James F. McKenzie, Jan L. Smeltzer. -- 2nd ed.
p. cm.
Includes bibliographical references and index.
ISBN 0-205-20069-9
1. Health promotion--Planning. 2. Health promotion--Evaluation.
I. Smeltzer, Jan L. II. Title.
RA427.8.M393 1996
613'.068--dc10 96-9109

CIP

Printed in the United States of America

10 9 8 7 6 5 4 3 2 1 01 00 99 98 97 96

Contents

Preface

As its title states, this textbook is a primer and was written for students who are enrolled in their first professional course in health promotion program development. It was designed to help them understand and develop the skills necessary to carry out program development regardless of the setting. The book is unique among the health program–planning textbooks on the market in that it provides readers with both theoretical and practical information. A straightforward, step-by-step format is used to make concepts clear and the full process of health promotion programming understandable. This book also provides, under a single cover, material on all three areas of program development—planning, implementing, and evaluating.

LEARNING AIDS

Each chapter of the book includes chapter objectives, a list of key terms, presentation of content, chapter summary, review questions, and activities. In addition, many of the key concepts are further explained with information presented in figures, tables, and the appendixes.

Chapter objectives. The chapter objectives identify the content and skills that should be mastered after reading the chapter, answering the end-of-chapter questions, and completing the activities. Most of the objectives are written using the cognitive and psychomotor (behavior) educational domains. For most effective use of the objectives, we suggest that they be reviewed before reading the chapter. This will help readers focus on the major points in each chapter and will facilitate answering the questions and completing the activities at the end.

Key terms. Key terms are introduced in each chapter of the textbook and are important to the understanding of the chapter. The terms are presented in a list at the beginning of each chapter and then are printed in boldface at the appropriate points within the chapter. Again, as with the chapter objectives, we suggest that readers skim the list before reading the chapter. Then as the chapter is read, particular attention should be paid to the definition of each term.

Presentation of content. Although each chapter in this book could be expanded—in some cases, entire books have been written on topics we have covered in a chapter or less—we believe that each chapter contains the necessary information to help readers understand and develop many of the skills required to be a successful health promotion program planner, implementor, and evaluator.

Chapter summary. At the end of each chapter, readers will find a one- or two-paragraph review of the major concepts contained in the chapter.

Review Questions. The purpose of the questions at the end of each chapter is to provide readers with some feedback regarding their mastery of the content. We have endeavored to ask questions that would reinforce the chapter objectives and key terms presented in each chapter.

Activities. The final portion of each chapter consists of several activities that will allow readers to put their new knowledge and skills to use. The activities are presented in several different formats for the sake of variety and to appeal to the different learning styles of readers. It should be noted that, depending on the ones selected for completion, the activities in one chapter can build on those in a previous chapter and lead to the final product of a completely developed health promotion program.

NEW TO THIS EDITION

In revising this textbook, we incorporated as many suggestions from reviewers, colleagues, and former students as possible. In addition to updating material throughout the text, the following points reflect the major changes in this new edition:

- Chapter 4 on needs assessment and how to acquire needs assessment data has been reformatted to make it more usable for students.
- A new Chapter 5 consolidates all data collection information to eliminate any confusion over data collection for needs assessment and evaluation.
- In Chapter 6, an expanded section on writing objectives for health promotion programs now differentiates between *program objectives* and *learning objectives.*
- More information on applying theory to practice has been added to Chapter 7 to assist students in making that transition.
- In Chapter 14, evaluation models and designs have been reworked to focus the material in a single chapter.

Readers will find this textbook easy to understand and use. We are confident that if the chapters are carefully read and an honest effort is put into completing the activities, readers will gain the essential knowledge and skills for program planning, implementation, and evaluation.

ACKNOWLEDGMENTS

A project of this nature could not have been completed without the assistance and understanding of many individuals. First, we thank all our past and present students, who have had to put up with our "working drafts" of the manuscript.

Second, we are grateful to those professionals who took the time and effort to review and comment on various editions of this book. For the first edition, they include Vicki Keanz, Eastern Kentucky University; Susan Cross Lipnickey, Miami University; Fred Pearson, Ricks College; Kerry Redican, Virginia Tech; John Sciacca, Northern Arizona University; and William K. Spath, Montana Tech. For the second edition, reviewers include Gordon James, Weber State; John Sciacca, Northern Arizona University; and Mark Wilson, University of Georgia.

Third, we thank our friends Robert J. Yonker, Ph.D., professor in the Department of Educational Foundations and Inquiry, Bowling Green State University, and Lawrence W. Green, Dr.P.H., director of the Institute of Health Promotion Research and professor in the Department of Health Care and Epidemiology at the University of British Columbia, for providing valuable feedback on selected portions of our manuscript.

Fourth, we appreciate the work of Allyn and Bacon employees Suzy Spivey, senior acquisitions editor for health and physical education, and Lisa Davidson, editorial assistant, for their work. We also appreciate the careful work of Karen Mason, who oversaw production of this edition.

Finally, we want to express our deepest appreciation to our families for their support, encouragement, and understanding of the time that writing takes away from our family activities.

J. F. M.
J. L. S.

1

Health Education, Health Promotion, Health Educators, and Program Development

After reading this chapter and answering the questions at the end, you should be able to:

- Explain the relationship between good health behavior, health education, and health promotion.
- Write your own definition of health education.
- Explain the role of the health educator as defined by the Role Delineation Project.
- Explain how the Framework for Competency-Based Health Education is used by the National Council for the Accreditation of Teacher Education (NCATE), the National Commission for Health Education Credentialing, Inc. (NCHEC), and the SOPHE/AAHE Baccalaureate Program Approval Committee (SABPAC).
- Identify the assumptions upon which health education is based.
- Name the generic components for developing a program.

Key Terms

entry-level health educator
health behavior
health education
health educator
health promotion
health promotion and disease prevention
primary care givers
primary prevention
Role Delineation Project
secondary prevention
target population
tertiary prevention

The concern of American people about good health, wellness, and health behavior has reached new heights in recent years, and rightfully so. We now know that better control of behavioral risk factors alone—such as lack of exercise, poor diet, use of tobacco and drugs, and alcohol abuse—could prevent between 40 and 70% of all premature deaths, one-third of all acute disabilities, and two-thirds of chronic disabilities (USDHHS, 1990b).

Although many events, research studies, and publications have contributed to this focus on health and **health behavior** (those behaviors that impact a person's health), there may be none more important than the government publication *Healthy People: The Surgeon General's Report on Health Promotion and Disease Prevention* (*Healthy People*, 1979). This document brought together much of what was known about the relationship of personal behavior and health status. The document also presented a "personal responsibility" model that provided Americans with a prescription for reducing their health risks and increasing their chances for good health.

It may not have been the content of *Healthy People* that made the publication so significant, because several publications written before it provided a similar message. *Healthy People* was important because it summarized the research available up to that point, presented it in a very readable format, and made the information available to the general public. *Healthy People* launched us into the health promotion phase of public health history. The message of *Healthy People* was spread so well that there are few Americans today who do not know the importance of good health behavior.

This focus on health has given many people in the United States a desire to do something about their health. This desire in turn has created a greater need for good health information that can be easily understood by the average person. One need only look at the current best-seller list, read the daily newspaper, observe the health advertisements delivered via the mass media, or consider the increase in the number of health-promoting facilities (not illness or sickness facilities) to verify the interest that American consumers have in health. Because of the increased interest in health, health professionals are now faced with providing the public with the health information they want and need.

HEALTH EDUCATION AND HEALTH PROMOTION

In the simplest terms, **health education** is the process of educating people about health. However, two more formal definitions of health education have been frequently cited in the literature. The first comes from the Joint Committee on Health Education Terminology report (1991, p. 103). The committee defined the health education process as the "continuum of learning which enables people, as individuals and as members of social structures, to voluntarily make decisions, modify behaviors, and change social conditions in ways which are health enhancing." The second definition was proposed by Green, Kreuter, Deeds, and Partridge (1980, p. 7). They defined health education as "any combination of learning experiences designed to facilitate voluntary adaptations of behavior conducive to health." The learning experiences noted in this definition are innumerable and could be placed on a continuum anchored by self-taught learning experiences on one end and by highly sophisticated, thoroughly planned, multiactivity learning experiences on the other. Obviously, each type of learning experience has the potential for educating the intended **target population** and has its own strengths and weaknesses.

Another term that is closely related to health education, and sometimes incorrectly used in its place, is **health promotion**. Health promotion is a broader term than health education. One of the early definitions of this term stated that health promotion was "any combination of health education and related organizational, political and economic interventions designed to facilitate behavioral and environmental adaptations that will improve or protect health" (USDHHS, 1980, p. 1). In this definition, *interventions* refers to systematically planned health promotion programs. A more recent definition of health promotion was offered by Green and Kreuter (1991, p. 4). They simplified the earlier definition to read: "the combination of educational and environmental supports for actions and conditions of living conducive to health." In this definition, *educational* refers to health education, and *environmental* refers to social, political, organizational, policy, economic, and regulatory circumstances bearing on health. A third definition of health promotion was provided in the Joint Committee on Health Education Terminology report (1991, p. 102). The committee defined **health promotion and disease prevention** as "the aggregate of all purposeful activities designed to improve personal and public health through a combination of strategies, including the competent implementation of behavioral change strategies, health education, health protection measures, risk factor detection, health enhancement and health maintenance." According to all three of these definitions of health promotion, health education is an important component of health promotion and firmly implanted in it (Figure 1.1). In other words, health education is one of several different intervention activities that can be used to promote health. "Without health education, health promotion would be a manipulative social engineering enterprise" (Green & Kreuter, 1991, p. 14).

The effectiveness of health promotion programs can vary greatly. However, the success of a program can usually be linked to the planning that takes place before implementation of the program. Programs that have undergone a thorough planning process are usually the most successful.

HEALTH EDUCATORS

The role of the **health educator** in the United States has evolved over time based upon the need to provide the public with good health information. The earliest signs of the role of the health educator appeared in the mid-1800s with school hygiene education, which was closely associated with physical activity. By the early 1900s, the need for health education spread to the public health arena, but it was the writers, journalists, social workers, and visiting nurses who were doing the educating—not health educators as we know them today (Deeds, 1992). As we gained

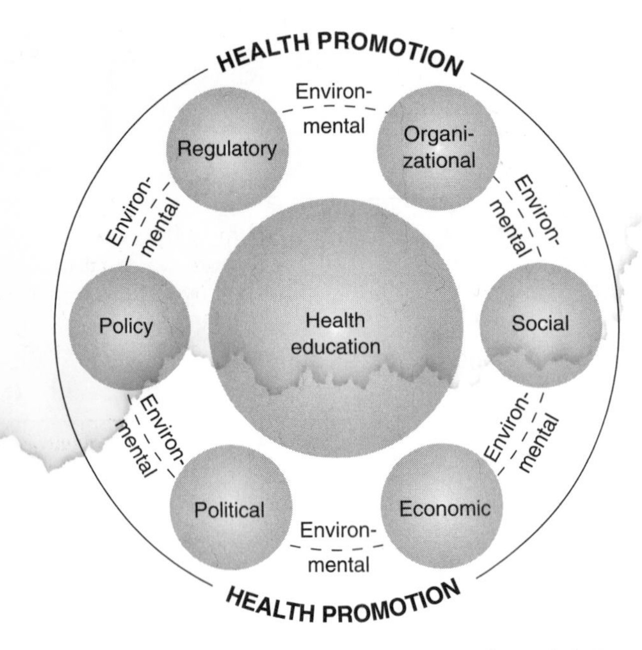

FIGURE 1.1 Relationship of Health Education and Health Promotion

more knowledge about the relationship between health, disease, and health behavior, it was obvious that the writers, journalists, social workers, visiting nurses, and **primary caregivers**—mainly physicians, dentists, other independent practitioners, and nurses—were unable to provide the needed health education. The combination of the heavy workload of the primary caregivers, the lack of formal training in the process of educating others, and the desire for education in the importance of **primary and secondary prevention** (see Figure 1.2) created a need for health educators.

Today, health educators can be found working in a variety of settings, including schools (K–12, colleges, and universities), community health agencies (official and nonofficial), worksites (business, industry, and other work settings), and medical settings (clinics, hospitals, and health maintenance organizations, or HMOs).

Though the need for health educators grew out of the need to deliver health information, the role has expanded over the years such that health educators are now involved in all aspects of health promotion. As the role of health educators has grown, there has been a movement by those in the discipline to clearly define their role so that people inside and outside the discipline would have a better understanding of what the health educator does. In 1978 the **Role Delineation Project** was begun (National Task Force [on the Preparation and Practice of Health Educators, Inc.], 1985). Through a comprehensive process, this project yielded a generic role for the **entry-level health educator**—that is, responsibilities for health educators taking their first job regardless of the work setting. In more recent years, the list of responsibilities has become known as "A Competency-Based Framework for Professional Development of Certified Health Education Specialists." This framework

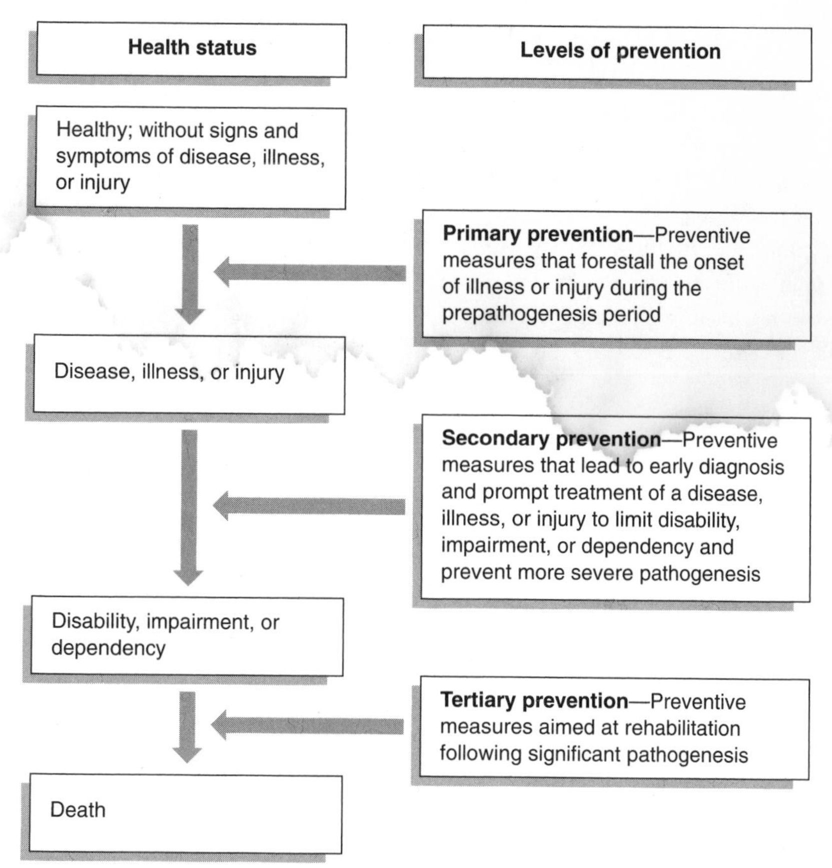

FIGURE 1.2 Levels of Prevention

Source: Adapted from *Public Health: Administration and Practice* by G. Pickett and J. J. Hanlon, 1990, St. Louis: Times Mirror/Mosby College Publishing.

comprises seven major areas of responsibility and several different competencies and subcompetencies, which further delineate the responsibilities. The seven major areas of responsibility identified through the Role Delineation Project include:

1. Assessing individual and community needs for health education.
2. Planning effective health education programs.
3. Implementing health education programs.
4. Evaluating the effectiveness of health education programs.
5. Coordinating provision of health education services.
6. Acting as a resource person in health education.
7. Communicating health and health education needs, concerns, and resources (National Task Force, 1985, pp. 15–16).

In reviewing the seven areas of responsibility, it is obvious that four of the seven are directly related to program planning, implementation, and evaluation and that

TABLE 1.1 Number of Certified Health Education Specialists

Year	Period	Number Certified
1989	Charter period (no certification test)	1,559
1990	Beginning of window period (certification test begins)	646
1991	End of window period	1,312
1992	Beginning of health education preparation required	199
1993	Health education preparation required	324
1994	Health education preparation required	315
1995	Health education preparation required	392

the other three could be associated with programming depending on the type of program being planned. In effect, these responsibilities distinguish health educators from other professionals who try to provide health education experiences.

The importance of the defined role of the health educator is becoming greater as the discipline of health education continues to grow. This is shown by its use in three major professional activities. First, the National Council for the Accreditation of Teacher Education (NCATE) uses the framework in reviewing and accrediting teacher education programs in institutions of higher education. If a college or university now wants its health education program to have NCATE accreditation, it must show how its curriculum provides opportunities for students to learn the knowledge and skills listed in the framework.

Second, the framework is used by the National Commission for Health Education Credentialing, Inc. (NCHEC) for certifying individuals as health educators (Certified Health Education Specialist, or CHES). In 1988, experienced health educators were permitted to apply for charter certification. Since 1990, individuals become certified by passing a national certification examination that is given annually in the fall. Table 1.1 provides information on those who have become certified through 1995.

Third, the framework is used by a joint committee of the Society for Public Health Education (SOPHE) and the Association for the Advancement of Health Education (AAHE), known as the SOPHE/AAHE Baccalaureate Program Approval Committee (SABPAC). The committee used the framework to develop a process by which colleges and universities could review their undergraduate health education programs. This framework is used as part of a self-study and by external reviewers to determine if the program being offered is of high quality.

ASSUMPTIONS OF HEALTH PROMOTION

So far we have discussed the need for health, what health education and health promotion are, and the role health educators play in delivering successful health promotion programs. We have not yet discussed the assumptions that underlie health promotion—all the things that must be in place before the whole process of health promotion begins. In the mid-1980s, Bates and Winder (1984) outlined what they saw as four critical assumptions of health education. We have modified their list by adding several items and referring to them as "assumptions of health promotion." We see this expanded list of assumptions as being critical to understanding what we can expect from health promotion programs. Health promotion is by no means the sole answer to the nation's health care problem or, for that matter, the sole means of getting the smoker to stop smoking or the nonexerciser to exercise. Health promotion is an important part of the health care system, but it does have limitations. Here are the assumptions:

1. Health status can be changed.
2. Disease occurrence theories and principles can be understood (Bates and Winder, 1984).
3. Appropriate prevention strategies can be developed to deal with the identified health problems (Bates and Winder, 1984).
4. An individual's health is affected by a variety of factors, not just lifestyle. Other factors include heredity, environment, and the health care system.
5. Changes in individual and societal health behaviors and lifestyles will affect an individual's health status positively (Bates and Winder, 1984).
6. "Individuals, families, small groups, and communities can be taught to assume responsibility for their health, which in turn changes their health behaviors and lifestyles" (Bates and Winder, 1984, p. 2).
7. Individual responsibility should not be viewed as victim blaming.
8. For health behavior change to be permanent, an individual must be motivated and ready to change.

The importance of these assumptions is made clearer if we refer to the definitions of health education presented earlier in the chapter. Implicit in those definitions was a goal of having the participants of health education programs voluntarily adopt health-enhancing behavior. To achieve such a goal, the assumptions must indeed be in place. We cannot expect people to adopt lifelong health-enhancing behavior if we force them into such change. Nor can we expect people to change their behavior just because they have been exposed to a health education program. Health behavior change is very complex, and health educators should not expect to change every person with whom they come in contact. However, the greatest chance for success will come to those who have the knowledge and skills to plan, implement, and evaluate appropriate programs.

PROGRAM DEVELOPMENT

Since many of health educators' responsibilities are involved in some way with program planning, implementation, and evaluation, health educators need to become

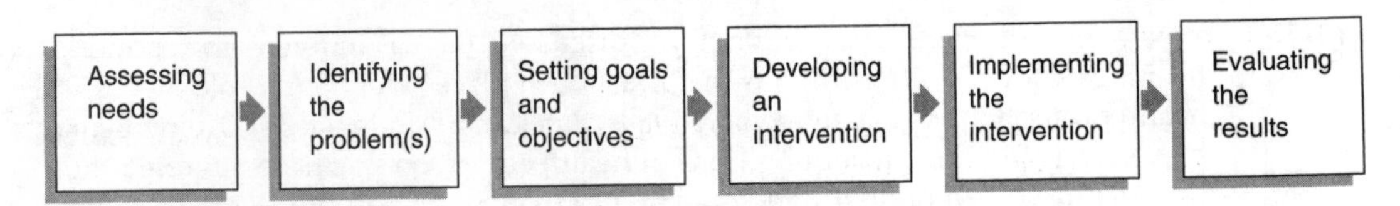

FIGURE 1.3 A Generalized Model for Program Development

well versed in these processes. "Planning an effective program is more difficult than implementing it. Planning, implementing, and evaluating programs are all interrelated, but good planning skills are prerequisite to programs worthy of evaluation" (Breckon, Harvey, and Lancaster, 1994, p. 115). All three processes are very involved, and much time, effort, practice, and on-the-job training are required to do them well. Even the most experienced health educators find program planning challenging because of the constant changes in settings, resources, and target populations.

Today, it is generally accepted that the process of health promotion can take many different forms. That is, there are many different ways of getting from point A to point B. However, all approaches usually center on a generic set of tasks that include:

1. Assessing the needs of the target population.
2. Identifying the problem(s).
3. Developing appropriate goals and objectives.
4. Creating an intervention that considers the peculiarities of the setting.
5. Implementing the intervention.
6. Evaluating the results (see Figure 1.3).

The remaining chapters of this book present a process that health educators can use to plan, implement, and evaluate successful health promotion programs and will introduce readers to the necessary knowledge and skills to carry out these tasks.

SUMMARY

The increased interest in personal health and the flood of new health information have created a need to provide quality health promotion programs. Individuals are seeking guidance to enable them to make sound decisions about behavior that would be conducive to their health. Those best prepared to help these people are health educators who have received appropriate training. Properly trained health educators are aware of the limitations of the discipline and understand the assumptions on which health promotion is based.

QUESTIONS

1. Explain the role *Healthy People* played in the relationship between the American people and health.
2. How is *health education* defined by the Joint Committee on Health Education Terminology (1991)?
3. What are the key phrases in the definition of health education presented by Green, Kreuter, Deeds, and Partridge (1980)?
4. What is the relationship between health education and health promotion?
5. Why is there a need for health educators?
6. What is the Role Delineation Project?
7. How is the Framework for Competency-Based Health Education used by NCATE? By NCHEC? By SABPAC?
8. What are the seven major responsibilities of health educators?
9. What assumptions are critical to health promotion?
10. What are the components of the generalized model for program development?

ACTIVITIES

1. Based upon what you have read in this chapter and your knowledge of the discipline of health education, write your own definitions for *health, health education, health promotion,* and *health promotion program.*
2. Write a response indicating what you see as the importance of each of the eight assumptions presented in the chapter. Write no more than one paragraph per assumption.
3. With your knowledge of health promotion, what other assumptions would you add to the list presented in this chapter? Provide a one-paragraph rationale for each.
4. If you have recently graduated from college or will be graduating soon, write or call the National Commission for Health Education Credentialing, Inc. (NCHEC) and request an application for the certification examination for health education specialists. NCHEC can be contacted at 944 Marcon Blvd., Suite 310, Allentown, PA 18103, by telephone (610) 264-8200, by fax (800) 813-0727, or by e-mail cogs101w@wonder.em.cdc.gov.
5. If you have not already done so, go to the government documents section of the library on your campus and read *Healthy People: The Surgeon General's Report on Health Promotion and Disease Prevention (Healthy People,* 1979).

2

Models for Health Education and Health Promotion Programming

After reading this chapter and answering the questions at the end, you should be able to:

- Explain the importance of using a model for planning a program.
- Identify the models most commonly used in planning health education and health promotion programs and briefly explain each.
- Identify the major components of the planning models.

Key Terms

administrative and policy diagnosis
behavioral and environmental diagnosis
educational and organizational diagnosis
EMPOWER
enabling factors
epidemiological diagnosis
evaluation
impact evaluation
outcome evaluation
PRECEDE-PROCEED
predisposing factors
process evaluation
reinforcing factors
social diagnosis

As noted in Chapter 1, a major portion of the role of the health educator is associated with health promotion programming—planning, implementing, and evaluating health education programs. Good health promotion programs are not created by chance; they are the product of much effort and should be based on well-developed models. Models are the means by which planners give structure and organization to the programming process. They provide planners with direction and supply a frame on which to build. Many different planning models have been developed, some of which are used more frequently than others. Although many of the models have common elements (sometimes with different labels), each has a slightly different perspective. No perfect model yet exists; instead, each has its own strengths and weaknesses.

Most planners find occasions when they do not need to use a model in its entirety or when it is necessary to combine parts of different models to meet specific needs and situations. As Gilmore, Campbell, and Becker (1989, p. 13) have pointed out, "It may not be feasible for every programming effort to use all of the cited considerations at each stage, [but] they do provide prompters for planning committee, and administrative discussions."

The remainder of this chapter will present the models most commonly used in planning health promotion programs. These are tried-and-true models that have been used in a variety of settings with many successes and some failures.

PRECEDE-PROCEED

Currently, the best known and most often used model for health promotion programming is the **PRECEDE-PROCEED** model. PRECEDE is an acronym for Predisposing, Reinforcing, and Enabling Constructs in Educational/Environmental Diagnosis and Evaluation. PROCEED stands for Policy, Regulatory, and Organizational Constructs in Educational and Environmental Development (Green & Kreuter, 1991).

PRECEDE-PROCEED is a model with which all students should become very familiar. It is considered "the model" by most in our profession and has been the basis for many professional projects at the national level. PRECEDE-PROCEED is well received because it is theoretically grounded and comprehensive in nature; it combines a series of phases in the planning, implementation, and evaluation process.

PRECEDE-PROCEED was developed over the course of about 15 to 20 years. The PRECEDE framework was conceived in the early 1970s (Green, 1974) and evolved as a planning model during the late 1970s (Green, 1975, 1976; Green, Levine, & Deeds, 1975; Green et al., 1978; Green, Kreuter, Deeds, & Partridge, 1980). This portion of the model "takes into account the multiple factors that shape health status and helps the planner arrive at a highly focused subset of those factors as targets for intervention. PRECEDE also generates specific objectives and criteria for evaluation" (Green & Kreuter, 1991, p. 22).

The PROCEED framework was developed in the 1980s (Green, 1979, 1980, 1981a, 1981b, 1982, 1983a, 1983b, 1984a, 1984b, 1984c, 1984d, 1986a, 1986b, 1986c,

1986d, 1986e, 1987a, 1987b; Green & Allen, 1980; Green & McAlister, 1984; Green, Mullen, & Friedman, 1986; Green, Wilson, & Lovato, 1986; Green, Wilson, & Bauer, 1983) and "is essentially an elaboration and extension of the administrative diagnosis step of PRECEDE, which was the final and least developed link in the PRECEDE framework" (Green & Kreuter, 1991, p. 25). It was influenced by the participation of the authors in national policy initiatives and the development of community health promotion programs such as Planned Approach to Community Health (PATCH) (Green & Kreuter, 1992).

The Nine Phases of PRECEDE-PROCEED

As can be seen in Figure 2.1, PRECEDE-PROCEED is composed of nine phases or steps. At first glance, the model seems overly complicated, but on close examination, the continuous series of steps reveals a very logical sequence for health promotion programming. The underlying approach of this model is to begin by identifying the desired outcome, to determine what causes it, and finally to design an intervention aimed at reaching the desired outcome. In other words, PRECEDE-PROCEED begins with the final consequences and works backward to the causes.

Phase 1 in the model is called **social diagnosis** and seeks to subjectively define the quality of life (problems and priorities) of those in the target population. The designers of this model suggest that this is best accomplished by involving individuals in the target population in a self-study of their own needs. Some of the social indicators of quality of life include absenteeism, alienation, crime, discrimination, happiness, illegitimacy, riots, self-esteem, unemployment, and welfare.

Phase 2, **epidemiological diagnosis,** is the step in which the planners use data to identify and rank the health goals or problems that may contribute to the needs identified in Phase 1. Those data might include disability, discomfort, fertility, fitness, morbidity, mortality, and physiological risk factors and their dimensions (distribution, duration, functional level, incidence, intensity, longevity, and prevalence). It is important to note that ranking the health problems in this phase is critical, because there are rarely, if ever, enough resources to deal with all or multiple problems.

Phase 3, **behavioral and environmental diagnosis,** involves determining and prioritizing the behavioral and environmental factors that might be linked to the health problems selected in Phase 2. Behavioral indicators include such things as compliance, consumption patterns, coping, preventive actions, self-care, and utilization. These indicators can be expressed in the dimensions of frequency, persistence, promptness, quality, and range (Green & Kreuter, 1991). As we mentioned in Chapter 1, *environmental* refers to the factors outside an individual that can be modified to support behavior, health, and quality of life. Examples of environmental indicators include economic, physical, services, and social, and their dimensions (access, affordability, and equity) (Green & Kreuter, 1991). Note that in Figure 2.1 arrows connect both of the boxes in Phase 3 with Phases 1 and 2. This suggests that programs attacking specific risk factors can also have an impact on social forces. The prioritization needed in this phase can be accomplished by first ranking the

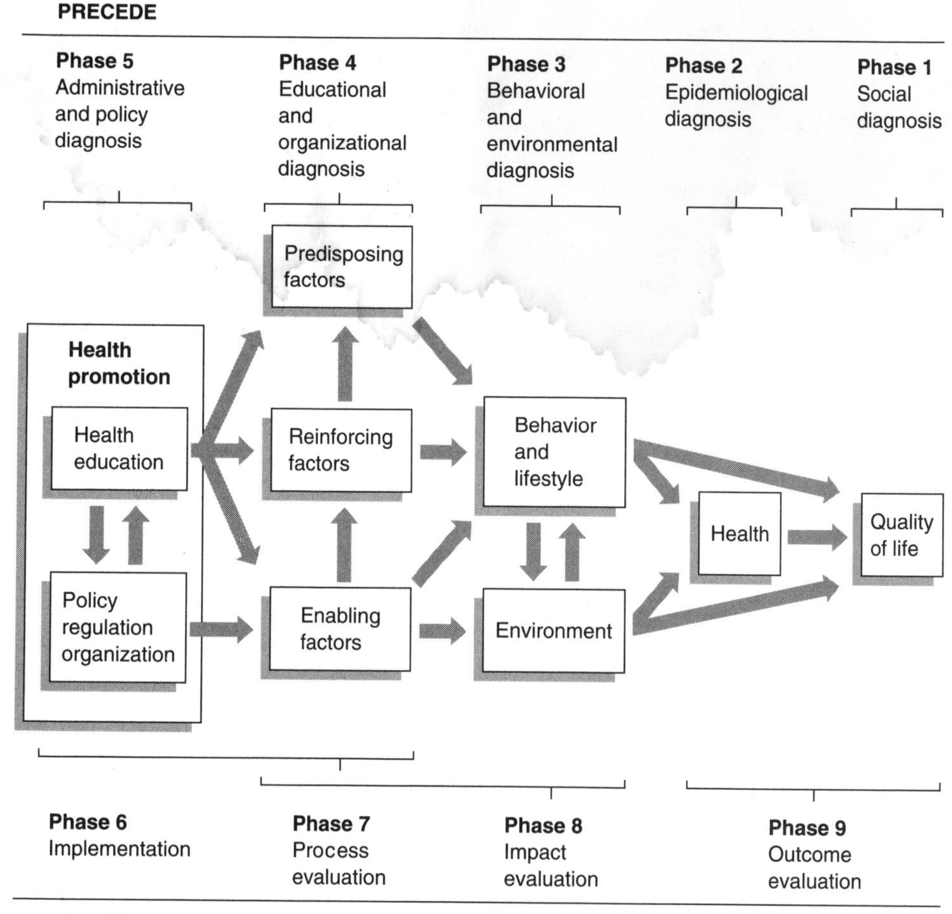

FIGURE 2.1 The PRECEDE-PROCEED Model for Health Promotion Planning and Evaluation

Source: Health Promotion Panning: An Educational and Environmental Approach, 2d ed. (p. 23) by L. W. Green and M. W. Kreuter, 1991, Palo Alto, CA: Mayfield Publishing. Copyright 1991 by Mayfield Publishing. Reprinted by permission.

factors by importance and changeability and then using the 2 × 2 matrix presented in Figure 2.2.

Phase 4, **educational and organizational diagnosis,** identifies and classifies the literally hundreds of factors that have the potential to influence a given behavior into three categories: predisposing, reinforcing, and enabling. **Predisposing factors** include knowledge and many affective traits such as a person's attitude, values, beliefs, and perceptions. These factors can facilitate or hinder a person's motivation to change and can be altered through *direct* communication. Barriers created mainly by

	More important	Less important
More changeable	High priority for program focus (quadrant 1)	Low priority except to demonstrate change for political purposes (quadrant 3)
Less changeable	Priority for innovative program; evaluation crucial (quadrant 2)	No program (quadrant 4)

FIGURE 2.2 Prioritization Matrix

Source: Health Promotion Panning: An Educational and Environmental Approach, 2d ed. (p. 140) by L. W. Green and M. W. Kreuter, 1991, Palo Alto, CA: Mayfield Publishing. Copyright 1991 by Mayfield Publishing. Reprinted by permission.

societal forces or systems make up **enabling factors,** which include access to health care facilities, availability of resources, referrals, rules or laws, and skills. These can be changed primarily through training for skills and community organization for barriers and resources. **Reinforcing factors** comprise the different types of feedback and rewards that those in the target population receive, which may either encourage or discourage them in changing their behavior. The reinforcing factors can be changed mainly by indirect communication through family, peers, teachers, employers, and others who control social rewards. As with the previous phases, planners must set priorities. The factors identified in this phase become the focus of the intervention that will be planned (Green & Kreuter, 1991).

Phase 5 consists of an **administrative and policy diagnosis,** in which planners determine if the capabilities and resources are available to develop and implement the program. It is between Phases 5 and 6 that PRECEDE (the diagnostic portion of the model) ends and PROCEED (implementation and evaluation) begins. However, there is not a clean break between the two phases; they really run together, and planners can move back and forth between them.

The four final phases of the model—Phases 6, 7, 8, and 9—make up the PROCEED portion. In Phase 6, with appropriate resources in hand, planners select the methods and strategies of the intervention and implementation begins. Phases 7, 8, and 9 focus on the **evaluation, process, impact,** and **outcome,** respectively and are based on the earlier phases of the model, when objectives were outlined in the diagnostic process. Whether all three of these final phases are used depends on the evaluation requirements of the program. Obviously, the resources needed to conduct evaluations of impact (Phase 8) and outcome (Phase 9) are much greater than those needed to conduct process evaluation (Phase 7). (See Chapter 6 for a discussion on the relationship of objectives to evaluation.)

Expert Methods for Planning and Organization within Everyone's Reach (EMPOWER)

Using the PRECEDE-PROCEED model to plan, implement, and evaluate a health promotion program requires that a certain level of knowledge, experience, and resources are available to planners. Unfortunately, this is not always the case. However, there is now a computer program, EMPOWER, developed by a group of health educators (Bob Gold, Larry Green, and Marshall Kreuter), that allows users to work through a decision matrix based on the PRECEDE-PROCEED model (Gilbert & Sawyer, 1995). This program is designed to help planners design community-based cancer prevention and control programs targeted to the health education needs of communities with diverse minority and other high-risk populations. The technology in the program is related to artificial intelligence and expert systems, and provides users with access to experts for help and advice, external databases, and other planning documents as they work through the planning and evaluation processes (Green, Gold, Tan, & Kreuter, 1994; Gold, 1995). EMPOWER and the training to use it are available by contacting Dr. Robert S. Gold, Macro International, Inc., 11785 Beltsville Dr., Calverton, MD 20705.

MODEL FOR HEALTH EDUCATION PLANNING (MHEP)

The MHEP (Ross & Mico, 1980), first developed by Mico in 1966 and periodically updated, analyzes planning through six phases and the dimensions of content (subject matter), method (steps and techniques), and process (interactions). The model is outlined in Table 2.1. Phase 1 is the initiation of the planning activity. To carry out this phase, planners must

1. Understand the target population's problem and something about its system.
2. Enter into an initial contract.
3. Make the client aware that a problem exists.

Phase 2 of the MHEP involves completing a needs assessment. Ross and Mico (1980) suggest that to complete a needs assessment planners should first identify how the problem was measured in the past, determine what data need to be collected now and how best to gather them, collect and analyze the data, and finally describe the nature and extent of the problem.

Phase 3 of the model deals with goal setting. The goals should be based on the problems identified in the needs assessment. They should be appropriate and realistic, and should include input from those who will be affected. Also, in this goal-setting phase planners should develop strategies for implementing the goals. Phase 4, called planning/programming, "converts the agreed-upon strategies into a rational implementation plan or program, designs systems and tools for manag-

TABLE 2.1 Model for Health Education Planning (MHEP)

	Content Dimension
Phase 6 **Evaluation**	4. Knowledge of problem and client system 3. Technology of feedback systems 2. Language and systems 1. Nature of evaluation
Phase 5 **Implementation**	4. Writing skills 3. Dynamics of problem solving 2. Knowledge of subject and content; Training and Technical Assistance being provided for 1. Knowledge of plan, how it is to work
Phase 4 **Planning and programming**	3. Nature of political process 2. Systems analysis and management science 1. Techniques of planning
Phase 3 **Goal setting**	5. Theory of change 4. Management by Objectives technology 3. Forecasting 2. Nature of policy 1. Role of goals, how to set them, measure
Phase 2 **Needs assessment**	4. Relevance of data 3. Language and systems 2. Data sources 1. Standards and criteria
Phase 1 **Initiate**	3. Power and influence structures, community organization, culture 2. Contract terminology and resources 1. Knowledge of problem and client system

Source: From *Theory and Practice in Health Education* (pp. 214–215) by Helen S. Ross and Paul R. Mico, 1980, Palo Alto, CA: Mayfield Publishing. Reprinted by permission.

ing the activity, and negotiates commitments among those involved" (Ross & Mico, 1980, p. 224).

The final two phases of the MHEP are implementation (Phase 5) and evaluation (Phase 6). In Phase 5, planners offer the program, provide any needed assistance to facilitators and participants, and keep track of the progress. Phase 6, as described by Ross and Mico (1980), includes the following steps:

1. Clarifying the evaluation measures.
2. Collecting and analyzing evaluation data.

Method Dimension	Process Dimension
4. Redefine problem and standards 3. Feedback to activity, reporting, accountability 2. Data collection and analysis 1. Clarify evaluation measures	4. Consensus of new definitions 3. Communication, threat reduction 2. Learning assimilation 1. Agreement
4. Reporting 3. Problem solving 2. Training and technical assistance, consultation 1. Initiate activity	4. Communications 3. Creativity conflict resolution, win-win 2. Skill development, helping 1. Communications, orientations
3. Negotiate commitments, Memorandums of Agreement 2. Design management systems and tools 1. Develop implementation plan	3. Negotiation 2. Role clarification, communications 1. Understanding and commitment
5. Determine strategies for implementation 4. Select goals and objectives 3. Alternative goals statement, force-field analysis 2. Link to policy development 1. Establish criteria for goals	5. Consensus 4. Decision making, consensus 3. Reality testing, creative problem solving 2. Understanding of process and roles 1. Agreement
4. Describe nature and extent of problem 3. Data collection and analysis 2. Determine data to be collected 1. Identify and review present criteria	4. Reduce fantasy by fact 3. Open communications, sensitivity to data sources 2. Agreement 1. Agreement on starting point
3. Organize concerned 2. Develop initial contract 1. Entry or intervention strategy, force-field analysis, interviewing	3. Involvement, leadership, values clarification 2. Legitimacy, commitment, trust, readiness 1. Unfreezing, threat reduction, credibility, awareness of need

3. Providing appropriate feedback.
4. Redefining the problem and standards.

COMPREHENSIVE HEALTH EDUCATION MODEL (CHEM)

The CHEM (Sullivan, 1973) comprises six major steps and several suggested procedures within each of the steps (Table 2.2, page 18). The first step is to involve people. Step 1 includes identifying the target population and those needed to carry out

TABLE 2.2 Comprehensive Health Education Model (CHEM)

Steps	Activities
1. Involve people	Planners need to identify the individuals affected by the problem, identify those who have needed skills to help deal with the problem, and determine the roles and relationships of these people. In addition, planners need to network with people involved in related programs.
2. Set goals	Planners need to set ultimate goals related to health status, personal action, health education practices, and health education resources.
3. Define problems	Planners need to conduct a needs assessment. They need to do this by determining: a. the health status gaps and trends caused by personal actions, b. gaps and trends in personal health action, c. characteristics of the affected persons and the trends in these characteristics, d. the positive and negative forces affecting personal health actions, e. gaps, trends, and forces regarding health education practices, and f. gaps, trends, and forces regarding health education resources. With this information, planners then need to determine the aspects of the problem that should be tackled, such as health, personal actions, education, resources, and/or forces.
4. Design plans	Planners need to list and analyze alternative approaches for dealing with and moving toward the program goals. The analysis should lead to selecting, pretesting, and revising a tentative approach. With the approach selected, specific operational objectives, subobjectives, activities, timetables, and resources need to be set. Next, planners need to pretest and revise their plans. Finally, in this step planners need to specify their evaluation plans, obtain the approval for the plans, and get commitments for resources.
5. Conduct activities	Planners need to obtain the necessary resources to conduct the program, including financial, personnel (staff, volunteers, consultants), facilities, equipment, and supplies. With these resources, specific duties and relationships need to be defined, and management policies and procedures need to be developed. Finally, in this step the plans need to be implemented.
6. Evaluate results	Planners need to determine a. to what extent the objectives and subobjectives have been achieved, b. to what extent the activities were carried out and the resources were used as planned, and c. the relationship between achievement of objectives, carrying out activities, and the use of resources. With this information, the planners can determine the strengths and weaknesses of the program, what the favorable and unfavorable by-products are, how important this program is as compared to others, and whether or not to continue the program. If so, recommendations need to be made on how to improve the program.

Source: Adapted from "Model for Comprehensive, Systematic Program Development in Health Education," by Daniel Sullivan, 1973, *Health Education Report, 1*(1), pp. 4–5.

the program, determining the roles of those involved, and establishing the necessary relationships among the people.

Step 2 involves setting the ultimate goals for the program. In Step 3, defining the problems, planners determine the gaps between what is and what could be. Once they have identified the problems, planners need to determine what problems to tackle. Next, they design the program plans (Step 4). This includes identifying the most appropriate approach; setting specific operational objectives; defining a timetable, activities, and resources; conducting a pretest; and developing evaluation procedures. The fifth step consists of obtaining the necessary resources to implement the program and then implementing it. In the sixth and final step, planners evaluate the program, based on the program objectives. Results of the evaluation then provide data for later decision making regarding the program.

FIGURE 2.3 A Conceptual Model for the Analysis of Health Education Planning and Resource Development (MHEPRD)

Source: Adapted from *Introduction to Health Education* (p. 103) by I. J. Bates and A. E. Winder, 1994, Mountain View, CA: Mayfield Publishing. Reprinted by permission.

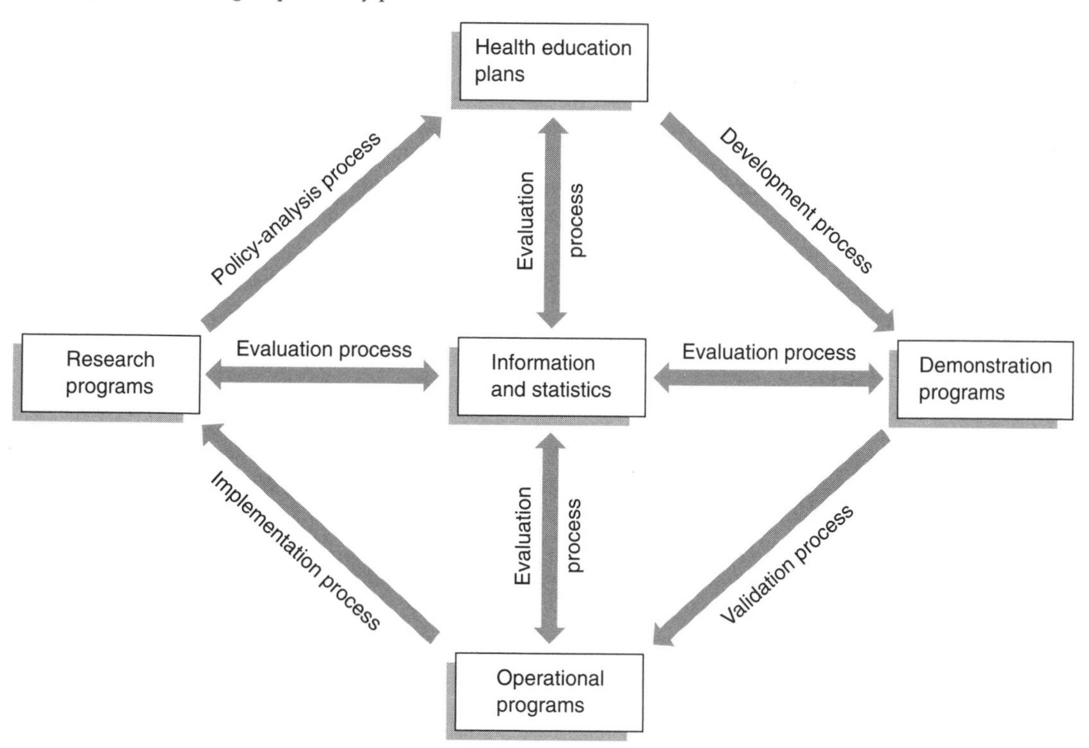

MODEL FOR HEALTH EDUCATION PLANNING AND RESOURCE DEVELOPMENT (MHEPRD)

A less well-known model than those already presented is the MHEPRD introduced by Bates and Winder (1984), shown in Figure 2.3 (page 19). The creators of this model state that it can be distinguished from others because it separates process from end results, and because of the use of evaluation. Each of the five major components in the MHEPRD—health education plans, demonstration programs, operational programs, research programs, and information and statistics—represents an end result of the planning process. The creators do not see evaluation as a separate phase of the model. Instead it plays an integral part in each phase by testing and validating program assumptions throughout the entire process (Bates & Winder, 1984).

FIGURE 2.4 Generic Health/Fitness Delivery System (GHFDS)

Source: Reprinted, by permission from R. P. Patton, J. M. Corry, L. R. Gettman, and J. S. Graff, 1986, *Implementing Health/Fitness Programs* (Champaign, IL: Human Kinetics Publishers), 83.

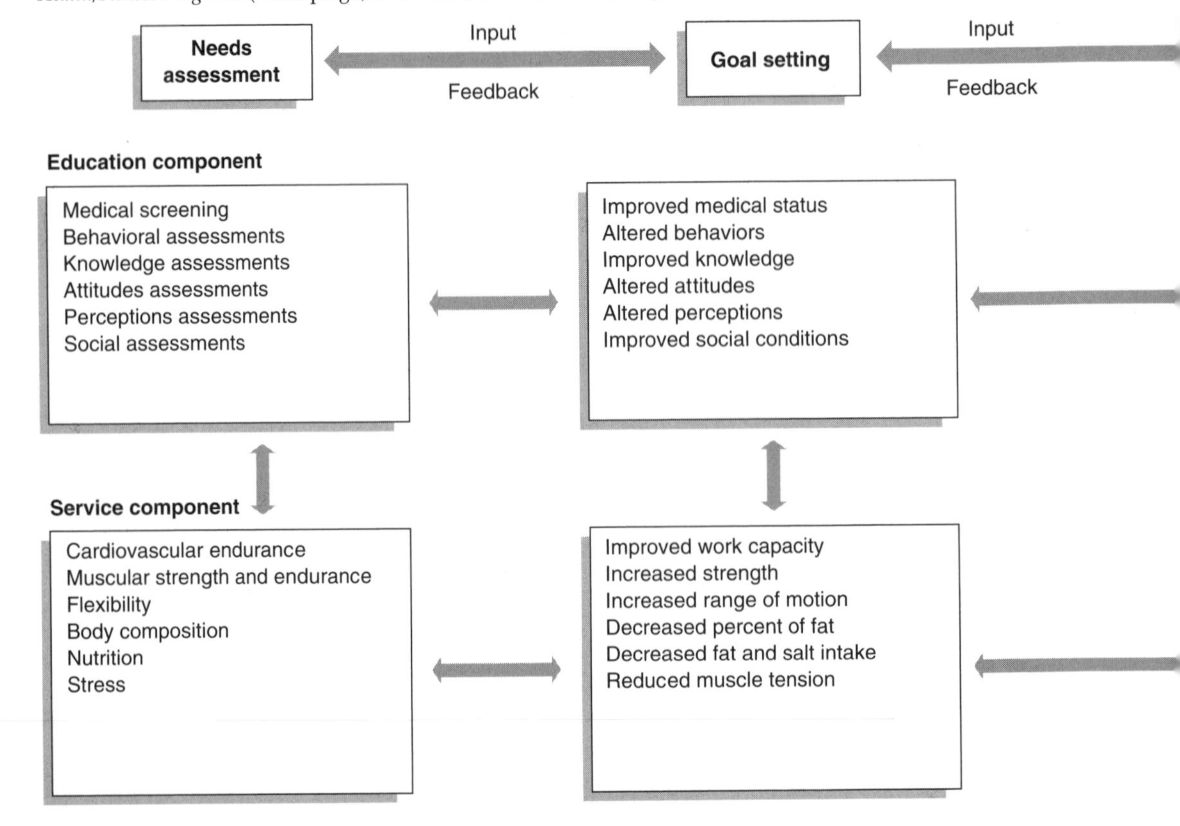

In Phase 1 of the model, health education plans are an end result of a needs assessment (or, as Bates and Winder call it, a "policy-analysis process") and ongoing evaluation of information and statistics. The plans developed in Phase 1 are treated as hypotheses to be tested in Phase 2. To validate their effectiveness, planners create demonstration programs. Phase 3 examines the results of the demonstration programs to determine which should continue and thus become operational programs. This phase also includes the development of an implementation plan that reflects the experiences learned during the demonstration. This process should yield operational programs that are based on a sound rationale of research, planning, and demonstrations.

Phase 4 implements the operational programs. During this phase, steps that are commonly used in a research project are put to use. The problems that surface during implementation provide the basis for research questions for the program planners. The planners in turn formulate possible answers to the questions through appropriate experimentation. The data generated through the experimen-

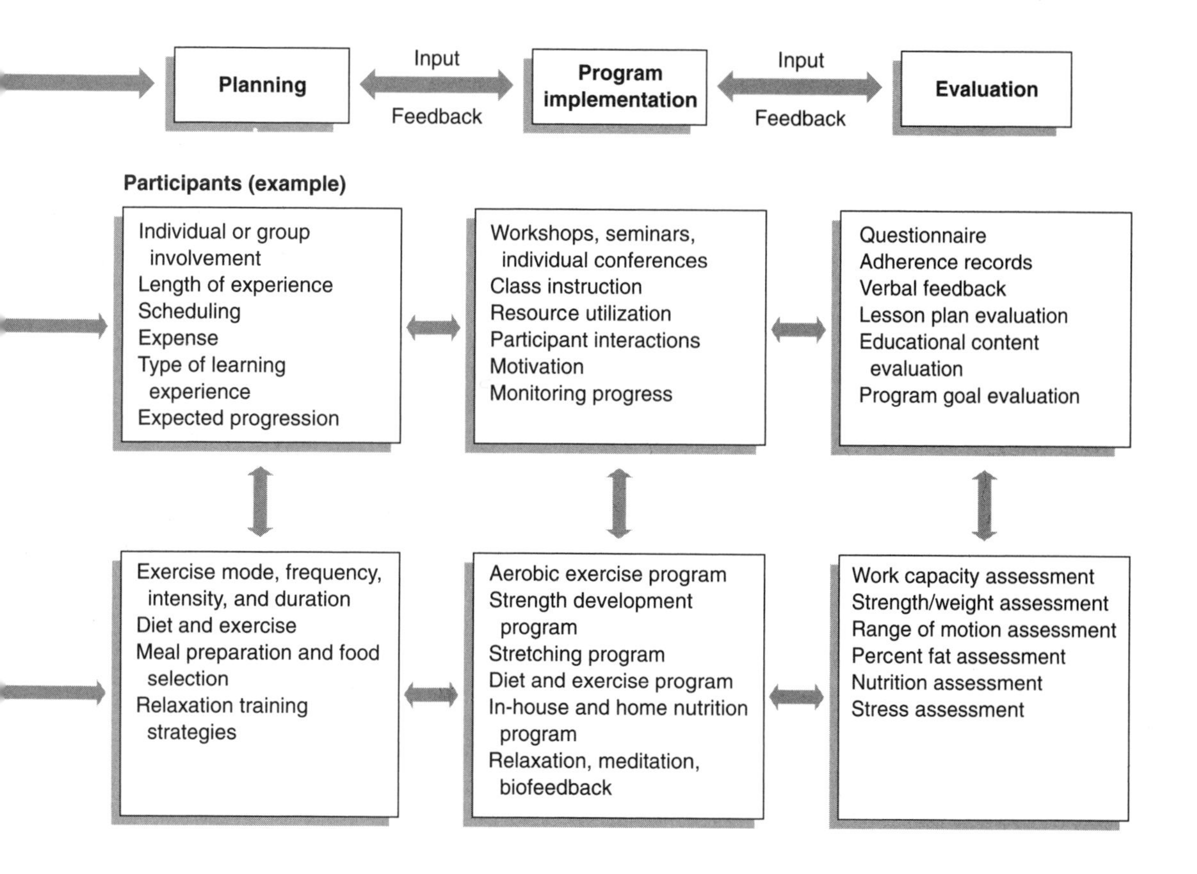

tation are used for future policy analysis and planning. Thus the planning process becomes cyclic in nature since it always builds on previous planning. As the process continues, the result should be better organized and more effective health education services (Bates & Winder, 1984).

GENERIC HEALTH/FITNESS DELIVERY SYSTEM (GHFDS)

The final model to be presented in this chapter is the Generic Health/Fitness Delivery System, or GHFDS (Patton, Corry, Gettman, & Graff, 1986). As its name suggests, this model was not developed specifically for health education but can easily be applied to it. This goal-oriented planning model suggests five steps: needs assessment, goal setting, choice of strategies to meet goals, delivery of program, and evaluation. Each of the steps has two components, education and service. The education component provides a cognitive experience in each step, while the service component provides a hands-on experience. As can be seen in the visual presentation of the model (Figure 2.4, pages 20–21), this approach to program planning is dynamic and interactive. It provides constant insight and feedback so as best to meet the needs of those in the target population. Input from a previous step in the GHFDS modifies the approach used in delivering the later steps in the model. Feedback from the later steps becomes most useful in modifying program delivery (Patton et al., 1986).

SUMMARY

A model can provide the framework for planning and evaluating a health promotion program. Several different planning models have been developed and revised over the years. The five planning models for health education/promotion presented in this chapter are the following:

1. PRECEDE-PROCEED (Predisposing, Reinforcing, and Enabling Constructs in Educational/Environmental Diagnosis and Evaluation; Policy, Regulatory, and Organizational Constructs in Educational and Environmental Development);
2. MHEP (Model for Health Education Planning);
3. CHEM (Comprehensive Health Education Model);
4. MHEPRD (Model for Health Education Planning and Resource Development); and
5. GHFDS (Generic Health/Fitness Delivery System).

To date, probably the best-known model and the one most often used in health promotion is the PRECEDE-PROCEED model; however, the others have made and continue to make valuable contributions (Table 2.3).

TABLE 2.3 Summary of Health Education/Promotion Planning Models (by author & year)

PRECEDE-PROCEED (Green & Kreuter, 1991)	MHEP (Ross & Mico, 1980)	CHEM (Sullivan, 1973)	MHEPRD (Bates & Winder, 1984)	GHFDS (Patton et al., 1986)
Phase 1 Social diagnosis	Phase 1 Initiate	Step 1 Involve people	Health education plans	Needs assessment
Phase 2 Epidemiological diagnosis	Phase 2 Needs assessment	Step 2 Set goals	Demonstration programs	Goal setting
Phase 3 Behavioral and environmental diagnosis	Phase 3 Goal setting	Step 3 Define problems	Operational programs	Planning
Phase 4 Educational and process diagnosis	Phase 4 Planning and programming	Step 4 Design plans	Research programs	Program implementation
Phase 5 Administrative and policy diagnosis	Phase 5 Implementation	Step 5 Conduct activities	Information and statistics	Evaluation
Phase 6 Implementation	Phase 6 Evaluation	Step 6 Evaluate results	Evaluation process	Educational component
Phase 7 Process evaluation			Various other processes	Service component
Phase 8 Impact evaluation				
Phase 9 Outcome evaluation				

QUESTIONS

1. Why is it important to use a model when planning?
2. Name the five models presented in this chapter, and list one distinguishing characteristic of each.
3. Of the models presented, which one has been most commonly used? Name the different phases of this model.
4. What five or six components seem to be common to all the models? (Note that the names of the components may not be the same, but the concepts are.)

ACTIVITIES

1. After reviewing the five models presented in this chapter, create your own model by identifying what you think are the common key components of the models. Provide a rationale for including each component. Then draw a diagram of your model and put it on a transparency so that you can share it with the class. Be prepared to explain your model.
2. In a one-page paper, defend what you believe is the best planning model presented in this chapter.
3. Using a hypothetical health problem for a specific target population, explain the steps/phases for each of the models presented in this chapter.

3

Starting the Planning Process

After reading this chapter and answering the questions at the end, you should be able to:

- Explain the importance of gaining the support of decision makers.
- Develop a rationale for planning and implementing a health promotion program.
- Identify the individuals who could make up a planning committee.
- Explain what program parameters are and the impact they have on program planning.

Key Terms

advisory committee
institutionalized
organizational culture
parameter
pilot program
planning committee
program ownership
stakeholders
steering committee
vendor

Planning a health promotion program is a multiphase process. "'To plan' is to engage in a process or a procedure to develop a method for achieving an end" (Breckon, Harvey, & Lancaster, 1994, p. 115). At the start of the planning process, program planners need to gain the support of key people in order to ensure that the planning process proceeds as smoothly as possible. This chapter presents the initial steps of obtaining the support of decision makers, identifying those who may be interested in helping to plan the program, and establishing the parameters in which the planners must work.

GAINING SUPPORT OF DECISION MAKERS AND EXECUTIVES

No matter what the setting of a health promotion program—whether a business, an industry, the community, a clinic, a hospital, or a school—it is most important that the program have support from the highest level (the administration, chief executive officer, church elders, board of health, or board of directors) (Wolfe, Slack, & Rose-Hearn, 1993) of the "community" for which the program is being planned. These top-level people in decision-making positions are able to provide the necessary support, moral as well as financial, for the program. There will be times when the idea for, or the motivating force behind, a program comes from the top-level people. When this happens, it is a real boon for the program planners because they do not have to "sell" the idea to these people to gain their support. However, this scenario does not occur frequently.

More often than not, the idea or the big push for a health promotion program comes from someone other than one who is part of the top level of the "community." The idea could start with an employee, an interested parent, a health educator within the organization, a member of the parish or congregation, or a concerned citizen. The idea might even be generated by an individual outside the "community," such as a **vendor** trying to sell a program to a business. When the scenario begins at a level below the decision makers, those who want to create a program must "sell" it to the decision makers. Without the support of decision makers, it becomes more difficult to plan and implement a program. Behrens (1983) has stated that health promotion programs in business and industry have a greater chance for success if all levels of management, including the top, are committed and supportive. This seems to be true of health promotion programs in all settings, not just programs in business and industry.

If they need to gain the support of decision makers, program planners should develop a rationale for the program's existence. Why is it necessary to "sell" something that everyone knows is worthwhile? After all, does anyone doubt the value of trying to help people gain and maintain good health? The answer to these and similar questions is that few people are motivated by health concerns alone. Decisions by top-level management to develop new programs are based on a variety of factors, including finances, policies, public image, and politics, to name a few. Thus, to "sell" the program to those at the top, planners need to develop a rationale that shows how the new program will help those at the top to meet the organi-

TABLE 3.1 Summary of Information Sources for Building a Rationale

1. Needs assessment data
2. Epidemiological data about a specific health problem
3. Merits common to most health promotion programs
4. Results of other successful programs in similar settings
5. Compatibility between the proposed program and the health plan of a state or the nation
6. Protecting human resources
7. What is best for the stakeholders

zation's goals and in turn to carry out its mission. In other words, program planners need to position their program rationale politically, in line with the organization. To do this, planners need to amass as many "political data" (data that help to align the program with the organization's mission) as possible; this will enable them to put together a sound rationale to "sell" program development. There are several different sources of information (see Table 3.1) that can be used in developing a rationale. One source would be the results of a needs assessment showing that such a program is needed and wanted. An example of such a situation is the result of a recent Gallup poll conducted for the American Cancer Society that indicated that there was overwhelming support for comprehensive school health education from adolescent students (ages 12–17), parents, and school administrators (Seffrin, 1994). However, more than likely, a formal needs assessment will not yet have been completed at this point in the planning process, since an assessment usually takes place after permission has been given for planning to begin. However, if an assessment has been completed for this or another related or similar program, data from it can be used to help develop the rationale.

The rationale for the program may also be built on the merits common to most health promotion programs. These merits include the following: increased awareness and knowledge; change in attitudes, such as improvement of feelings of general well-being and self-concept (Blair, Collingwood, Reynolds, Smith, Hagen, & Sterling, 1984); improvement in workers' job-related attitudes (Allensworth & Kolbe, 1987; Spilman, Goetz, Schultz, Bellingham, & Johnson, 1986); skill development or acquisition; lowering of health risks (Edington & Yen, 1992; Spilman et al., 1986); reduction in rates of absenteeism (Baun, Bernacki, & Tsai, 1986; Blair et al., 1984; Blair, Smith, Collingwood, Reynolds, Prentice, & Sterling, 1986; Chenoweth, 1987; Cox, Shepard, & Corey, 1981; Jones, Bly, & Richardson, 1990); reduction in employee turnover (Chenoweth, 1987; Cox et al., 1981; Shepard, 1992; Tsai, Baun, Bernacki, 1987); enhanced employee recruitment (Sciacca, Seehafer, Reed, & Mulvaney, 1993; Wolfe et al., 1993); lowering of health insurance premiums; reduction in numbers of workers' compensation claims (Chenoweth, 1987; Sciacca et al., 1993); fewer hospital admissions and shorter lengths of stay (Bly, Jones, & Richardson, 1986); good examples (role models) for others (Allensworth & Kolbe, 1987); enhanced public relations (Sciacca et al., 1993); and improved level of individual well-being, health status, and quality of life (Blair, Tritsch, & Kutsch, 1987, Edington & Yen, 1992; Sciacca et al., 1993).

When citing the merits common to most health promotion programs, planners should use the "reduction in health care costs" rationale with caution. Initial works (Bowne, Russell, Morgan, Optenberg, & Clarke, 1984; Minter, 1986; Shepard, Corey, Renzland, & Cox, 1982) indicated that there might be some savings. However, further study indicates that in the long run such a positive relationship may not exist (Edington & Yen, 1992; Sciacca et al., 1993; Warner, 1987; Warner, Wickizer, Wolfe, Schildroth, & Samuelson, 1988). Edington & Yen (1992) note a paradox that has occurred in the United States over the past thirty plus years: a continued increase in the percentage of Americans adopting health-enhancing behavior, a decrease in the rate of mortality, yet a continuing increase in the cost of health care. Health care costs have continued to rise no matter how they are measured—in dollars per capita per year, dollars per employee per year, percentage of payroll, or percentage of the Gross National Product (GNP).

Epidemiological data about a specific health problem are another information source for building a rationale. Seffrin (1994, p. 399) presents a good example when he talks about the impact of cigarette smoking on the forty-five million smokers in the United States and the United States population in general. He writes, "Not only does tobacco addiction exact an unacceptable burden in health care costs—about $65 billion annually—and a true carnage in human lives—20% of all deaths in 1993—it also strips one-fourth of our population of significant freedom of choice through addiction, and sets an unnecessary and undesirable limit on each smoker's human potential."

A fourth source of data is other successful programs that have been conducted in similar settings. For example, planners may know of other successful programs in surrounding communities, companies, churches, or schools; the people associated with those programs may be able to provide data they generated or may be willing to share their thoughts on how they "sold" their program to those at the top. Of course, planners can always refer to successes reported in the professional literature.

A fifth source of information for a rationale is a comparison between the proposed program and the health plan for the nation or a state. Comparing the health needs of the target population with those of other citizens of the state or of all Americans, as outlined in the goals and objectives of the nation (USDHHS, 1990a), should enable program planners to show the compatibility between the goals of the program and those of the nation's health plan. A discussion of these national health goals and objectives is presented in Chapter 6.

When preparing a rationale to gain the support of decision makers, program planners should emphasize the importance of people as a resource to any "community." Andrew J. J. Brennan, director of Metropolitan Life Insurance Company's Center for Health Help, sums up this point nicely by stating, "People are our company's single biggest asset. It makes good business sense to invest wisely in our employees' good health" (quoted in Novelli & Ziska, 1982). In addition, planners should be sure their rationale answers the question of what is best for the **stakeholders**—those who have something to gain or lose by having or not having the program.

CREATING A RATIONALE

Planners must realize that gaining the support of decision makers is the most important step in the planning process and should not be taken lightly. Many program ideas have died at this stage because the planners were not well prepared. Before making an appeal to decision makers, planners need to be thoroughly prepared. "The 'selling job' should be backed by a soundly researched idea" (McKenzie, 1988, p. 149). Therefore, planners need to put much care into developing their rationale. No formula or recipe has been put forward for writing a rationale, but through our experience we have found a logical format for putting ideas together (see Figure 3.1). Begin the rationale by titling it and indicating who contributed to its authorship. The first paragraph or two of the rationale should identify the health problem in global terms. This is where you can use epidemiological and other needs assessment data. Most local health problems are also present on the international, national, and/or state levels. Presenting the problem at these higher levels shows decision makers that dealing with the health problem is consistent with the concerns of others.

Showing the relationship of the local health problem to the "bigger problem" at the international, national, and/or state levels is the next logical step in presenting the rationale. Thus the next portion of the rationale should identify the local health problem and state *why* it is a problem and *why* it should be dealt with.

At this point in the rationale, you should state your solution to the problem. In other words, state the name and purpose of the proposed health promotion program. The statement of the purpose of the program should be followed by a statement of what can be gained from the program. The benefits of the program should be given in terms that are meaningful to the decision makers. This can be done by:

1. Comparing the proposed program with other successful programs,
2. Stating what is best for the stakeholders, and
3. Stating that the program will protect human resources.

Next, state why you believe this program will be successful. It can be helpful to point out the similarity of this target population to others with which similar programs have been successful. Using the argument that the "timing is right" for the program can also be useful.

Finally, make sure to include a list of the references used to prepare the rationale. This shows decision makers that you have researched your idea. (See the examples of rationales presented in the Activities at the end of the chapter.)

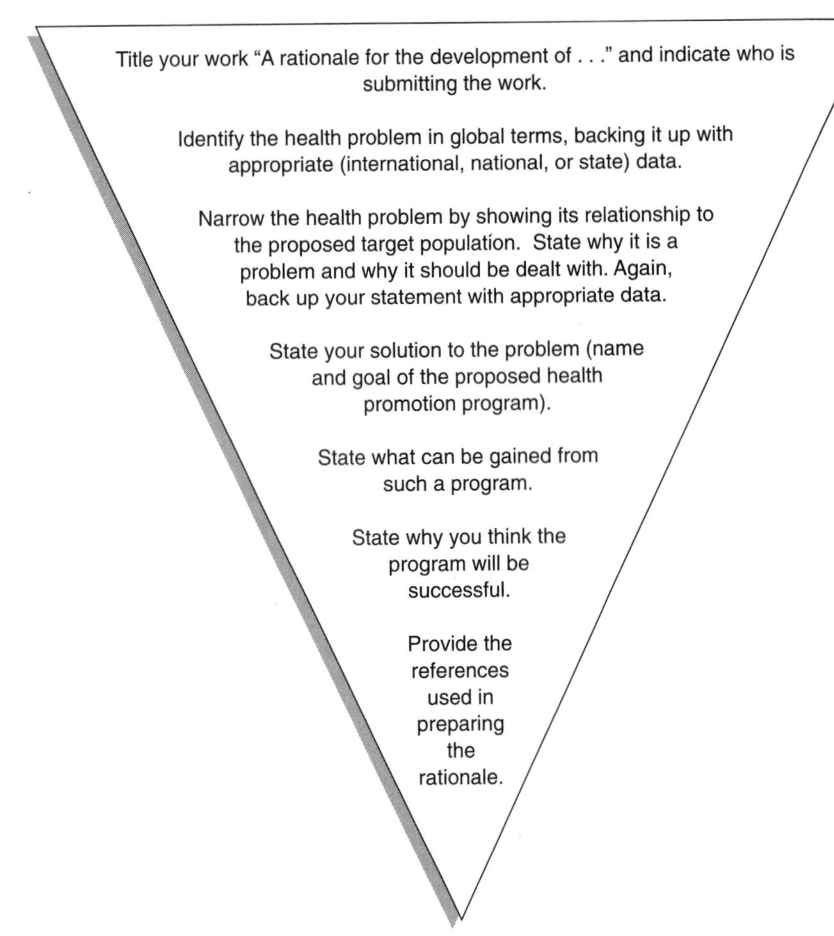

FIGURE 3.1 Creating a Rationale

IDENTIFYING A PLANNING COMMITTEE

"One very helpful method to develop a clearer and more comprehensive planning approach is to establish a committee" (Gilmore & Campbell, 1996, p. 16). Identifying individuals who would be willing to serve as members of the **planning committee** (sometimes referred to as a **steering committee**) becomes one of the planner's first tasks. The number of individuals on a planning committee can differ depending on the setting for the program and the size of the target population. For example, the size of a planning committee for a safety belt program in a community of 50,000 people would probably be larger than that of a committee planning a similar program for a business with 50 employees. There is no ideal size for a planning committee, but the following guidelines, which have been presented earlier

(McKenzie, 1988) and are given here in a modified form, should be helpful in setting up a committee.

1. Select individuals who represent a variety of groups in the target population. If possible, the committee should have representation from all segments of the target population (e.g., administrators/students/teachers, age groups, health behavior participants/nonparticipants, labor/management, race/ethnic groups, different sexes, socioeconomic groups, union/nonunion members, etc.). The greater the number of individuals who are represented by committee members, the greater the chance of the target population's developing a feeling of **program ownership**. With program ownership will come better planned programs, greater support for the programs, and people who will be willing to help "sell" the program to others because they feel it is theirs.
2. Select willing individuals who are interested in seeing the program succeed. Select a combination of "doers" and "influencers." Doers are people who will be willing to roll up their sleeves and do the physical work needed to see that the program is implemented. Influencers are those who with a single phone call or signature on a form will enlist other people to participate or will help provide the resources to facilitate the program. Both doers and influencers are important to the planning process.
3. Ensure that the committee includes an individual who has a key role within the organization sponsoring the program—someone whose support would be most important to ensure a successful program and institutionalization.
4. Include representatives of other stakeholders not represented in the target population.
5. Reevaluate committee membership regularly to ensure that the composition lends itself to fulfilling program goals and objectives.
6. Add new individuals periodically to generate new ideas and enthusiasm. It may be helpful to set a term of office for committee members.
7. Be aware of the politics that are always present in an organization or target population. There are always some people who bring their own agendas to committee work.
8. Make sure the committee is large enough to accomplish the work, but small enough to be able to make decisions and reach consensus. If necessary, subcommittees can be formed to handle specific tasks.

The actual means by which the committee members are chosen varies according to the setting. Commonly used techniques include:

1. Asking for volunteers by word of mouth, a newsletter, a needs assessment, or some other widely distributed publication;
2. Holding an election, either community-wide or by subdivisions of the community;

FIGURE 3.2 Make-Up of a Solid Planning/Steering Committee

3. Inviting people to serve; and
4. Having members appointed by a governing group or individual.

Figure 3.2 illustrates the composition of a well-chosen planning committee.

Once the planning committee has been formed, someone must be designated to lead it. This is an important step. The leader (chairperson) "should be interested and knowledgeable about health education programs, and be organized, enthusiastic, and creative" (McKenzie, 1988, p. 149). One might think that most program planners, especially health educators, would be perfect for the committee chairperson's job. However, sometimes it is preferable to have someone other than the program planners serve in the leadership capacity. For one thing, it helps to spread out the workload of the committee. Planners who are not good at delegating responsibility may end up with a lot of extra work when they serve as the leaders. Second, having someone else serve as the leader allows the planners to remain objective about the program. And third, the planning committee can act as an **advisory committee** to the planners, if this is considered desirable.

PARAMETERS FOR PLANNING

Once the support of the decision makers has been gained and a planning committee formed, planners must identify the **parameters** within which they can work. There are several questions to which planners should have answers before they become too deeply involved in the planning process. In an earlier work (McKenzie, 1988), six such questions were presented, using the example of school-site health education/promotion programs. The six questions are modified for presentation here. It should be noted, however, that not all of the questions would be appropriate for every program because of the different circumstances of each setting.

1. What is the decision makers' philosophical perspective on health promotion programs? Do they see the programs as something important or as "extras"?
2. What type of commitment to the program are the decision makers willing to make? Are they interested in the program becoming **institutionalized**? That is, are they interested in seeing that the "program becomes imbedded within the host organization, so that the program becomes sustained and durable" (Goodman, McLeroy, Steckler, & Hoyle, 1993, p. 163)? Or

are they more interested in providing a one-time or **pilot program**? (Note: Goodman et al. [1993] have developed a scale for measuring institutionalization.)

3. What type of financial support are the decision makers willing to provide? Does it include personnel for leadership and clerical duties? Released time for managing the program and participation? Space? Equipment? Materials?
4. Are the decision makers willing to consider changing the **organizational culture**? For example, are they interested in "well" days instead of sick days? Would they like to create employee smoking and safety belt policies? Change vending machine selections to more nutritious foods? Set aside an employee room for meditation? Develop a health promotion corner in the organization library?
5. Will all individuals in the target population have an opportunity to take advantage of the program, or will it only be available to certain subgroups?
6. What is the authority of the planning committee? Will it be an advisory group or a programmatic decision-making group? What will be the chain of command for program approval?

After the parameters have been defined, the planning committee should understand how the decision makers view the program, and should know what type and amount of commitment and support to expect. Setting the parameters early will save the planning committee a great deal of effort and energy throughout the planning process.

SUMMARY

Gaining the support of the decision makers is an important initial step in program planning. Planners should take great care in developing a rationale for "selling" the program idea to these important people. A planning committee can be most useful in helping with some of the planning activities and in helping to "sell" the program to the target population. Therefore, the committee should be composed of interested individuals who are representative of the target population. If the planning committee is to be effective, it will need to be aware of the parameters set for the program by the decision makers.

QUESTIONS

1. Why is the support of the decision makers important in planning a program?
2. What kinds of reasons should be included in a rationale for planning and implementing a health promotion program?
3. How important is "selling" the idea of a program to decision makers?

4. What items should be addressed when creating a program rationale?
5. Who should be selected as the members of a planning committee?
6. What are *parameters?* Give a few examples.
7. Why is it important to know the parameters at the beginning of the planning process?

ACTIVITIES

1. Write a two-page rationale for "selling" a program you are planning to decision makers, using the guidelines presented in this chapter.
2. Write a two-page rationale for beginning an exercise program for a small company with 200 employees. A needs assessment of this target population indicates that the number one cause of lost work time of this cohort is back problems and the number one cause of premature death is heart disease.
3. For a program you are planning, write a two-page description of the individuals (by position/job title, not name) who will be asked to serve on the planning committee, and provide a rationale for asking each to serve.
4. Provide a list (by position/job title, not name) and a rationale for each of the ten individuals you would ask to serve on a community wide safety belt program. Use the town or city in which your college/university is located as the community.
5. Below are two program rationales written by former students at Ball State University. Read each of the rationales and then select one to critique using the guidelines presented in this chapter. Critique by describing the following: (a) the strengths of the rationale, (b) the weaknesses, and (c) how you would change the rationale to make it stronger. Be critical! Closely examine the content, reasoning, and references.

   A. **A Rationale for Offering a Violence Education Program in the Schools**
   During the past ten years, many programs have been implemented in an attempt to curb the use of tobacco products by our country's high school students. As a result, the nation has witnessed a reduction in such activity. Also, programs to increase awareness about drinking and driving have been introduced in abundance. A dramatic decrease has followed there as well. But the amount of crime and violence in our nation's schools and the number of deviant acts committed by our nation's adolescents have continued to rise throughout the 1980s with relatively little intervention by comparison, though the issue is of equal if not greater importance. It is reported that 91% of all high school seniors worry about crime and violence, an increase of over 10% since 1980 (*Sourcebook of Criminal Justice Statistics,* 1992). The number of inmates under the age of eighteen in U. S. state prisons increased from 2,057 in 1986 to 4,552 in 1991 (U.S. Bureau of Justice Statistics, 1992). Although the problem has

been addressed in *Healthy People 2000*, very few programs are currently being implemented at the school level to aid in rectifying the problem.

Many reasons have been proposed for the increase in juvenile crime. Some of the more commonly cited reasons are family breakdown and lack of parental supervision, increased prevalence of gang activity, violence portrayed in movies and on television, increased availability of drugs, and the "softness" of the court system regarding juvenile punishment. Other reasons cited include the fast pace of life in the United States, and increased levels of stress on the family as a result of economics and divorce (Smith & Gunason, 1994). While not in a position to solve all of these social problems, the public schools are in a position to offer anti-violent and positive conflict-resolution alternatives in a comprehensive health education program.

Who stands to gain from such a program? First and foremost, students can gain a future from such a program. Students who commit major criminal violations reduce their chances of landing a job with adequate upward mobility to support a household, while dramatically decreasing their overall job opportunities. Without this ability to choose a profession, their futures are often thrust upon them by circumstance. As crime and violence in the schools are reduced, a better education is also made possible. Where gangs are prevalent, 35% of students report that they feared an attack at school (Smith & Gunason, 1994). Optimal learning does not take place under such circumstances. Teachers also find it difficult to perform adequately under the constant demands of disciplinary action. When violence runs rampant in the school systems, the students and teachers are unable to concentrate solely on education.

Taxpayers also stand to gain immensely from an anti-violent conflict-resolution program in the schools. It is estimated that hospital costs and long-term rehabilitation costs for treating gunshot wounds amounted to $14.4 billion in 1985 (Smith & Gunason, 1994). Taxpayers paid for 80% of these costs. Gunshot wounds are now the second leading cause of death among individuals between the ages of ten and thirty-four (Smith & Gunason, 1994). With 48% of males reporting carrying a weapon to school in Indiana, and weapon law violations among blacks increasing by an estimated 103% since 1980, the cost to taxpayers will continue to increase unless intervention programs are planned and implemented in the near future (Ellis & Torabi, 1992; Smith & Gunason, 1994).

Another burden to the taxpayers is the state detention centers—in Indiana, $31 million was spent in one year in caring for youngsters in these centers. The cost to the Indiana taxpayer for adolescents needing these facilities is nearly $30,000 per day (Smith & Gunason, 1994).

Finally, the community at large benefits from a school-based program. Economically, the community becomes recognized as safer, encouraging more individuals to purchase housing in the community and thus creating a larger base for companies wishing to do business in the community. The result is greater economic freedom and opportunity. Socially, the community benefits by the reduced amount of fear of and contempt for the younger generations. Such a program reinforces the idea that our children are indeed our future, and that it is well worth it to invest in that future, not only for their sake, but for the sake of the country as a whole.

References

Ellis, N. T., & Torabi, M. (1992). *The Indiana student health survey: Surveillance of 9th and 12th grade youth health behaviors.* Indianapolis, IN: Indiana Department of Education.

Smith, D. L., & Gunason, S. (Ed.). (1994). *Kids, crime, and court: The juvenile justice system in Indiana.* Indianapolis, IN: Indiana Youth Institute.

Sourcebook of Criminal Justice Statistics. (1992). Washington, D.C.: Government Printing Office.

U.S. Bureau of Justice Statistics. (1992). Washington, D.C.: Government Printing Office.

This rationale was written by Brian Allred and Jenni Robison while they were graduate students at Ball State University, Muncie, Indiana, in 1994–1995. It is used here with permission.

B. A Rationale for Condom Awareness Week

Students on college campuses are having sex. And, more often than not, they are not using protective measures. One study reported that only 20 percent of sexually active college students consistently used condoms (Boyd & Wandersman, 1991). In fact "most of those engaging in sexual intercourse do not use any form of protection from sexually transmitted diseases (STDs) the first time they engage in the behavior" (Caron, Davis, Halteman, & Stickle, 1993, p. 252). The same study revealed that only 13% of sexually active college students always use a condom. This is partially due to the negative attitudes toward condom use. Men and women both report negative beliefs regarding condoms, such as embarrassment, reduction of enjoyment, and interruption of the "romance" in intercourse (Boyd & Wandersman, 1991).

Common health risk factors rationalizing condom use include the increasing incidences of STDs (Boyd & Wandersman, 1991), unplanned pregnancy, and, most importantly, increasing incidence of HIV infection. The spread of HIV on college campuses is enough to warrant programs devoted to condom awareness as infection rates for HIV and other STDs are "increasing at an alarming rate among heterosexual adults" (DeBro, Campbell, & Peplau, 1994, p. 166). It has been suggested that students still believe condoms are solely for birth control (Oswalt & Matson, 1993). This exhibits yet another need for condom awareness.

There are several purposes for this program, encompassing both short- and long-term goals. Initially, the program is designed to increase awareness of proper condom usage and define exactly what proper condom usage is. An understanding of which products are considered oil based and which are water based is also essential. Collegians must be made aware that condoms are readily available in several different varieties.

In the long term, increased acceptability of condoms predicts an increase in usage (Caron et al., 1993). Increased condom usage should lead to a decrease in the transmission rates of STDs, a decrease in number of unintentional pregnancies, and a decrease in sexual transmission of HIV.

Providing a forum for education about condoms should meet these short- and long-term goals. Hands-on demonstrations of proper usage along with games to increase knowledge can help remove some of the stigmas against condom use. Furthermore, a week-long "celebration" of condoms will catch the eyes of most college students. Raising awareness and increasing the knowledge level can promote student discussions among themselves. Additionally, raising awareness of STD morbidity for college students may help increase students' likelihood of using condoms.

Through tasteful, educational programming, student knowledge can be increased and attitudes toward condoms can become more positive. In return, increased condom usage, decreased STD incidence, fewer unplanned pregnancies, and decreased HIV infection can be expected.

References

Boyd, B., & Wandersman, A. (1991). Predicting undergraduate condom use with the Fishbein and Ajzen and the Triandis attitude-behavior models: Implications for public health interventions. *Journal of Applied Social Psychology,* 21(22), 1810–1831.

Caron, S., Davis, C., Halteman, W., & Stickle, M. (1993). Predictors of condom-related behaviors among first-year college students. *The Journal of Sex Research,* 30(3), 252–259.

DeBro, S., Campbell, S., & Peplau, L. (1994). Influencing a partner to use a condom. *Psychology of Women Quarterly,* 18, 165–182.

Oswalt, R., & Matson, K. (1993). Sex, AIDS, and the use of condoms: A survey of compliance in college students. *Psychology Reports,* 72, 764–766.

This rationale was written by Lisa G. Fields and Anissa L. Conley while they were graduate students at Ball State University, Muncie, Indiana, in 1994–1995. It is used here with permission.

4

Assessing Needs

After reading this chapter and answering the questions at the end, you should be able to:

- Define needs assessment.
- Explain why a needs assessment must be completed.
- Differentiate between primary and secondary data sources.
- Explain how a needs assessment can be completed.
- Conduct a needs assessment on a given group of people.

Key Terms

APEX/PH
community analysis/community diagnosis
Delphi technique
eyeballing the data
needs assessment
networking
opinion leaders
primary data
secondary data
segmenting
service demands
service needs
significant others
social diagnosis/epidemiological diagnosis
target population

Once the planning committee is in place, the next step in the planning process is to identify the need(s) or problem(s) of those to be served—the **target population**. Assessing the needs of the target population may be the most critical step in the planning process. Without determining these needs, there is really no way to know whether a program is warranted. Many fine programs have failed because there was no need for them. An example of such a scenario might be a program planned by a voluntary health agency that has a national goal to offer more smoking cessation programs in the workplace. If we look at the national figures, there may appear to be a need for such a program. Approximately 26% of the adult population in the United States today smokes; that figure is even higher among skilled and unskilled labor. So it appears that there is a need on the national level. But it is necessary to consider the local level, where the program must be implemented. What about Blue Earth County, Minnesota? Delaware County, Indiana? Wood County, Ohio? Do 26% of the adults in these counties smoke? What percentage of county residents who work in industry smoke? Do those smokers want to quit? Do employers mind if their employees smoke? Is there really a need for smoking cessation programs in these counties? No one can say for sure until a needs assessment has been completed, and even then the need for such a program may not be clear.

WHAT IS A NEEDS ASSESSMENT?

Up to this point, we have used the term **needs assessment** several different times, without defining it. Now, let's take a closer look at the term and what it means. First, it should be noted that other terms have been used in a similar context: **social diagnosis/epidemiological diagnosis** (Green & Kreuter, 1991) and **community analysis/community diagnosis** (Dignan & Carr, 1992). All these terms are used to describe the process by which those who are planning programs can determine what health problems might exist in any given group of people. Windsor, Baranowski, Clark, and Cutter (1994, p. 63) have defined *needs assessment* as "the process by which the program planner identifies and measures gaps between what is and what ought to be." Stated a bit differently, "needs assessment is a planned process that identifies the reported needs of an individual or a group" (Gilmore & Campbell, 1996, p. 5). No matter how it is defined, the concept is the same: identifying the health needs of the target population and deciding whether or not these needs are being met.

Although determining the needs of a target population at first seems a straightforward task, planners must ask, Through whose eyes is the need determined or evaluated? Windsor and colleagues (1994) have applied the vocabulary of marketing to the needs assessment process, identifying two types of health needs. The first type is **service needs.** These are the things that "health professionals believe a given population must have or be able to do in order to resolve a health problem." The other type consists of the things that those in the target population "say they must have or be able to do in order to resolve a health problem" (Windsor et al., 1994, p. 64). These needs are referred to as **service demands.**

Both types of needs are important, and if either is ignored, the true need of a given target population may not be understood. A program that is based entirely upon service needs (from the planners' point of view) may not interest or appeal to the target population even though a serious problem exists that the program could help solve. On the other hand, a program that is planned around service demands (from the viewpoint of those being served) may not contribute to solving the real health problem. Therefore, it is important for program planners to identify both types of needs. Once this has been done, planners must blend the two to reflect both perspectives.

In addition to identifying the needs of the target population, a needs assessment can also provide valuable information that can help segment the target population according to demographic variables, such as age, gender, or socioeconomic status; behaviors, such as exercisers versus nonexercisers; and attitudes, for example, those who are for or against permitting smoking in public places. Such **segmenting** allows program planners to design programs for a specific subgroup of the target population and thus increase the program's chance of being effective. This is a key strategy in helping to market a health promotion program; it is discussed in greater detail in Chapter 11.

ACQUIRING NEEDS ASSESSMENT DATA

Program planners can gather needs assessment data in one of two ways. They can use data that are "available from other sources" (Windsor et al., 1994, p. 72), called **secondary data,** or they can collect their own data, thus generating **primary data.**

The advantages of using secondary data are that (1) they already exist, and thus time to collect them is not needed, and (2) they are usually fairly inexpensive to access. Both of these advantages are important to program planners because programs are often planned when both time and money are limited. However, a drawback of using secondary data is that the information might not identify the true needs of the target population—perhaps because of how the data were collected, when they were collected, what variables were considered, or from whom the data were collected. A good rule is to move cautiously and make sure the secondary data are applicable to the immediate situation before using them.

Primary data have the advantage of directly answering the questions planners want answered by those in the target population. The data are specific to the target population. However, collecting primary data can be expensive and when done correctly can take a great deal of time.

An overview of the means of acquiring primary and secondary data are presented in the following pages. The different sources of data are presented using the classification system presented in Gilmore and Campbell (1996). For those readers who need a much more detailed explanation of the needs assessment process, we refer you to the text by Gilmore and Campbell (1996).

Sources of Primary Needs Assessment Data

Primary data can be divided into two large categories: data gathered from individuals and data gathered from groups.

Gathering Data from Individuals

Primary data are collected from individuals through the use of a survey. Surveys can take many different forms. One way of classifying surveys is by the number of times those collecting the data ask those in the target population for information. Single-step and multistep surveys are discussed here.

Single-Step Survey. Single-step surveys are a means of collecting primary data in which those collecting the data gather the data from the target population with a single contact. The most commonly used means of surveying the target population are by paper-and-pencil questionnaires, telephone interviews, or face-to-face interviews (see Table 5.4 for a comparison of the advantages and disadvantages of these techniques). The means used to collect the data are probably not as important as the specific procedures used. When collecting data, planners must take the necessary steps to ensure that the data collected are representative of the target population. The concept of representativeness will be discussed later (see Chapter 5), but two major questions that must be considered are (1) how the survey sample is chosen, and (2) whether the data collection instrument is valid and reliable. A valid instrument is one that measures what it is supposed to measure. A reliable instrument is one that will provide consistent results in subsequent uses. One other point should be noted here about surveying the target population: It provides an opportunity to obtain answers to marketing questions as well as questions of needs. Marketing questions might be concerned with the best location for the program, the best time of day, and how much participants would be willing to pay to participate. These questions can help to segment the target population.

In addition to surveying the target population, there are two other groups of individuals who are commonly asked to respond to single-step surveys for the purpose of collecting primary needs assessment data. They include significant others of the target population and community opinion leaders. **Significant others** may include family members and friends. Collecting data from the significant others of a group of heart disease patients is a good example. Program planners might find it difficult to persuade the heart disease patients themselves to share information about their outlook on life and living with heart disease. A survey of spouses or other family members might help elicit this information so that the program planners could best meet the needs of the heart disease patients.

Opinion leaders are individuals who are well respected in a community and who have an overall view of its needs. These leaders are:

1. Active users of the media.
2. Demographically similar to the target group.

3. Knowledgeable about community issues and concerns.
4. Early adopters of innovative behavior (see Chapter 10 for an explanation of these terms).
5. Active in persuading others to become involved in innovative behavior.

Opinion leaders include political figures, chief executive officers (CEOs) of companies, union leaders, administrators of local school districts, and other highly respected individuals.

Multistep Survey. As its title might suggest, a multistep survey is one in which those collecting the data contact those who will provide the data on more than one occasion. The technique that uses this process is called the **Delphi technique.** It is a process that generates consensus through a series of questionnaires, which are usually administered via the mail or electronic mail. The process begins with those collecting the data asking the target population to respond to one or two broad questions. The responses are analyzed, and a second questionnaire, with more specific questions, is developed and sent to the target population. The answers to these more specific questions are analyzed again, and a new questionnaire is sent out, requesting additional information. If consensus is reached, the process may end here; if not, it may continue for another round or two (Gilmore, Campbell, & Becker, 1989). Most often this process continues for five or fewer rounds.

Gathering Data from Groups

There are several different techniques available to those collecting primary data from groups. The more commonly used techniques used by health educators include the community forum, the focus group, the nominal group process, and observation.

Community Forum. Put simply, the community forum approach brings together people from the target population to discuss what they see as their group's health problems. It is not uncommon for a community forum to be organized by a group representing the target population, in conjunction with the program planners. Such groups include labor, civic, religious, or service organizations, or groups like the Parent Teacher Association (PTA) or Parent Teacher Organization (PTO). Once people have arrived, a moderator explains the purpose of the meeting and then asks those from the target population to share their concerns. One or several individuals from the organizing group, called recorders, are usually given the responsibility for taking notes or taping the session to ensure that the responses are recorded accurately. However, when moderating a community forum, it is important to be aware that the silent majority may not speak out and/or a vocal minority may speak too loudly. For example, an individual parent's view may be wrongly interpreted to be the view of all parents.

At a community forum, participants may also be asked to respond in writing (1) by answering specific questions or (2) by completing some type of instrument. Figure 4.1 is an example of an instrument that could be used to collect data from a group of people.

Directions: Please rank the need for each program in the community by placing a number in the space to the left of the programs. Use 1 to rank the program of greatest need, 2 for the next greatest need, and so forth, until you have ranked all seven programs. The program with the highest number next to it should be the one that, in your opinion, is least needed. If you feel that a program should not be considered for implementation in our community, please place an X in the space to the left of the program instead of a number. Please note that the number you place next to each program represents its need in the community, not necessarily your desire to participate in it. After ranking the program, place an X to the right of the program in the column(s) that represents the age group(s) to which you feel the program should be targeted.

	Program	All ages	Children 5–12	Teens 13–19	Adults 20–64	Older adults 65+
____	Alcohol education:	____	____	____	____	____
____	Exercise/fitness:	____	____	____	____	____
____	Nutrition education:	____	____	____	____	____
____	Safety belt use:	____	____	____	____	____
____	Smoking cessation:	____	____	____	____	____
____	Smoking education:	____	____	____	____	____
____	Weight loss:	____	____	____	____	____

FIGURE 4.1 Instrument for Ranking Program Need

Source: Modified from a form developed by Amy L. Bernard, Ph.D., CHES; Assistant Professor, University of Cincinnati. Adapted by permission.

Focus Group. Focus groups are a form of qualitative research that grew out of group therapy. They are used to obtain information about the feelings, opinions, perceptions, insights, beliefs, misconceptions, attitudes, and receptivity of a group of people concerning an idea or issue. Focus groups are rather small compared to community forums and usually include only 8–12 people. If possible, it is best to have a group of people who do not know one another so that their responses are not inhibited by acquaintance. Participation in the group is by invitation. People are invited about one to three weeks in advance of the session. At the time of the invitation, they receive general information about the session but are not given the specifics. This precaution helps ensure that responses will be on target yet spontaneous.

Once assembled, the group is led by a skilled moderator who has the task of obtaining candid responses from the group to a set of predetermined questions. In addition to eliciting responses to the questions, the moderator may ask the group to prioritize the different responses. As in a community forum, the answers to the questions are recorded through either written notes and/or audio or video recordings, so that at a later date the interested parties can review and interpret the results.

For any one project, it may be necessary to hold several different focus groups to collect the needed information. For example, if planners are using focus groups to find out what the people in the community think about a proposed sex education curriculum, it would be helpful to organize focus groups based on the beliefs of certain subsets within the target population. Otherwise, if liberals were brought together with conservatives or pro-choice advocates were brought together with pro-life people, the focus groups would turn into shouting matches and little would be accomplished. Usually, the more controversial the topic, the greater the need to organize several focus groups with segments of the population.

Focus groups are not easy to conduct. Special care must be given to developing the questions that will be asked. Poorly written questions will yield information that is less than useful. In addition, the facilitator should be one who is skilled in leading a group. As might be surmised, the level of skill needed to conduct a focus group increases as the topic of discussion becomes more controversial.

Although focus groups have been shown to be an effective way of gathering data, they do have one major limitation. Participants in the groups are usually not selected through a random-sampling process. They are generally selected because they possess certain attributes (individuals of low income, city dwellers, parents of disabled children, or chief executive officers of major corporations). Participants are typical, not representative, of the target population. Therefore, the results of the focus group are not generalizable. "Findings [of focus groups] should be interpreted as suggestive and directional rather than as definitive" (Schechter, Vanchieri, & Crofton, 1990, p. 254).

Nominal Group Process. The nominal group process is a highly structured process in which a few knowledgeable representatives of the target population (5–7 people) are asked to qualify and quantify specific needs. Those invited to participate are asked to record their responses to a question without discussing it among themselves. Once all have recorded a response, each participant shares his or her response in a round-robin fashion. While this is occurring, the facilitator is recording the responses on a chalkboard/paper/etc. for all to see. The responses are clarified through a discussion. After the discussion, the participants are asked to rank-order the responses by importance to the target population. This ranking may be considered either a preliminary or a final vote. If it is preliminary, it is followed with more discussion and a final vote.

Observation. Gathering primary needs assessment data via observation can be accomplished in several different ways. It can be done by the planners or their workers, who can become a part of the day-to-day events where the health problems may occur, so that they can observe the actions of the target population. Examples of such fieldwork may include watching the eating patterns of teachers in a school lunchroom, observing workers on an assembly line to see if they are wearing their protective glasses, checking the smoking behavior of employees on break, and observing community members for safety belt use.

Observational data can also be collected by those in the target population through self-directed assessments. Self-directed assessments include techniques such as breast self-examination (BSE), testicular self-examination (TSE), skin cancer detection (SCD), and health risk appraisals (HRA) or health hazard appraisals (HHA). The HRA/HHA, a relatively recent means of determining an individual's health risks as compared to the other techniques mentioned in this chapter, has also been found useful in helping to determine the needs of a target population. The HRA/HHA is an instrument that requires people to answer a number of questions about their health behavior, health history, and the results of a few clinical screenings (height, weight, blood pressure, and cholesterol). This information is then entered into a computer that has been programmed to compare the entered data against a database that contains information from individuals of the same gender, race, and age. The result of such a comparison tells people their risk of dying in the next ten years from the leading causes of death as compared to others of the same gender, race, and age. Most HRA/HHA computer programs are designed to provide not only individual results but also the collective results for any given group of people. The HRA/HHA can therefore provide program planners with valuable needs assessment data. Most of these instruments have been developed to determine overall health risks, but some programs are designed to calculate the risk from a single disease.

To date, several different HRA/HHA instruments have been developed. The most frequently used HRA/HHA computer program is an adaptation of the Canadian health risk appraisal developed by the Centers for Disease Control and Prevention, advanced by the Carter Center at Emory University; it is now available from Risk Assessment Systems, Inc. (5846 Distribution Drive, Memphis, TN 38141; 1-800-421-7000). It is called Healthier People. Other individuals, organizations, and companies have taken this instrument and adapted it for their own use or to market it to others. In addition to the often used HRA/HHA computer programs, several paper-and-pencil HRA/HHA instruments have been developed. Many of these are made up of relatively few questions and are intended to determine the risk of a specific disease.

Although this discussion has revolved around the use of HRAs/HHAs as means of providing information for a needs assessment, they have also been used in recent years for other purposes: to help motivate people to act on their health, to increase awareness, to serve as cues to action, and to contribute to program evaluation. However, it should be noted that the instruments were originally developed for physicians to use as an educational tool with their patients. The expanded use of these instruments has prompted several researchers (Alexy, 1985; Best & Milsum, 1978; Elias & Dunton, 1981; Sachs, Krushat, & Newman, 1980; Smith, McKinlay, & McKinlay, 1989) to question the reliability of HRA/HHA data (see Chapter 14 for a discussion of reliability). In general, it has been found that

1. The reliability of HRA/HHA risk scores can vary greatly from one instrument to another.

2. Reliability scores decrease when users calculate their own score as opposed to computer scoring.
3. There is a great variance in the self-reporting of specific risk factors and clinical physiologic measurements.
4. Only those HRAs/HHAs for which reliability can be demonstrated should be used for evaluating the effectiveness of health education.

Sources of Secondary Needs Assessment Data

The sources of secondary needs assessment data for program planners are many. The main sources include data collected by governmental agencies at any level (international, national, state, or local), data available from health records, and data that are presented in the literature.

Data Collected by Governmental Agencies

Certain governmental agencies collect data on a regular basis. Some of the data collection is mandated by law (i.e., census, births, deaths, notifiable diseases, etc.), whereas other data are collected voluntarily (i.e., usage rates for safety belts) for use by the public. Since the data are collected by the government, program planners can gain free access to them by contacting the agency that collects the data or by finding them in a library that serves as a United States government depository for government documents. Many college and university libraries and large public libraries serve as such depositories. Presented here is information about some of the more useful sources of data collected by governmental agencies.

From the U.S. Department of Commerce. Within the U.S. Department of Commerce is located the Bureau of Census. The bureau is responsible for taking a census of the United States every ten years. The first census was ordered by George Washington in 1790 for the purpose of apportioning representation to the House of Representatives. The most recent census, taken in 1990, includes data on number of people, income, employment, family size, education, type of dwelling, and many other social indicators.

Another Bureau of Census publication is the *Statistical Abstract of the United States* (SA). This book, published since 1878, provides a summary of statistics on the social, political, and economic organization of the United States. Recent volumes of the book include a selection of data from both government and private statistical publications (U.S. Bureau of Census, 1994). Major sections of the book cover population, vital statistics, health and nutrition, education, law enforcement, courts and prisons, and many other areas. A new edition of SA is published each January and includes data for years up to two years prior to the publication date. It can be purchased from the U.S. Government Printing Office for approximately $30 (McKenzie & Pinger, 1995).

From the National Center for Health Statistics (NCHS). The NCHS is one of the seven major divisions of the Centers for Disease Control and Prevention (CDC). As the nation's keeper of health data, the NCHS maintains several ongoing data systems. However, "budgetary constraints have caused the center staff to establish priorities for those systems and reduce the frequency of their operation" (Pickett & Hanlon, 1990, p. 138). Though all the data systems are useful, four that have proved very helpful to health promotion program planners have been basic vital statistics, National Health Interview Survey (NHIS), National Health and Examination Survey (NHANES), and the Youth Risk Behavior Surveillance System (YRBSS). Basic vital statistics are published in the *Monthly Vital Statistics Report: Provisional Data from the National Center for Health Statistics* and in annual volumes making up the *Vital Statistics of the United States.* Data from the two surveys are published in the *Vital and Health Statistics* series, whereas data from the YRBSS were published in the *Morbidity and Mortality Weekly Report* (MMWR) in 1995. The MMWR is prepared by CDC staff but published by the Massachusetts Medical Society, publishers of the *New England Journal of Medicine.*

Of special note to program planners is the availability of the survey questionnaires used in the NHIS and NHANES. These instruments provide good starting points for program planners who need to collect primary needs assessment data. The instruments are also available from the NCHS or the government depositories.

As a final note about sources of data available from national-level governmental agencies, planners should consider contacting the National Health Information Clearinghouse at P.O. Box 1133, Washington, D.C. 20013–1133.

From State and Local Agencies. Although the discussion to this point has centered on national data, similar data are available from state and local governmental agencies. Program planners should consult with their local and state health departments to see what is available to them. For example, many, but not all, states have collected behavioral risk factor survey data. State and local agencies are also mandated by law to collect specific data (i.e., vital statistics).

Data Available from Health Records

Health data are often "collected as a by-product of a service effort, such as managing a clinic, an immunization program, or a water pollution control program" (Pickett & Hanlon, 1990, p. 151). Although not immediately used by those who collect them, these data can serve as very useful secondary needs assessment data. Clinical indicators, such as blood pressure, height, weight, body composition, or blood analysis, are routinely collected by health care professionals. Also often available are records that deal with the utilization or cost of medical services. These data include such items as health insurance claims paid, hospital utilization rates, visits to a doctor's office, disability benefits and insurance premiums paid, and incidental and disability absenteeism.

Data from the Literature

Program planners might also be able to identify the needs of a target population by reviewing any available current literature about that target population. An example would be a planner who is developing a health promotion program for individuals infected by the Human Immunodeficiency Virus (HIV). Because of the relative newness and seriousness of this disease and the number of people who have studied and written about it, there is a good chance that present literature could reflect the need of a certain target population.

The best means of accessing data from the literature is by using the available literature databases. Some are also available via the Internet. Most literature databases today are available in book form and via the computer on either CD-ROM or data tapes. Computer access would depend upon the capacity of the library or unit housing the databases. Depending on the database used, program planners can expect to find comprehensive listings of citations of journal articles, book chapters, and books, and in some databases, abstracts of the literature. Within the listings, most databases cite sources by both author and subject/title. Figure 4.2 provides an example of what planners might find when searching a database.

There are many literature databases available to program planners. Below is a short discussion of those databases that have proven helpful to health educators.

PsycLIT. This is a database produced by the American Psychological Association (APA) that includes journal articles, book chapters, and book citations on literature in psychology and related subjects. The database is divided into several major cat-

FIGURE 4.2 Sample Citations

Source: Adapted from *Index Medicus,* by D. A. B. Lindberg (ed.), 1995 (NIH Publication No. 95- 252), Washington, D.C.: U.S. Government Printing Office.

Author Citation

author ↓ article title ↓

O'Brien, K., Using focus groups to develop health surveys: An example from research on social relationships and AIDS-preventive behavior. Health Educ Q 1993 Fall; 20 (3): 361-372.

↑ journal

Subject/Title Citation

article title ↓

Using focus groups to develop health surveys: An example from research on social relationships and AIDS-preventive behavior. O'Brien, K. Health Educ Q 1993 Fall; 20 (3):

egories, but two of particular interest to health educators are (1) psychological and physical disorders and (2) health and mental health treatment and prevention.

Index Medicus. This is produced monthly by the National Library of Medicine and contains citations to the biomedical journal literature. A companion volume is the annual *Cumulated Index Medicus,* which comprises the contents of the twelve monthly issues (January through December). Indexed in *Index Medicus* are journal articles and those letters, editorials, biographies, and obituaries that have substantive contents (Lindberg, 1995).

Medline. Medline, available on CD-ROM, is an enlarged version of the printed *Index Medicus* (Baumgartner & Strong, 1994). It covers the international literature on biomedicine, including the allied health fields and the biological and physical sciences, humanities, and information science as they relate to medicine and health care. Information is indexed from approximately 3,600 journals and selected monographs of congresses and symposia.

Education Resources Information Center (ERIC). ERIC "is a national information system established in 1966 by the federal government to provide ready access to educational literature by and for educational practitioners and scholars" (Houston, 1987, p. x). Today it is funded by the Office of Educational Research and Improvement in the U.S. Department of Education. ERIC is available on data tapes that include all the information from the printed indexes *Current Index to Journals in Education (CIJE)* and *Resources in Education (RIE),* which are printed monthly. *CIJE* includes annotated journal articles, whereas *RIE* comprises abstracted citations for nonjournal literature (Baumgartner & Strong, 1994; Houston, 1987).

Cumulative Index to Nursing & Allied Health Literature (CINAHL). CINAHL grew out of the work of a hospital librarian in the 1940s who created an index for nursing journals. Demand for this work grew over the years until in 1961 the first volume of *Cumulative Index to Nursing Literature (CINL)* was published. "In order to keep pace with the trend toward a multidisciplinary approach to health care, the scope of coverage was expanded in 1977 to include allied health journals. To reflect this change *CINL* changed its title to *CINAHL*" (Marcarin, 1995, p. 3). This database went online in 1984 and is available today on magnetic tape and CD-ROM (Marcarin, 1995).

Steps for Conducting a Literature Search

The process of searching a database is not difficult, and with the exception of a few individual differences, most indexes are arranged in a similar format. As Figure 4.2 indicated, most indexes include both an author and a subject/title index. An item that is specific to each index is its thesaurus, a listing of the key words the indexes use to index the subject/titles. Program planners can find the thesauri in a separate volume with or near the indexes.

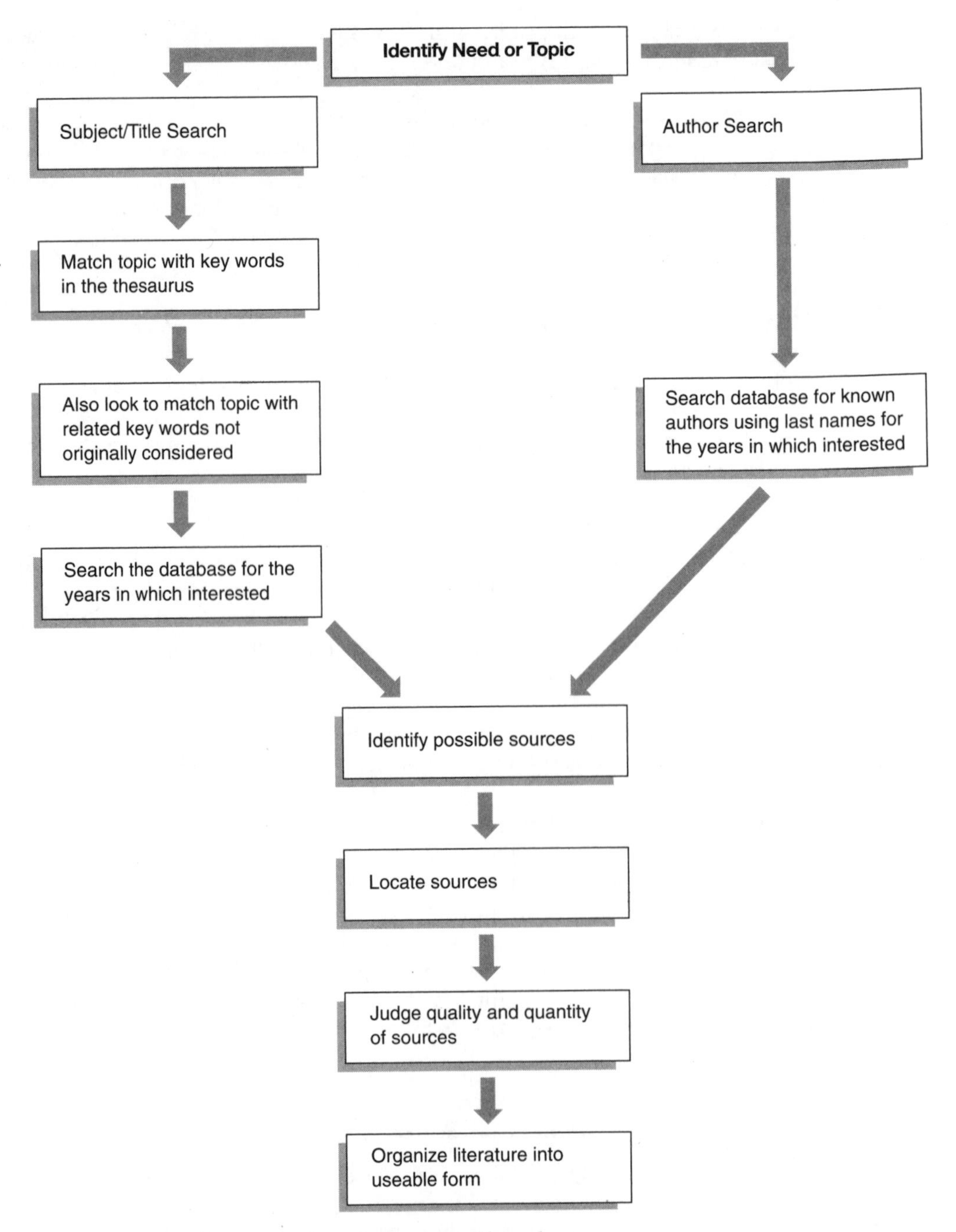

FIGURE 4.3 Literature Search Strategy Flowchart

Source: Adapted from *The Health Education Specialist: Self-Study for Professional Competence,* by S. G. Deeds, 1992, Los Alamitos, CA: Loose Canon Publications, and *Cumulative Index to Nursing and Allied Health Literature (CINAHL),* by S. Marcarin (ed.), 1995, Volume 40, Part A, Glendale, CA.

Figure 4.3 provides program planners with a literature search strategy in the form of a flowchart. The chart begins by identifying the need of the target population or topic to be searched. At this point, planners can search either by subject/title or by author. If planners know of an author who has done work on their topic, they can search the database using the author's last name. If they do not know of any such authors, they will need to match their topic with the key words presented in the thesaurus. Since there are times when a topic is not expressed in the same terms used in the thesaurus, planners will need to look for related terms. Once they have a list of key words, they need to search the database for possible matches. In conducting this search, they need to ensure that they are using the database that covers the years of literature in which they are interested. This search should identify possible sources and citations.

Once the sources are identified, planners will need to locate the sources, judge the quality and quantity of the literature, then organize it in a useful form (Deeds, 1992).

One means by which planners can judge the quality and quantity of the literature is to examine the references at the end of the publications. First, this reference list may lead planners to other sources not identified in the original search. But second, if the sources found in the database include all those commonly cited in the literature, this can verify the exhaustiveness of the search.

CONDUCTING A NEEDS ASSESSMENT

Having explained the general categories of needs assessment data, let's consider how a needs assessment is actually conducted. The process of conducting a needs assessment includes gathering data about the needs of a target population, analyzing the data, identifying and prioritizing the needs based upon the ability to meet each need and the importance of the need with regard to the health problem, and validating the need. As presented here, the process includes four steps. This is not the only way to conduct a needs assessment, but it serves to identify and explain the necessary steps.

Step 1: Determining the Present State of Health of the Target Population

The first step in the needs assessment process involves establishing the existing conditions, that is, the present state of health of the target population. To do this, planners must consider sources of data that reflect needs from the viewpoint of the planners and also needs perceived by those in the target population. At this point in time, planners need to determine if they are going to use both primary and secondary data or just one exclusive of the other. If primary data are going to be used, planners need to decide whom to collect the data from and take the necessary steps to collect the data. The data collection process is presented in Chapter 5. If secondary data are going to be used, planners need to decide which sources will be used. If it is feasible, we recommend that planners use both sources of data in order to gain a clear picture of both the service needs and demands.

Step 2: Analyzing the Data Collected

At this point in the needs assessment process, the planners must analyze all the data collected. The analysis of the data may be formal or informal. The approach used would depend upon what data were collected and how exact the planners wanted to be. Formal analysis would consist of some type of statistical analysis. This approach could be used only when appropriate statistical criteria (see any introductory statistics book) have been met. Much of the time, a less formal means of analyzing the data is used. This approach is commonly referred to as **eyeballing the data**—that is, looking at the data for obvious differences between health status, and health promotion and care. As Windsor and colleagues (1994, p. 63) have stated, eyeballing the data means looking for differences between "what is and what ought to be."

Sometimes this step in the needs assessment process is not very complicated because the need is obvious. For example, breast cancer rates may have risen in a given community, the number of breast screenings may be low, and the consumers may recognize this. Or, in another setting, the planners may find a direct correlation between the health status of a community and the lack of health care. However, not all needs assessments yield an obvious problem. The data may be mixed or confusing. In such cases, it is probably a good idea to see if additional data might be collected to paint a clearer picture. If obtaining additional data does not help, then asking other professionals for their opinions or relying on one's own "gut reactions" may aid in reaching a conclusion.

What conclusion should planners be looking for? At the end of Step 2, the planners should be able to list the problems, with a description of the nature and extent of each.

Step 3: Prioritizing the Identified Needs

This third step in the needs assessment process will set the program direction. Step 2 identified the problems; Step 3 is the stage at which planners prioritize the needs. Needs must be prioritized not because the lowest-priority needs are not important, but because organizations have limited resources. Thus planners need to see how the health promotion dollars can best be used. Therefore, in setting priorities, the planners should seek answers to these questions:

1. What is the most pressing need?
2. Are there resources adequate to deal with the problem?
3. Can the problem best be solved by a health promotion intervention, or could it be handled better through administration, politics, or changes in the economy?

4. Can the problem be solved in a reasonable amount of time?

After answering these questions, the planners should be able to prioritize the identified problems.

The actual process of setting priorities can take many different forms and range from basic rank ordering by a group of stakeholders, to use of the nominal group process, to a more complex process called the priority ranking process. The priority ranking process was first presented by Hanlon (1974) (it has been more recently presented in Pickett & Hanlon, 1990) and will be discussed here in greater detail because it can greatly help program planners quantify the subjective process of prioritizing. The process requires program planners to rate four different components of the identified needs and insert the ratings into a formula in order to determine a rating between 0 and 100. The components and their possible scores (in parenthesis) are:

A size of the problem (0 to 10)
B seriousness of the problem (0 to 20)
C effectiveness of the possible interventions (0 to 10)
D propriety, economics, acceptability, resources, and legality (PEARL) (0 or 1)

The formula in which the scores are placed is:

$$\text{Basic priority rating (BPR)} = \frac{(A + B)\,C}{3} \times D$$

Component A, size of the problem, can be scored by using epidemiological rates or determining the percentage of the target population at risk. The higher the rate or percentage, the greater the score. Pickett and Hanlon (1990) offer the scale noted in Table 4.1 for scoring the size of the problem when using incidence and prevalence rates.

TABLE 4.1 Scoring the Size of the Problem

Incidence or Prevalence per 100,000 Population	Score
50,000 or more	10
5,000 to 49,999	8
500 to 4,999	6
50 to 499	4
5 to 49	2
0.5 to 4.9	0

Source: Public Health: Administration and Practice, by G. Pickett and J. J. Hanlon, 1990, St. Louis: Mosby-Year Book, Inc.

Component *B*, seriousness of the problem, is examined using four factors: economic loss to community, family, or individuals; involvement of other people who were not initially affected by the problem, as with the spread of an infectious disease; the severity of the problem measured in mortality, morbidity, or disability; and the urgency of solving the problem because of additional harm. Although the maximum score for this component is 20, raters can use a 0 to 10 score for each of the factors. If the score for the component adds up to more than 20, a 20 is used.

Component *C*, effectiveness of the interventions, is often the most difficult of the four components to measure. The efficacy of some interventions is known, such as immunizations (close to 100%) and smoking cessation classes (around 30%), but for many, it is not. Program planners will need to estimate this score based upon the work of others or their own best guess.

Component *D*, PEARL, consists of several factors that determine whether a particular intervention can be carried out at all. The score is 0 or 1; any need that receives a zero will automatically drop to the bottom of the priority list because a score of zero for this component will yield a total score of zero in the formula. Examples of when a zero may result are if an intervention is economically impossible, unacceptable to the target population or planners, or illegal.

Once the score for the four components is determined, an overall priority rating for each need can be calculated, and the prioritizing can take place.

Other means of quantifying the prioritization of the needs may include getting the target population or key people from the community, like opinion leaders, to rank-order the identified needs.

Finally, when prioritizing needs, planners also need to consider the existing health promotion programs to avoid any duplication with planning efforts. Therefore, program planners should seek to determine the status of existing health promotion programs by trying to answer as many questions as possible from the following list:

1. What health promotion programs are presently available to the target population?
2. Are the programs being utilized? If not, why not?
3. How effective are the programs? Are they meeting their stated goals and objectives?
4. How were the needs for these programs determined?
5. Are the programs accessible to the target population? Where are they located? When are they offered? Are there any qualifying criteria that people must meet to enroll? Can the target population get to the program? Can the target population afford the programs?
6. Are the needs of the target population being met? If not, why not?

There are several ways to seek answers to these questions. Probably the most common way is through **networking** with other people working in health promotion and the health care system—that is, communicating with others who may know about existing programs. (See Chapter 9 for a more detailed discussion of networking.) These people may be located in the local or state health department, in voluntary health agencies, or in health care facilities, such as hospitals, clinics, nursing homes, extended care facilities, or Health Maintenance Organizations (HMOs).

Planners might also find information about existing programs by checking with someone in an organization that serves as a clearinghouse for health promotion programs or by using a community resource guide. The local or state health department, a local chamber of commerce, a coalition, the local medical/dental societies, a community task force, or a community health center may serve as a clearinghouse or produce such a guide. Another avenue is to talk with people in the target population. Although they may not know about all existing programs, they may be able to share information on the effectiveness and accessibility of some of the programs. Finally, some of the information could be collected in Step 1 through separate community forums, focus groups, or surveys.

Step 4: Validating the Prioritized Needs

The final step in the needs assessment process is to validate the identified need(s). By validate, we mean to confirm that the need that was identified is the need that should be addressed. Obviously, if great care was taken in the needs assessment process, validation should be a perfunctory step. However, there have been times when a need was not properly validated; much energy and many resources have thereby been wasted on unnecessary programs.

Validation amounts to "double checking," or making sure that an identified need is the real need. Any means available can be used, such as (1) rechecking the steps followed in the needs assessment to eliminate any bias; (2) conducting a focus group with some individuals from the target population to determine their reaction to the identified need (if a focus group was not used earlier to gather the data); and (3) getting a "second opinion" from other health professionals.

ASSESSMENT PROTOCOL FOR EXCELLENCE IN PUBLIC HEALTH (APEX/PH)

A discussion of the needs assessment process would not be complete without mention of **APEX/PH** (NACHO, 1991), a needs assessment instrument for local health departments. APEX/PH was developed in 1991 by the National Association of County Health Officials (NACHO) and a number of collaborative groups. (Note: In July 1994, NACHO combined with the United States Conference of Local Health Officers [USCLHO] to form a new organization called the National Association of County and City Health Officials [NACCHO]). APEX/PH was developed to help local health departments respond to the Institute of Medicine's (IOM) report "The Future of Public Health," in which it was stated every public health agency should regularly and systematically collect, assemble, and analyze information on community health needs (IOM, 1988).

The APEX/PH Workbook is divided into two parts: Part I focuses on assessing and improving the organizational capacity of the local health department, and Part II is aimed at identifying and prioritizing the community health needs. Specifically, Part II uses demographic, socioeconomic, and morbidity and mortality data to determine the health status of those in the community. One criticism of Part II of APEX/PH has been the lack of attention given to the assessment of environmental health needs (McDonald, Treser, & Hatlen, 1994). Therefore, an environmental health addendum was created to supplement the APEX/PH Workbook. Since the development of this addendum, the Centers for Disease Control and Prevention have provided the Washington State Department of Health with a grant to pilot-test the addendum in that state (McDonald, Treser, & Hatlen, 1994).

The APEX/PH is not an assessment tool that would be useful in all needs assessment activities, but it makes good sense for planners working on community-wide programs to use it or the data collected from its use. Planners will need to check with the local health departments to see if APEX/PH data have been collected on the target population communities.

SUMMARY

This chapter presented several definitions of needs assessment and a discussion of primary and secondary data. The sources of these data were discussed at length. Also, presented in this chapter was a four-step approach that health planners can follow in conducting a needs assessment on a given group of people. It is by no means the only way of conducting an assessment, but it is workable.

No matter what procedure is used to conduct a needs assessment, the end result should be the same. Planners should finish with a list of clearly defined, prioritized problems of the target population.

QUESTIONS

1. What does *needs assessment* mean?
2. Why must a needs assessment be viewed through the eyes of both the planners and the consumers?
3. What is the difference between primary and secondary data?
4. Name several different sources of both primary and secondary data.
5. What advice might you give to someone who is interested in using previously collected data (secondary data) for a needs assessment?
6. What are the four steps in the needs assessment process, as identified in the chapter?
7. Explain the difference between a community forum and a focus group.
8. What is APEX/PH?

ACTIVITIES

1. Assume that you have been hired by the board of trustees of your college or university to conduct a needs assessment on the student body for the possibility of developing a health promotion program. Assume that there are few secondary data on this group of people, other than national norms for college students. You could conduct a "university forum" or hold a series of focus groups, but instead you have decided to survey a random sample of the population with a paper-and-pencil instrument. Your task now is to develop a needs assessment instrument. When developing the instrument, use questions that will collect data that are reflective of your target population's awareness of health, attitudes about health, knowledge of health, health behavior, health interests, and demographics, as well as marketing possibilities. After completing the instrument, pilot-test it on 10 students (for the purposes of this assignment, this does not need to be a random group). Use the results of the pilot-test to complete Steps 2 and 3 in the needs assessment process.
2. Develop a needs assessment instrument for a program you will be planning. Collect the same type of data noted in Activity 1, administer the instrument to a small group of people, then complete Steps 2 and 3 in the needs assessment process.
3. Using secondary data provided by your instructor (such as data from a Behavioral Risk Factor Survey, state or local secondary data, or data from the National Center for Health Statistics), analyze the data and determine the needs of the target population. Finally, prioritize the needs using the criteria noted in Step 3 of the needs assessment process.
4. Administer an HHA/HRA to a group of 25–30 people. Using the data generated, identify and prioritize a collective list of health problems of the group.
5. Plan and conduct a focus group on an identified health problem on your campus. Develop a set of questions to be used, identify and invite people to participate in the group, facilitate the process, and then write up a summary of the results based upon your written notes and an audio tape of the session.
6. Using the data (paper-and-pencil instruments, clinical tests, and health histories) generated from a local health fair, identify and prioritize a collective list of health problems of those who participated.

5

Measurement, Measures, and Data Collection

After reading this chapter and answering the questions at the end, you should be able to:

- Briefly describe the four levels of measurement.
- Describe several methods of data collection.
- Define *bias* in data collection and discuss how it can be reduced.
- Discuss the advantages and disadvantages of data collection from self-report (written surveys, telephone interviews, and face-to-face interviews), direct observation, existing records, and meetings.
- Explain the various types of validity.
- Define *reliability* and explain why it is important.
- Describe how a sample can be obtained from a population.
- Differentiate between probability and nonprobability samples.
- Describe how a pilot test is used.

Key Terms

anonymous
bias
census
cluster sample
concurrent validity
confidential
construct validity
content validity
criterion-based validity
direct observation
field study
frame
internal consistency
interrater reliability
interval
levels of measurement
nominal
nonprobability sample
ordinal
parallel forms reliability
parameters
pilot test
predictive validity
prepilot
probability sample
random-digit dialing
randomization
ratio
reliability
respondents
response rate
sample
sampling
self-report
simple random sample
stability reliability
statistics
stratified random sample
survey population
systematic sample
validity

In the process of planning and evaluating health promotion programs, it is necessary to collect data. This information can be used for a needs assessment when designing a program or used in the evaluation of a program. The techniques used to collect the data in both cases are the same; the difference lies in how the information is used. In needs assessment, the data are used to determine the initial need for the program; in an evaluation, the information collected is used to make decisions about the program or to determine the value of the program.

An extremely important aspect of data collection is consistency. All participants must be treated in the same manner in order to reduce the possibility of error that will affect the final results. Another consideration is the number of people who are willing to participate when asked, which is referred to as the **response rate**. More accurate results are gained when the response rate is high.

The response rate is usually higher when the responses are anonymous or confidential. **Anonymous** refers to data collected without requiring the person's name, Social Security number, or other identifying information. **Confidential** data may include information that would serve to identify the respondent, but this information is not released without the person's permission.

*Bias** is defined as the difference between the score obtained and the true score. Windsor and colleagues (1994) describe ways in which bias can occur in data collection: for example, when participants change behavior because they are being tested, when certain characteristics of the interviewer influence a response, and when participants answer questions in a particular way regardless of the questions. Using techniques to reduce bias during data collection helps increase the accuracy of the results.

LEVELS OF MEASUREMENT

When planners/evaluators begin to think about data collection, they need to consider the type(s) of data they want to use. Not all data are the same.

There are four **levels of measurement** used to determine how something is to be quantified. They are heirarchical in nature, and the type of data collected determines what statistical tests can be used to analyze them. The four levels of measurement are:

1. **Nominal** provides a label to classify into a group (sex, city of residence, nationality). The categories represent differences from each other and not amounts of a characteristic.
2. **Ordinal** provides a label to classify into a group and rank-orders according to intensity or severity (academic achievement, level of satisfaction with a program, or socioeconomic status). Likert scales are commonly used in collecting ordinal data.
3. **Interval** ranks data, but also provides a standard unit of measure along a scale (temperature, standardized test scores). The one drawback of interval scales is that there is no absolute zero value. For example, a temperature of zero does not mean that there is no temperature; zero is only a point on the scale.
4. **Ratio** provides a standard unit of measure along a scale with an absolute zero (height, weight, dollars).

If given the choice, planners/evaluators should strive to collect ratio data. This is the highest level in the hierarchy and allows the planner/evaluators the greatest flexibility in data analysis.

TYPES OF MEASUREMENT

Many types of measurement can be utilized to assess needs or conduct an evaluation. The type chosen should reflect the program goals and objectives, which will be discussed in detail in Chapter 6. Table 5.1 presents seven types of measurement, with examples of how the information can be obtained.

TABLE 5.1 Types of Measurement

Type of Measurement	Example Means of Obtaining Data
Awareness	• Written instruments (e.g., true-false items, completion items) • Proxy measures (see Ward, 1981)
Knowledge	• Written/oral knowledge test (e.g., completion items, short- and extended-answer essay items, multiple-choice items, true-false items) • Proxy measures (see Ward, 1981)
Attitudes	• Written instrument (e.g., summated Likert scale items, cumulative scale items, equal-appearing interval scale items, value scale items, semantic differential items, forced choice items)
Behavior	• Self-report written instrument (e.g., completion items, short- and extended-answer essay items, multiple-choice items, true-false items) • `Observation (obtrusive and unobtrusive) • Proxy measures (see Ward, 1981)
Skills	• Observation (obtrusive and unobtrusive) • Skills test (e.g., CPR)
Health status	• Medical tests and screenings (e.g., blood pressure, cholesterol level, TB screenings) • Health risk/hazard appraisals
Quality of life	• Written instrument • Proxy measures (see Ward, 1981) • Other proxy measures noted by Green and Kreuter (1991) (e.g., absenteeism, comport, crime, discrimination, illegitimacy, welfare)

METHODS OF DATA COLLECTION

Self-Report

Written questionnaires, telephone interviews, and face-to-face interviews are methods of collecting data from **respondents,** that is, the individuals who supply this information. In **self-report,** each respondent is asked to recall and report accurate information; inaccurate information may lead to bias in the data collected. The results are influenced by the person's ability to remember information ("When was your last visit to the dentist?") and report it honestly ("Do you floss your teeth daily?"). Some questions may be viewed as too personal; if this information they provide is essential, such questions should be worded carefully and included at the end of the instrument. Offering anonymity is helpful in gaining honest answers from respondents.

Another possible bias in self-report is the desire to please the interviewer or to give a socially acceptable answer. If information is requested about a smoking cessation program, the respondent may want to give the "right" answer ("Yes, I quit smoking"). This bias may also work in reverse: A respondent may not like one aspect of a program and may give negative responses to all questions to emphasize displeasure. For example, a respondent may indicate that the time the class was offered was not convenient, the materials were not useful, and the location was not suitable, in order to downgrade the program because he feels that the instructor was ineffective. Skilled interviewing techniques can aid evaluators in obtaining correct information.

BOX 5.1 Sample Cover Letter

Lake County
Community
Health Coalition

10 East Washington Street
Painesville, OH 44077-3472

January 14, 1995

Dear Community Member,

The goal of the Lake County Community Health Coalition is to work together to improve the health of the residents of our county. In order to effectively focus our efforts on current needs, we are asking for your help. Enclosed is a survey for you to complete. Please take a few minutes to tell us what you think are the most important health needs.

There is no need to put your name on the survey; no individual responses will be reported. We will compile the results in February and provide this information to Coalition members. Please return your survey in the enclosed, postage-paid envelope by February 10.

If you have questions about the survey or would like more information about the Community Health Coaltion, please call our office at 555-4561. Thank you for your help.

Sincerely,

Lloyd Chapman
Coalition Chairperson

Source: Lake County Community Health Coalition. Reprinted by permission.

Questions Used in Self-Report

The presentation, wording, and sequence of questions in self-report questionnaires and interviews can be critical in gaining the necessary information. The questionnaire or interview should begin by explaining the purpose of the study and why the individual's responses are important. A cover letter should accompany a mailed questionnaire, explaining the need for the information and including very clear directions for supplying it (see Box 5.1 for an example of a cover letter). The name, address, and telephone number of the planner/evaluator or another contact person can also be included in case the respondent needs additional information to complete the questionnaire. A stamped, addressed envelope should be enclosed. Udinsky, Osterlind, and Lynch (1981) have developed guidelines for writing a cover letter, which are presented in Table 5.2.

With telephone or face-to-face interviews, the interviewer can give information about the study and explain the need for information from the individual contacted. This introduction can be followed by general questions to put the respondent at ease or to develop a rapport between the interviewer and the respondent.

After several general questions come the questions of interest. Any questions that deal with sensitive topics should be posed at the end of the questionnaire or interview. Answers to questions about drug use, sexuality, or even demographic information such as income level are more readily answered when the respondents understand the need for the information, are assured of confidentiality or anonymity, and feel comfortable with the interviewer or the questionnaire. If the

TABLE 5.2 Guidelines for a Cover Letter

1. This letter should contain a clear, brief, yet adequate statement of the purpose and value of the questionnaire.
2. It should be addressed to the respondent specifically.
3. It should provide good reason for the respondent to reply.
4. It should involve the respondent in a constructive and appealing way.
5. The respondent's professional responsibility, intellectual curiosity, personal worth, etc., are typical of response appeals.
6. The letter should establish a reasonable, but firm, return date.
7. An offer to send the respondent a report of the findings is often effective, though it carries with it the ethical responsibility to honor such a pledge.
8. The use of a letterhead, signature, and organizational endorsements lends prestige and official status to the letter.
9. The letter should guarantee anonymity and confidentiality.
10. Each letter should be signed individually by the researcher.
11. The researcher should include a stamped, self-addressed envelope for the return of the instrument.

Source: From *Evaluation Resource Handbook: Gathering, Analyzing, Reporting Data* (p. 120), by B. F. Udinsky, S. J. Osterlind, and S. W. Lynch, 1981, San Diego, CA: EdITS Publishers. Reprinted by permission of EdITS Publishers.

respondent ends the interview or does not complete the survey when asked sensitive questions, the other information collected can still be used; this is another advantage of putting these questions at the end.

The actual questions should be clear and unbiased. It is important to avoid questions with a specific direction ("How have you enjoyed the class?") that would guide the respondent's answer. Two-part (double-barreled) questions should also be avoided ("Do you brush and floss your teeth?"). Another problem with question design occurs when the question assumes knowledge that individuals may not have or includes terminology that they may not understand ("What cardiovascular benefits do you feel you gain from aerobic exercise?").

The way in which data collection questions are worded is extremely important in gaining the needed information. The result of a poorly worded question was evident to one health promotion planner who was planning a smoking cessation program for employees. When asked, "Do you feel we need a smoking cessation program?" most employees said yes. The planner realized later that he should also have asked the question, "Would you attend a smoking cessation program?" since very few employees participated.

If possible, planners/evaluators should use existing questionnaires. This requires gaining permission from the author if the document is not in the public domain. (Documents in the public domain can be freely used without requesting permission.) The advantages to using questionnaires that have been developed by experts include increased credibility, lower cost, less planning time needed, and more documentation of validity and reliability. The major disadvantage—one that prevents the use of existing questionnaires in many cases—is that the items used to evaluate one program may not all be relevant or appropriate to evaluate a similar program. Adaptations may be needed so that the questionnaire will fit with program objectives or the local target population.

If an existing questionnaire is not available, one must be developed. When designing a questionnaire (see Box 5.2 for a list of steps to follow when developing a data collection instrument) to collect self-reported data, evaluators can use several types of questions. The most structured or closed types of questions have yes-no or multiple-choice responses, and are most often used for knowledge questions. These types of responses are the easiest to tabulate but do not allow the individual to elaborate on the answers. They may also force a person into a choice because of the limited number of responses to each question. An "other" category, with space to list the exact nature of the "other" response, may serve to give the respondent another option. However, giving the respondents an opportunity to provide their own answers on multiple-choice questions makes it more difficult to categorize responses when the data are analyzed, thus reducing one of the main benefits of such questions. One way to ensure that the most common responses to questions are included in the multiple choices is to involve several individuals (especially those in the target population) in the formation of the instrument.

Attitude questions generally use less structured forms. Scales, such as Likert or semantic differentials, are often used, with the respondent choosing a response

BOX 5.2 Steps in the Development of a Data Collection Instrument

1. Determine the purpose and objectives of the proposed instrument.
2. Develop instrument specifications.
3. Review existing instruments.
4. Develop new instrument items.
5. Develop directions for administration and examples of how to complete items.
6. Establish procedures used for scoring the instrument.
7. Conduct a preliminary review of the instrument with colleagues.
8. Revise the instrument based on review.
9. Pilot test the instrument with twenty to fifty subjects.
10. Conduct item analysis, reliability, and validity studies.
11. Provide instrument specifications and pilot study data to a panel of experts for review.
12. Revise the instrument based on comments from the panel of experts.
13. Conduct a second pilot test.
14. Conduct item analysis, reliability, and validity studies.
15. Provide instrument specifications and pilot study data to a panel of experts for a second review.
16. Make final changes.
17. Determine cut score (for criterion-referenced tests or screening tests).
18. Produce the final instrument for evaluation study.

Source: From Paul D. Sarvela and Robert J. McDermott, *Health Education Evaluation and Measurement: A Practitioner's Perspective.*

along a continuum, generally ranging from a five- to a seven-point scale. For example, responses to the statement, "I feel that it is important to limit my use of salt," might be rated on a seven-point scale ranging from "strongly agree" to "strongly disagree" (see examples in Table 5.3).

Unstructured or open-ended questions, such as essay questions, short-answer questions, journals, or logs, may be used to gain descriptive information about a program, but are generally not used when collecting quantitative data. Such responses are often difficult to summarize or to code for analysis. Table 5.3 provides examples of structured and unstructured types of questions.

Self-report, while widely used in evaluating health promotion programs, has limitations. To maximize the usefulness of self-report, Baranowski (1985, pp. 181–82) has developed eight steps to increase the accuracy of this method of data collection. These steps include:

TABLE 5.3 Examples of Self-Report Questions

Structured

I. Dichotomy

1. What is your gender?
   a. Female b. Male
2. A risk factor for heart disease is sedentary lifestyle.
   a. True b. False

II. Multiple Choice

1. The leading cause of death in the United States for adults is
   a. Cancer b. Heart disease
   c. Injuries d. AIDS
2. What type of computer do you use?
   a. IBM b. Apple
   c. Radio Shack d. Other (please specify) ____________________

III. Matching

Vitamin deficiencies

1. Vitamin A	a. Frequent infection
2. Vitamin C	b. Slow blood clotting
3. Vitamin D	c. Night blindness
4. Vitamin K	d. Bone softening

Grams of saturated fats

1. Butter, 1 tbsp.	a. 9
2. Ice cream, 4 oz.	b. 7.1
3. Chicken, 3 oz.	c. 5
4. One hot dog	d. 1.2

Less Structured (But Still Closed)

I. Likert

1. Women should be able to have an abortion if they choose to do so.	Strongly agree	Agree	Neutral	Disagree	Strongly disagree
2. I feel I can exercise regardless of weather conditions.	Strongly agree	Agree	Neutral	Disagree	Strongly disagree

II. Semantic Differentials

1. Smokeless tobacco is Good ___ ___ ___ ___ ___ Bad
2. When taking a test, I feel Nervous ___ ___ ___ ___ ___ Calm

III. Rank Order

1. Put the following values in order, from most important in your life to least important:
   a. health ___ d. emotional security ___
   b. love ___ e. financial security ___
   c. friendship ___

2. Rank-order the following servings of foods from highest to lowest sources of protein:

a.	tuna	___	d.	cottage cheese	___
b.	rice	___	e.	bread	___
c.	sirloin steak	___	f.	broccoli	___

Unstructured (Open)

I. Completion

1. I like to exercise because ______________________________
2. The types of foods I generally eat are ______________________________

II. Short-answer

1. List five advantages to conducting a worksite health promotion program.
2. Describe the correct way to lift a heavy object to avoid straining your back.

III. Essay

1. Explain the difference between aerobic and anaerobic exercise. Include examples of each type of exercise, and discuss the importance of each in total fitness.
2. Discuss the incidence of tuberculosis in the world today, including who is at risk and the public health measures to reduce the problem.

---

1. Select measures that clearly reflect program outcomes.
2. Select measures that have been designed to anticipate response problems and that have been validated.
3. Conduct a pilot study with the target population.
4. Anticipate and correct major sources of unreliability.
5. Employ quality control procedures to detect other sources of error.
6. Employ multiple methods.
7. Use multiple measures.
8. Use experimental and control groups with random assignment to control for biases in self-report.

By following these steps, evaluators can enhance the accuracy of self-report, making this a more effective method of data collection.

Written Questionnaires

Probably the most often used method of collecting self-reported data is the written questionnaire. It has several advantages, notably the ability to reach a large number of respondents in a short period of time, even if there is a large geographic area to be covered. This method offers low cost with minimum staff time needed. However, it often has the lowest response rate.

With a written questionnaire, each individual receives the same questions and instructions in the same format, so that the possibility of response bias is lessened. The corresponding disadvantage, however, is the inability to clarify any questions or confusion on the part of the respondent.

As mentioned, the response rate for mailed questionnaires tends to be low, but there are several ways to overcome this problem. One way is to include with the questionnaire a postcard that identifies the person in some way (such as by name or identification number). The individual is asked to return the questionnaire in the envelope provided and to send the postcard back separately. Anonymity is thus maintained, but the evaluator knows who returned a questionnaire. The evaluator can then send a follow-up mailing (including a letter indicating the importance of a response and another copy of the questionnaire with a return envelope) to the individuals who did not return a postcard from the first mailing. The use of incentives also can increase the response rate. For example, some hospitals offer free health risk appraisals to those who return a completed needs assessment instrument.

Another way to overcome the drawback of a low response rate from a mailed questionnaire is to use this method for a homogeneous group, that is, one composed of similar individuals. The problem of underrepresentation of certain types of individuals may still occur, but if the group is homogeneous in, for example, age or health behaviors, the likelihood that the missing data will be different from the data collected is much less.

The appearance of the questionnaire is extremely important. It should be attractive, be easy to read, and offer ample space for the respondent's answers. It should also be easy to understand and complete, since written questionnaires provide no opportunity to clarify a point while the respondent is completing the questionnaire. All mailed questionnaires should be accompanied by a cover letter, as previously discussed.

Short questionnaires that do not take a long time to complete and questionnaires that clearly explain the need for the information are more likely to be returned. Evaluators should give thought to designing a questionnaire that is as easy to complete and return as possible.

Telephone Interviews

Compared to mailed surveys or face-to-face interviews, the telephone interview offers a relatively easy method of collecting self-reported data at a moderate cost. The evaluator must choose a way of selecting individuals to participate in this type of data collection; this method will reach only those individuals who have access to a telephone. One possibility is to call a randomly selected group of people who have completed a health promotion program. Another method is to select telephone numbers at random from a telephone directory, for example, a local telephone book, student directory, church directory, or employee directory. This method will not reach all the population since some people have unlisted telephone numbers. One way to overcome this problem is a method known as **random-digit dialing,** in which telephone number combinations are chosen at random. This method would include businesses as well as residences and nonworking as well as valid numbers, making it more time-consuming. The numbers may be obtained from a table of random numbers or generated by a computer. The advantage of random-digit dialing is that it includes all the survey population with a telephone in the area, including people with unlisted numbers. Drawbacks to this method include some people's resistance to answer questions over the telephone or resentment in being interrupted with an unwanted call. Those conducting the interviews may also have difficulty reaching individuals because of unanswered phones or answering machines.

Telephone interviewing requires trained interviewers; without proper training and use of a standardized questionnaire, the interviewer may not be consistent during the interview. Explaining a question or offering additional information can cause a respondent to change an initial response, thus creating a chance for interviewer bias. The interviewer does have the opportunity to clarify questions, which is an advantage over the written questionnaire, but does not have the advantage of visual cues that the face-to-face interview offers.

Face-to-Face Interviews

At times it is advantageous to administer the instrument to the respondents in an interview setting. This method is time-consuming, since it may require not only time for the actual interview but also travel time to the interview site and/or waiting time between interviews. As with telephone interviews, the interviewer must be carefully trained to conduct the interview in an unbiased manner. It is important to explain the need for the information in order to conduct the evaluation and to accurately record the responses. Methods of probing, or eliciting additional information about an individual's responses, are used in the face-to-face interview, and the interviewer must be skilled at this technique.

This method of self-report allows the interviewer to develop rapport with the respondent. The flexibility of this method, along with the availability of visual cues, has the advantage of gaining more complete evaluation data from respondents. Smaller numbers of respondents are included in this method, but the rate of participation is generally high. It is important to establish and follow procedures for selecting the respondents. There are also several disadvantages to the face-to-face interview. It is more expensive, requiring more staff time and training of interviewers. Variations in the interviews, as well as differences between interviewers, may influence the results.

Direct Observation

Direct observation can be used to obtain information regarding the behavior of participants in a program. For example, planners/evaluators might observe students in the cafeteria to gain information about actual food choices and consumption. This method is somewhat time-consuming, but it seldom encounters the problem of people refusing to participate in the evaluation, resulting in a high response rate.

Observation is generally more accurate than self-report, but the presence of the observer may alter the behavior of the people being observed. For example, having someone observe smoking behavior may cause smokers to smoke less out of self-consciousness due to their being under observation, not as a result of the program. Observers must be unobtrusive; conspicuous note taking or recording behavior may bias a needs assessment or evaluation.

Differences among observers may also bias the results, since different observers may not observe and report behaviors in the same manner. Some behaviors, such as safety belt use, are very easy to observe accurately. Others, such as degree of tension, are more difficult to observe. This method of data collection requires a clear definition of the exact behavior to observe and how to record it, in order to avoid subjective observations. Observer bias can be reduced by providing training and by determining interrater reliability (see page 73 for a discussion of interrater reliability). If the observers are skilled, observation can provide accurate evaluation data at a moderate cost.

Indirect methods or proxy measures can also be used to determine whether a behavior has occurred. Examples of indirect methods include measuring weight loss and monitoring blood pressure. These measures can be used to verify self-reports when observations of the actual changes in behavior cannot be observed.

Existing Records

Using existing records may be an efficient way to obtain the necessary information for a needs assessment or evaluation without the need for additional data collection. The advantages include low cost, minimum staff needed, and ease in randomization. The disadvantages to using this method of data collection include difficulty in gaining access to necessary records and the possible lack of availability of all the information needed for program evaluation.

Examples of the use of existing records include checking physician records to monitor blood pressure and cholesterol levels of participants in an exercise program, reviewing insurance usage of employees enrolled in an employee health promotion program, and comparing the academic records of students engaging in an after-school weight loss program. In these situations, as with all needs assessments or evaluations using existing records, the cooperation of the agencies that hold the records is essential. At times, agencies may be willing to collect additional information to aid in the evaluation of a health promotion program. Keepers of records are concerned about confidentiality and the release of private information. Evaluators can deal with this by getting permission from all participants in the evaluation to use their records or by using only anonymous data.

Meetings

Meetings are a good source of information for process evaluation. For example, if a fitness program is being evaluated, the evaluators, staff, and some participants may meet early in the planning and implementation stages to discuss the status of the program. Focus groups or community forums are other examples of engaging potential program participants in discussions to gain insight for program planning

TABLE 5.4 Methods of Data Collection

Method	Advantages	Disadvantages
Self-report		
Written questionnaire	Large outreach No interviewer bias Convenient Low cost Minimum staff time required Easy to administer Quick Standardized	Possible low response rate Possible unrepresentation No clarification of questions Need homogeneous group if response is low
Telephone interview	Moderate cost Relatively easy to administer Good response rate	Possible problem of representation Possible interviewer bias Requires trained interviewers
Face-to-face interview	High response rate Flexibility Gain in-depth data Develop rapport	Expensive Requires trained interviewers Possible interviewer bias Limits sample size Time-consuming
Observation	Accurate behavioral data Can be unobtrusive Moderate cost	Requires trained observers May bias behavior Possible observer bias May be time-consuming
Existing records	Low cost Easy to randomize Avoid data collection Minimum staff needed	May need agency cooperation Certain data may be unavailable
Meetings	Good for formative evaluation Low cost Flexible	Possible result bias Limited input from participants

(see Chapter 4 for a discussion of the use of focus groups and community forums in needs assessment).

The meeting structure can be flexible to avoid limiting the scope of the information gained. The cost of this form of evaluation is minimal. Possible biases may occur, however, when meetings are used as a source of evaluation data. Those involved may give "socially acceptable" responses to questions rather than discussing actual concerns. There also may be limited input if relatively few participants are included, or if one or two participants dominate the discussion.

Summarized in Table 5.4 are the advantages and disadvantages of the various methods of data collection. As discussed in Chapter 14, it may be beneficial to combine methods of data collection as well as to incorporate quantitative and qualitative data.

QUALITY OF DATA COLLECTION

The results of a needs assessment or program evaluation are only as good as the data that are used to gain the results. If a questionnaire was filled with ambiguous questions and the respondents were not sure how to answer, it is highly likely that the data collected will not be reflective of the true knowledge, attitudes, etc., of those responding. Therefore, it is of vital importance that planners and evaluators make sure that the data they collect are both reliable and valid.

Reliability

Reliability refers to consistency in the measurement process. A reliable instrument gives the same (or nearly the same) result every time. However, no instrument will ever provide perfect accuracy in measurement. Green and Lewis (1986) illustrate the theory of reliability with an equation, where total score (obtained score) equals the true score (unobservable) plus an error score. The total score represents the individual's score obtained on the measuring instrument. The true score represents the score for the same individual if all conditions and the measuring instrument were perfect. An error score must be included since conditions are never perfect in the real world. Several methods of determining reliability are available.

Internal Consistency

Internal consistency refers to the intercorrelations among the individual items on the instrument, that is, whether all items on the instrument are measuring part of the total area. This can be done by logically examining the instrument to ensure that the items reflect what is to be measured and that the level of difficulty of all items is the same. Statistical methods can also be used to determine internal consistency by correlating the items on the test with the total score.

Stability Reliability

Stability reliability, or test-retest reliability, examines whether the results would be the same if the instrument were administered to the same person at a later date. The length of time between test and retest may vary from hours to weeks to years. A maximum amount of time should be allowed so that individuals are not answering on the basis of remembering responses they made on the first test, but it should not be so long that other events could occur in the intervening time to influence their responses. To avoid the problems of retesting, parallel forms of the test can be administered to the participants and the results can be correlated.

Interrater Reliability

Interrater reliability focuses on the consistency between test administrators. This comes into play when information is collected by observing or rating, or in other situations that could be affected by human error. It is measured as an agreement or correlation between the raters, as in the consistency of measurement between observers when measuring the amount of time preschool children spend in active play. This type of reliability is reported as a percentage.

Parallel Forms Reliability

Parallel forms reliability determines whether different forms of the same test instrument have equal means, standard deviations, and item intercorrelations. Parallel forms reliability is used to determine if different forms of standardized tests (e.g., college entrance exams) include the same content and are of the same degree of difficulty.

Validity

When designing a data collection instrument, planners/evaluators must ensure that it measures what it is intended to measure. This refers to the **validity** of the measurement—whether it is correctly measuring the concepts under investigation. Using a valid instrument increases the chance that planners/evaluators are measuring what they want to measure, thus ruling out other possible explanations for the results. We will discuss several types of validity.

Content Validity

The first type of validity, **content validity**, is based on the measurement's reflecting the area(s) of information—that is, the items on the instrument come from each content area measured. A review of the literature is a good means of establishing content validity since current information about the topic is used to develop the instrument. For example, when planning a risk reduction program for cardiovascular disease, the program planner can conduct a review of the literature in the area of cardiovascular risk reduction in order to ensure that all major risk factors, such as smoking, exercise, and diet, are included on a questionnaire.

Another means of establishing content validity is to use a group (jury or panel) of experts to review the instrument. After such a group is identified, they would be asked to review each element of the instrument for its appropriateness to be included. The collective opinion of the experts is then used to determine the content of the instrument.

Criterion-Based Validity

Criterion-based validity is determined by established criteria and looks at the degree of relationship between two measures of the same phenomenon. If the two measurements are focused on the present, such as scores on a knowledge test about AIDS and current grade point average, the type of criterion validity is known as **concurrent validity.** If the measurement used will be correlated with a future measurement of the same phenomenon, as with the use of standardized test scores to predict future college success, the criterion validity is known as **predictive validity**.

Construct Validity

Another type of validity is **construct validity**. This deals with psychological constructs, such as self-esteem, self-efficacy, or locus of control, which are difficult to define but have characteristics that are recognized. Individuals with high levels of the trait (as determined by experts) are given the instrument. If they receive high scores on the instrument, it is determined to have high construct validity—that is, it is measuring the construct as intended.

SAMPLING

Once a reliable and valid method of collecting the data has been chosen, evaluators should consider how to select the group of individuals who will be included. Depending on the size of the population, they may want to collect data from all participants **(census)** or from only some of the participants **(sample).** Evaluators must exercise care in selecting the sample: The sample should be representative of the total target group included in the program, and the selection procedure should be unbiased.

Figure 5.1 illustrates the relationship between groups of individuals. All individuals, unspecified by time or place, constitute the universe—for example, all U.S. citizens, regardless of where they reside in the world. Within the universe is a population of individuals specified by time or place, such as all U.S. residents in the fifty United States on January 1, 1997. Within this population is a **survey population,** composed of all individuals who can be contacted. The key term here is *accessible.* For example, all U.S. citizens who can be reached by telephone would be a survey population. Obviously, this would not include those without telephones, such as those who chose not to own them, those institutionalized, and the homeless.

A survey population may still be too large to include in its entirety. For this reason, a sample is chosen from the survey population, a process called **sampling**. These are the individuals who will be included in the data collection process. Using a sample rather than an entire survey population helps contain costs. For example, using a sample reduces the amount of staff time needed to conduct interviews, the cost of postage for written questionnaires, and the time and cost of travel to conduct observations.

How the sample is chosen is critical to the result of the needs assessment or evaluation: does the information gained from the sample reflect the knowledge, attitudes, and behaviors of the population? According to Green and Lewis (1986), the sampling bias is the difference between the sampling estimate and the actual population value. The sampling bias can be controlled by controlling the sampling pro-

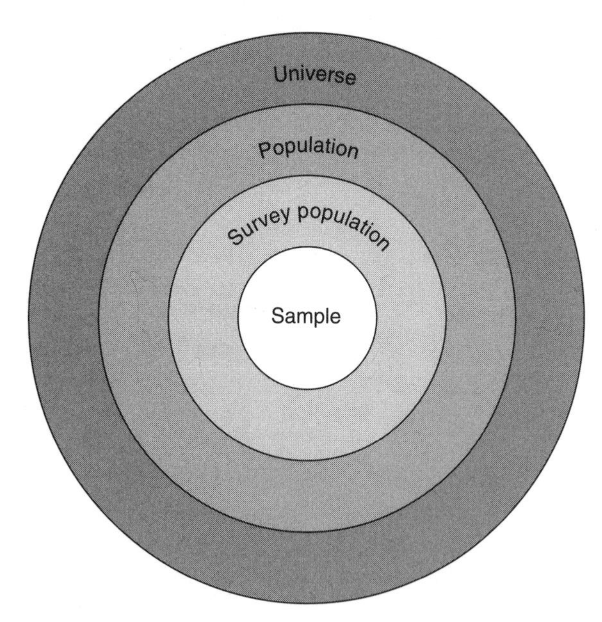

FIGURE 5.1 Relationship of Groups of Individuals

cedure, that is, how the sample is chosen. The ability to generalize the results to the population is greater when the sampling bias is reduced.

Probability Sample

Increasing the chance that the sample is representative of the population is achieved by **randomization**. This assures that each person in the survey population has an equal chance and known probability of being selected, thus creating a **probability sample**. A **simple random sample** can be obtained by taking a list of all participants **(frame)** and choosing the sample by following a list of random numbers, giving each individual an equal chance of being selected. A **systematic sample** also uses a list of participants and takes every *N*th person beginning with a randomly selected individual. For example, suppose that we want to choose a sample of 10 people from a survey population of 100. We start by randomly choosing a number between 1 and 100, such as 26, using a table of random numbers. We then choose every tenth (10/100) person (36, 46, 56, 66, 76, 86, 96, 06, 16) until we have the 10 subjects for the sample. In this way, everyone in the survey population has an equal chance of being selected. A simple random sample or systematic sample can also be used to select groups instead of individuals. When this occurs, it is called **cluster sampling.**

If it is important that certain groups should all be represented in a sample, a **stratified random sample** can be obtained. For example, if representatives from all age groups are needed, a predetermined number from each age group would be

TABLE 5.5 Summary of Probability Sampling Procedures

Sample	Primary Descriptive Elements
Simple random	Each subject has an equal chance of being selected if table of random numbers is used.
"Fishbowl" (or "out of a hat")	Approximates simple random sampling, but not as precise. Can be done with or without replacement.
Systematic	Using a list (e.g., membership list or telephone book), subjects are selected at a constant interval (N/n) after a random start.
Stratified random	The population is divided into subgroups based on key characteristics (strata), and subjects are selected from the subgroups at random to ensure representation of the characteristic.
Proportional stratified	Like the stratified random sample, but subjects are selected in proportion to the numerical strength of strata in the population.
Cluster or area	Random sampling of groups (e.g., teachers' classes) or areas (e.g., city blocks) instead of individuals.
Matrix	The responses of several randomly selected subjects to different items are combined to form the response of one.

Source: Adapted from *The Practice of Social Research,* 6th ed., by E. R. Babbie, 1992, Belmont, CA: Wadsworth, Inc.; *Methods in Behavioral Research,* 3d ed., by P. C. Cozby, 1985, Palo Alto, CA: Mayfield Publishing Company; *Practical Research: Planning and Design,* 5th ed., by P. D. Leedy, 1993, New York: Macmillan Publishing Company; and *Health Education Evaluation and Measurement: A Practitioner's Perspective,* by P. D. Sarvela and R. J. McDermott, 1993, Madison, WI: WCB Brown & Benchmark Publishers.

randomly chosen. The predetermined number is based upon representation. For example, if the evaluator is selecting 100 out of a population of 1,000 college students (1 in 10), it may be important to ensure that all class ranks are represented. If 400 of the students are freshmen, 300 sophomores, 200 juniors, and 100 seniors, then the representative sample would contain 1 in 10 of each of those subgroups: 40 freshmen, 30 sophomores, 20 juniors, and 10 seniors. Within each class rank, the appropriate number of students would be randomly selected. (See Table 5.5 for a summary of probability sampling procedures.)

Nonprobability Sample

There are times when a probability sample cannot be obtained. In such cases, planners/evaluators can take **nonprobability samples**, samples in which all individuals in the survey population did not have a known probability of being selected to participate in the evaluation. Participants can be included on the basis of convenience (because they have volunteered or because they are available or can be easily contacted) or because they have a certain characteristic.

TABLE 5.6 Summary of Nonprobability Sampling Procedures

Sample	Primary Descriptive Elements
Convenience	Includes any available subject meeting some minimum criterion usually being part of an accessible intact group.
Volunteer	Includes any subject motivated enough to self-select for a study.
Grab	Includes whomever investigators can access through direct contact, usually for interviews.
Homogeneous	Includes individuals chosen because of a unique trait or factor they possess.
Judgmental	Includes subjects whom the investigator judges to be "typical" of individuals possessing a given trait.
Snowball	Includes subjects identified by investigators, and any other persons referred by initial subjects.
Quota	Includes subjects chosen in approximate proportion to the population traits they are to "represent."

Source: From Paul D. Sarvela and Robert J. McDermott, *Health Education Evaluation and Measurement: A Practitioner's Perspective.* Copyright © 1993 Wm. C. Brown Communications, Inc. Reprinted by permission of Times Mirror Higher Education Group, Inc., Dubuque, Iowa. All Rights Reserved.

Nonprobability samples have limitations in the extent to which the results can be generalized to the total survey population. Bias may also occur since those who are not included in the sample may differ in some way from those who are included. For example, including only the individuals who complete a health promotion program may bias the results; the findings might be different if all participants, including those who attended but did not complete the program, were surveyed.

Nonprobability samples can be used when planners/evaluators are unable to identify or contact all those in the survey population. These samples can also be used when resources are limited and a probability sample is too costly or time-consuming. It is important that planners/evaluators understand the limitations of this type of sample when reporting the results. (See Table 5.6 for a summary of nonprobability sampling procedures.)

Sample Size

How many individuals to include in the sample is difficult to determine. Green and Lewis (1986) give guidelines for determining the sample size, with the objective being to obtain the highest level of precision for a given cost. Precision refers to how accurately the sample values **(statistics)** reflect the actual values **(parameters)** in the population. Another consideration is variability in the survey population: The greater the differences among the survey population, the larger the sample size needed.

Additional guidelines refer to the sampling method selected, with stratified random sampling offering the greatest level of precision for a given cost. The cost of the evaluation is also a consideration in determining whether a desired sample size is affordable. Planners/evaluators can choose actual numbers of participants with the help of statistics textbooks, giving consideration to statistical power and level of statistical significance.

PILOT TEST

Once a method of data collection has been selected and the instrument selected or developed, a trial run of the instrument, data collection procedures, and analyses should be conducted. This is known as a **pilot test,** or piloting. The purpose of the pilot test is to refine the method of data collection on the basis of comments from those reviewing the instrument and suggestions from the respondents. Any problems in the data collection process should be evident in the pilot test, such as ambiguous questions, difficulty with code sheets, and misunderstood directions. The data collected in the pilot test should be statistically analyzed or compiled to make sure that there is no difficulty with this step in the evaluation process. Revising the data collection process using the information gained from the pilot test helps ensure that the actual data collection will proceed smoothly.

Sarvela and McDermott (1993) discuss using a hierarchy of piloting techniques: **prepilots,** pilot tests, and **field studies.** Prepilots are used by evaluators with five or six target subjects to assess the quality of materials, instruments, and data collection techniques. Methods used to collect this information include observations, interviews, and focus groups. The pilot test requires the actual implementation of the instrument, program, data collection procedures, curriculum materials, and public awareness campaigns. A representative sample of the target population is used to determine the quality of the program. A field study is a final pilot test, combining all materials previously tested separately (e.g., instrument, curriculum materials) into a complete program. If at all possible, the use of this sequence of piloting techniques is desirable, but planners and evaluators are often limited by time and resources, and so not all the steps can be completed.

Stacy (1987) feels that the piloting process should include reviews by three different groups: colleagues, potential users of the data, and a sample of program participants. The person reviewing the instrument is asked to complete a short questionnaire. For example, the colleague would answer questions on the appropriateness of the title, the introductory statement explaining the purpose of the study, the directions, the grouping of the questions, and the length of the questionnaire. The individuals in the sample population are questioned on the directions, the title, the appropriateness of the questions (unclear, too personal), the length of the instrument, the purpose of the study, and the method for returning the questionnaire. The potential users of the data could review the instrument with regard to how well the questions reflect the topic being studied, whether the questions are consistent with current knowledge of the topic, and whether questions should be added or deleted. Information collected from this process can then be used to revise the questionnaire.

SUMMARY

This chapter presented four main areas of data collection: self-report, direct observation, existing records, and meetings. Advantages and disadvantages of each method of data collection should be considered when selecting an appropriate method. Many steps can be taken to reduce bias, or error, in information gained, such as selecting a representative sample and conducting a pilot test.

QUESTIONS

1. What is bias in data collection? Name some ways in which it can be reduced.
2. Describe each method of data collection (self-report, direct observation, existing data, and meetings), and list two advantages and disadvantages of each.
3. Name and give an example of each of the four levels of measurement.
4. What are the advantages and disadvantages of using an existing data collection instrument?
5. What is validity? What is reliability? Why are they so important?
6. How does an evaluator determine who will participate in the data collection?
7. Describe three types of probability samples.
8. When, if ever, should nonprobability samples be used?
9. What is the purpose of a prepilot, a pilot test, and a field study? How is each conducted?

ACTIVITIES

1. Construct a three-page written questionnaire on a health promotion topic of your choice that could be administered to a group of college students.
2. Conduct a pilot test of your written questionnaire on ten of your friends, colleagues, or classmates. After the pilot test, identify any flaws you see in the questionnaire or data collection process.
3. Assume that you are charged with the responsibility of collecting data from all the students on your campus who have enrolled in a jogging course. Assume also that this group of students is too large to collect data from everyone. Explain how you would obtain a representative sample from this population.
4. Visit a survey research center on your campus or in your community. Ask about the methods of data collection, and if possible arrange to observe a

face-to-face or telephone interview. Write a two-page paper describing your reaction to this experience.

5. Review a needs assessment or evaluation instrument. Identify the level of measurement for the questions, types of measurement, and the type of question.
6. Photocopy a page from a local telephone book. Let's assume that this page represents a sampling frame for your target population. Go through the frame and divide it into groups of ten by using the first ten numbers as group one, the second ten as group two, etc., until all the numbers are used. Be sure you do not use fax or business numbers. If you have an odd number of telephone numbers (not an even ten), do not use that group. With this information, explain how you would select a simple random sample of twenty numbers, a systematic sample of ten numbers, a stratified sample of forty numbers stratified on the first three numbers of the telephone numbers, and a cluster sample of ten groups, assuming that the groups of tens you formed are your clusters.

6

Mission Statement, Goals, and Objectives

After reading this chapter and answering the questions at the end, you should be able to:

- Explain what is meant by the term *mission statement.*
- Define *goals* and *objectives,* and distinguish between the two.
- Identify the different levels of objectives as presented in the chapter.
- State the necessary elements of an objective as presented in the chapter.
- Specify an appropriate criterion for objectives.
- Write program goals and objectives.
- Describe the use for *Healthy People 2000.*

Key Terms

conditions
criterion
goal
mission statement
objectives
outcomes
target population

To plan, implement, and evaluate effective health promotion programs, planners must have a solid foundation in place to guide them through their work. The mission statement, goals, and objectives of a program can provide such a foundation. If prepared properly, a mission statement, goals, and objectives should not only give the necessary direction to a program but also provide the groundwork for the eventual program evaluation. There are two old sayings that help express the need for a mission statement, goals, and objectives. The first is, If you do not know where you are going, then any road will do—and you may end up someplace where you do not want to be, or you may eventually end up where you want to be, but after wasted time and effort. The second is, If you do not know where you are going, how will you know when you have arrived? Without a mission statement, goals, and objectives, a program may lack direction, and at best it will be difficult to evaluate. Figure 6.1 shows the relationship between a mission statement, goals, and objectives.

MISSION STATEMENT

Sometimes referred to as a program overview or program aim, a **mission statement** is a short narrative that describes the general focus of the program. The statement not only describes the intent of a program but also may reflect the philosophy behind it. The mission statement also helps to guide program planners in the development of program goals and objectives. Table 6.1 presents examples of mission statements for several different settings.

PROGRAM GOALS

Although some individuals use the terms *goals* and *objectives* synonymously, they are not the same: There are important differences between them. Ross and Mico (1980, p. 219) have stated that "a goal is a future event toward which a committed endeavor is directed; objectives are the steps to be taken in pursuit of a goal." Deeds (1992, p. 36) defines a goal as a "broad timeless statement of a long-range program purpose." In comparison to objectives, a **goal** is an expectation that:

FIGURE 6.1 Relationship of Mission Statement, Goals, and Objectives

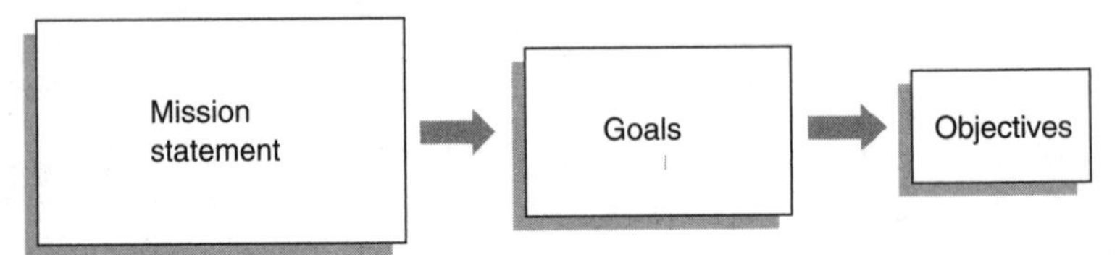

TABLE 6.1 Examples of Mission Statements

Setting	Mission Statement
Community Setting	The mission of the Walkup Health Promotion Program is to provide a wide variety of primary prevention activities for residents of the community.
Medical-Care Setting	This program is aimed at helping patients and their families to understand and cope with physical and emotional changes associated with recovery following cancer surgery.
School Setting	School District #77 wants happy and healthy students. To that end, the district's personnel strives, through a comprehensive school health program, to provide students with experiences that are designed to motivate and enable them to maintain and improve their health.
Worksite Setting	The purpose of the employee health promotion program is to develop high employee morale. This is to be accomplished by providing employees with a working environment that is conducive to good health and by providing an opportunity for employees and their families to engage in behavior that will improve and maintain good health.

1. Is much more encompassing, or global.
2. Is written to include all aspects or components of a program.
3. Provides overall direction for a program.
4. Is more general in nature.
5. Usually takes longer to complete.
6. Usually is not observed, but rather must be inferred because it includes words like *evaluate, know, improve,* and *understand* (Jacobsen, Eggen & Kauchak, 1989).
7. Is often not measurable in exact terms.

Program goals are not difficult to write and need not be written as complete sentences. They should, however, be simple and concise, and should include two basic components: Who will be affected, and what will change as a result of the program. A program need not have a set number of stated goals. It is not uncommon for some programs to have a single goal while others have several. Table 6.2 presents some examples of goals for health promotion programs.

TABLE 6.2 Examples of Program Goals

- To reduce the incidence of cardiovascular disease in the employees of the Smith Company.
- All cases of measles in the City of Kenzington will be eliminated.
- To stop the spread of HIV in the youth of Indiana.
- To reduce the cases of lung cancer caused by exposure to secondhand smoke.
- To reduce the incidence of influenza in the residents of the Delaware County Home.
- The survival rate of breast cancer patients will be raised through the optimal use of community resources.

OBJECTIVES

As Ross and Mico (1980) have indicated, **objectives** are more precise and represent smaller steps than program goals—steps that, if completed, will lead to reaching the program goal(s). Objectives outline in measurable terms the specific changes that will occur in the target population at a given point in time as a result of exposure to the program. "Objectives are crucial; they form a fulcrum, converting diagnostic data into program direction" (Green & Kreuter, 1991, p. 118). Objectives can be thought of as the bridge between needs assessment and a planned intervention. Knowing how to construct objectives for a program is a most important skill for program planners.

Different Levels of Objectives

There are several different levels of objectives associated with program planning. The different levels are sequenced or placed in a hierarchical order to allow for more effective planning (Deeds, 1992; Parkinson & Associates, 1982). Objectives are created at each level in order to help attain the program goal. The "objectives should also be coherent across levels, with objectives becoming successively more refined and more explicit, level by level" (Green & Kreuter, 1991, p. 119). Achievement of the lower-level objectives will contribute to the achievement of the higher-level objectives and goals. Table 6.3 presents the hierarchy of objectives and indicates their relationship to program outcomes and evaluation.

Administrative Objectives

The administrative objectives are the daily tasks, activities, and work plans that lead to the accomplishment of all other levels of objectives (Deeds, 1992). They help to shape or form the program and thus focus on all program inputs (all that are needed to carry out a program), implementation activities (actual presentation of the program), and stakeholder reactions (Green & Kreuter, 1991). More specifically, these objectives would focus on such things as program resources (materials, funds, space); appropriateness of intervention activities; target population exposure, attendance, participation, and feedback; feedback from other stakeholders such as the funding and sponsoring agencies; and data collection techniques, to name a few.

Learning Objectives

The second level of objectives in the hierarchy comprises learning objectives. They are the educational or learning tools that are needed in order to achieve the desired behavior change. They are based upon the analysis of educational and organizational diagnosis of the PRECEDE-PROCEED model. They address the predisposing, reinforcing, and enabling factors (Deeds, 1992).

Within this level of objectives, there is another hierarchy (Parkinson & Associates, 1982). This hierarchy includes four types of objectives, beginning with the

TABLE 6.3 Hierarchy of Objectives and Their Relation to Evaluation

Type of Objective	Program Outcomes	Possible Evaluation Measures	Type of Evaluation
Administrative objectives	Activities presented and tasks completed	Number of sessions held, exposure, attendance, participation, staff performance, appropriate materials, adequacy of resources	Process (form of formative)
Learning objectives	Change in awareness, knowledge, attitudes, and skills	Increase in awareness, knowledge, attitudes, and skill development/acquisition	Impact (form of summative)
Behavioral and environmental objectives	Behavior adoption, change in environment	Change in behavior, hazards or barriers removed from the environment	Impact (form of summative)
Program objectives	Change in quality of life (QOL), health status, or risk, and social benefits	QOL measures, morbidity data, mortality data, measures of risk (i.e., HRA)	Outcome (form of summative)

Source: Adapted from *The Health Education Specialist: Self Study for Professional Competence,* by S. G. Deeds, 1992, Los Alamitos, CA: Loose Canon Publications.

least complex and moving toward the most complex. Complexity is defined in terms of the time, effort, and resources necessary to accomplish the objective. The learning objectives hierarchy begins with awareness objectives and moves through knowledge, attitude, and skill development or acquisition objectives. This hierarchy indicates that if those in the target population are going to adopt and maintain a health-enhancing behavior to alleviate a health concern or problem, they must first be aware of the health concern. Second, they must expand their knowledge and understanding of the concern. Third, they must attain and maintain an attitude that enables them to deal with the concern. And fourth, they need to possess the necessary skills to engage in the health-enhancing behavior.

Behavioral and Environmental Objectives

Behavioral objectives describe the behaviors or actions in which the target population will engage that will resolve the health problem and move you toward achieving your program goal (Deeds, 1992). Environmental objectives outline the nonbehavioral causes of a health problem that are present in the social, physical, or psychological environment. These objectives are based upon the results of the behavioral and environmental diagnosis of the PRECEDE-PROCEED model or the behavior and environmental changes indicated by the needs assessment of another planning model. Behavioral objectives are commonly written about adherence (e.g., regular exercise), compliance (e.g., taking medication as prescribed), consumption patterns (e.g., diet), coping (e.g., stress reduction activities), preventive actions (e.g., brushing and flossing teeth), self-care (e.g., first aid), and utilization (e.g, appropriate use of the emergency room). Environmental objectives are written about such things as the state of the physical environment (e.g., clean air or water), the social environment (e.g., access to health care), or the psychological environment (e.g., the emotional learning climate).

Program Objectives

Program objectives are the ultimate objectives of a program and are aimed at changes in health status, social benefits, or quality of life. "They are outcome or future oriented" (Deeds, 1992, p. 36). If these objectives are achieved, then the program goal will be achieved. These objectives are commonly written in terms of reduction of risk, morbidity, disability, mortality, or quality of life measures.

Developing Objectives

Does every program require objectives from each of the levels just described? The answer is yes! Too often, health promotion programs have too few objectives, all of which fall into one or two levels. Many planners have developed programs hoping solely to change the health behavior of a target population. For example, a smoking cessation program may have an objective of getting 30% of the participants to stop smoking. Perhaps this program is offered, and only 10% of the participants quit smoking. Is the program a failure? If the program has a single objective of changing behavior, its sponsors would have a good case for saying that the program was not effective. However, it is quite possible that as a result of participating in the smoking cessation program, the participants increased their awareness of the dangers of smoking. They probably also increased their knowledge, changed their attitudes, and developed skills for quitting or cutting back on the number of cigarettes they smoke each day. These are all very positive outcomes—and they could be overlooked when the program is evaluated, if the planner did not write objectives that cover a variety of levels.

Criteria for Developing Objectives

In addition to making sure that the objectives are written in an appropriate manner, planners also need to be realistic with regard to the other parameters of the program. These are some of the questions that program planners should consider when writing objectives.

1. Can the objective be realized during the life of the program or within a reasonable time thereafter? It would be quite realistic to assume that a certain number of people will not be smoking one year after they have com-

pleted a smoking cessation program, but it would not be realistic to assume that a group of elementary school students could be followed for life to determine how many of them die prematurely due to inactivity.

2. Can the objective realistically be achieved? It is probably realistic to assume that 30% of any smoking cessation class will stop smoking within one year after the program has ended, but it is not realistic to assume that 100% of the employees of a company will participate in its fitness program.
3. Does the program have enough resources (personnel, money, and space) to obtain a specific objective? It would be ideal to be able to reach all individuals in the target population, but generally there are not sufficient resources to do so.
4. Are the objectives consistent with the policies and procedures of the sponsoring agency? It would not be realistic to expect to incorporate a no-smoking policy in a tobacco company.
5. Do the objectives violate any of the rights of those who are involved (participants or planners)? Right-to-know laws make it illegal to withhold information that could cause harm to a target population.

Elements of an Objective

For an objective to provide direction and to be useful in the evaluation process, it must be written in such a way that it can be clearly understood, states what is to be accomplished, and is measurable. To ensure that an objective is indeed useful, it should include the following elements:

1. The outcome to be achieved, or what will change.
2. The conditions under which the outcome will be observed, or when the change will occur.
3. The criterion for deciding whether the outcome has been achieved, or how much change.
4. The target population, or who will change.

The first element, the **outcome,** is defined as the action, behavior, or something else that will change as a result of the program. In a written objective, the outcome is usually identified as the verb of the sentence. Thus, words such as *apply, argue, build, compare, demonstrate, evaluate, exhibit, judge, perform, reduce, spend, state,* and *test* would be considered outcomes (see Table 6.4 for a more comprehensive listing of appropriate outcome words). It should be noted that not all verbs would be considered appropriate outcomes for an objective; the verb must refer to something measurable and observable. Words such as *appreciate, know, internalize,* or *understand* by themselves do not refer to something measurable and observable, and therefore they are not good choices for outcomes.

The second element of an objective is the **conditions** under which the outcome will be observed, or when it will be observed. "Typical" conditions found in objec-

TABLE 6.4 Outcome Verbs for Objectives

abstract	copy	gather	order	round
accept	count	(information)	organize	score
adjust	create	generalize	pair	seek
adopt	criticize	generate	participate	select
advocate	deduce	group	partition	separate
analyze	defend	guess	perform	share
annotate	define	hypothesize	persist	show
apply	delay (response)	identify	plan	simplicity
approximate	demonstrate	illustrate	practice	simulate
argue	derive	imitate	praise	solve
(a position)	describe	improve	predict	sort
ask	design	infer	prepare	spend (money)
associate	determine	initiate	preserve	state
attempt	develop	inquire	produce	structure
balance	differentiate	integrate	propose	submit
build	discover	interpolate	prove	subscribe
calculate	discriminate	interpret	qualify	substitute
categorize	dispute	invent	query	suggest
cause	distinguish	investigate	question	summarize
challenge	effect	join	recall	supply
change	eliminate	judge	recite	support
choose	enumerate	justify	recognize	symbolize
clarify	estimate	keep	recommend	synthesize
classify	evaluate	label	record	tabulate
collect	examine	list	reduce	tally
combine	exemplify	locate	regulate	test
compare	exhibit	manipulate	reject	theorize
complete	experiment	map	relate	translate
compute	explain	match	reorganize	try
conceptualize	express	measure	repeat	unite
connect	extend	name	replace	visit
construct	extract	obey	represent	volunteer
consult	extrapolate	object (to an idea)	reproduce	weigh
contrast	find	observe	restructure	write
convert	form	offer		

tives might be "upon completion of the exercise class," "as a result of participation," "by the year 2000," "after reading the pamphlets and brochures," "orally in class," "when asked to respond by the facilitator," "one year after the program," "by May 15th," or "during the class session."

The third element of an objective is the **criterion** for deciding when the outcome has been achieved, or how much change will occur. The purpose of this element is to provide a standard by which the program planners/evaluators can determine if an outcome has been performed in an appropriate and/or successful manner. Examples might include "to no more than 105 per 1000," "with 100% accuracy," "as presented in the lecture," "300 pamphlets," "according to the criteria developed by the American Heart Association," "95% of the motor vehicle occupants," or "using the technique outlined in the American Cancer Society's pamphlet."

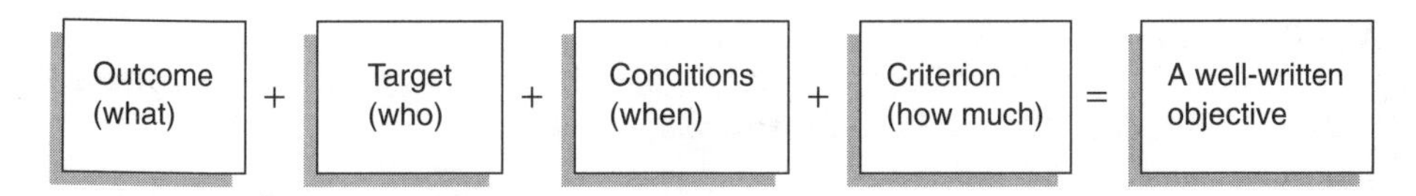

FIGURE 6.2 Elements of a Well-Written Objective

The last element that needs to be included in an objective is mention of the **target population,** or who will change. Examples are "1,000 teachers," "all employees of the company," and "those residing in the Muncie and Bowling Green areas." Figure 6.2 summarizes the key elements in an objective.

GOALS AND OBJECTIVES FOR THE NATION

A chapter on goals and objectives would not be complete without at least a short discussion of the health goals and objectives of the nation. These goals and objectives have been most helpful to program planners throughout the United States.

The U.S. government is very interested in improving the health status of Americans. It is concerned about individuals and the population as a whole. The country is facing many problems and issues that revolve around health; the cost of ill health is the most obvious. Therefore, for at least some parts of the federal government, there is a goal to improve the health status of the public. Objectives have been developed to guide the work of reaching this goal. Some people have referred to these statements of objectives as the health plan for the United States.

The first set of objectives was developed by many health professionals throughout the country; it was published in 1980 under the title *Promoting Health/ Preventing Disease: Objectives for the Nation* (USDHHS, 1980). This volume was divided into three main areas: preventive services, health protection, and health promotion. Each of these contained 5 focus areas, or 15 in all. From these 15 areas came a total of 226 objectives. These objectives, which were based upon the data collected for the U.S. Surgeon General's report *Healthy People* (1979), were the basis for health promotion and disease prevention planning during the 1980s.

Data for 1987 give evidence that nearly half of those objectives had been achieved or were likely to be achieved by 1990, while about a quarter were unlikely to be achieved; the status of the remaining quarter was in doubt because tracking data were not available. Progress was slow for some of the 15 priorities identified in 1980, such as pregnancy and infant health, nutrition, physical fitness and exercise, family planning, sexually transmitted diseases, and occupational safety and health. Substantial progress was made, however, in high blood pressure control, immunization, unintentional injury prevention and control, control of infectious diseases, smoking, and alcohol and drugs (Mason & McGinnis, 1990, p. 442).

As the 1980s came to a close, it was obvious from the evaluation conducted on these national goals and objectives (USDHHS, 1986b) that there was a need to de-

BOX 6.1 Examples of Objectives to Support the Program Goal "to reduce the amount of heart disease in the residents of Franklin County"

Administrative Objectives

A. During the next six months, 300 community residents will participate in one of the health department's health promotion activities.
Outcome (what): Will participate in an activity.
Target population (who): Community residents.
Conditions (when): During the next six months.
Criterion (how much): 300 residents.

B. By August 4, heart disease brochures will be distributed to all residences in the county.
Outcome (what): Will be distributed.
Target population (who): To all residences.
Conditions (when): By August 4.
Criterion (how much): All.

C. During the pilot testing, the program facilitators will receive a "good" rating from the program participants.
Outcome (what): Will receive.
Target population (who): Program facilitators.
Conditions (when): During the pilot testing.
Criterion (how much): "good" rating.

D. The reading materials will be made available to the program participants 10 days prior to the start of the activity.
Outcome (what): Materials made available.
Target population (who): Program participants.
Conditions (when): Prior to the start.
Criterion (how much): 10 days prior.

Learning Objectives

A. Awareness level: After the American Heart Association's pamphlet on cardiovascular health risk factors has been placed in grocery bags, at least 20% of the shoppers will be able to identify their own risks.
Outcome (what): Identify their own risks.
Target population (who): Shoppers.
Conditions (when): After distribution of the pamphlet.
Criterion (how much): 20%.

B. Knowledge level: When asked over the telephone, one out of three viewers of the heart special television show will be able to accurately explain the four principles of cardiovascular conditioning.
Outcome (what): Able to explain.
Target population (who): Television viewers.
Conditions (when): When asked over the telephone.
Criterion (how much): One out of three.

C. Attitude level: During one of the class sessions, the participants will defend their views about regular exercise.
Outcome (what): Defend their views.
Target population (who): Class participants.
Conditions (when): During one of the class sessions.
Criterion (how much): All.

D. Skill development/acquisition level: After viewing the video "How to Exercise," those participating will be able to locate their pulse and count it for 60 seconds.
Outcome (what): Locate their pulse and count it.
Target population (who): Those participating.
Conditions (when): After viewing the video.
Criterion (how much): For 60 seconds.

Behavioral and Environmental Objectives

A. One year after the formal exercise classes have been completed, 40% of those who completed 80% of the classes will still be involved in a regular aerobic exercise program.

Outcome (what): Will still be involved.
Target population (who): Those who completed 80% of the classes.
Conditions (when): One year after the classes.
Criterion (how much): 40%.

B. During the telephone interviews follow-up, 50% of the residents will report having had their blood pressure taken during the previous six months.

Outcome (what): Will report.
Target population (who): Residents.
Conditions (when): During the telephone interview follow-up.
Criterion (how much): 50%.

C. The percentage of household wells checked by the Franklin County Health Department will increase to 95% by the year 2000.

Outcome (what): Wells checked.
Target population (who): Household wells.
Conditions (when): By the year 2000.
Criterion (how much): 95%.

D. By the end of the year, all senior citizens will be provided transportation to the congregate meals.

Outcome (what): Provided transportation.
Target population (who): Senior citizens.
Conditions (when): By the end of the year.
Criterion (how much): All.

Program Objectives

A. By the year 2000, heart disease deaths will be reduced to no more than 100 per 100,000 in the residents of Franklin County.

Outcome (what): Reduce heart disease deaths.
Target population (who): Residents of Franklin County.
Conditions (when): By the year 2000.
Criterion (how much): To no more than 100 per 100,000.

B. By 1998, increase to at least 25% the proportion of men in Franklin County with hypertension whose blood pressure is under control.

Outcome (what): Increase the proportion.
Target population (who): Men in Franklin County.
Conditions (when): By 1998.
Criterion (how much): To at least 25%.

C. Half of all those in the county who complete a regular, aerobic, 12-month exercise program will reduce their "risk age" on their follow-up health risk appraisal by a minimum of two years compared to their preprogram results.

Outcome (what): Will reduce their "risk age."
Target population (who): Those who complete an exercise program.
Conditions (when): After the 12-month exercise program.
Criterion (how much): Half.

D. Those who participate in a formal exercise and fitness program will use 10% fewer sick days during the life of the program than those who do not participate.

Outcome (what): Use fewer sick days.
Target population (who): Those who participate.
Conditions (when): During the life of the program.
Criterion (how much): 10% fewer sick days.

TABLE 6.5 Twenty-Two Priority Areas of the National Health Objectives and the Lead Governmental Agency Responsible for Each

Priority Area	Lead Agency or Agencies
01 Physical Activity and Fitness	President's Council on Physical Fitness and Sports
02 Nutrition	National Institutes of Health Food and Drug Administration
03 Tobacco	Centers for Disease Control and Prevention
04 Alcohol and Other Drugs	Substance Abuse and Mental Health Services Administration
05 Family Planning	Office of Population Affairs
06 Mental Health and Mental Disorders	Substance Abuse and Mental Health Services Administration
07 Violent and Abusive Behavior	Centers for Disease Control and Prevention
08 Educational and Community-Based Programs	Centers for Disease Control and Prevention Health Resources and Services Administration
09 Unintentional Injuries	Centers for Disease Control and Prevention
10 Occupational Safety and Health	Centers for Disease Control and Prevention
11 Environmental Health	National Institutes of Health Centers for Disease Control and Prevention
12 Food and Drug Safety	Food and Drug Administration
13 Oral Health	National Institutes of Health Centers for Disease Control and Prevention
14 Maternal and Infant Health	Health Resources and Services Administration
15 Heart Disease and Stroke	National Institutes of Health
16 Cancer	National Institutes of Health
17 Diabetes and Chronic Disabling Conditions	National Institutes of Health Centers for Disease Control and Prevention
18 HIV Infection	National AIDS Program Office
19 Sexually Transmitted Diseases	Centers for Disease Control and Prevention
20 Immunization and Infectious Diseases	Centers for Disease Control and Prevention
21 Clinical Preventive Services	Health Resources and Services Administration Centers for Disease Control and Prevention
22 Surveillance and Data Systems	Centers for Disease Control and Prevention

Source: Healthy People 2000 Review, 1993 (p. 151), by U.S. Department of Health and Human Services (USDHHS), 1994 (DHHS Publication No. [PHS] 94-1232-1), Washington, DC: U.S. Government Printing Office.

velop new goals and objectives to guide the country through the 1990s. Therefore, a second set of goals and objectives (USDHHS, 1990a) was developed. The newest set is much more detailed than the first and has been more useful to all program planners. The three broad goals for public health that will guide us until the year 2000 are:

1. Increase the span of healthy life for Americans.
2. Reduce health disparities among Americans.
3. Achieve access to preventive services for all Americans.

As in the previous version, the newer objectives were divided into 3 categories—preventive services, health protection, and health promotion—but now there are 22 priority areas and approximately 300 objectives. Within the 22 priority areas are guidelines for surveillance and data systems and suggested actions that individuals and community organizations should take in pursuit of these goals and objectives. In addition, subobjectives were established for people with low incomes, people who are members of some racial and ethnic minority groups, and people with disabilities to help meet their unique needs and health problems (USDHHS, 1994). Table 6.5 lists the 22 priority areas and the lead governmental agency or agencies responsible for working toward the accomplishment of the objective.

DOCUMENTS RELATED TO HEALTHY PEOPLE 2000

Since the development of *Healthy People 2000* there have been a number of other documents created that can help planners develop or adopt appropriate objectives for their programs. The most notable is *Healthy Communities 2000: Model Standards.* It was jointly prepared by the American Public Health Association, American Society of State and Territorial Health Officers, National Association of County Health Officers, U.S. Conference of Local Health Officers, and the Association of Schools of Public Health (1991), in conjunction with the Centers for Disease Control and Prevention, to assist states and localities in putting the year 2000 objectives into practice. Specifically, this document provides "skeleton" objectives for each of the priority areas in which state and local agencies can create target population specific objectives based on the framework of *Healthy People 2000.*

The spin-off of the *Healthy People 2000* goals and objectives is apparent in several other documents as well. Individual states have taken the national objectives and created similar documents specific to their own residents. For example, in Indiana, the Indiana State Department of Health created *Healthy Hoosiers 2000: Health Promotion and Disease Prevention Objectives* (ISDH, 1992). Other organizations have taken similar steps to make the national goals and objectives appropriate for their target populations. A few examples include objectives for college campuses (*Healthy Campus 2000: Making It Happen* [ACHA, no date]), objectives for school-age children (*Healthy Kids for the Year 2000: An Action Plan for Schools* [AASA, 1990]), nutrition objectives (*2000 and Counting!* [National Dairy Council, 1992]), and objectives for Native Americans (*Promoting Healthy Traditions Workbook—A Guide to the Healthy People 2000 Campaign* [AIHCA, no date]).

The national goals and objectives have been important components in the process of health promotion planning since 1980. We highly recommend that planners review these objectives before developing goals and objectives for programs. The national objectives may be helpful in providing a rationale for a program and in focusing program goals and objectives toward the areas of greatest need, as planners work toward the year 2000.

SUMMARY

The mission statement provides an overview of a program and is most useful in the development of goals and objectives. The terms *goals* and *objectives* are sometimes used synonymously, but they are quite different. Together the two provide a foundation for program planning and evaluation. Goals are more global in nature and often are not measurable in exact terms, whereas objectives are more specific and consist of the steps used to reach the program goals. Program objectives can and should be written for several different levels. For objectives to be useful, they should be written so as to be observable and measurable. At a minimum, an objective should include the following elements: a stated outcome (what), conditions under which the outcome will be observed (when), a criterion for considering that the outcome has been achieved (how much), and mention of the target population (who).

QUESTIONS

1. Why is a mission statement important?
2. What is (are) the difference(s) between a goal and an objective?
3. What is the purpose of program goals and objectives?
4. What are the different levels of objectives?
5. What are the necessary elements of an objective?
6. What are the goals and objectives for the nation? How can they be used by program planners?

ACTIVITIES

1. Write a mission statement, a goal, and supporting objectives (one at each level) for a program you are planning.
2. Identify which of the following objectives include all four elements necessary for a complete objective; revise those objectives that do not include all the elements.
   a. After the class on objective writing, the student will know the difference between a goal and an objective.
   b. The student knows how a skinfold caliper works.
   c. After completing this chapter, the student will be able to write objectives for each of the levels based on the four elements outlined in the chapter.

d. Given appropriate instruction, the employees will be able to accurately take blood pressure readings of fellow employees.
e. Program participants will be able to list the reasons why people do not exercise.

3. Write a mission statement, a goal, and supporting objectives (one at each level) for a workshop on responsible use of alcohol by college students.

7

Theories and Models Commonly Used for Health Promotion Interventions

After reading this chapter and answering the questions at the end, you should be able to:

- Define *theory, model,* and *constructs.*
- Explain why health promotion interventions should be planned using theoretical frameworks.
- Briefly explain the theories and models identified in the chapter.

Key Terms

action stage
aversive stimulus
behavioral capability
constructs
contemplation
direct reinforcement
ecological perspective
efficacy expectations
emotional-coping responses
expectancies
expectations
field test
health belief model
likelihood of action
locus of control
maintenance
model
negative punishment
negative reinforcement
outcome expectations
perceived barriers
perceived benefits
perceived seriousness
perceived susceptibility
perceived threat
positive punishment
positive reinforcement
precontemplation stage
preparation
punishment
recidivism
reciprocal determinism
reinforcement
relapse
relapse prevention
self-control
self-efficacy
self-management
self-regulation
theory
vicarious reinforcement

Whenever there is a discussion about the theoretical bases for health education and health promotion, we often find the terms *theory* and *model* used. Some use the terms correctly, while others either use them synonymously or confuse their meaning. We begin this chapter with a brief explanation of these terms, to establish a common understanding of their meaning.

According to one definition, a **theory** is "an integrated set of propositions that serves as an explanation for a class of phenomena. In general, theories are introduced into a science only after a class of phenomena has already revealed a systematic set of uniformities" (Chaplin & Krawiec, 1979, p. 67). "A theory is then intended to provide deeper understanding by presenting those phenomena as manifestations of certain underlying processes, governed by characteristic laws which account for, and usually correct and refine, the previously established generalizations" (Hempel, 1977, p. 244). In other words, a theory is a systematic arrangement of fundamental principles that provide a basis for explaining certain happenings of life. Hochbaum, Sorenson, and Lorig (1992, p. 298) defined theories in relationship to health education as "tools to help health educators better understand what influences health—relevant individuals, group, and institutional behaviors—and to thereupon plan effective interventions directed at health-beneficial results."

In comparison, a **model** is a subclass of a theory. It provides researchers with a plan for investigating the phenomena. Unlike theories, a model "does not attempt to explain the processes underlying learning, but only to represent them" (Chaplin & Krawiec, 1979, p. 68).

Based on these descriptions, it seems logical to think of theories as the backbone of the processes used to plan, implement, and evaluate health promotion interventions. "A theory based approach provides direction and justification for program activities and serves as a basis for processes that are to be incorporated into the health promotion program" (Cowdery, Wang, Eddy, & Trucks, 1995, p. 248). For example, developmental theories can be used to ensure that the goals and objectives of programs are consistent with the participants' developmental stages and abilities. Theories also can guide program planners in selecting the types of interventions that are needed to accomplish the stated goals and objectives. Appropriate use of learning and behavioral theories can help to ensure congruence between the planned interventions and expected outcomes. Stated a bit differently, "theories can provide answers to program developers' questions regarding *why* people aren't already engaging in a desirable behavior of interest, *how* to go about changing their behaviors, and *what* factors to look at when evaluating a program's focus" (van Ryn & Heaney, 1992, p. 326). In addition, theoretical frameworks can alert planners to consider important influences outside the teaching-learning process, such as social support and environment, that have an impact on targeted program outcomes (Parcel, 1983). Models provide the vehicle for applying the theories.

All health promotion interventions should be planned and evaluated based upon proven theories. "Theory is not a substitute for professional judgment, but it can assist health educators in professional decision making. Insofar as the application of theory to practice strengthens program justification, promotes the effective and efficient use of resources, and improves accountability, it also assists in establishing professional credibility" (D'Onofrio, 1992, p. 394). However, this is not to say that a theory cannot be modified or expanded to include a logically valid idea or parts of other theories. "In fact, it is well understood that working with a theory has certain disadvantages; one of which is leaving out or ignoring factors that happen not to be theoretically relevant, even though they may be empirically significant" (Jessor & Jessor, 1977).

The importance of theory in planning health promotion interventions is best shown by the large number of health promotion programs that are designed to help facilitate health behavior change in the target population. Getting people to engage in health behavior change is a complicated process that is very difficult under the best of conditions. Without the direction that theories provide, planners can easily waste valuable resources in trying to achieve the desired behavior change. Therefore, program planners should ground their programming process in the theories that have been the foundation of other successful health promotion efforts. An article by Shea and Basch (1990) provides a good review and rationale of the theories behind and the models used in some of the most successful health promotion programs: the North Karelia Project, the Stanford Three Community Study, the Stanford Five-City Project, the Minnesota Heart Health Program, and the Pawtucket Heart Health Program. Table 7.1 summarizes the theories and models used in these programs, based on the information provided by Shea and Basch (1990). As can be seen by the information presented in the table, each of these programs is well grounded in theory.

Essentially, the principles and practices of health education are "derived from the egalitarian spirit and progressive theories of education and the fundamental theories of the behavioral sciences" (National Task Force, 1985, p. vii). The remaining sections of this chapter present an overview of the theories and models that are most often used in planning and evaluating health promotion interventions.

BEHAVIORAL CHANGE THEORIES

Stimulus Response (SR) Theory

One of the theories used to explain and modify behavior today is the stimulus response, or SR, theory (Thorndike, 1898; Watson, 1925; Hall, 1943). This theory reflects the combination of classical conditioning (Pavlov, 1927) and instrumental conditioning (Thorndike, 1898) theories. These early conditioning theories explain learning based upon the associations among stimulus, response, and reinforcement (Parcel & Baranowski, 1981; Parcel, 1983). "In simplest terms, the SR theorists believe that learning results from events (termed 'reinforcements') which reduce physiological drives that activate behavior" (Rosenstock, Strecher, & Becker, 1988, p. 175). The behaviorist B. F. Skinner believed that the frequency of a behavior was determined by the reinforcements that followed that behavior.

In Skinner's view, the mere temporal association between a behavior and an immediately following reward is sufficient to increase the probability that the behavior will be repeated. Such behaviors are called *operants;* they operate on the en-

TABLE 7.1 Theories and Models Used in Five Community-Based Cardiovascular Disease Prevention Programs

Program	Year Begun	Theories and Models Used
Minnesota Heart Health Program	1980	• Social learning theory[a] • Communication–persuasion model[b] • Model of innovation diffusion[d] • Community development[c] • Problem-behavior theory[a]
North Karelia Project	Late 1950s	• Social learning theory[a] • Theory of reasoned action[a] • Communication–persuasion model[b] • Model of innovation diffusion[d] • Community organization model[c]
Pawtucket Heart Health Program	1980	• Community organization model[c] • Social behavioral community psychology theory[a]
Stanford Five-City Project	1978	• Social learning theory[a] • Theory of reasoned action[a] • Communication–persuasion model[b] • Model of innovation diffusion[d]
Stanford Three Community Study	1972	• Social learning theory[a]

[a] =Discussed in Chapter 7
[b] =Discussed in Chapter 8
[c] =Discussed in Chapter 9
[d] =Discussed in Chapter 11

vironment to bring about changes resulting in reward or reinforcement (Rosenstock et al., 1988, p. 176). Stated another way, operant behaviors are behaviors that act on the environment to produce consequences. These consequences, in turn, either reinforce or do not reinforce the behavior that preceded.

The consequences of a behavior can come as either **reinforcement** or **punishment**. Individuals can learn from both. Reinforcement has been defined by Skinner (1953) as any event that follows a behavior, which in turn increases the probability that the same behavior will be repeated in the future. Stated differently, reinforcement has "a *strengthening effect* that occurs when operant behaviors have certain consequences" (Nye, 1992, p. 16). Behavior has a greater probability of occurring in the future (1) if reinforcement is frequent, and (2) if reinforcement is provided soon after the desired behavior. This immediacy clarifies the relationship between the reinforcement and appropriate behavior (Skinner, 1953). If a behavior is complex in nature, smaller steps working toward the desired behavior with appropriate reinforcement will help to shape the desired behavior. This was found to be true in getting pigeons to play Ping-Pong, and it can be useful in trying to change a complex health behavior like smoking or exercise. While reinforcement will increase the frequency of a behavior, punishment will decrease the frequency of a behavior. However, both reinforcement and punishment can be either positive or negative. The terms *positive* and *negative* in this context do not mean good and bad; rather, *positive* means adding something (effects of the stimulus) to a situation, while *negative* means taking something away (removal or reduction of the effects of the stimulus) from the situation.

If individuals act in a certain way to produce a consequence that makes them feel good or that is enjoyable, it is labeled **positive reinforcement**. Examples of this would be an individual who is involved in an exercise program and "feels good" at the end of the workout, or one who participates in a weight loss program and receives verbal encouragement from the facilitator, again making that person "feel good." SR theorists would note that in both of these situations, the pleasant experiences (internal feelings and verbal encouragement, respectively) occur right after the behavior, which in turn increases the chances that the frequency of the behavior will increase.

While positive reinforcement helps individuals learn by shaping behavior, behavior that avoids punishment is also learned because it reduces the tension that precedes the punishment (Rosenstock et al., 1988). "When this happens, we are being conditioned by *negative reinforcement*: A response is strengthened by the *removal* of something from the situation. In such cases, the 'something' that is removed is referred to as a *negative reinforcer* or *aversive stimulus* (these two phrases are synonymous)" (Nye, 1979, p. 33). A good example of **negative reinforcement** is a weight loss program that requires weekly dues. When participants stop paying dues because they have met their goal weight, this removal of an obligation should increase frequency of the desired behavior (weight maintenance).

Some people think of negative reinforcement as a form of punishment, but it is not. While negative reinforcement increases the likelihood that a behavior will be repeated, punishment typically suppresses behavior. "Skinner suggests two ways in which a response can be punished: by *removing a positive reinforcer* or by *presenting a negative reinforcer* (aversive stimulus) as a consequence of the response" (Nye, 1979, p. 43). Punishment is usually linked to some uncomfortable (physical, mental, or otherwise) experience and decreases the frequency of a behavior. An aversive smoking cessation program that circulates cigarette smoke around those enrolled in the program as they smoke is an example of **positive punishment**. It decreases the frequency of smoking by presenting (adding) a negative reinforcer or **aversive stimulus** (smoke) as a consequence of the response. Examples of **negative punishment** (removing a positive reinforcer) would include not allowing teachers to use the teacher's lounge if they continue to smoke while using it or reducing the health insurance benefits of employees who continue to participate in health-harming behavior like not wearing a safety belt. SR theorists would note that taking

FIGURE 7.1
2 × 2 Table of the Stimulus Response Theory

		Consequences	
		Positive (adding to)	Negative (taking away)
Behavior	Increase in frequency	Positive reinforcement	Negative reinforcement
	Decrease in frequency	Positive punishment	Negative punishment

away the privilege of using the teacher's lounge or enhanced health insurance benefits would cause a decrease in frequency of smoking among the teachers and an increase in the wearing of safety belts, respectively. Figure 7.1 illustrates the relationship between reinforcement and punishment.

Finally, if reinforcement is withheld—or, stating it another way, if the behavior is ignored—the behavior will become less frequent and eventually will not be repeated. Skinner (1953) refers to this as extinction. Teachers frequently use this technique with disruptive children in the classroom. If a child is acting up in class, the teacher may choose to ignore the behavior in hopes that the nonreinforced behavior will go away.

Social Cognitive Theory (SCT)

The social learning theories (SLT) of Rotter (1954) and Bandura (1977b)—or, as Bandura (1986) relabeled them, the *social cognitive theory (SCT)*—combine SR theory and cognitive theories. SR theorists emphasize the role of reinforcement in shaping behavior and believe that no "thinking" or "reasoning" is needed to explain behavior. Those who espouse SCT believe that reinforcement is an integral part of learning, but emphasize the role of subjective hypotheses or expectations held by the individual (Rosenstock et al., 1988). In other words, reinforcement contributes to learning, but reinforcement along with an individual's expectations of the consequences of behavior determine the behavior. "Behavior, in this perspective, is a function of the subjective value of an outcome and the subjective probability (or 'expectation') that a particular action will achieve that outcome. Such formulations are generally termed 'value-expectancy' theories" (Rosenstock et al., 1988, p. 176). In brief, SCT describes learning as a reciprocal interaction between the individual's environment, cognitive processes, and behavior (Parcel, 1983). SCT explains learning through **constructs** (synthesized thoughts or key concepts). Those that have been most often used in designing health education/promotion interventions will be presented here.

Parcel and Baranowski (1981) have provided an explanation of several constructs of SCT and health education, starting with reinforcement. As already noted, reinforcement is an important component of SCT. According to SCT, reinforcement can be accomplished in one of three ways: directly, vicariously, or through self-management. An example of **direct reinforcement** is a group facilitator who provides verbal feedback to participants for a job well done. **Vicarious reinforcement** is having the participants observe someone else being reinforced for behaving in an appropriate manner. This is often referred to as social modeling. In a system of reinforcement by **self-management,** the participants would keep records of their own behavior, and when the behavior was performed in an appropriate manner, they would reinforce or reward themselves.

In addition to the constructs dealing with reinforcement, SCT has other constructs applicable to health promotion. Although there may be some situations in which more than one construct will be applicable to a learning situation, program planners will find that certain constructs will be more useful than others, depending on the type of learning taking place. Those constructs identified by Parcel and Baranowski (1981) include behavioral capability, expectations, expectancies, self-control, self-efficacy, emotional-coping responses, and reciprocal determinism.

If individuals are to perform specific behaviors, they must know first what the behaviors are and then how to perform them. This is referred to as **behavioral capability.** For example, if people are to exercise aerobically, first they must know that aerobic exercise exists, and second they need to know how to do it properly. Many people begin exercise programs, only to quit within the first six months (Dishman, Sallis, & Orenstein, 1985), and some of those people quit because they do not know how to exercise properly. They know they should exercise, so they decide to run a few miles, have sore muscles the next day, and quit. Skill mastery is very important. The construct of **expectations** refers to the ability of human beings to think and thus to expect certain things to happen in certain situations. For example, if people are enrolled in a weight loss program and follow the directions of the group facilitator, they will expect to lose weight. **Expectancies**, not to be confused with expectations, are the values that individuals place on an expected outcome. If people value an expected outcome, they are more likely to perform the necessary behavior to yield the outcome. Someone who enjoys the feeling of not smoking more than that of smoking is more likely to try to do the things necessary to stop. The construct of **self-control** or **self-regulation** states that individuals may gain control of their own behavior through monitoring and adjusting it (Clark, Janz, Dodge, & Sharpe, 1992). When helping individuals to change their behavior, it is a common practice to have them monitor their behavior over a period of time, through 24-hour diet or smoking records or exercise diaries, and then to have them reward (reinforce) themselves based upon their monitored performance.

One construct of SCT that has received special attention in health promotion programs is **self-efficacy** (Strecher, DeVellis, Becker, & Rosenstock, 1986). Self-efficacy refers to the internal state that individuals experience as "competence" to perform certain desired tasks or behavior. This state is situation specific, that is, someone may be self-efficacious when it comes to aerobic exercise but not so when faced with reducing the amount of fat in her diet. People's competency feelings have been referred to as **efficacy expectations**. Thus, someone who thinks she can exercise on a regular basis no matter what the circumstances has efficacy expectations.

FIGURE 7.2
Diagrammatic Representation of the Difference between Efficacy and Outcome Expectations

Source: Social Learning Theory by Albert Bandura, © 1977. Reprinted by permission of Prentice-Hall, Inc., Upper Saddle River, NJ.

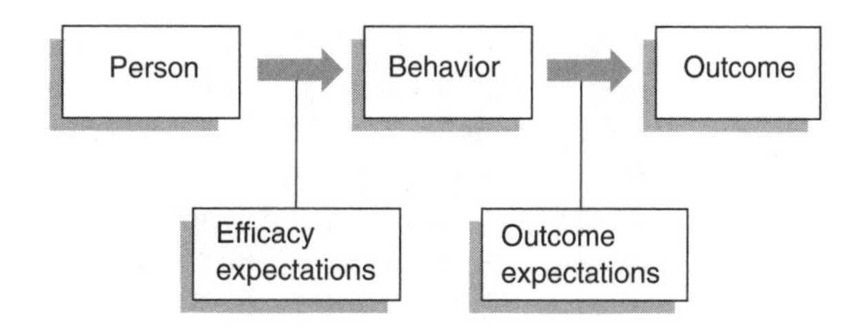

Even though people have efficacy expectations, they still may not want to engage in a behavior because they may not think the outcomes of that behavior would be beneficial to them. Stated another way, they may not feel that the reward (reinforcement) of performing the behavior is great enough for them. These beliefs are called **outcome expectations.** For example, in order for a person to quit smoking for health reasons (behavior), she must believe both that she is capable of quitting (efficacy expectation) and that cessation will benefit her health (outcome expectation) (I. M. Rosenstock, personal communication, April 1986). Figure 7.2 (Bandura, 1977b) illustrates efficacy and outcome expectations.

Individuals become self-efficacious in four main ways:

1. Through performance attainments (personal mastery of a task).
2. Through vicarious experience (observing the performance of others).
3. As a result of verbal persuasion (receiving suggestions from others).
4. Through emotional arousal (interpreting one's emotional state).

The construct of **emotional-coping responses** states that for a person to learn, she must be able to deal with the sources of anxiety that may surround a behavior. For example, fear is an emotion that can be involved in learning; according to this construct, participants would have to deal with the fear before they could learn the behavior.

The construct of **reciprocal determinism** states, unlike SR theory, that there is an interaction among the person, the behavior, and the environment, and that the person can shape the environment as well as the environment shaping the person. All these relationships are dynamic. Glanz and Rimer (1995, p. 15) provide a good example of this construct.

> *A man with high cholesterol might have a hard time following his prescribed low-fat diet because his company cafeteria doesn't offer low-fat food choices that he likes. He can try to change the environment by talking with the cafeteria manager or the company medical or health department staff, and asking that healthy food choices be added to the menu. Or, if employees start to dine elsewhere in order to eat low-fat lunches, the cafeteria may change its menu to maintain its lunch business.*

Finally, there is one other construct that grew out of the social learning theory of Rotter (1954) that needs to be mentioned because of its association with health behavior. "Rotter posited that a person's history of positive or negative reinforcement across a variety of situations shapes a belief as to whether or not a person's own actions lead to those reinforcements" (Wallston, 1994, p. 187). Rotter referred to this construct as **locus of control.** Thus, he felt that people with internal locus of control perceived that reinforcement was under their control, whereas those with external locus of control perceived reinforcement to be under the control of some external force. In the 1970s, Wallston and his colleagues at Vanderbilt University began testing the usefulness of this construct in predicting health behavior (Wallston, 1994). They explored the concept of whether individuals with internal locus of control were more likely to participate in health-enhancing behavior than those with external locus of control. They began their work by examining locus of control as a two-dimensional construct (internal vs. external), then moved to a multidimensional construct when they split the external dimension into "powerful others" and "chance" (Wallston, Wallston, & DeVellis, 1978). After a number of years of work by many different researchers, Wallston has come to the conclusion that locus of control accounts for only a small amount of the variability in health behavior (Wallston, 1992). The internal locus of control belief about one's own health status is a necessary but not sufficient determinate of health-enhancing behavior (Wallston, 1994). Since the rise of the construct of self-efficacy, Wallston (1994) feels that self-efficacy is a better predictor of health-promoting behavior than locus of control. This not to say that locus of control is not a useful construct in developing health promotion programs. Knowing the locus of control orientation of those in the target population can provide planners with valuable information when considering social support as part of a planned intervention.

Theory of Reasoned Action (TRA)

Another theory that has received considerable attention in the literature of health behavior change is Fishbein's *theory of reasoned action (TRA)* (Fishbein & Ajzen, 1975). Like the theories already discussed, this theory was developed to explain not just health behavior but all volitional behaviors. However, while the theories discussed earlier in this chapter were directly concerned with behavior, this one provides a framework to study attitudes toward behaviors.

Fishbein and Ajzen distinguish among attitude, belief, behavioral intention, and behavior, and they present a conceptual framework for the study of the relationship among these four constructs. According to the model, an individual's intention to perform a given behavior is a function of her attitude toward performing the behavior and normative beliefs about what relevant others think she should do, weighted by motivation to comply with those others. Behavioral intention is viewed as a special type of belief and is indicated by the person's subjective perception and report of the probability that she will perform the behavior (Parcel, 1983, p. 41).

In our opinion, this theory has one element that distinguishes it from other theories that try to explain human behavior: This is the construct that deals with the normative beliefs about what relevant others think the person should do. This con-

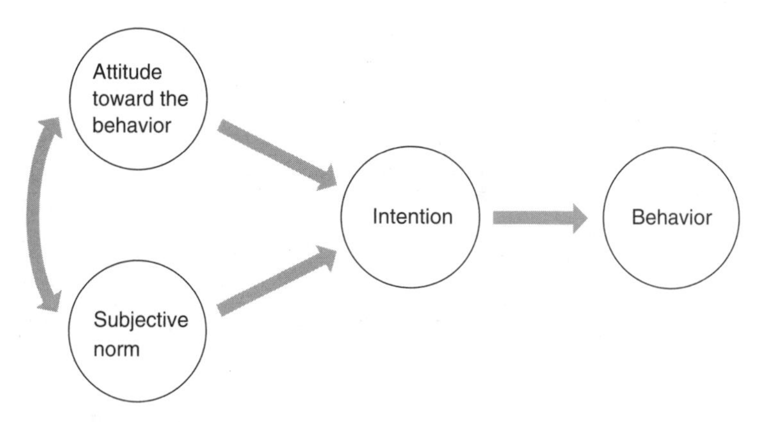

FIGURE 7.3 Diagram of the Theory of Reasoned Action

Source: From *Attitudes, Personality, and Behavior* (p. 118), by I. Ajzen, 1988, Chicago: Dorsey Press. Copyright 1988. Reprinted by permission of Open University Press.

struct states that individuals' intent to perform a given behavior is dependent partly on their belief that others (individuals or groups) think they should do so, and partly on the fact that they care about what these others think. This construct is often referred to as the subjective norm. An example of this construct applied to health promotion is the employee who intends to participate in the company's exercise program because she believes her boss thinks she should engage in exercise. For many behaviors, the relevant others may include a person's parents, spouse, close friends, and coworkers, as well as experts or professionals like physicians or lawyers. Figure 7.3 shows the major elements of TRA.

Theory of Planned Behavior (TPB)

TRA has proved to be most successful when dealing with purely volitional behaviors, but complications are encountered when the theory is applied to behaviors that are not fully under volitional control. A good example of this is a smoker who intends to quit but fails to do so. Even though intent is high, nonmotivational factors, such as lack of requisite opportunities and resources, could prevent success (Ajzen, 1988).

The *theory of planned behavior (TPB)* (see Figure 7.4) is an extension of the theory of reasoned action that addresses the problem of incomplete volitional control. The major difference between TPB and TRA is the addition of a third, conceptually independent determinant of intention. Like TRA, TPB includes attitude toward the behavior and subjective norm, but it has added the concept of perceived behavioral control. This refers to the perceived ease or difficulty of performing the behavior and is assumed to reflect past experience as well as anticipated impediments and obstacles. As a general rule, the more favorable the attitude and subjective norm

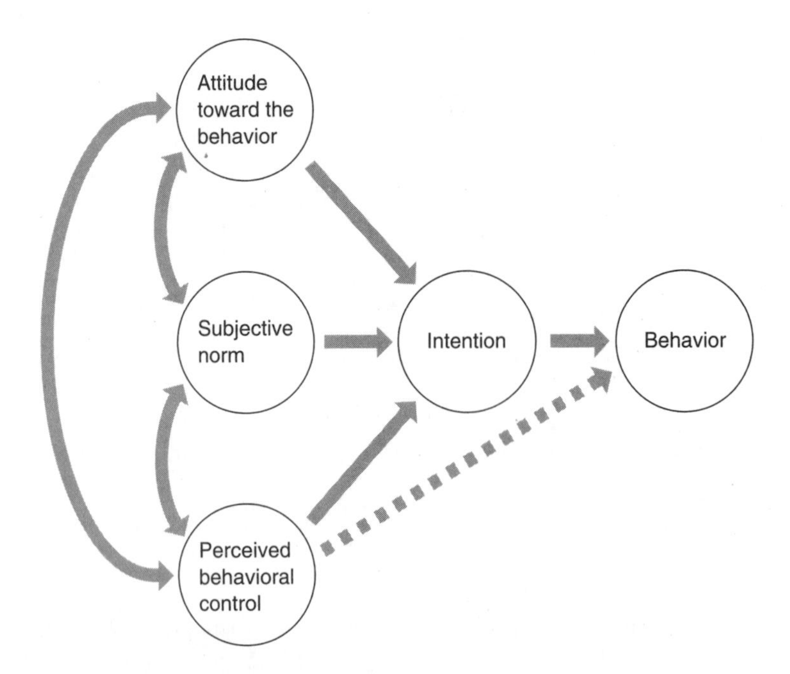

FIGURE 7.4 Diagram of the Theory of Planned Behavior

Source: From *Attitudes, Personality, and Behavior* (p. 118), by I. Ajzen, 1988, Chicago: Dorsey Press. Copyright 1988. Reprinted by permission of Open University Press.

with respect to a behavior, and the greater the perceived behavioral control, the stronger should be the individual's intentions to perform the behavior under consideration (Ajzen, 1988, pp. 132–33).

Figure 7.4 illustrates two important features of this theory. First, perceived behavioral control has motivational implications for intentions. That is, without perceived control, intentions could be minimal even if attitudes toward the behavior and subjective norm were strong. Second, there may be a direct link between perceived behavioral control and behavior. Behavior depends not only on motivation but also on adequate control. Thus, it stands to reason that perceived behavioral control can help predict goal attainment independent of behavioral intention (Ajzen, 1988). To use the example of smoking once again as a behavior not fully under volitional control, TPB predicts that a person will give up smoking if she:

1. Has a positive attitude toward quitting.
2. Thinks others whom she values believe it would be good for her to quit.
3. Perceives that she has control over whether or not she quits.

Because this theory is comparatively new, there have been few references to it in the health promotion literature. However, an article by Murphy and Brubaker

(1990) very nicely explains the application of this theory to testicular self-examination in high school males. We believe this theory will have a significant impact on the development of future health promotion interventions.

Theory of Freeing (TF)

A theory that takes a much different approach from the other theories presented is the *theory of freeing (TF)* (Freire, 1973, 1974). Like the others, it is not specific to health promotion, but it does have application to health promotion. It is a theory aimed at empowering education. Wallerstein and Bernstein (1988, p. 380) define *empowerment* as "a social action process that promotes participation of people, organizations, and communities in gaining control over their lives in their community and larger society. With this perspective, empowerment is not characterized as achieving power to dominate others, but rather power to act with others to effect change."

The theory was first used in the late 1950s when Paulo Freire, a Brazilian educator, initiated a successful literacy and political consciousness program for shantytown dwellers and peasants in Brazil (Freire, 1973). Since that time, the theory has been applied to many other problems.

One of the first to apply this theory to health promotion was Greenberg. He stated (1978, p. 20) that the task of health education should be to "free people so they may make health-related decisions based upon their needs and interests as long as these needs and interests do not adversely affect others." In essence, Freire's concept of freeing contrasts "being free with being oppressed" (Walker & Bibeau, 1985/1986, p. 5). People become free by being critically conscious.

The underlying concept of this theory is that critical consciousness is determined by the interaction with culture. Consciousness is influenced by and influences the culture. Oppressed people are "of the world," and their consciousness is a product of the culture. Being "of the world" is defined by the lack of the person's ability to perceive, respond, and act with power to change concrete reality (Walker & Bibeau, 1985/1986). Free people are "in the world," and their consciousness is a producer of culture.

Education is the key to becoming critically conscious. However, the education that is meant here is not education in the traditional sense. Education occurs through dialogue, not through lecture. People who use dialogue are teachers, whereas those who just talk are lecturers. And in this type of education, participants replace pupils. All those involved in the educational process learn from one another.

A very nice summary of the applications of Freire's work to health promotion has been presented by Wallerstein and Bernstein (1988) and Wallerstein (1994). They state that Freire's theory includes three stages. Stage 1 is the listening stage, in which those in the target population have the opportunity to share their thoughts, identify the problems, and set the priorities. Unlike in a more traditional planning process, the program planners do not collect data and determine the needs. Instead, the target population is identifying the issues and prioritizing the needs.

Stage 2 is a dialogue process. The dialogue revolves around a *code*. "A 'code' is a concrete physical representation of an identified community issue in any form:

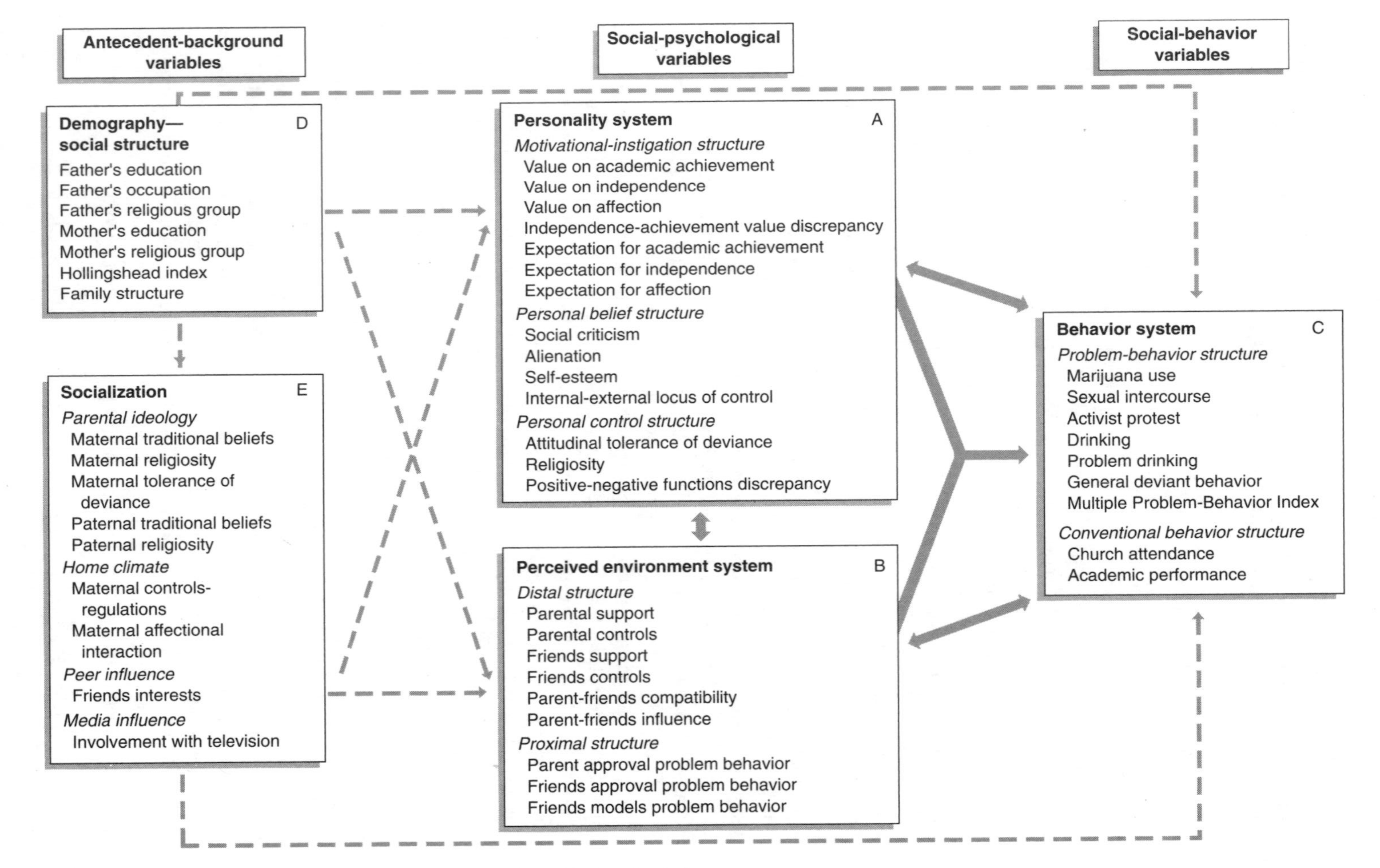

FIGURE 7.5 Conceptual Structure of Problem-Behavior Theory

Source: From *Problem Behavior and Psychosocial Development: A Longitudinal Study of Youth* (p. 36), by R. Jessor and S. L. Jessor, 1977, New York: Academic Press. Copyright 1977. Reprinted by permission of Academic Press and Richard Jessor.

role plays, stories, slides, photographs, songs, etc." (Wallerstein & Bernstein, 1988, p. 383). After experiencing a code, group facilitators lead the target population through a discussion that helps the people move from a personal to a social analysis and action level. They do this by asking the target population to respond to these five statements (Wallerstein & Bernstein, 1988):

1. Describe what you see and feel.
2. As a group, define the many levels of the problem.
3. Share similar experiences from your lives.
4. Question why this problem exists.
5. Develop action plans to address the problem.

Stage 3 of this theory is the action stage, in which those in the target population try out the plans that came from the listening and dialogue stages. As the people put their plans into action, they reflect on their new experiences and create a thinking-acting cycle. "This recurrent spiral of action-reflection-action enables people to learn from their collective attempts at change and to become more deeply involved to surmount the cultural, social, or historic barriers" (Wallerstein & Bernstein, 1988, p. 383).

Problem-Behavior Theory (PBT)

Because many health promotion programs focus on problem behaviors, program planners have found *problem-behavior theory (PBT)* to be a useful framework for guiding program development. This theory rests upon the social-psychological relationships that occur within and among the three major systems of personality, perceived environment, and behavior. Each of these systems includes a variety of variables that are interrelated and organized in such a manner as to generate a greater or lesser likelihood of occurrence of problem behavior (Jessor & Jessor, 1977).

The logic and rationale of the original formulation of PBT were presented by Jessor, Graves, Hanson, and Jessor (1968), and the present content and structure of the framework were presented in detail by Jessor and Jessor (1977). This later presentation of the theory was based upon the study of adolescence and youth in American society in the late 1960s and early 1970s. As such, the theory is designed to account for problem behaviors that organize the daily lives of young people (Jessor & Jessor, 1977). A schematic representation of this theory is presented in Figure 7.5.

The personality system, found in box A of the schematic diagram in Figure 7.5, contains three major structures: motivational-instigation, personal belief, and personal control. The interaction of these three structures determines a person's personality as it relates to a problem behavior. The motivational-instigation structure is concerned with the directional orientation of the action or goals (not directly related to problem behavior) toward which the individual strives and the motivation to begin behaviors to work toward the goals. The greater the value placed on a goal, the greater the likelihood of action directed toward the goal. The personal belief structure deals with the cognitive controls exerted against the occurrence of a problem behavior. There are four variables in this structure: social criticism, alienation, self-esteem, and locus of control. The third structure in this system, personal control, includes variables that are directly linked to the problem behaviors.

The second system in this theory is the perceived environment system (box B), which Jessor and Jessor describe as "the environment that is contributed by the actor from his experience with it" (1977, p. 27). This structure includes both distal variables (those that are remote from the causal chain) and proximal variables (those obviously related to the occurrence of problem behavior). Both types of variables deal with the individual's interactions with friends and parents/family. The distal variables can be thought of as the social content in which a person is located, while the proximal variables determine the degree to which the person is located in the social content.

The third system of the theory is the behavior system, represented by box C. This component contains two major areas: problem behavior and conventional behavior. *Problem behavior* refers to behavior that is undesirable by the norms of society and needs some type of social control, whereas *conventional behavior* includes what are seen as desirable behaviors by society.

Two other boxes (D and E) shown in Figure 7.5 contain antecedent and background variables, mainly demography—social structure and socialization. These variables affect both the personality and perceived environment systems, but the amount of impact is hard to measure.

In applying this theory to health promotion programs, we would refer to a problem behavior as one that is detrimental to good health. This detrimental health behavior is thus related to the personality and perceived environment systems, which in turn are affected by the social structure and socialization of a person. In other words, if a person is an overeater or a nonexerciser, there are many variables that could lead to this behavior and would need to be examined if the behavior is to be changed.

COMBINATION HEALTH BEHAVIOR MODELS

Several models have been developed (Becker & Maiman, 1983) to explain the various types of health behavior. Several of these models are based upon parts of theories that have been discussed earlier in this chapter. This section presents the best known of these models, the health belief model and the transtheoretical model. It also presents the cognitive-behavioral model of the relapse process. Each of these models should provide program planners with frameworks for helping to develop appropriate interventions.

Health Belief Model (HBM)

The **health belief model (HBM)**, which is the one most frequently used in health behavior applications, was developed in the 1950s by a group of psychologists to help explain why people would or would not use health services (Rosenstock, 1966). The HBM is based upon Lewin's decision-making model (Lewin, 1935, 1936; Lewin, Dembo, Festinger, & Sears, 1944). Since its creation, the HBM has been used to help explain a variety of health behaviors (Janz & Becker, 1984).

The HBM hypothesizes that health-related action depends upon the simultaneous occurrence of three classes of factors:

1. The existence of sufficient motivation (or health concern) to make health issues salient or relevant.
2. The belief that one is susceptible (vulnerable) to a serious health problem or to the sequelae of that illness or condition. This is often termed **perceived threat**.
3. The belief that following a particular health recommendation would be beneficial in reducing the perceived threat, and at a subjectively acceptable cost. Cost refers to the **perceived barriers** that must be overcome in order to follow the health recommendation; it includes, but is not restricted to, financial outlays (Rosenstock et al., 1988, p. 177).

Figure 7.6 on page 112 provides a diagram of the HBM as presented by Becker, Drachman, and Kirscht (1974).

As noted, the HBM has been applied to all types of health behavior. Here is an example of the HBM applied to exercise. Someone watching television sees an advertisement about exercise. This is a cue to action that starts her thinking about her own need to exercise. There may be some variables (demographic, sociopsychological, and structural) that cause her to think about it a bit more. She remembers her college health course that included information about heart disease and the importance of staying active. She knows she has a higher than normal risk for heart disease because of family history, poor diet, and slightly elevated blood pressure. Therefore, she comes to the conclusion that she is susceptible to heart disease **(perceived susceptibility).** She also knows that if she develops heart disease, it can be very serious (**perceived seriousness**/severity). Based upon these factors, she thinks that there is reason to be concerned about heart disease (perceived threat). She knows that exercise can help delay the onset of heart disease and can increase the chances of surviving a heart attack if one should occur **(perceived benefits).** But exercise takes time from an already busy day, and it is not easy to exercise in the variety of settings in which she typically finds herself, especially during bad weather (perceived barriers). She must now weigh the threat of the disease against the difference between benefits and barriers. This decision will then result in a likelihood of exercising or not exercising **(likelihood of taking recommended preventive health action)**.

The Transtheoretical Model or Stages of Change

The *transtheoretical model,* or the *stages of change* (summarized in Table 7.2), as it has more commonly been named, is a model that helps to explain the stages that a ma-

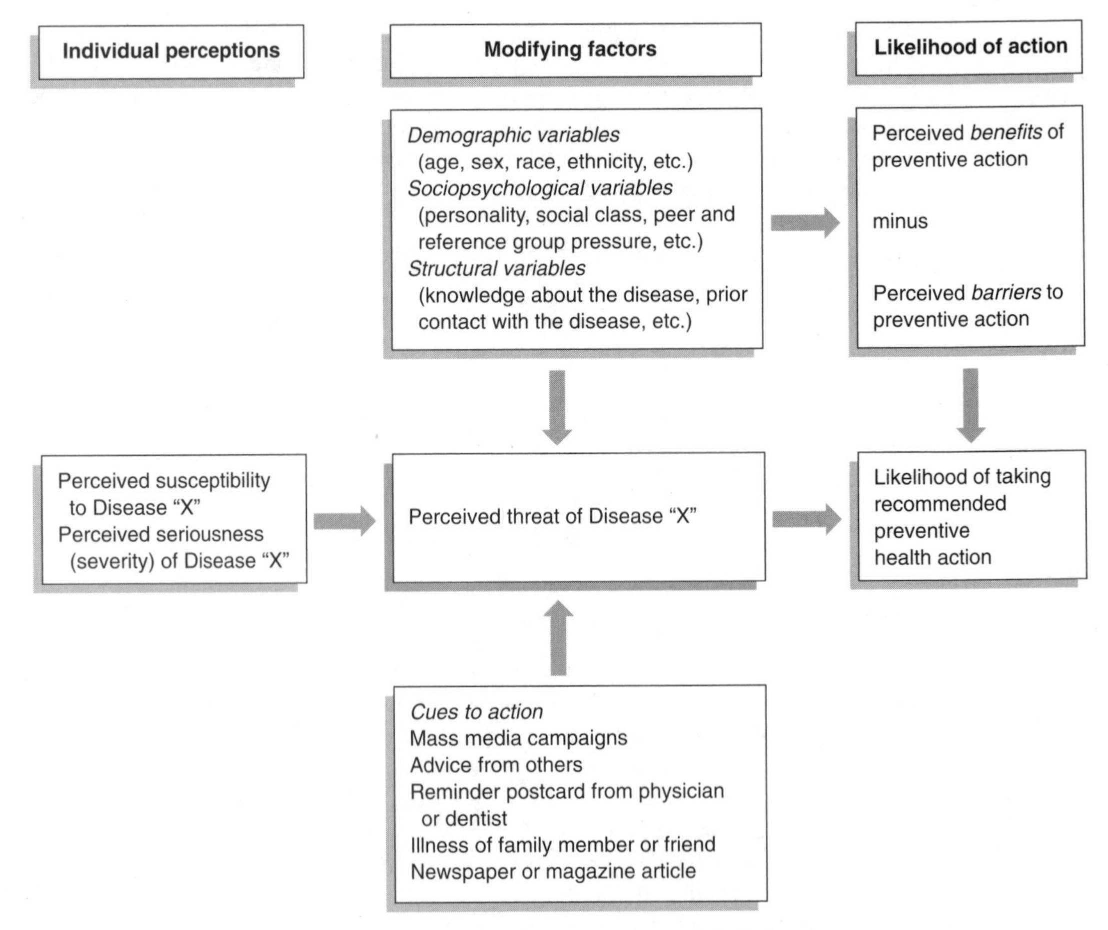

FIGURE 7.6 The HBM as a Predictor of Preventive Health Behavior

Source: From "A New Approach to Explaining Sick-Role Behavior in Low Income Populations," by M. H. Becker, R. H. Drachman, and J. P. Kirscht, 1974, *American Journal of Public Health,* 64 (March), pp. 205–216. Copyright 1974. Reprinted by permission of APHA and Marshall H. Becker.

jority of people experience as they attempt to change their health behavior over time. The model has its roots in psychotherapy and was developed by Prochaska (1979) after he completed a comparative analysis of eighteen therapy systems and a critical review of three hundred therapy outcome studies. From the analysis and review, Prochaska found that some common processes were involved in change.

As this model has evolved, researchers have applied it to many different types of health behavior change, including but not limited to contraceptive use (Grimley, Riley, Bellis, & Prochaska, 1993; Grimley, Prochaska, Velicer, & Prochaska, 1995), addictive behaviors (Prochaska, DiClemente, & Norcross, 1992), smoking cessation (DiClemente, Prochaska, Fairhurst, Velicer, Velasquez, & Rossi, 1991; DiClemente & Prochaska, 1982; Prochaska & DiClemente, 1983; Prochaska, DiClemente, Velicer, Ginpil,

TABLE 7.2 Stages of Change

Stages	Timeframe
Precontemplation	Not thinking about change in the next six months
Contemplation	Seriously thinking about change in the next six months
Preparation	Actively planning change
Action	Overly making changes
Maintenance	Taking steps to sustain change and resist temptation to relapse

& Norcross, 1985), condom use (Prochaska, Harlow, Redding, Snow, Rossi, & Velicer, 1990), alcohol abuse (Norcross, Prochaska, & Hambrecht, 1991), HIV prevention (Prochaska, Redding, Harlow, Rossi, & Velicer, 1994), and weight control (Prochaska, Norcross, Fowler, Follick, & Abrams, 1992; Prochaska & DiClemente, 1985).

The transtheoretical model suggests that "people move from *precontemplation,* not intending to change, to *contemplation,* intending to change within 6 months, to *preparation,* actively planning change, to *action,* overtly making changes, and into *maintenance,* taking steps to sustain change and resist temptation to relapse" (Prochaska et al., 1994). The **precontemplation stage** is defined as a time when people are not seriously thinking about changing their behavior during the next six months. "Many individuals in this stage are unaware or underaware of their problems" (Prochaska, DiClemente et al., 1992, p. 1103). The second stage, **contemplation** occurs when people are aware that a problem exists and are seriously thinking about a behavior change but have not yet made a commitment to take action. For example, most smokers know that smoking is bad for them and consider quitting, but are not quite ready to do so. The third stage is called **preparation** and combines intention and behavioral criteria. "Individuals in this stage are intending to take action in the next month and have unsuccessfully taken action in the past year" (Prochaska, DiClemente et al., 1992, p. 1104). In this stage, they may have taken some small steps toward action, such as buying the necessary clothes for exercising or cutting back on the fat grams they consume or the cigarettes they smoke, but they have not reached an effective criterion for effective action (Prochaska et al., 1992).

People are in the fourth stage, the **action stage,** when they are overtly making changes in their behavior, experiences, or environment in order to overcome their problems. This stage of change reflects a consistent behavior pattern, is usually the most visible, and receives the greatest external recognition (Prochaska, DiClemente et al., 1992). If those making the changes continue with their new pattern of behavior, they will move into the fifth stage, maintenance.

Maintenance is a continuation of the change started in the action stage. For addictive behaviors, the beginning of this stage has been defined as six months after taking overt action to change these behaviors (Prochaska, DiClemente et al., 1992).

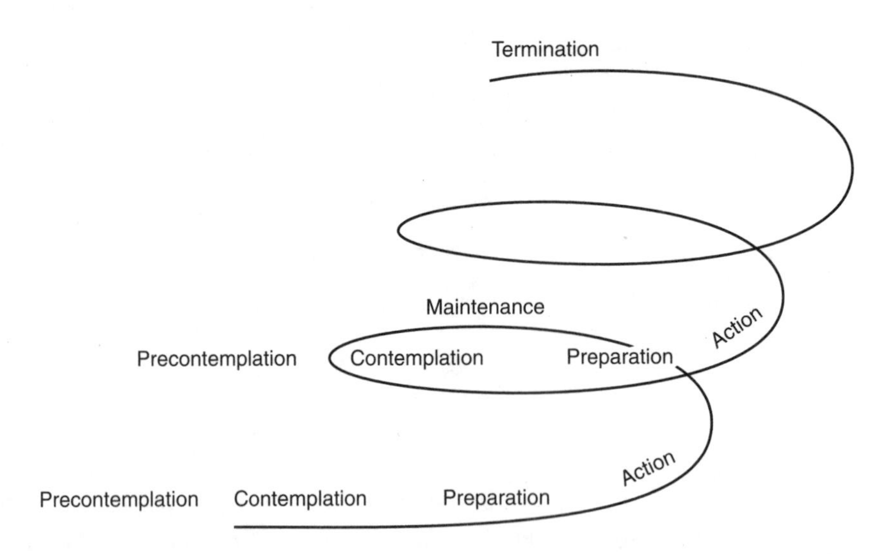

FIGURE 7.7 A Developmental Sequence for the Stages of Change

Source: From "The Transtheoretical Model of Change and HIV Prevention: A Review," by J. O. Prochaska, C. A. Redding, L. L. Harlow, J. S. Rossi, and W. F. Velicer, *Health Education Quarterly,* 21(4), pp. 471–486. Copyright © 1994 by John Wiley & Sons, Inc. Reprinted by permission of John Wiley & Sons, Inc. and the author.

The initiation of this stage has not been defined for many other health behaviors. However, it is safe to say that a goal of health promotion is to have health-enhancing behaviors last a lifetime, no matter when they begin.

It was once thought that movement through these stages was linear. However, as noted in the next section of this chapter, "for most health behavior problems the majority of people relapse and return to the precontemplation or contemplation stage of change, before eventually succeeding in maintaining change. In this model, relapse is not extraordinary, but a natural part of the change cycle" (Prochaska et al., 1994, p. 473). Because relapse is a part of the change cycle, the model is represented in Figure 7.7 as a spiral. This suggests that most people learn from their relapse episodes instead of going in circles and making no progress toward change (Prochaska, 1989, August).

Since its development, the transtheoretical model has been useful in several different ways. The first is that it makes program planners aware that not everyone is ready for change "right now," even though there is a program that can help them modify their behavior. People proceed through behavior change at different paces. Second, if individuals are not ready for action right now, then other programs can be developed to help them become ready for action. Third, the model has been very useful in helping to identify individuals who are truly ready for change and in predicting who may be successful in trying to change a health behavior. This third aspect fits in nicely with the effort to market a program and is discussed further in Chapter 11.

COGNITIVE-BEHAVIORAL MODEL OF THE RELAPSE PROCESS

As noted in the transtheoretical model, for most people, relapse is a part of change. It has been said that getting people to change behavior is hard, but having them maintain the behavior is much harder. This is nicely illustrated by the old saying "Giving up smoking is easy, I've done it a hundred times." At one time, it was enough for health promotion program planners just to get people to change their behavior, now they need to do more. Because of the difficulty of maintaining a new behavior, program planners need to give special attention to helping those in the target population avoid slipping back to their previous behaviors.

Although much of the early research dealing with this concept of slipping back was conducted using addictive behaviors, such as substance abuse and gambling, the concept applies to all behavior change, including preventive health behaviors. Marlatt (1982) indicates that a high percentage of individuals who enter programs for health behavior change **relapse** to their former behaviors within one year. More specifically, researchers have warned program planners of **recidivism** problems with participants in exercise (Dishman, Sallis, & Orenstein, 1985; Horne, 1975), weight loss (Stunkard & Braunwell, 1980), and smoking cessation (Leventhal & Cleary, 1980) programs. Therefore, planners need to make sure that program interventions include the skills necessary for dealing with those difficult times during behavior change.

Marlatt (1982) has referred to the process of trying to prevent slipping back as relapse prevention. **Relapse prevention,** which is based on social cognitive theory, "is a self-control program designed to teach individuals who are trying to change their behavior how to anticipate and cope with the problem of relapse" (Marlatt, 1982, p. 329). Relapse is triggered by *high-risk situations.* "A high-risk situation is defined broadly as any situation which poses a threat to the individual's sense of control and increases the risk of potential relapse" (Marlatt, 1982, p. 338). Cummings, Gordon, and Marlatt (1980), in a study of clients with a variety of problem behaviors (drinking, smoking, heroin addiction, gambling, and overeating), found high-risk situations to fall into two major categories—intrapersonal and interpersonal determinants. They found that 56% of the relapse situations were caused by intrapersonal determinants, such as negative emotional states (35%), negative physical states (3%), positive emotional states (4%), testing personal control (5%), and urges and temptations (9%). The 44% of the situations represented by interpersonal determinants included interpersonal conflicts (16%), social pressure (20%), and positive emotional states (8%). These determinants can be referred to as the covert antecedents of relapse. That is to say, these high-risk situations do not just happen; instead, they are created by what Marlatt (1982) calls lifestyle imbalances.

People who have the coping skills to deal with a high-risk situation have a much greater chance of preventing relapse than those who do not. Figure 7.8 illustrates the possible paths one may take in a high-risk situation (Marlatt, 1982).

Marlatt has developed both global (Figure 7.9 on page 117) and specific (Figure 7.10 on page 118) self-control strategies for relapse intervention. Specific intervention procedures are designed to help participants anticipate and cope with the

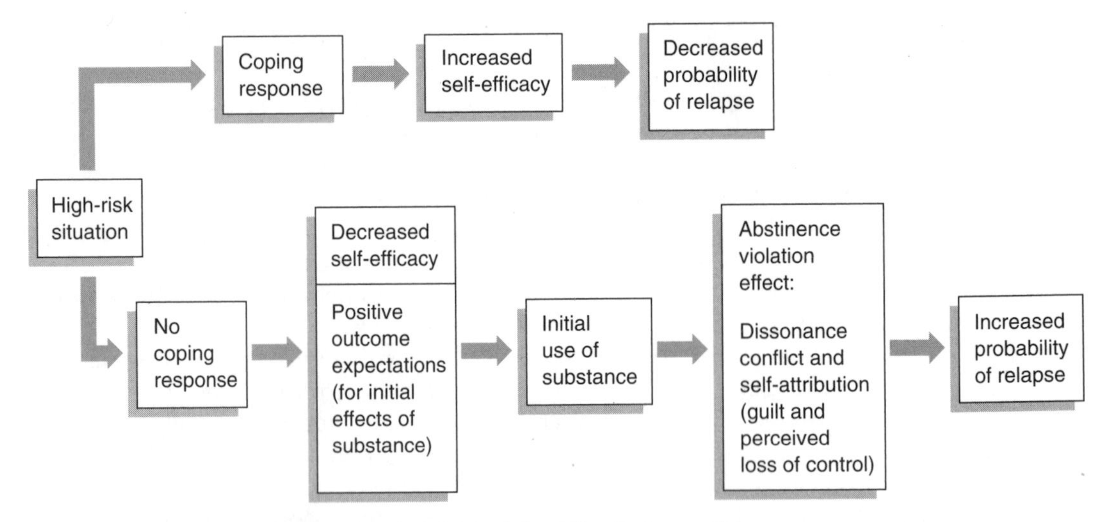

FIGURE 7.8 Cognitive-Behavioral Model of the Relapse Process

Source: From "Relapse Prevention: Theoretical Rationale and Overview of the Model," by G. A. Marlatt, in G. A. Marlatt and J. R. Gordon (Eds.), *Relapse Prevention* (p. 38), 1985, New York: Guilford Press. Reprinted by permission of Guilford Press.

relapse episode itself, while the global intervention procedures are designed to modify the early antecedents of relapse, including restructuring of the participant's general style of life. A complete application of the relapse prevention model would include both specific and global interventions (Marlatt, 1982).

APPLYING THEORY TO PRACTICE

Learning and understanding the theories presented in this chapter are manageable tasks. However, learning "how to apply given theories to 'real life' projects where theories usually have to be bent and twisted and adapted to uncontrollable conditions" (Hochbaum et al., 1992, p. 311) is a much more difficult task. Several authors (Burdine & McLeroy, 1992; D'Onofrio, 1992; Hochbaum et al., 1992; McLeroy, 1993; van Ryn and Heaney, 1992) have reported the difficulties practitioners have had in applying theory. In the sections below, we will discuss the reported barriers to applying theory in the field and provide suggestions for choosing and applying theory.

Barriers to Applying Theory

Burdine and McLeroy (1992) have reported on semistructured interviews with health professionals on the use of theory in practice. Though the group was not randomly selected—it was part of a workgroup in eastern Pennsylvania—it was thought to be broadly representative of "practicing health educators." From these

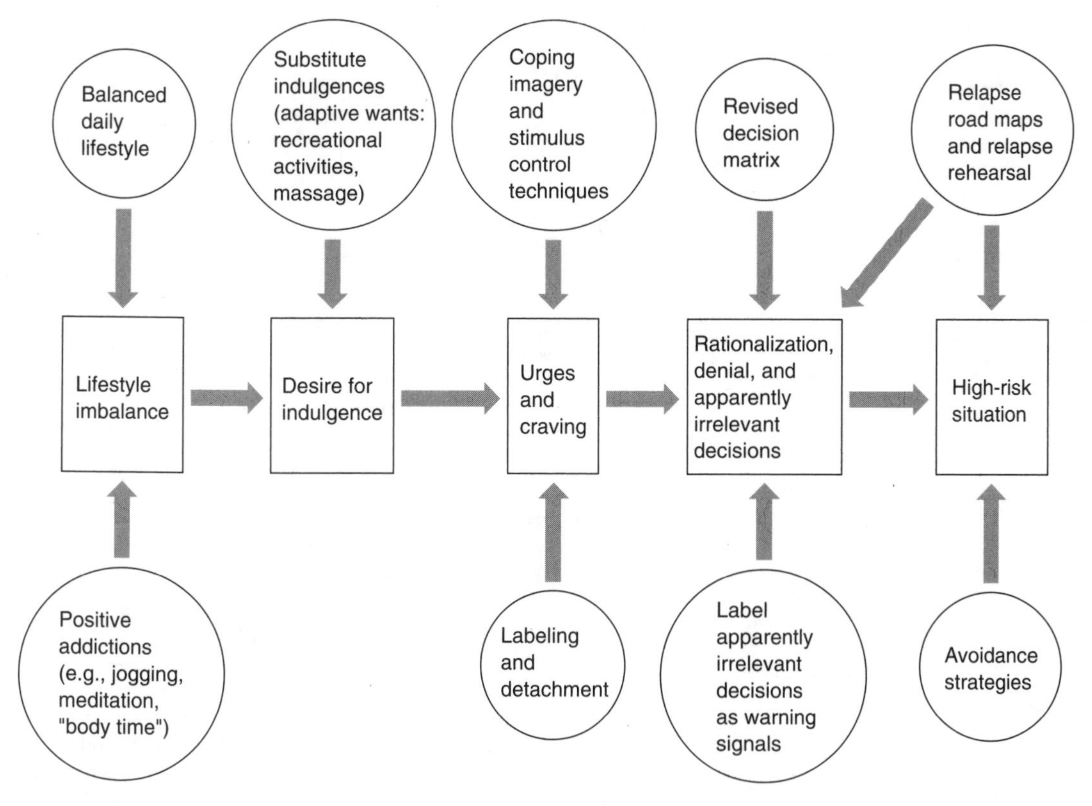

FIGURE 7.9 Relapse Prevention: Global Self-Control Strategies

Source: From "Relapse Prevention: Theoretical Rationale and Overview of the Model," by G. A. Marlatt, in G. A. Marlatt and J. R. Gordon (Eds.), *Relapse Prevention* (p. 61), 1985, New York: Guilford Press. Reprinted by permission of Guilford Press.

interviews came three primary reasons why practitioners were not using theory learned in their professional preparation courses in college. They included "(1) the failure of theory to adequately guide practice in specific settings or contexts; (2) the lack of appropriate theories to guide community-oriented interventions; and (3) difficulties in transferring theories from the academic training context to the practice environment." (Burdine & McLeroy, 1992, p. 336).

The concern about the failure of theory to adequately guide practice in specific settings or contexts stems from the fact that the theory on which the health education discipline was built is borrowed from the social and behavioral sciences. It primarily revolves around individual behavior change. Even though behavior change is an important part of the work of health educators, the theories do not match well with the expanded role of health educators when they address problems such as controlling environmental health hazards, increasing access to and utilization of health care facilities, limiting the commercial promotion of alcohol

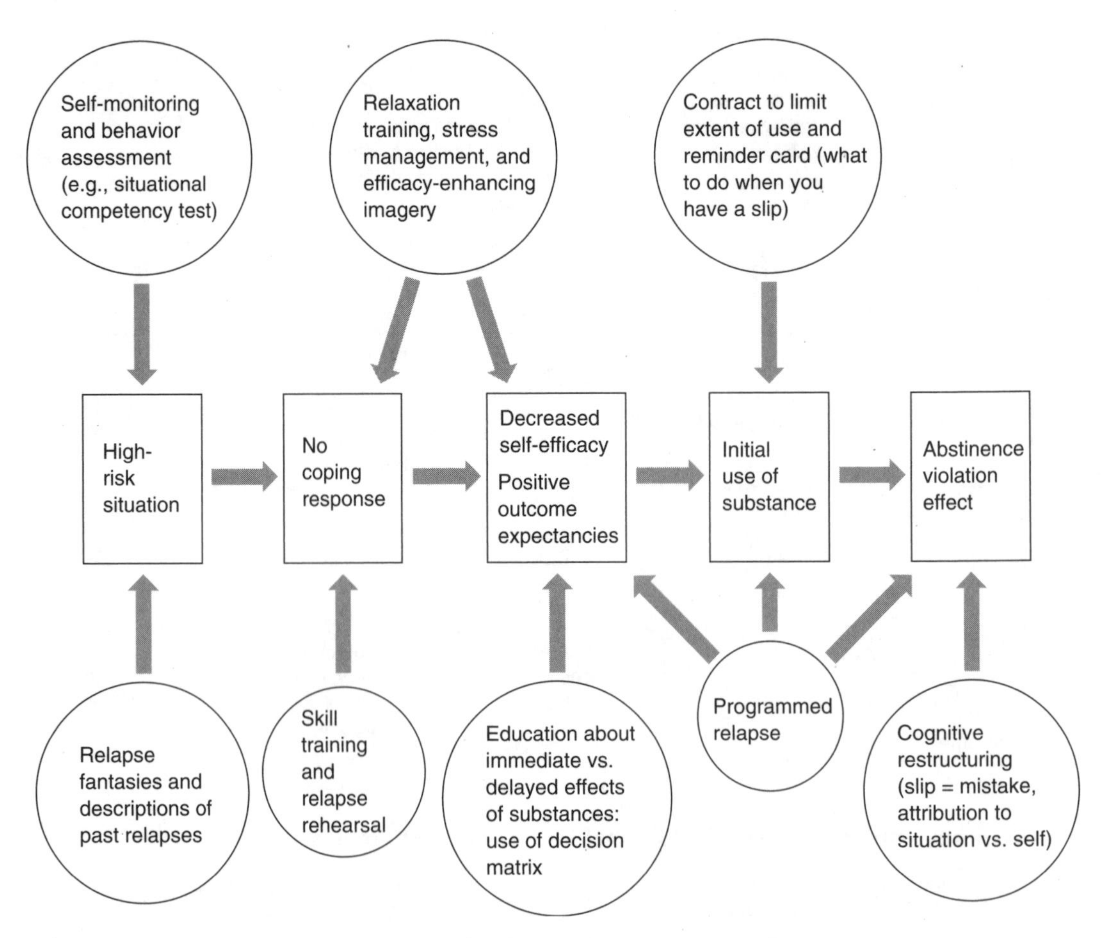

FIGURE 7.10 Relapse Prevention: Specific Intervention Strategies

Source: From "Relapse Prevention: Theoretical Rationale and Overview of the Model," by G. A. Marlatt, in G. A. Marlatt and J. R. Gordon (Eds.), *Relapse Prevention* (p. 54), 1985, New York: Guilford Press. Reprinted by permission of Guilford Press.

and tobacco (D'Onofrio, 1992), and organizing committees to deal with these problems (Burdine & McLeroy, 1992).

The issue of the lack of appropriate theory to guide community-oriented interventions speaks to the fact that the discipline lacks process or practical guide theory. The discipline needs a theory to take us from the social science theory to creating appropriate interventions for a specific target population (Burdine & McLeroy, 1992).

The third reason shared by Burdine and McLeroy (1992) for practitioners not using theory in practice is the means by which theory is taught by academicians. Instead of presenting the theories and asking how they apply to a problem, it is suggested (Burdine & McLeroy, 1992; D'Onofrio, 1992) that academicians should be teaching theory by starting with a specific health problem and asking how each of the theories helps us to understand the problem.

Now that we know a bit about what appear to be some of the reasons for not using theory in practice, let's look at how it can be implemented.

Suggestions for Applying Theory to Practice

Several authors (D'Onofrio, 1992; Hochbaum et al., 1992; van Ryn & Heaney, 1992) have suggested ideas for applying theory to practice. Below is a summary compilation of their ideas.

The first step is having a basic grasp of the theories—old and new (D'Onofrio, 1992). Practitioners should take the time to review the theories and not depend on their memory. Theories, like most other knowledge, are forgotten over time if they are not used. Also, the very nature of theory suggests that it can change and be updated. The theory of reasoned action and the theory of planned behavior are good examples. Practitioners also need to become familiar with new theories and models, such as the recently developed transtheoretical model.

Once practitioners feel comfortable with the theories and models, they should examine the applicability of these theories and models to the problem they are addressing (D'Onofrio, 1992; van Ryn & Heaney, 1992). This can be done by taking the goals of a proposed program and matching them with the most applicable theories. For example, some theories address only behavior change, while others address organization change. Further, some behavior change theories, such as the theory of planned behavior, address only volitional behavior, while others generalize to addictive behaviors, like Marlatt's cognitive-behavioral model of relapse (van Ryn & Heaney, 1992). Glanz and Rimer (1995) have organized this concept of appropriate theory selection by noting which theories are best suited when attacking a health problem through the five different levels within the **ecological perspective** (McLeroy, Bibeau, Steckler, & Glanz, 1988). The five levels of influence for health-related behaviors and conditions that need to be considered when developing interventions include:

1. Intrapersonal, or individual factors.
2. Interpersonal factors.
3. Institutional, or organizational factors.
4. Community factors.
5. Public policy factors.

For the purpose of this discussion, Glanz and Rimer (1995) grouped the latter three levels into a single level referred to as *community.* Three theories that are especially useful at the intrapersonal level are the transtheoretical or stages of change model (Prochaska, 1979), the health belief model (Rosenstock, 1966), and the consumer information processing model (Bettman, 1979). The theory that has been useful when attacking a health problem from the interpersonal level is the social learning/cognitive theory (Rotter, 1954; Bandura, 1977b). The theories that have been used successfully at the community level are community organization (see Chapter 9), the diffusion theory (see Chapter 11), and various theories of organizational change.

Knowing that several theories or models are applicable to the problem they are addressing, planners should look for evidence that the theories or models will work in their situation. Have others used theories or models with success with the same or a similar problem or target population (van Ryn & Heaney, 1992)? Some theories or models may have to be adjusted or modified to be applicable to certain target populations. For example, can the same theory apply to people from different cultural backgrounds within the United States? Or, what is the applicability of behavioral theories based on Western thought to people from non-Western cultures (D'Onofrio, 1992)?

It is also important to remember that seldom does a single theory or model address all the complexities of a problem. Planners will more than likely have to use more than one theory or model to adequately address all the components of the problem. To do so, planners will need to synthesize and integrate the theories and models to fit their particular situation (D'Onofrio, 1992). In bringing theories or models together, planners are warned against using only selected parts of a theory or model. Theories are based upon the interaction of several variables. When some of those variables are removed, the theory or model is not the same. For example, if cues to action or motivation are removed from the health belief model, planners will not know the true effectiveness of the model. Thus, the most effective use of a theory or model is to use it in total (Hochbaum et al., 1992).

In the final step in choosing a theory, planners need to select "a theory that makes sense to them, given their experience and what they know and believe about the world" (van Ryn & Heaney, 1992, p. 320). This is not to say that planners should not consider theories and models that may be different from their own views, but it "does not make sense to base a program on theoretical ideas that are at odds with one's own philosophy or belief system" (van Ryn & Heaney, 1992, p. 320).

An Example of Applying Theory to Practice

To help planners move from theory to practice, we thought it would be helpful to provide an example. We have chosen to apply the social cognitive theory and the cognitive-behavioral model of the relapse process to creating a comprehensive behavior change intervention. The intervention, which is presented in Figure 7.11 and discussed below, includes eight different components.

First Component: Education and Awareness Building

The first two components of this intervention are based upon a portion of the construct of behavioral capability. If people are going to behave in health enhancing ways, they first must know what those behaviors are. For instance, if a program is aimed at changing the behavior of people in order to lower their serum cholesterol

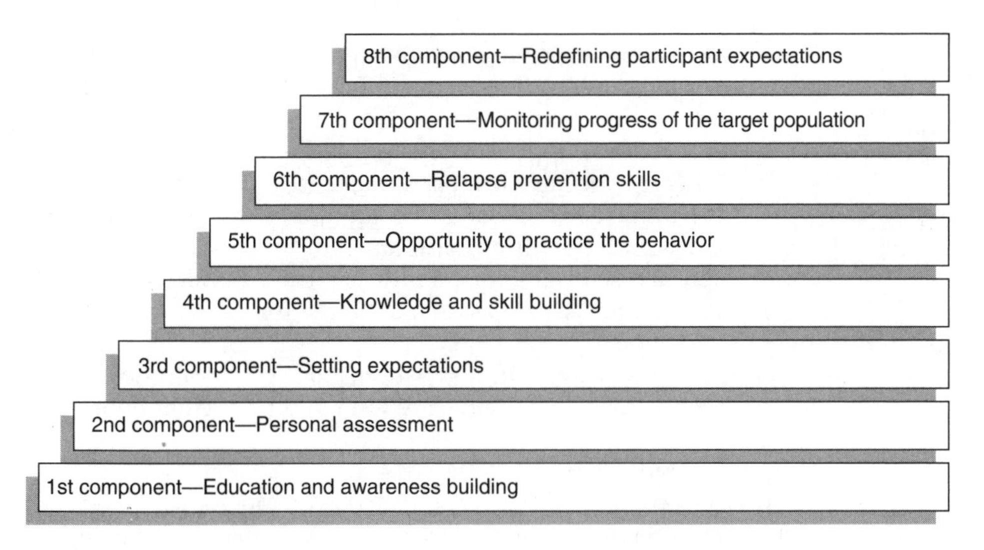

FIGURE 7.11 Model for Building a Comprehensive Intervention

levels, after experiencing this component of the intervention those in the target population should know:

1. What cholesterol is.
2. Why it is a health concern.
3. What contributes to the cholesterol level found in one's blood.
4. What are acceptable cholesterol readings.

The purpose of this component is not to provide in-depth information on the health concern or problem; rather, it should provide an overview. After experiencing this component, the participants should have a general understanding of the health concern or problem and should not be mystified by medical jargon and statistics. This component could be accomplished through an introductory session of a program, through a pamphlet distributed to all those in the target population, or through a series of public service announcements on television or radio.

Second Component: Personal Assessment

Once the program participants have an overall understanding of the health concern or problem, they need to see how the problem relates to their own life or situation. Therefore, we suggest that planners allow the participants either to assess themselves or, if that is not possible, to be assessed by someone else to find out how they compare to norms or averages with regard to the health concern or problem. This component will help make the program more relevant to the individual participants, thus increasing their interest and motivation. Typical assessments could include:

1. A health risk appraisal (HRA).
2. Disease-specific risk appraisals like Risko or Cancer Risks.
3. A **field test**, such as Cooper's 12-minute or 1.5-mile run (Cooper, 1982) or a treadmill test for physical fitness.
4. A health screening (blood pressure, body composition, or cholesterol).
5. A paper-and-pencil assessment for stress, stress management, or personality type.
6. A record of consumption patterns for tobacco, alcohol, or food, as is commonly done with the twenty-four- and forty-eight-hour diaries.

This last technique is a part of the construct of self-control.

The personal assessment is completed primarily for the benefit of the program participants, even though it can also provide valuable information for the program facilitators. There is, however, another assessment that can be very helpful for the program planners at this point of the intervention: one that is used to determine participants' attitude toward health in general and toward the specific health concern or problem being addressed in the program (Cummings, K. et al., 1980). What value do the program participants put on health? Are the program participants self-efficacious with regard to skills or behavior necessary to deal with the concern or problem? What type of health locus of control do the program participants have? Are the participants ready for change? Answers to these questions could go a long way to help program planners select and design appropriate program interventions. There are several instruments available to help collect this type of data. They include the Value Survey (K. A. Wallston, personal communication, 1984), Multidimensional Health Locus of Control (MHLC) Scales (Wallston, Wallston, & DeVellis, 1978), Terminal Values (Rokeach, 1969), Stages of Change (McConnaughy, Prochaska, & Velicer, 1983), and the Rotter Internal-External Locus of Control Scale (Rotter, 1966). Other valuable assessment scales may be found in a set of books from IOX Assessment Associates (1988) that should be useful with this component of the model.

Third Component: Setting Expectations

Once those in the target population have an understanding of the health concern or problem and know what their own status is in relationship to it, they are ready to set expectations for themselves. In other words, what can they expect to happen if they engage in this behavior change? This step should help to maintain participants' interest, individualize the program as much as possible, and motivate the participants to continue their participation in the program. In this component, program planners need to make sure that the participants set realistic expectations for themselves. An unrealistic expectation can be just as detrimental to a participant as a realistic one can be motivating. In addition to being realistic, expectations should be based upon the best available information and research on the health concern or problem.

To guide health planners in understanding the difference between appropriate (realistic and soundly based) and inappropriate (unrealistic or not based on sound information) expectations, we present several examples of each. After each inappropriate expectation, the reason why it is inappropriate is stated in parentheses.

Inappropriate expectations for program participants

1. I plan to lose thirty pounds during this four-week weight loss program. (Research has shown that a healthy weight loss rate is one to two pounds per week.)
2. I will lose ten pounds using the grapefruit diet. (Weight loss should incorporate sound eating habits and exercise.)
3. I want to lose ten pounds during my participation in the program. (Why ten pounds? Is this figure based upon a body composition test or weighing oneself, or is it based on the feeling that "I look better when I am ten pounds lighter"?)
4. As an alcoholic, I plan to reduce my alcohol intake to zero, then just drink socially. (Recovering alcoholics cannot drink socially.)
5. After the first six weeks of my aerobics exercise program, I want to be in good enough shape to run a marathon. (Training for a long endurance race takes much longer than six weeks, especially for the beginning exerciser.)

Appropriate participant expectations

1. Based upon my body composition test, I will lose ten pounds over the next four weeks. This will put my percentage of body fat at 15% (for males; 22% for females).
2. One year after the last class of the smoking cessation program, I will no longer be smoking.
3. I will burn 400 calories more per day than I am doing now.
4. At the end of this program, I will be able to conduct a breast self-examination (or a testicular self-examination) and explain it to someone else.
5. I will incorporate one stress management technique into my daily schedule.

Fourth Component: Knowledge and Skill Building

Upon completion of any health promotion program, those in the target population should possess the necessary knowledge and skills to behave in a healthy manner with regard to the health concern of interest. This is the second part of the behavioral capability construct. If people want to eat in a healthy manner, they must first know what the "healthy manner" is and second have the necessary skills to prepare or choose the appropriate foods to eat. If people want to begin an aerobic exercise program, they need to know how to exercise and have the skills to do so properly.

This is the component of the model in which those in the target population learn most of the information about the concern or problem, and also learn the skills necessary to deal with it. The actual time needed to incorporate this component may be just a one-hour session, as with a breast self-examination or a testicular self-examination program; it may take four to twelve hours, as for a course in cardiopulmonary resuscitation (CPR); or it may take weeks, as with weight loss, exercise, or nutrition programs.

Fifth Component: Opportunity to Practice the Behavior

This component has three major aspects. The first is to make sure that the planned intervention includes activities for removing barriers that stand between those in the target population and healthier behavior. Planners should consider barriers such as limited access, availability, and resources, and prohibitive policies and laws.

The second aspect of this component is to give those in the target group an opportunity to put into practice the new knowledge and skills learned in the fourth component. Too many health promotion programs provide people with the knowledge and skills to behave in a healthy manner, but never give them an opportunity to practice the activity. Thus they cannot become self-efficacious with regard to the newly learned behavior. If people are going to stop smoking, they need to practice the skills needed to stop. If people want to become involved in a program of regular exercise, they need to experience it, not just read or be told about exercising (Dennison, 1984).

Most, but not all, interventions can be planned to incorporate this "get them involved" step, in which program participants can experience the new behavior. In preparing the program participants for situations in which they cannot actually experience the new behavior, a lifelike experience may be the next best thing. An example of this may be the social pressure people experience when trying to break a habit, like smoking. There always seems to be someone around who tries to pressure the person to have "just one." In this case, a lifelike experience could include a role-playing activity; other possibilities would be responding to a case study or analyzing a critical incident. All of these "next best" experiences allow people to think about and react to a situation before they experience it in real life.

The third important aspect of this component is letting the program participants see others practicing healthy behaviors. Not only do people learn vicariously, but also they can become self-efficacious from watching others. Allowing new participants in a weight loss program to interact with those who have been through it previously, letting new exercise participants watch an exercise class in session, or making sure employees see the executives wearing their safety belts while driving company-owned cars are all very important.

Sixth Component: Relapse Prevention Skills

In this component, planners want to prepare program participants for the high-risk situations they will encounter when changing behavior. First, with the help of the program facilitator, program participants need to identify those times when they may be tempted to relapse. Once such situations have been identified, a strategy can be planned to counter them. For example, if people who are trying to quit smoking know that they will have a difficult time not smoking in times of stress, a plan for dealing with stressful situations in ways other than smoking needs to be ready. These alternatives could include things like taking a walk, talking to a friend, or practicing a meditation exercise. Each of these experiences can be a coping response to replace smoking.

Seventh Component: Monitoring Progress of the Target Population

After those in the target population have had the opportunity to experience their new behavior, either actually or through a lifelike situation, they need to reflect on, critique, and monitor their progress. This monitoring process will provide the participants and planners with feedback that can be used to:

1. Reinforce what is being done.
2. Check learning.
3. Help prevent relapse.
4. Identify areas that should be corrected and not reinforced.

The monitoring process can be completed by anyone involved in the program; it may take many different forms depending on the program goals and objectives. It can be completed by the participants themselves, by other participants, by the facilitators of the program, or by a combination of these individuals. Commonly used techniques for participants to self-monitor their progress are keeping logs of their activity or behavior (weight loss, miles walked, percentage of a particular group adhering to a specific behavior) or charting or graphing their progress. Other participants could be involved in the monitoring process by providing verbal feedback on the behavior of their peers after a role-playing situation, by giving their opinion on progress made to date, or by reviewing a videotape of a role-playing situation, a critical incident, or even a real situation. This responsibility has traditionally been approached by having program facilitators monitor the target population's progress. Techniques have included various forms of testing, verbal feedback, written critiques of work, and use of checklists.

No matter what technique is used, it is most important that progress be monitored and feedback provided.

Eighth Component: Redefining Participant Expectations

After the program participants have had the opportunity either to monitor their own progress or to have it monitored by another, they need to compare their progress to the expectation(s) they set in the third component of the model. If their expectations are still realistic, given the progress made to date, they should continue. If not, they should rework their expectations with the program facilitator to make them realistic. This would mean repeating the activity described in component 3 concerning expectation setting and then working through the remaining components as they apply to the new expectation(s). This component could be completed in a group setting with discussion, in one-on-one sessions between participant and facilitator, or by the participants themselves.

SUMMARY

This chapter presented an overview of several theories and three models that underlie the interventions used in many of today's health promotion programs. These theories and models are important components for planning and evaluating health promotion programs because they provide planners with ideas that have been tried and tested. They provide the framework on which to build. The theories and models reviewed include stimulus response theory, the social cognitive theory, the theory of reasoned action, the theory of planned behavior, problem-behavior theory, the theory of freeing, the health belief model, the transtheoretical model, and the cognitive-behavioral model of the relapse process (see Table 7.3 for a summary of the major components).

TABLE 7.3 Major Components of the Theories and Models That Underlie Health Promotion Interventions

Stimulus Response Theory	Social Cognitive Theory	Theory of Reasoned Action	Theory of Planned Behavior
Operant behavior	Reinforcement 1. Direct 2. Vicarious 3. Self-management	Attitude toward behavior	Attitude toward behavior
Consequences	Behavioral capability	Subjective norm	Subjective norm
Positive reinforcement	Expectations	Intentions	Perceived behavioral control
Negative reinforcement	Expectancies	Behavior	Intentions
Positive punishment	Self-control		Behavior
Negative punishment	Self-efficacy		
	Emotional coping response		
	Reciprocal determinism		

Finally, the chapter provides a discussion of some of the roadblocks to using theory, suggestions for applying theory to practice, and an example of how theory can be applied to practice.

QUESTIONS

1. Define *theory*, using your own words.
2. Why is it important to use theories when planning and evaluating health promotion programs?
3. What is the underlying concept for each of the following theories?
   a. Stimulus response theory
   b. Social cognitive theory
   c. Theory of reasoned action
   d. Theory of planned behavior
   e. Theory of freeing
   f. Problem-behavior theory

Problem-Behavior Theory	Theory of Freeing	Health Belief Model	Transtheoretical Model	Cognitive-Behavior Model of the Relapse Process
Personality system	Free	Perceived susceptibility	Precontemplation	Global self-control strategies
Perceived environment system	Oppressed	Perceived seriousness	Contemplation	High-risk situation
Behavior system	Critical consciousness	Perceived benefits	Preparation	Specific intervention strategies
Antecedent variables	Education	Perceived barriers	Action	
Background variables		Motivation	Maintenance	
			Relapse	
			Termination	

4. What are the major components of the health belief model? Explain each.
5. What are the stages of the transtheoretical model? Why is it important to understand this model?
6. How can program planners help to prepare those in the target population for relapse prevention?

ACTIVITIES

1. Assume that you have identified a need (health problem) for a given target population. In a two-page paper:
   a. State who the target population is and what the need is.
   b. Select a theory or model to use as a guide in developing an intervention to address the problem.
   c. Explain why you chose the theory or model that you did.
   d. Defend why you think this is the best theory or model to use.
   e. Show how the problem "fits into" the theory or model.
2. In a two-page paper, identify a theory or model that you plan to use in developing the intervention for the program you are planning. Explain why you chose the theory or model, and why you think it is a good fit for the problem you are addressing.
3. Write a paragraph on each of the following:
   a. Using the stimulus response theory, explain why a person might smoke.
   b. Using the social cognitive theory, explain how you could help people change their diets.
   c. Explain how the SCT construct of behavioral capability applies to managing stress.
   d. Explain the differences between and the relationship of the SCT constructs of expectations and expectancies.
   e. Explain what would have to take place for a person to be self-efficacious with regard to being able to take her insulin.
   f. According to the theory of reasoned action, what would increase intent to exercise?
   g. Use the theory of planned behavior to explain how a smoker stops smoking.
   h. Using the theory of freeing, describe an ideal teacher.
   i. Apply the health belief model to getting a person to take a "flu shot."
   j. Apply the transtheoretical model to getting a person to change any health behavior.

8

Interventions

After reading this chapter and answering the questions at the end, you should be able to:

- Define the word *intervention* and apply it to a health promotion setting.
- Provide a rationale for selecting an intervention strategy.
- Explain the advantages of using a combination of several intervention activities rather than a single intervention activity.
- Explain the difference between micro and macro interventions.
- List and explain the different categories of intervention activities.
- List some of the documents that provide guidelines or criteria for developing health promotion programs and interventions.
- Discuss the ethical concerns related to intervention development.
- Create an intervention for a health promotion program.

Key Terms

codes of practice
ethics
incentives
intervention
intervention activity
macro intervention
mandated activities
micro intervention
penetration rate
risk appraisal
risk reduction
treatment

Once goals and objectives have been developed, program planners need to decide on the most appropriate means of reaching, or attaining, the goals and objectives. The planners must identify an activity or set of activities that would permit the most *effective* (leads to desired outcome) and *efficient* (uses resources in a responsible manner) achievement of the outcomes stated in the goals and objectives. These planned activities make up the **intervention**, or what some refer to as **treatment**. The intervention is the activity or experience to which those in the target population will be exposed or in which they will take part. In the strictest sense, *intervention* means "to occur, fall, or come between points of time or events" (Woolf, 1979, p. 600). When applied to the planning of health promotion programs, it is usually thought of as something that occurs between the beginning and the end of a program or between pre- and postprogram measurements. For example, let's say that we want the employees of Company S to increase their use of safety belts while riding in company-owned vehicles. We can measure their safety belt use before doing anything, by observing them driving out of the motor pool; this would be a preprogram measure. Then we can intervene in a variety of ways. For example, we could provide an incentive by stating that all employees seen wearing their safety belt would receive a ten-dollar bonus in their next paycheck. Or we could put a pamphlet on the importance of wearing safety belts in each employee's pay envelope. We could institute a company policy requiring all employees to wear safety belts while driving company-owned vehicles. Each of these activities for getting employees to increase their use of safety belts would be considered part of an intervention. After the intervention, we would complete a postprogram measurement of safety belt use to determine the success of the program.

The term *intervention* is used to describe all the activities that occur between the two measurement points. Thus an intervention may be a single activity, or it may be a combination of two or more activities. In the case of the example just given, we could use an incentive by itself and call it an intervention, or we could use an incentive, pamphlets, and a company policy all at the same time to increase safety belt use and refer to the combination as an intervention.

With regard to the number of activities that should be included in an intervention, research (Erfurt, Foote, Heirich, & Gregg, 1990; Shea & Basch, 1990) shows that interventions that include several activities are more likely to have an effect on the target population than are those that consist of only a single activity. In other words, "dosage" is important in health promotion. Few people change their behavior based on a single exposure (or dose); instead, multiple exposures (doses) are generally needed to change most behaviors. It stands to reason that "hitting" the target population from several angles or through multiple channels should increase the chances of making an impact. Although research has shown that several activities are better than one, it has not identified an exact number of activities or a specific combination of activities that yields the best results. It is still a best-guess situation. It is possible, however, to determine the effectiveness of an **intervention activity** or activities by measuring the number of people who comply with the health message of the intervention. The specifics of how to measure the effectiveness of an intervention are discussed in detail beginning in Chapter 13.

MACRO VERSUS MICRO INTERVENTIONS

Interventions can be classified into two major categories—macro and micro. **Macro interventions** are usually planned and implemented for a group of people (or a community or society) and are not aimed at a specific individual. Mandates to use safety belts are a good example. These interventions may take the form of a company's chief executive officer creating a policy that requires employees to wear a safety belt while driving a company-owned vehicle, or they may come in the form of a state law concerning safety belt use. In both cases, these interventions affect large groups of people: all those who work for the company that establishes such a policy and all those who drive or ride in motor vehicles in the state that has such a law. No single person is identified as the recipient of the intervention; rather, the intervention is aimed at a group of people. Health messages sent as public service announcements in the mass media (television, radio, or newspapers) are another example of macro interventions.

Micro interventions, on the other hand, are aimed at individuals, even though those individuals may meet in a group. For example, a smoking cessation program for a group of ten employees is considered a micro intervention. Individually prescribed diet and exercise regimens for those in a weight loss program would be considered micro interventions.

Usually it is thought that macro interventions affect a relatively larger number of people than micro interventions, but that is not always the case. For example, a small business with, say, thirty employees may be exposed to a macro intervention in the form of a safety belt policy, and there may be thirty people enrolled in a micro intervention program for smoking cessation. The real distinction between macro and micro interventions is whether the intervention is aimed at specific individuals or at groups. The old concept of public or community health interventions (macro) versus personal health interventions (micro) may be one way to keep the distinction clear.

To date, much of the work of health promotion planners has dealt with micro interventions. O'Rourke and Macrina (1989) believe that continued emphasis on micro interventions will limit the approaches that can be taken in improving the level of health of American society. They have suggested that health promotion planners redirect their efforts to work toward more public policies that combine micro and macro interventions.

Another way to explain the concept embedded in the micro and macro intervention activities discussion is through the ecological perspective (McLeroy et al., 1988) presented in Chapter 7. This approach identifies five different levels of influence for health-related behaviors and conditions that need to be considered when developing interventions. Whether it is referred to as the ecological perspective or the combining of micro and macro activities, interventions must be planned to attack the multiple levels of influence on health.

SELECTING APPROPRIATE INTERVENTION ACTIVITIES

Selection of intervention activities for a health promotion program should be based upon a sound rationale as opposed to chance; an activity should not be selected just because the planners think it "sounds good," or because they have a "feeling" that it will work. As mentioned earlier, planners should choose an intervention that will be both effective and efficient. Although no prescription for an appropriate intervention has been developed, experience has indicated that the results of some in-

FIGURE 8.1 Items to Consider when Creating a Health Promotion Intervention

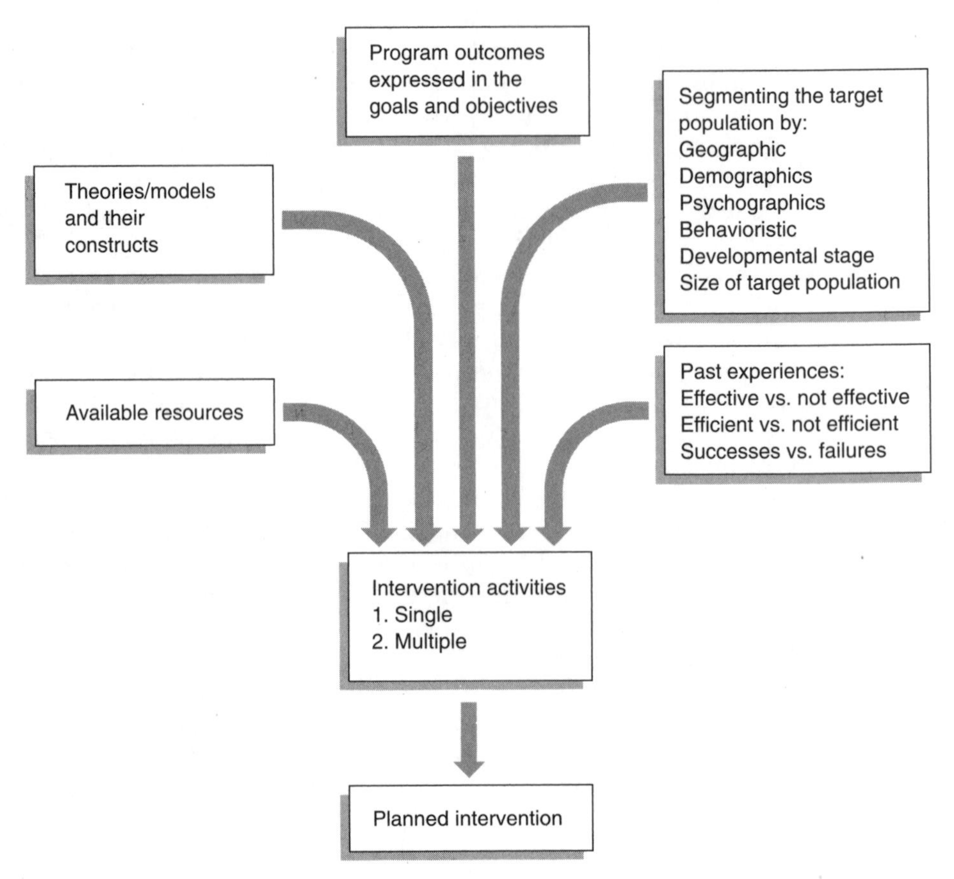

terventions are more predictable than others. In this section, we present six major questions that planners need to consider when creating health promotion interventions. Figure 8.1 summarizes these major considerations.

Are the activities based upon an appropriate theory?

Interventions have a much greater chance of reaching the desired outcome if they are planned using sound learning and educational theories and models that have proved their worth through experience and social science research. Interventions should not be without a solid basis in theory. Readers are referred back to Table 7.3 for a listing of the constructs from these theories and models.

Do the intervention activities fit the goals and objectives of the program?

It is important that there be a good fit between the goals and objectives of a program and the intervention activities used to reach the desired outcomes. If the single purpose of a program was to increase the awareness of the target population, the intervention would be very different from what it would be if the purpose was to change behavior. Matching goals and objectives sounds easy enough, but creating such a match is a bit more difficult because of the "gray areas" created by the lack of empirical data to support such claims. Anderson and O'Donnell (1994) created such an intervention-outcome matrix based upon work presented in the *American Journal of Health Promotion.* Figure 8.2 on page 134 presents a similar matrix using the terminology presented in this textbook.

Are the necessary resources available to implement the intervention selected?

Obviously, some intervention activities require more money, time, personnel, or space to implement than others. For example, it may be prudent to provide each person in the target population with $100 for participating in the health promotion program, but it may not be possible because of budget limitations.

Is the intervention appropriate for the segmented target population?

Experience has shown that intervention activities need to "fit" the segmented target population. Figure 8.1 and Table 11.3 provide several different ways by which program planners can segment the target population. Below are a few examples of why segmentation and intervention activities need to fit. If program planners are developing written materials as part of their intervention, they need to make sure that the materials are written at an acceptable reading level for the target population. From a developmental stage perspective, it is not reasonable to expect kindergartners to sit still for a one-hour lesson. Intervention activities developed primarily for white majority target groups will probably not be culturally relevant and applicable for minority or ethnic groups (Pahnos, 1992; LeMaster & Connell, 1994). And planners would probably not use the same intervention activities if their target population happened to be a handful of employees trying to stop smoking as they would when they try to persuade a community of 50,000 people to get flu shots.

Type of objective	Program outcome	Intervention activities									
		Educational	Behavior modification	Environmental	Regulatory	Community advocacy	Organizational culture	Communication	Incentives	Social	Health status evaluation
Administrative	1. Activities presented	X	X	X	X	X	X	X	X	X	X
	2. Tasks completed	X	X	X	X	X	X	X	X	X	X
Learning	1. Awareness	X	X	?	X	X	?	X	?	X	X
	2. Knowledge	X	?	?	?	X	?	X	?	X	X
	3. Attitudes	X	?	?	?	X	?	X	?	X	X
	4. Skills	X	X	X	X	?	?	X	X	X	?
Behavioral	1. Behavior change	?	X	X	X	?	X	X	X	X	X
Program	1. Quality of life	?	?	?	?	?	?	X	?	X	?
	2. Health status	?	X	X	X	?	?	X	X	X	?
	3. Health risks	?	X	X	X	?	?	X	X	X	?
	4. Social benefits	?	?	?	?	X	X	X	X	X	?

FIGURE 8.2 Matrix of Intervention Activities, Objectives, and Program Outcomes

What types of intervention activities are known to be effective (i.e., have been successfully used in previous programs) in dealing with the program focus?

By networking with other health educators and by reviewing the literature, planners can find out what interventions have been effective with certain target populations or in dealing with specific health problems.

Would it be better to use an intervention that consists of a single activity or one that is made up of multiple activities?

A single-activity intervention would most likely be easier and less expensive to implement and easier to evaluate. There are, however, some real advantages to using several activities. These advantages include: (1) "hitting" the target population with a message in a variety of ways; (2) appealing to the variety of learning styles within any target population; (3) keeping the health message constantly before the target population; (4) hoping that at least one activity appeals enough to the target population to help bring about the expected outcome; and (5) appealing to the various senses (such as sight, hearing, or touch) of each individual in the target population. Probably the biggest drawback to using multiple activities is the difficulty of separating the effects of one activity from the effects of others in evaluating the impact of the total program and of individual components (Ad Hoc Work Group, 1987).

TYPES OF INTERVENTION ACTIVITIES

As mentioned earlier, there are many different types of activities that planners can use as part of an intervention. We present here several categories covering the more common activities, but in actuality the variety of activities is limited only by the planner's imagination. We have categorized activities into the following groups:

1. Educational activities or methods.
2. Behavior modification activities.
3. Environmental change activities.
4. Regulatory activities.
5. Community advocacy activities.
6. Organizational culture activities.
7. Communication activities.
8. Economic and other incentives.
9. Health status evaluation activities.
10. Social intervention activities.

Educational Activities

Educational activities are those usually associated with formal education in courses, seminars, and workshops. This includes educational methods such as lecture, discussion, and group work, as well as audiovisual materials, laboratory exercises, and written materials (books and periodicals). Table 8.1 on page 136 provides a more complete listing of educational activities, and Gilbert and Sawyer (1995) have provided a detailed discussion of these methods.

Behavior Modification Activities

This group of activities, most often used in micro interventions, includes techniques intended to help those in the target population experience a change in behavior. *Behavior modification* is usually thought of as a systematic procedure for changing a specific behavior. The process is based on the stimulus response theory. As applied to health behavior, emphasis is placed on a specific behavior that one might want either to increase (such as exercise or stress management techniques) or to decrease (such as smoking or consumption of fats). Particular attention is then given to changing the events that are antecedent or subsequent to the behavior that is to be modified.

TABLE 8.1 Commonly Used Educational Activities

A. Audiovisual materials and equipment
  1. Audio tapes, records, and compact disks
  2. Bulletin, chalk, cloth, flannel, magnetic, and peg boards
  3. Charts, pictures, and posters
  4. Computers
  5. Films and filmstrips
  6. Instructional television
  7. Opaque projector
  8. Slides and slide projectors
  9. Transparencies and overhead projector
  10. Video disks and tapes

B. Printed educational materials
  1. Instructor-made handouts and worksheets
  2. Pamphlets
  3. Study guides (commercial and instructor-made)
  4. Text and reference books
  5. Workbooks

C. Teaching strategies and techniques for the classroom
  1. Brainstorming
  2. Case studies
  3. Cooperative learning
  4. Debates
  5. Demonstrations and experiments
  6. Discovery or guided discovery
  7. Discussion
  8. Group discussion
  9. Guest speakers
  10. Lecture
  11. Lecture/discussion
  12. Newspaper and magazine articles
  13. Panel discussions
  14. Peer group teaching/coaching
  15. Poems, songs, and stories
  16. Problem solving
  17. Puppets
  18. Questioning
  19. Role playing and plays
  20. Simulation, games, and puzzles
  21. Tutoring
  22. Values clarification activities

D. Teaching strategies and techniques for outside of the classroom
  1. Community resources
  2. Field trips
  3. Health fairs
  4. Health museums

In changing a health behavior, the behavior modification activity often begins by having those in the target population keep records (diaries, logs, or journals) for a specific period of time (twenty-four to forty-eight hours, one week, or one month) concerning the behavior (such as eating, smoking, or exercise) they want to alter. Using the information recorded, one can plan an activity to modify that behavior. For example, facilitators of smoking cessation programs often will ask participants to keep a record of all the cigarettes they smoke from one class session to the next (see Figure 8.3 for an example of such a record). After keeping the record, participants are asked to analyze it to see what kind of smoking habit they have. They may be asked questions such as these: "What three cigarettes seem to be the most important of the day to you?" "In what three places or activities do you find yourself smoking the most?" "With whom do you find yourself smoking most often?" "Is there a primary reason or mood for your smoking?" "When during the day do you find yourself smoking the most and the least?" Once the participant has answered these questions, appropriate interventions can be designed to deal with the

Name ______________

Date ______________

Number of cigarettes during the day	Time of day	Need rating*	Place or activity	With whom	Mood or reason
1.	______	1 2 3	______	______	______
2.	______	1 2 3	______	______	______
3.	______	1 2 3	______	______	______
4.	______	1 2 3	______	______	______
5.	______	1 2 3	______	______	______
6.	______	1 2 3	______	______	______
7.	______	1 2 3	______	______	______
8.	______	1 2 3	______	______	______
9.	______	1 2 3	______	______	______
10.	______	1 2 3	______	______	______
11.	______	1 2 3	______	______	______
12.	______	1 2 3	______	______	______
13.	______	1 2 3	______	______	______
14.	______	1 2 3	______	______	______
15.	______	1 2 3	______	______	______
16.	______	1 2 3	______	______	______
17.	______	1 2 3	______	______	______
18.	______	1 2 3	______	______	______
19.	______	1 2 3	______	______	______
20.	______	1 2 3	______	______	______
21.	______	1 2 3	______	______	______
22.	______	1 2 3	______	______	______
23.	______	1 2 3	______	______	______
24.	______	1 2 3	______	______	______
25.	______	1 2 3	______	______	______
26.	______	1 2 3	______	______	______
27.	______	1 2 3	______	______	______
28.	______	1 2 3	______	______	______
29.	______	1 2 3	______	______	______
30.	______	1 2 3	______	______	______

*Need rating: How important is the cigarette to you at this time?
1 = Most important, I would miss it very much.
2 = Average
3 = Least important, I would not miss it.

FIGURE 8.3 Twenty-Four-Hour Cigarette Count

problem behavior. For example, if a participant says he only smokes when he is by himself, then activities would be planned so that he does not spend a lot of time alone. If another participant seemed to do most of his smoking while drinking coffee, an activity would be developed to provide some type of substitute. If a person seemed to smoke the most while sitting at the table after meals, activities could be planned to get the person away from the dinner table and doing something that would occupy his hands.

Another way of leading into a behavior modification activity is through a health status evaluation, or what is often referred to as a health screening. Such screenings could happen at home (e.g., BSE, TSE, hemocult, etc.), at a community health fair, or in the office of a health care professional. Like record keeping via diaries, logs, or journals, health screenings can "grab the attention" (develop awareness) of those in the target population to begin the behavior modification process.

Environmental Change Activities

Another group of activities that have proved useful in reaching desired outcomes falls into the category of environmental change. These activities are more often used in macro interventions because they usually affect a group of people. They are characterized by changes in those things "around" individuals that may influence their awareness, knowledge, attitudes, skills, or behavior. Some of these activities provide a "forced choice" situation, as when the selection of foods and beverages in vending machines or cafeterias is changed to include only "healthy" foods. If people want to eat foods from these sources, they are forced to eat certain types of foods. Other activities in this category may provide those in the target population with health messages and environmental cues for certain types of behavior. Examples would be the posting of no-smoking signs, elimination of ash trays, provision of lockers and showers, use of role modeling by others, playing of soft music in a work area, a shuttle service or some other type of transportation system to get seniors to congregate meals or to a health care provider, and point-of-purchase education, such as a sign on a vending machine or food labeling on the food lines in the cafeteria.

Regulatory Activities

This group of activities includes executive orders, laws, policies, position statements, regulations, and rules. These could be classified as **mandated activities** or regulated activities because they are activities that are required by an administrator, board, or legislative body. These activities are commonly part of macro interventions. Examples include state laws requiring the use of safety belts and motorcycle helmets or raising the taxes on cigarettes, company policy stating that there will be no smoking in corporate offices and company-owned vehicles, and a board of education adopting a position statement that it will provide only well-balanced meals in its cafeterias.

This type of intervention activity may be controversial. It has been criticized by some because it mandates a particular response from an individual. It takes away individual freedoms and sometimes plays on a person's pride, "pocketbook," and psyche. This type of activity must be sold on the basis of "common good." That is, the justification for this type of societal action is to protect the public's health. Regulatory activities exist for the protection of the community and of individual rights. In other words, "officials are willing to intercede into the private activities and lives of people in order to protect the larger population. When such intervention occurs it is usually very narrow and very specifically defined. There also tend to be sanctions attached if people do not comply. For example, in the case of inoculations, if a mother and father did not have their child inoculated that child cannot attend school. If parents do not send their child to school they are in violation of the law, and there are criminal and civil penalties that are involved" (Rich & Sugrue, 1989, p. 33).

Some would say that regulatory activities do not allow for the "voluntary adaptations of behavior conducive to health" that are suggested by Green and colleagues (1980, p. 7) in their definition of health education. But, at the same time, this kind of activity can get people to change their behavior when other strategies have failed. For example, before the passage of safety belt laws, most states were reporting about a 14% use rate by drivers of automobiles and were trying to attack the problem through educational activities using the mass media. Now that safety belt laws are in effect in about half of the states, usage rates in those states are closer to 50%; in some states where there is strict enforcement, usage rates approach 80%. Another example is the work of Sorensen, Rigotti, Rosen, Pinney, and Prible (1991), which showed a 21% reduction in the number of employees who smoked in a company that put a nonsmoking policy in effect. Both of these examples show that regulatory activities are necessary to reinforce and support prevention messages.

Since regulatory activities are mandatory, it is particularly important to use good judgment and show respect for others when implementing them. In some instances, program planners will be faced with ethical decisions. If a program will make use of regulatory intervention activities, the planner should remember that, as in any political process, there is likely to be both pro and con feelings toward the "mandatory" action. Thus when developing and implementing any mandatory action, planners should bear in mind the following points:

1. Have top-level support for the mandated action (Emont & Cummings, 1989; Mikanowicz & Altman, 1995).
2. Have a representative group (committee) from the target population help formulate the "mandatory" action.
3. Consider surveying those in the target population to gain additional information regarding policy change (Mikanowicz & Altman, 1995).
4. Make sure expert advice on the subject of the mandated action is available to the group developing it.
5. Seek a legal opinion if necessary.
6. Examine the work of others and review the issues they faced when implementing "mandatory" actions.
7. Be sure that regulatory activities are based on sound principles.
8. Seek input and debate/discussion concerning the mandated action from the target population while it is being formulated.

9. Develop regulatory activities that are written simply and include a rationale, a general policy statement, specific areas affected, and clearly defined complaint, grievance, and enforcement procedures (Mikanowicz & Altman, 1995).
10. Consider phasing in the new regulation a little bit at a time. For example, if a no-smoking policy is going to be implemented, the planner may want to begin by restricting smoking in certain areas before banning it altogether. This not only helps people change gradually, but also expresses concern for them.
11. Provide education and behavior change programs to assist those in the target population with the implementation of the "mandatory" actions (Mikanowicz & Altman, 1995).
12. Ensure that, once formulated, the "mandatory" actions
    a. are actively communicated to those in the target population.
    b. are reviewed on a regular basis for the purposes of evaluating and revising if necessary.
    c. apply to all in the target population and not just to select groups.
    d. are consistently enforced. Be prepared to deal with the complaint and grievance processes (Mikanowicz & Altman, 1995).
    e. are enforced as a shared responsibility of all in the institution.

To help gain a sense of the difficulty of dealing with regulatory activities, let's examine the options available to a group of department heads who are trying to decide whether or not they should continue to allow the public to smoke in the lobby of the building and employees to smoke in their individual, self-contained offices. Several options are available to this administrative group:

1. Decide to have no explicit policy.
2. Make no changes and continue with the status quo.
3. Eliminate only public smoking in the building.
4. Designate a different area or room within the building for public smoking.
5. Allow smoking only in individual offices.
6. Designate the entire building as a "smoke-free building."
7. Request that all employees hired in the future be nonsmokers.
8. A combination of items 1–7.

Each of these options poses special concerns for administrative groups. Policies are seldom easy to develop, but looking at others that have already been developed helps in the creation of a new policy. For this reason, we provide several examples in the appendices to this book. Appendix A presents a model for developing an alcohol policy on a college campus (Sherwood, 1987). The steps outlined in this model could be useful in developing and implementing health-related mandates in other settings. Appendix B presents the smoking policy of the McSmeltzer Corporation. Appendix C presents a "Model Ordinance Eliminating Smoking in

Workplaces and Enclosed Public Places (100% Smokefree)" developed by Americans for Nonsmokers' Rights. (Note: Planners interested in developing policies regulating smoking should also review the works of Mikanowicz & Altman [1995] and USDHHS [1985]).

Community Advocacy Activities

Not to be confused with regulatory activities, community advocacy activities are used to influence social change. Community advocacy is a process in which the people of the community become involved in the institutions and decisions that will have an impact on their lives. It has the potential for creating more support, keeping people informed, influencing decisions, activating nonparticipants, improving service, and making people, plans, and programs more responsive (Checkoway, 1989). But community advocacy is not without costs: in most situations it requires time and effort, as well as persistence. Yet it can have a big impact on social change issues involving health. Community advocacy includes community organizing (see Chapter 9), coalition building (see Chapter 9), and education of the community and decision makers (Deeds, 1992). Techniques often used in trying to educate/influence decision makers are lobbying and letter-writing campaigns (see Figure 8.4 on page 142).

When trying to influence decision makers, it is important to do the following:

1. Gather and use data wisely.
2. Identify committed leadership.
3. Gain grassroots support.
4. Look for other related issues that could further the effort.
5. Gain bipartisan support.
6. Work with appropriate lobbyists.
7. Spend resources carefully.

Organizational Culture Activities

Closely aligned with environmental change activities is the category of activities that affect organizational culture. Culture is usually associated with norms and traditions that are generated by and linked to a "community" of people. Organizations, which are made up of people, also can have their own culture. The culture of an organization can be thought of as its personality. The culture expresses what is and what is not considered important to the organization. The nature of the culture depends on the type of organization—corporation, school, or nonprofit group.

Many people think that it takes a long time to establish norms and traditions, and it often does. Still, change can occur very quickly if the decision makers in an organization support it. For example, if organizational decision makers believe exercise is important, they may provide employees with an extra twenty minutes at lunchtime for exercise. Similarly, it is surprising to see how many young executives

Senators and Representatives pay attention to their mail. It is good politics. Responding to mail is crucial to reelection. A member knows your vote can be won or lost by her/his response. **The most effective letter is personal,** not a form letter. It should be concise, informed, and polite.

Date

Dear Senator/Representative,

- Try to stick to one typewritten page. Don't type or write on the back of the page. If writing longhand, take care to write legibly.
- In a short first paragraph, state your purpose. Stick with one subject or issue. Support your position with the rest of the letter.
- If a bill is the subject, cite it by name and number.
- Be factual and support your position with information about how legislation is likely to affect you and others. Avoid emotional philosophical arguments.
- Explain how you intend to help the cause. Ask what else you can do to help change things.
- State one more time what you would like your congress person to do.
- Be sure you include your name and address.
- Follow up your letter with a phone call.

Sincerely,

Jane Carcinogen

U.S. Congress Addresses

The Honorable . . .
U.S. Senate
Washington, DC 20510

The Honorable . . .
U.S. House of Representatives
Washington, DC 20515

Indiana General Assembly

Available by calling the following:

House (317) 232-9700 or
(D) 1-800-382-9842
(R) 1-800-382-9841

Senate (317) 232-9400 or
1-800-382-9467

FIGURE 8.4 Tips for Writing Effective Letters

Source: American Cancer Society, Indiana Division, Inc.

will use a corporation's exercise facility because the chief executive officer does. Other examples of organizational culture activities might include changing the types of foods found in vending machines, closing the "junk food" machines during lunch periods at school, and offering discounts on the healthy foods found in the company cafeteria. Because these activities have the potential to affect a large group of people, they are usually thought of as macro interventions.

Communication Activities

Communication activities have been recognized as important components of many different health promotion interventions. They have been shown to:

1. Increase awareness.
2. Increase knowledge.
3. Change attitudes (for example, about blood pressure, cancer screenings, and the ills of smoking).
4. Reinforce attitudes (for example, about smoking in public places).
5. Maintain interest (for example, for those contemplating a behavior change).
6. Provide cues for action.
7. Demonstrate simple skills (as in self-screening) (Bellicha & McGrath, 1990; Erickson, McKenna, & Romano, 1990).

Because of the techniques used, communication activities probably have the highest **penetration rate** (number in the target population exposed or reached) of any of the intervention activities. They are also much more cost effective and less threatening than many other types of intervention activities.

Probably the most visible forms of communication activities are those in the mass media (both electronic and print), which include daily newspapers with national or local circulation; local weekly newspapers; local, public, and network television, including cable television; public and commercial radio stations; and magazines with either a broad readership or a narrow focus. There are many ways to convey a message using the mass media. These include news coverage, public affairs coverage, talk shows, public service roundtables, entertainment, public service announcements (PSAs) (see Appendix D for examples of PSAs used by the Indiana State Department of Health), paid advertisements, editorials, letters to the editor, comic strips, and columnists' commentaries (Arkin, 1990). But communication activities are not limited to mass media; they can take many other forms. Information can be presented on billboards, in booklets, on bulletin boards, in church bulletins, in fliers, through direct mail (such as the mailing on the subject of AIDS sent by the Public Health Service to every U.S. household in 1988), on product labels (for alcohol, foods, and tobacco), in newsletters, in pamphlets, on posters (Miller, 1992), and through self-help materials in print or on audio and video, and, of course, through interpersonal communication, primarily involving health professional/client interactions (Clift & Freimuth, 1995). The cost of communication activities can range from almost nothing (e.g., elementary school children making posters for a health awareness campaign) to moderately priced (e.g., production of a brochure) to expensive (e.g., personal counseling) to very expensive (e.g., a prime-time television commercial). However, no matter what form the communication activities take or their cost, to be effective, they need to be carefully planned.

The knowledge and skills for planning effective communication activities vary from novice to expert. It is not the purpose of this book to make health educators communication experts; the experts are those with college degrees in the field of communication. Instead, in the space below, we present the procedures recommended by two different authors (McGuire, 1981; USDHHS, 1989) for planning effective communication activities, and we present guidelines (Meyer & Rainey, 1994) for a skill often used by health educators, preparing print communications.

One of the most often used procedures for developing communication activities for health educators was developed by McGuire (1981). McGuire set out a seven-step approach for designing a public health communications campaign. The first step involves analyzing the situation to determine if the health problem of concern is sufficiently severe, if corrective behaviors for the problem are available, and if such behaviors can be effectively promoted through communication activities. The second step determines whether the communication activity is cost beneficial compared to other means of dealing with the problem. The third step examines the sociocultural factors of the target population to determine which could facilitate or impede the campaign's effectiveness. In the fourth step, planners seek to find out the psychological matrix of thoughts, feelings, and behaviors that instigate and sustain undesirable health behavior. For example, do those in the target population not eat properly because they do not know any better, cannot afford it, or do not care? The fifth step consists of analyzing the data collected in the first four steps to pick out the most promising target groups and techniques for the communication activities. The sixth step includes the construction of the persuasive communication by choosing the source, message, channel, receiver, and destination variables that have the greatest promise for changing the undesirable behavior. The seventh and last step, as with many planning procedures, is to evaluate the effectiveness of the campaign by monitoring each of the previous six steps and examining the end results.

The National Cancer Institute compiled a book (USDHHS, 1989) that is most useful for developing communication activities in both mass media and printed materials (other than newspapers). The book is organized around six stages in health communication. Figure 8.5 graphically represents these stages. Stage 1 is planning and strategy selection. This includes studying the health problem and the target population, deciding what objectives are to be accomplished, and deciding what the target population should be told. Stage 2 deals with selecting the appropriate communication channels (worksite, mass media, face-to-face) to be used and deciding which format (booklets, videotapes, newsletters) will best suit the channels and messages. Stage 3 consists of developing the materials and pretesting them with the target population. Feedback from the target population is most important at this stage. Stage 4 is the implementation of the activity. During this stage,

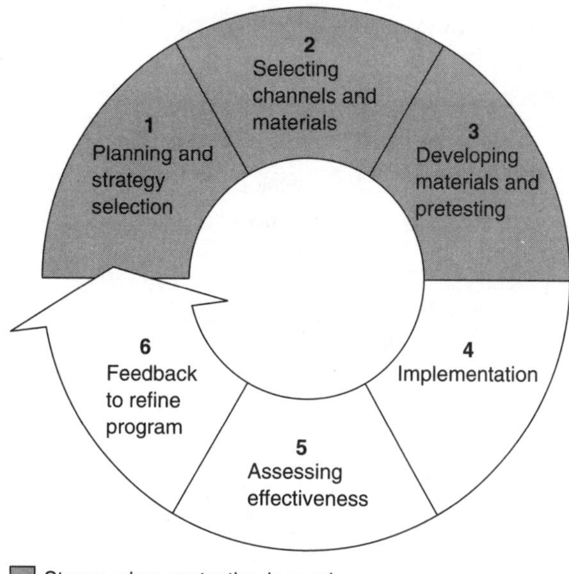

FIGURE 8.5 Stages in Health Communication

Source: From *Making Health Communication Programs Work: A Planner's Guide* (NIH Publication No. 89-1493, p. 5), by U.S. Department of Health and Human Services (USDHHS), 1989, Washington, DC: U.S. Government Printing Office.

the effect of the activity is tracked to determine if any alterations are needed. Stage 5 is evaluation, which should be based on the objectives identified in Stage 1. Stage 6, which loops right back to Stage 1, incorporates feedback gained in the other stages to prepare for a new cycle of the communication. This method answers many key questions: What worked and did not work? How can we improve it the next time? Knowing the answers to these questions will lead to improved future interventions.

Meyer and Rainey (1994) created a set of guidelines for health educators to follow when creating health education materials for low-literacy populations. We found their guidelines to be useful regardless of the target population. Their eight guidelines are summarized in Table 8.2 on page 146. The only addition we would make to their list would be to check the reading level of the written materials. "For the general public, writing at the 6th grade reading level is usually safe. You can check if you're on target by using a readability test such as the SMOG, the Fog-Gunning Index, or the Fry Readability Formula" (USDHHS, 1991, p. 3). You can find such formulas in most reading methods books. Box 8.1 on page 147 presents the steps in the process of testing readability using the SMOG.

TABLE 8.2 Guidelines for Preparing Written Materials

Guideline	Explanation
1. Needs and target population identification	Identify the topic and the target population, e.g., middle-aged women and mammography.
2. Plan the project	Develop a work plan and budget for your material.
3. Audience research	Segment your target population using such factors as experience, attitude, culture, etc.
4. Material development	
a. Style	Use an active voice with familar terms that highlight key points. If possible, develop a behaviorally oriented interactive message.
b. Organization	Sequence or prioritize the message.
c. Content	Write using words and terms that are understandable to lay people. Use short sentences and paragraphs.
d. Format	Make it appealing to the eye, making sure the reader can identify the main points.
5. Graphics and illustrations	Graphics and illustrations should be positive and easy to understand, and should summarize the message.
6. Pretesting	Make sure the materials work before you use them with the target population. Also, make sure the reading level is okay.
7. Printing	Consider paper color, size, and cost.
8. Distribution and training	Develop a distribution system and instructions for use.

Source: Adapted from "Writing Health Education Material for Low-Literacy Populations," by J. Meyer and J. Rainey, 1994, *Journal of Health Education, 25*(6), pp. 372–374.

Economic and Other Incentives

The use of **incentives** to influence health outcomes is a common type of activity. This activity is based upon the stimulus response theory, which holds that people are more likely to act in a certain manner if they are reinforced to do so. An incentive can increase the perceived value of an activity (Patton, Corry, Gettman, & Graff, 1986), motivate people to get involved, and remind program participants of their commitment to and goals for behavior change (Wilbur, 1983). The key to motivating someone with an incentive is to know what will incite an individual to action. Thus, for this type of activity to work, the planner needs to match the incentives with the needs, wants, or desires of the target population. However, this is not easy, for what is an incentive for one person may be a deterrent for another, and vice versa. It has been suggested that incentives should even be tailored to the socioeconomic characteristics of the participants (Chenoweth, 1987) and, for that matter, the individual characteristics of each person.

For the planners, the task becomes one of matching the needs of the program participant or potential program participant with available incentives. Two approaches have been used to accomplish this. The first is to include questions about

BOX 8.1 The SMOG Readability Formula

To calculate the SMOG reading grade level, begin with the entire written work that is being assessed, and follow these four steps:

1. Count off ten consecutive sentences near the beginning, in the middle, and near the end of the text.
2. From this sample of thirty sentences, circle all of the words containing three or more syllables (polysyllabic), including repetitions of the same word, and total the number of words circled.
3. Estimate the square root of the total number of polysyllabic words counted. This is done by finding the nearest perfect square, and taking its square root.
4. Finally, add a constant of three to the square root. This number gives the SMOG grade, or the reading grade level that a person must have reached if he or she is to fully understand the text being assessed.

A few additional guidelines will help to clarify these directions:

- A sentence is defined as a string of words punctuated with a period (.), an exclamation point (!), or a question mark (?).
- Hyphenated words are considered as one word.
- Numbers that are written out should also be considered, and if in numeric form in the text, they should be pronouned to determine if they are polysyllabic.
- Proper nouns, if polysyllabic, should be counted, too.
- Abbreviations should be read as unabbreviated to determine if they are polysyllabic.

Not all pamphlets, fact sheets, or other printed materials contain thirty sentences. To test a text that has fewer than thirty sentences:

1. Count all of the polysyllabic words in the text.
2. Count the number of sentences.
3. Find the average number of polysyllabic words per sentence as follows:

$$\text{Average} = \frac{\text{Total \# of polysyllabic words}}{\text{Total \# of sentences}}$$

4. Multiply that average by the number of sentences *short of thirty.*
5. Add that figure to the total number of polysyllabic words.
6. Find the square root and add the constant of three.

Perhaps the quickest way to administer the SMOG grading test is by using the SMOG conversion table. Simply count the number of polysyllabic words in your chain of thirty sentences and look up the appropriate grade level on the chart.

SMOG Conversion Table*

Total Polysyllabic Word Counts	Approximate Grade Level (±1.5 Grades)
0–2	4
3–6	5
7–12	6
13–20	7
21–30	8
31–42	9
43–56	10
57–72	11
73–90	12
91–110	13
111–132	14
133–156	15
157–182	16
183–210	17
211–240	18

*Developed by Harold C. McGraw, Office of Educational Research, Baltimore County Schools, Towson, Maryland.

Source: From *Making Health Communication Programs Work: A Planner's Guide* (NIH Pub. No. 89-1493), by Department of Health and Human Services, 1989, U.S. Government Printing Office.

incentives as part of any needs assessment conducted in program planning. For example, a workforce needs survey might include questions on incentives, such as "What incentives would entice you to participate in the exercise program?" or "What would it take to get you to participate in this program?" or "What would it take to keep you involved in a health promotion program?" or "Would you continue to participate in an exercise program if you knew you were going to be given a nice tee shirt after logging one hundred miles running or walking, or participating for fifty days in an aerobic dance or swimming program?" The responses to these questions should provide some indication of the type of incentives that would be most useful for this target population. The second is the shotgun approach, based upon previous experience or the experience reported by others. The shotgun approach offers a variety of incentives to meet the needs of a large percentage of the program's target population. However, we recommend the former approach as being more likely to meet the targeted needs and wants.

Based upon the idea that incentives should meet the individual needs of the target population, the number of different types of incentives is almost endless. Feldman (1983) has suggested two major categories of incentives or reinforcers. The first group includes incentives that would be considered social reinforcers, while the second group includes incentives that are considered material reinforcers, or what we refer to as economic incentives. A listing of such reinforcers is presented in Chapter 11.

Planners should remember that incentives can be used to keep the target population from doing something as well to get them to do something. For example, Penner (1989) reports on the use of a surcharge for health insurance to influence the behavior of those who continue to use tobacco products. Other examples include placing user taxes on a product to deter its use in a target population (e.g., cigarettes and adolescents), levying fines for health-harming behavior (e.g., not wearing safety belts), and not allowing the use of something because of a certain behavior (e.g., not allowing smokers to use the teachers' lounge or company vehicles).

As a final comment on incentives, several authors (French, Jeffery, & Oliphant, 1994; Jeffery, Forster, Baxter, French, & Kelder, 1993; Matson, Lee, & Hopp, 1993; Price, Telljohann, Roberts, & Smit, 1992) have reported on the effectiveness of using incentives for program participation and behavior change. From these works, it appears that incentives are useful in getting people to participate and change their behavior for a short period of time. Their effectiveness in long-term behavior change is not so clear.

Health Status Evaluation Activities

An activity aimed at making those in the target population more aware of their current health status is often used as part of a multiactivity intervention. These activities have involved the completion of a health risk appraisal (HRA) form (see Chapter 4 for a discussion of HRAs), self-screenings (e.g., breast self-examination or testicular self-examination), clinical screenings (e.g., blood pressure and cholesterol), and professional health checkups and examinations. The settings for such activities have included health fairs, worksites, personal residences, mobile units (e.g., vans equipped with mammography units), and health care facilities. These activities usually have high credibility with target populations because of their link with health care providers.

Social Intervention Activities

The importance of social support for behavior change and its relationship to health have been noted by several researchers (Becker & Green, 1975; Berkman & Syme, 1979; Cohen & Lichtenstein, 1990; Colletti & Brownell, 1982; Horman, 1989; Kviz, Crittenden, Madura, & Warnecke, 1994; Kaplan & Cassell, 1977; Cummings, Becker, & Maile, 1980). Many people find it much easier to change a behavior if those around them provide support or are willing to be partners in the behavior change process. One of the major reasons why worksite health promotion programs have been so well received is because of the built-in social support from coworkers (Behrens, 1983).

Reference has already been made to how social support could work as an incentive. That would be one form of a social activity. Other social interventions could include support groups or buddy support, social activities, and social networks. These intervention activities have been used in both micro and macro interventions with much success.

Support Groups and Buddy System

The importance of support groups as part of comprehensive interventions has been well established. One need only look to the twelve-step programs, such as Alcoholics Anonymous, Overeaters Anonymous, and Gamblers Anonymous, and also commercial programs (such as Weight Watchers and Optifast) to realize the importance of people coming together to share their experiences and support one another's efforts. A buddy system is an example of a two-person group. A support group need not be large; it might be as small as just two people. A buddy system can take one of two different forms. In the first, both individuals are trying to change a behavior. In such a relationship, the two individuals support each other, whether this means helping each other to stay on a special diet or meeting each other at 6 A.M. for exercise. In the other form, only one of the two is trying to change a behavior. The one not changing the behavior may have already changed (e.g., has already quit smoking or is exercising regularly) and is acting as a mentor to the one trying to change, or may not be trying to change but provides support at regular intervals or as problems arise.

Special elements that can be added to the support group or buddy system are the use of competition or a contract. Competition can take place between individual group members over such things as who can lose the most weight, who can walk/run the most miles, or who can go the longest without a cigarette. Competition could also be based upon teams within the target population (such as two different companies, two schools, or departments within an organization), using similar criteria but now based on group total figures (pounds, miles, or cigarettes). See Chapter 11 for more on competitions.

Contracts could be used by having one member of the target population enter into an agreement with another member or with another person (such as the program facilitator, a friend, or spouse) over a change in some health behavior. The major component of a contract is the contingency. The *contingency* is a statement of what will happen if a contract is met or not met. For example, if a person meets the terms of his contract by losing ten pounds in five weeks, he can then expect to receive something specified (an intangible, such as praise, or a material object) from the person who agreed to the contract. If the terms are not met, then the person for whom the contract was written must forfeit something specified (perhaps time volunteered to a community service or a material object of his own). See Chapter 11 for more on contracts.

Social Activities

Social activities can be an an important type of social intervention. Bringing together people who may be confronting similar problems for the purpose of purely social interaction not related to the problem can indirectly help them deal with the problem. Examples of such activities might be single parents having a cookout or a group of senior citizens attending a play. Although these activities do not deal directly with these people's common problems, they do help fill voids in their lives and thus indirectly help with the problem.

Social Networks

Social networks are another type of social intervention. *Networks* are matrices linked by relationships or "ties." The nature of a tie can be quite varied, consisting of almost anything that creates a special feeling: need, concern, loyalty, frustration, power, affection, or obligation, to name just a few. When people are "networking," they are said to be looking for relationships that would be useful in helping them with their concerns, such as problem solving, program development, resource identification, and others. As part of a health promotion intervention, social networking may take the form of having program participants trade telephone numbers for the purpose of calling each other when they are trying to resist smoking a cigarette or trying to locate a needed resource to solve a problem.

DESIGNING HEALTH PROMOTION INTERVENTIONS

Once program planners have completed a needs assessment, written program goals and objectives, and considered different types of intervention activities, they are in a position to begin designing an appropriate intervention.

Criteria and Guidelines for Developing a Health Promotion Intervention

There is no one best way of intervening to accomplish a specific program goal that can be generalized to all target populations. Each target population has its own needs and wants that must be addressed. Nevertheless, successful and responsible health promotion programs generally adhere to some common set of guidelines, standards, or criteria around which their interventions are planned (Ad Hoc Work Group, 1987). Such guidelines help to standardize and ensure the quality of the program, give credibility to a program, help with program accountability, provide a legal defense if a liability situation might arise, and identify ethical concerns that need to be addressed as a part of planning, implementing, and evaluating programs.

In 1987, the American Public Health Association (APHA), in collaboration with the Center for Health Promotion and Education of the Centers for Disease Control (CDC), developed a set of criteria to serve as guidelines for establishing the feasibility and/or the appropriateness of health education and promotion programs in a variety of settings (industrial, hospital, worksite, voluntary and official agencies) before making a decision to implement them. The criteria were not developed to assure successful programs, but rather to suggest issues that need to be considered in the decision-making process leading to the allocation of resources or the setting of program priorities (Ad Hoc Work Group, 1987, pp. 89–92). The five criteria suggested by the Work Group are:

1. A health promotion program should address one or more risk factors that are carefully defined, measurable, modifiable, and prevalent among the members of a chosen target group, factors that constitute a threat to the health status and the quality of life of target group members.
2. A health promotion program should reflect a consideration of the special characteristics, needs, and preferences of its target group(s).
3. Health promotion programs should include interventions that will clearly and effectively reduce a target risk factor and are appropriate for a particular setting.
4. A health promotion program should identify and implement interventions that make optimum use of the available resources.
5. From the outset, a health promotion program should be organized, planned, and implemented in such a way that its operation and effects can be evaluated.

In addition to the criteria set forth by APHA and CDC, other agencies and organizations have suggested criteria and guidelines. The Society of Prospective Medicine has developed some definitions of commonly used terms in health education and promotion and a set of "Guidelines for Health Risk Appraisal/Reduction Systems." This organization refers to the individual guidelines as essentials. The essentials are the basic attributes that need to be present in any **risk appraisal/risk reduction** program, no matter who provides it, where it is offered, or how long it runs. The seven essentials offered by the society (Task Force, 1981) state that every program should:

1. Have a written statement of objectives of the program and limitations.
2. Have evidence of a scientific base for the risk appraisal instrument.
3. Show that appropriate risk reduction resources are available to participants.
4. Be able to demonstrate the staff's capability to organize and conduct risk appraisal/reduction programs in accordance with stated objectives.
5. Ensure that participants receive the results of their appraisals in a form they can comprehend, including recommendations to consult an appropriate health provider when needed.
6. Have mechanisms to protect the confidentiality of the data on individual participants.
7. Have evidence of efforts to evaluate the program periodically in relation to objectives.

Some organizations and professionals have set guidelines, criteria, or **codes of practice** for specific types of health promotion programs. Examples are the criteria set forth by the American College of Sports Medicine (1980) for exercise programs, the guidelines established by the American College of Obstetricians and Gynecologists for exercise during pregnancy, and the "Code of Practice for Smoking Cessation Programs" (see Appendix E for a copy of this code) agreed upon by the American Cancer Society, the American Health Foundation, the American Heart Association, the American Lung Association, the Five-Day Plan to Stop Smoking, and Smok-Enders. Another example is the guidelines for conducting smoking cessation programs put forth by Bartlett, Windsor, Lowe, and Nelson (1986).

Obviously, the guidelines and criteria listed here are not all that are available. Prudent planners should seek out, through inquiry and networking, other criteria and guidelines that apply to programs they are planning.

Ethics and Health Promotion Interventions

It is not unusual for program planners to be faced with decisions about **ethics** when designing interventions. Is it ethical to require people to wear safety belts and fine them if they do not? To try to persuade people to do something they do not want to do? To try out a new smoking cessation treatment on a group without their knowledge? To withhold treatment from people because they cannot afford it? To help people lose weight in any way possible as long as they succeed in losing it? To use a sensationalist or fear-arousing method in teaching? To largely ignore the content recommendations of parents when teaching school health classes? To grade students on health behaviors or behavior change? These are just a few of the ethical questions that program planners may have to address.

As program planners begin to develop interventions, the following moral and ethical concerns need to be addressed (Shirreffs, Odom, McLeroy, Cryer, & Fors, 1990):

1. Respect the goals and values of those in the target population.
2. Be aware of the degrees of autonomy related to health behavior.
   a. Facilitation—assist in achieving objectives set by a target group (for example, putting safety belts in cars).
   b. Persuasion—argue and reason with others (for example, telling others about the importance of safety belts).
   c. Manipulation—modifying environment or psychic disposition (for example, automatic safety belts or passive restraints).
   d. Coercion—threat of deprivation (for example, a safety belt law and fine).
3. Follow the necessary steps to provide informed consent to those in the target population.
   a. Explanation of nature and purposes of procedures.
   b. Explanation of discomfort or risks.
   c. Explanation of expected benefits.
   d. Disclosure of alternative procedures.
   e. Offer to answer questions.
   f. Indication that the person is free to discontinue participation.
4. Be just and fair.
5. Protect the confidentiality and privacy of those in the target population.
6. Do not cause harm (nonmaleficence). Do not omit something you should include (omission), and do not do something you should not (commission).
7. Work to bring about or do good (beneficence).

A Model for Designing Interventions

What should be included in a health promotion intervention? This question is constantly asked by those who are responsible for planning programs. The criteria and guidelines listed earlier in this chapter and the theories presented in Chapter 7 provide a partial answer to this question, but more guidance is needed to help planners in the development of well-conceived interventions. For this reason, we felt it was important to present a model that would be useful in planning an intervention.

The conceptual model (see Figure 8.6 on page 154) is based upon a series of questions. Each question requires planners to consider the association of the planning steps discussed up to this point. Although planners may not be able to answer all the questions posed in the model because of limitations specific to their situation, the model does provide planners with a "skeleton" on which to build a com-

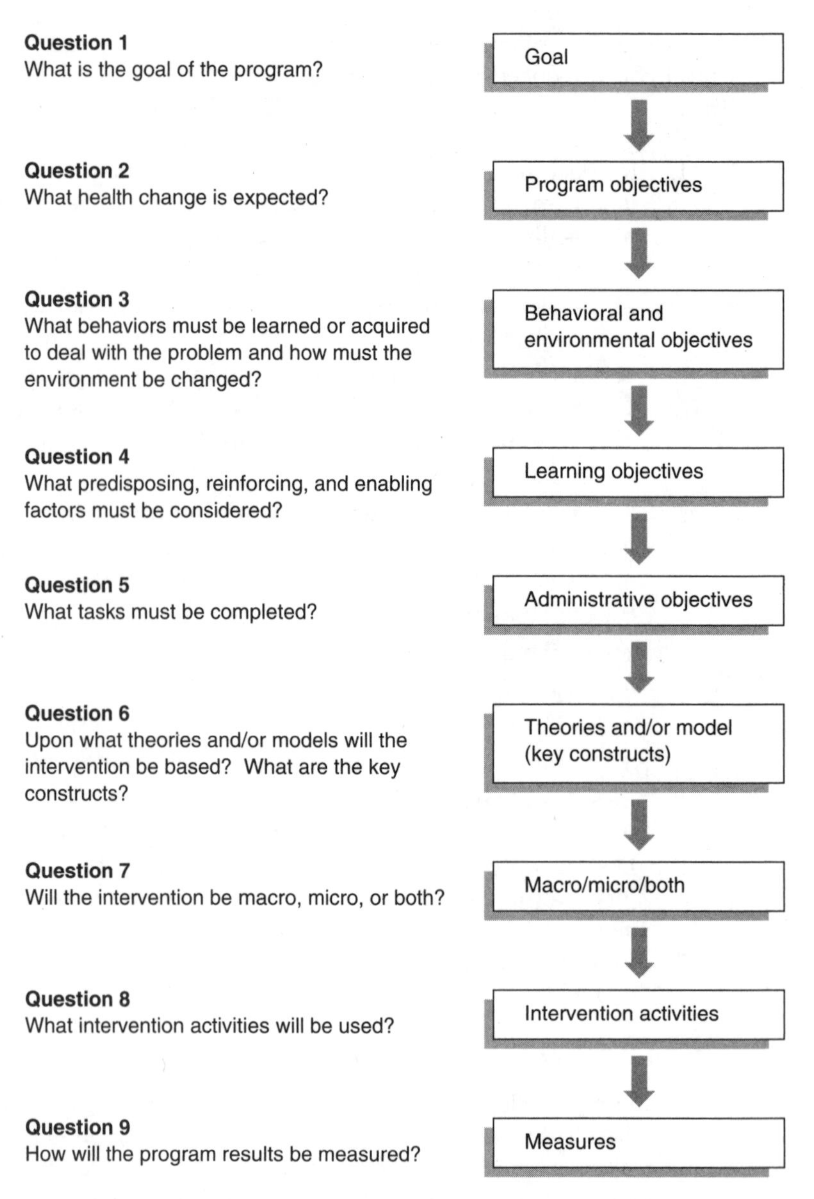

FIGURE 8.6 Conceptual Model for Designing an Intervention

prehensive intervention. However, whether program planners use this model or another, they should devote much thought to the health problem or concern, the desired program outcome(s), at what points to intervene, and the most effective intervention activities for the problem.

SUMMARY

Interventions are activities used by program planners to bring about the outcomes identified in the program objectives. These activities are also sometimes referred to as "treatments." Although many times an intervention is made up of a single activity, it is more common for planners to use a variety of activities to make up an intervention for a program. In this chapter, intervention activities were categorized into the following groups:

1. Educational activities or methods.
2. Behavior modification activities.
3. Environmental change activities.
4. Regulatory activities.
5. Community advocacy activities.
6. Organizational culture activities.
7. Communication activities.
8. Economic and other incentives.
9. Health status evaluation activities.
10. Social intervention activities.

Additionally, this chapter identified the need for program planners to be aware of recommended standards/criteria/guidelines when planning program interventions. Some examples were reviewed of general, as well as program-specific, guidelines that have been set forth by both professional organizations and individual professionals. Finally, this chapter presented a model that planners can use in developing health education interventions.

QUESTIONS

1. What is an intervention?
2. What are the advantages of using a multiactivity intervention over one that includes a single activity? Are there any disadvantages?
3. What are the major categories of interventions? Explain each.
4. Why should program planners be concerned with program guidelines that have been developed by professional organizations?
5. Name and briefly describe the major categories of ethical concerns related to intervention development.
6. What are some of the documents and sponsoring groups that have suggested standards, criteria, or guidelines for program development?
7. Briefly discuss the conceptual model set forth in this chapter for creating an intervention.

ACTIVITIES

1. Create a multiactivity intervention for a program you are planning.
2. Create a multiactivity intervention for a program that has as its goal "to get third-grade students to wear helmets while riding their bicycles."
3. Create a multiactivity intervention for a program that has as its goal "to eliminate smoking of all employees of Company X."
4. Create a multiactivity intervention for a program that has as its goal "the rehydration of young children in the small village of Y in the Third World country of Q."
5. Write a one-paragraph statement outlining the ethical stand your organization will take with regard to program development.
6. Develop a three-fold pamphlet that can be used as an informational piece for a program you are planning.
7. With other students in your class, write a PSA script for a program you are planning. Then rehearse the script and have it videotaped.
8. Write a two-page, double-spaced news release that describes a program you are planning.
9. Write a letter to your state or federal senators or representatives requesting their support of a piece of health-related legislation that is currently being considered.

9

Community Organization

After reading this chapter and answering the questions at the end, you should be able to:

- Define *community, community organization, community development,* and *coalitions.*
- Outline a process for organizing a community.
- Provide an overview of PATCH.

Key Terms

active participants
bottom-up
citizen initiated
citizen participation
coalitions
community
community empowerment
community organization
gatekeepers
grass-roots participation
locality development
network
networking
occasional participants
outside in
ownership
PATCH
social action
social planning
stakeholders
supporting participants
top down

A significant portion of the work of health educators involves implementing health promotion programs with small communities of people. By **community** we mean "a locale or domain that is characterized by the following elements: (1) membership—a sense of identity and belonging; (2) common symbol systems—similar language, rituals, and ceremonies; (3) shared values and norms; (4) mutual influence—community members have influence and are influenced by each other; (5) shared needs and commitment to meeting them; and (6) shared emotional connection—members share common history, experiences, and mutual support. Communality may be geographically bounded (e.g., a neighborhood) but is not necessary (e.g., an ethnic group)" (Israel, Checkoway, Schulz, & Zimmerman, 1994). Thus it is not uncommon for health educators to implement a smoking cessation program in a corporate setting, organize a support group for families affected by a chronic disease, or present a drug education program for school-age children. However, health educators sometimes work with large communities, a task that involves organizing the people in a community to work together to implement a solution to a communitywide problem, concern, or issue. This chapter addresses the fundamental elements of organizing large communities for action.

COMMUNITY ORGANIZATION AND ITS ASSUMPTIONS

When one begins to read the literature regarding community organization, it becomes apparent that not everyone defines community organization in the same way. As a matter of fact, several terms are used that have similar or overlapping definitions. Terms such as **citizen participation,** *community participation*, **grass-roots participation,** *macro practice*, and *community development* seem to be intertwined in the literature (Archer, Kelly, & Bisch, 1984; Brager, Specht, & Torczyner, 1987; Checkoway, 1989; Checkoway & Van Til, 1978; Connor, 1968; Kickbusch, 1989; Perlman, 1978; Perlman & Gurin, 1972; Rifkin, 1986; Ross, 1967; Rothman & Tropman, 1987). More recent discussions of **community empowerment** (Airhihenbuwa, 1994; Breslow, 1992; Israel et al., 1994; Labonte, 1994; Miner & Ward, 1992; Minkler, 1994; Robertson & Minkler, 1994; Wallerstein, 1992) have also included elements of *community development* and *community organization*. Probably the most accepted definition of *community development* is found in a United Nations (1955, p. 6) publication, where the term is defined as "a process designed to create conditions of economic and social progress for the whole community with its active participation and the fullest possible reliance on the community's initiative."

The term *community organization* comes from the social work literature and refers to various methods of intervention to deal with social problems. "Most problems or goals requiring a community organization effort are by definition larger than any one organization can be expected to handle, and stakes in the community issue often affect many different interest groups" (Green, 1990, pp. 175–76). **Community organization** has been defined as "the method of intervention whereby individuals, groups, and organizations engage in planned action to influence social problems. It is concerned with the enrichment, development, and/or change

TABLE 9.1 Terms Associated with Community Organization

Citizen participation	The bottom-up, grass-roots mobilization of citizens for the purpose of undertaking activities to improve the condition of something in the community.
Community development	A process designed to create conditions of economic and social progress for the whole community with its active participation and the fullest possible reliance on the community's initiative" (United Nations, 1955, p. 6).
Community organization	"The method of intervention whereby individuals, groups, and organizations engage in planned action to influence social problems. It is concerned with the enrichment, development, and/or change of social institutions" (Brager et al., 1987, p. 55).
Community participation	"A process of involving people in the institutions or decisions that affect their lives" (Checkoway, 1989, p. 18).
Empowered community	"One in which individuals and organizations apply their skills and resources in collective efforts to meet their respective needs" (Israel et al., 1994).
Grass-roots participation	"Bottom-up efforts of people taking collective actions on their own behalf, and they involve the use of a sophisticated blend of confrontation and cooperation in order to achieve their ends" (Perlman, 1978, p. 65).
Macro practice	The methods of professional change that deal with issues beyond the individual, family, and small group level.

of social institutions" (Brager et al., 1987, p. 55). It is not a science but an art of building consensus within a democratic process (Ross, 1967).

Even though formal community organization has taken place for a long time, the needs and efforts to organize communities now seem to be greater than in years past. In the early history of the United States, a sense of community was inherent in everyday life (Green, 1989, March). It was natural for communities to pool their resources to deal with shared problems. As time has passed, technology has improved greatly, resources have become more centralized, and American society has become more mobile. As a result of these changes, communities have become more dependent on those outside the community and have fewer reasons to interact with neighboring communities. "From self-sufficient farming communities of colonial America to the single-industry towns of the westward expansion and the industrial revolution to the Silicon Valleys of today's information and service era, communities have become increasingly dependent on other communities and on higher levels of organization and government to facilitate, coordinate, and regulate their interdependence" (Green, 1990, p. 165).

Although community organization may not be as "natural" as it once was, communities can still organize to analyze and solve problems through collective action (Table 9.1). In working toward this end, those who try to organize communities must make several assumptions. Ross (1967, pp. 86–92) has stated these as follows:

1. "Communities of people can develop capacity to deal with their own problems."

2. "People want to change and can change."
3. "People should participate in making, adjusting, or controlling the major changes taking place in their communities."
4. "Changes in community living that are self-imposed or self-developed have a meaning and permanence that imposed changes do not have."
5. "A 'holistic approach' can deal successfully with problems with which a 'fragmented approach' cannot cope."
6. "Democracy requires cooperative participation and action in the affairs of the community, and that the people must learn the skills which make this possible."
7. "Frequently communities of people need help in organizing to deal with their needs, just as many individuals require help in coping with their individual problems."

THE PROCESS OF COMMUNITY ORGANIZATION

There is no one specific method for organizing a community (Clapp, Packard, & Stanger, 1993). In fact, Rothman and Tropman (1987, pp. 4–5) have stated, "We should speak of community organization methods rather than the community organization method." Over the years, several different community organization methods have been used, including revolutionary techniques (Alinsky, 1971). However, in recent years, three models of community organization have been developed (Rothman & Tropman, 1987). They are locality development, social planning, and social action. **Locality development** is most like community development and seeks community change through broad self-help participation from the local community. The Peace Corps is a good example. **Social planning** emphasizes a technical process of problem solving that includes various levels of participation, ranging from a little to a lot, and involves outside planners. The United Way is an example of social planning. **Social action** deals with organizing a disadvantaged segment of the population. It aims at making changes in institutions and communities and often seeks a redistribution of resources and power. Although this model is no longer used as often as it once was, it was most useful during the civil rights and gay rights movements.

At the risk of violating Rothman and Tropman's (1987) maxim that there are various ways of organizing a community based upon existing resources and problems, and since our purpose in this chapter is to provide an overview of community organization, we present a very general or generic approach to organizing a community (see Figure 9.1). It does not include everything planners need to know about community organization, but it does present the basic elements. Our model relies heavily on social planning but also includes some specific elements from locality development and social action. For further information about community organization, readers should refer to any of several books listed in the References that are devoted entirely to the subject. Also, there are several works that deal specifi-

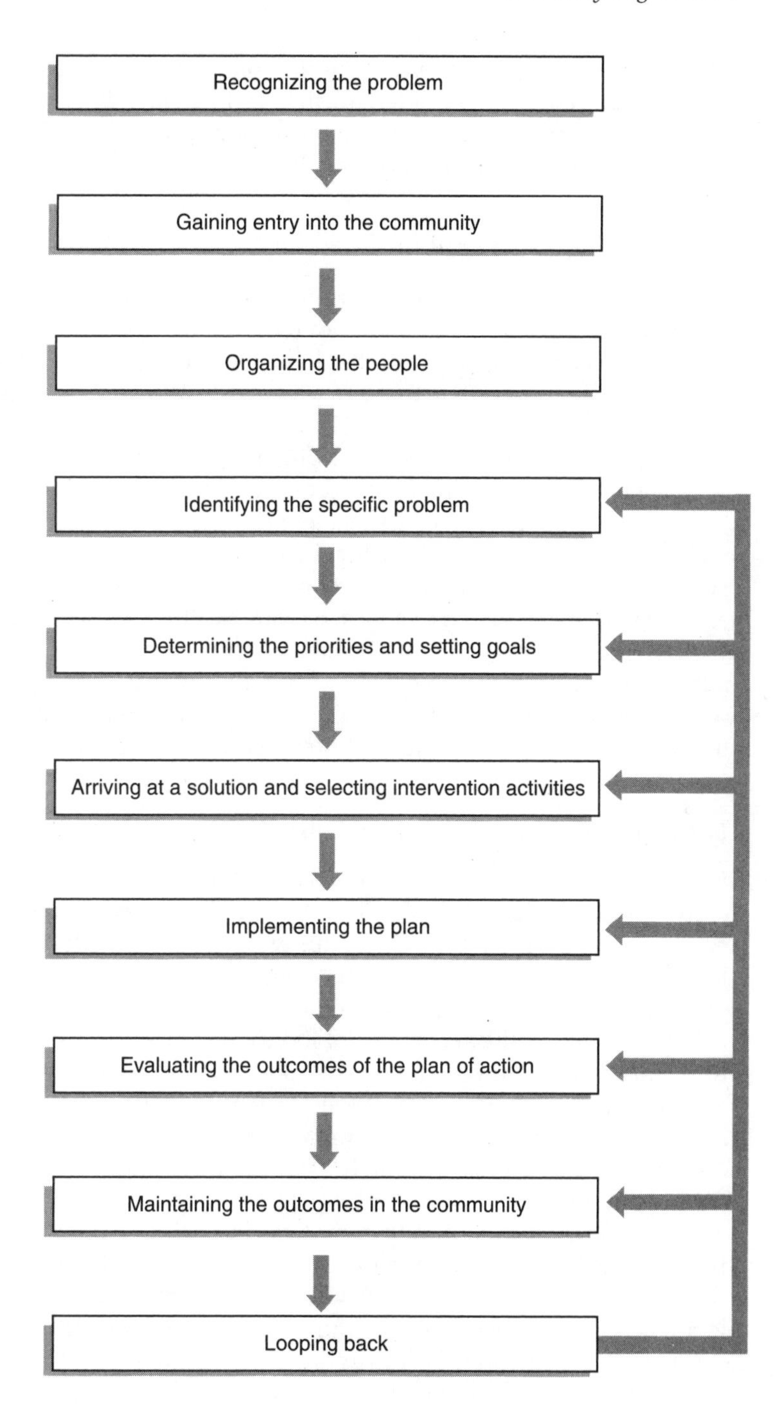

FIGURE 9.1 Summary of the Steps of Community Organization

cally with the application of community organization to health promotion activities (Blackburn, 1983; Kumpfer, Turner, & Alvarado, 1991; Maccoby & Solomon, 1981; McAlister, Puska, Salonen, Tuomilehot, & Koskelia, 1982, and Pentz, Johnson, Dwyer, MacKinnon, Hansen, & Flay, 1989).

Recognizing the Problem

The process of community organization begins when an individual, group, or organization recognizes that a problem (or concern or issue) exists in the community and that something needs to be done about it. For the purposes of our discussion, we will assume that the problem is a health problem, but the community organization process could be used with any type of problem found in a community. Problems can be as specific as trying to get a certain piece of legislation passed or as general as advocating for a drug-free community.

The recognition of a health problem can occur from inside or outside the community. A concerned citizen or a church leader from within the community may point out the problem, or it may first be identified by someone outside the community, such as an employee of a local or state health department, a state legislator, or someone from a local voluntary health agency. Internal recognition of the problem is referred to as **citizen initiated** and includes **bottom-up**, or grass-roots, groups. When community organization is initiated by individuals from outside of the community, the problem is said to be organized from the **top down** or **outside in** (Perlman, 1978).

Gaining Entry into the Community

Recognition of a problem does not mean that people should immediately set about correcting it. Instead, they should follow a set of steps to deal with the problem; gaining proper "entry" into the community is the first step. Braithwaite, Murphy, Lythcott, and Blumenthal (1989) have stressed the importance of tactfully negotiating entry into a community with the individuals who control, both formally and informally, the "political climate" of the community. These individuals are referred to as **gatekeepers**, or community opinion leaders. They may include people such as business leaders, education leaders, heads of law enforcement agencies, leaders of community activist groups, parent and teacher groups, clergy, politicians, and others. Their support is absolutely essential to the success of any attempt to organize a community.

To make entry, community organizers must first be familiar with the community they want to help. They must know: (1) with whom the power lies; (2) what type of political interactions take place within the community; and (3) whether the problem has been recognized before and, if so, how it was addressed. In other words, community organizers must have a thorough knowledge of the community and the people living there before they try to enter the informal boundaries of the community (Braithwaite et al., 1989). Having a thorough understanding of the community and tactfully approaching its gatekeepers will help community organizers to develop credibility and trust with those in the community. It is not easy to bring a problem to the attention of those in the community. Few people are glad to know they have a problem, and fewer still like others to tell them they have a problem. Move with caution, and do not be too aggressive!

When the top down approach is being used, organizers might find it advantageous to enter the community through an already established, well-respected organization or institution in the community, such as a church, a service group, or another successful local group. Green (1990) has suggested that the academic health center might be the ideal convener to address health services, health protection, or health promotion issues. "It has the deep roots in the community, it is not typically beholden to an out-of-state master, it can cut deals with local organizations, and it can draw upon resources to leverage commitments and resources from other organizations" (Green, 1990, p. 175). If such an organization/institution can be convinced that the problem exists and needs to be solved, it can help smooth the way to gaining entry and achieving the remaining steps in the process.

Organizing the People

Obtaining the support of the community members to deal with the problem is the next step in the process. It is best to begin with those individuals who are already interested in solving the problem. This is not the time either to try to convert people to the cause or to make sure that all the key players of the community are involved. It is best to begin with a core group of people who want to see change occur. Make sure this group includes people who are affected by the problem. For example, if you are dealing with a teenage drug problem, include teens in the core group. If you are trying to help low-income individuals who need housing, make sure they are involved. More often than not, this core group will be small and will consist of people who are committed to the resolution of the problem regardless of the time frame. Brager and colleagues (1987) have referred to this core group as executive participants. From among the core group, a leader or coordinator must be identified. If at all possible, the leader should be someone with leadership skills and a good knowledge of the problem. One of the early tasks of the leader will be to help build group cohesion.

With the core group in place, the next step is to expand the group to build support for dealing with the problem—that is, to broaden the constituency. Brager and colleagues (1987) have noted that other group participants will include active, occasional, and supporting participants. The **active participants** (who may also be executive participants) take part in most group activities and are not afraid to do the work that needs to be done. The **occasional participants** become involved on an irregular basis and usually only when major decisions are made. The **supporting participants** are seldom involved but help swell the ranks and may contribute in nonactive ways or through financial contributions. When expanding the group, look for others who may be interested in helping, and ask current group members for names of people who might be interested. Look for people who may already be dealing with the problem through their present work or who have resources to contribute. This search should include existing social groups, such as voluntary health agencies, agricultural extension services, church groups, hospitals, health care providers, political office-holders, policy makers, police, educators, lay citizens, or special interest groups.

Over the last thirty years, in many communities the number of people interested in volunteering their time has decreased. Today, if you ask someone to volunteer, you may hear the reply, "I'm already too busy." There are two primary reasons for this response. First, there are many families in which both husband and wife work outside the home. Between 1970 and 1990, the proportion of married women with preschool-aged children who were in the labor force almost doubled, from 30% to 59%. Also during this same period of time, the proportion of married women with children of school age who were in the labor force jumped from 49% to 75%. In 1990, 70% of married couples with children reported that both husband and wife were employed outside the home (USDC, 1992). Second, there are more single-parent households. Between 1970 and 1988, the number of single parents who maintained their own households and had their own children living with them rose from 3.8 million to 9.4 million. Today they constitute about one-fourth of all family households with children, and most headed by women (USDC, 1989).

Therefore, when organizers are expanding their constituencies, they should be sure to:

1. Identify people who are affected by the problem that they are trying to solve.
2. Provide "perks" for or otherwise reward volunteers.
3. Keep volunteer time short.
4. Match volunteer assignments with the ability and expertise of the volunteers.
5. Consider providing appropriate training to make sure volunteers are comfortable with their tasks.

For example, if the organizers need someone to talk with law enforcement groups, it would probably be a good idea to solicit the help of someone who feels comfortable around such groups and who is respected by them, such as another law enforcement person.

These expanded community groups are sometimes referred to as associations, task forces, or coalitions. These types of groups build a constituency in support of the problem; there is power in numbers, and pooled resources can maximize the energy of those involved. Of these types of community groups, the coalition is probably considered the most formal. A **coalition** can be defined as a temporary union of two or more individuals and/or organizations to achieve a common purpose (often, to compensate for deficits in power, resources and expertise). The underlying concept behind coalitions is collaboration, for several individuals, groups, or organizations with their collective resources have a better chance of solving the problem than any single entity.

Table 9.2 provides a modified list of guidelines (Lindsay & Edwards, 1988) for keeping a coalition dynamic, viable, and effective.

TABLE 9.2 Guidelines for Effective Coalitions

1. Be sensitive to turf issues.
2. Make sure the coalition is genuine.
3. Clarify the exact purpose of the coalition.
4. Limit the number of agencies involved in the coalition.
5. Allow enough time for decisions to be made.
6. Communicate with other coalitions from other geographic areas dealing with the same problem.
7. Make sure the visibility and recognition of the agencies involved in the coalition are increased as a result of their participation.
8. Secure a financial commitment from agencies involved in the coalition.
9. Have infrequent but worthwhile meetings.
10. Make sure someone is accountable for the work of the coalition.
11. Be sure to distribute the workload of the coalition among participating agencies.

Source: From "Creating Effective Health Coalitions" by G. B. Lindsay and G. Edwards, 1988, *Health Education, 19*(4), pp. 35–36.

Identifying the Specific Problem

With the expanded community group in place, the next task is to isolate the specific problem (or problems) that need to be resolved. For example, consider a community in which community organizers initially saw the problem to be drug abuse by teens. What are the underlying problems that lead to teenage drug abuse? Answering this question will help to guide the group in its work.

An appropriately conducted needs assessment can help to identify these underlying problems. The needs assessment should be thorough enough to provide the expanded group with the knowledge needed to begin tackling the problem. This assessment is also useful in setting priorities and providing a baseline for further evaluation. An important follow-up to the needs assessment is an assessment of the "culture" of the community. This should identify the values of the community—what is seen as important. It should also identify the skills and limitations of the community, and the formal and informal political influences in the community.

A good way to approach this step in the community organization process is through **networking**. A **network** is a system of elements (professional counterparts) who work collaboratively as consultants and consultees. For example, if community organizers are interested in determining what resources there are in a community to deal with drug abuse, they may network with education leaders, church leaders, law enforcement agencies, hospitals, mental health centers, treatment centers, and the local health department. As a part of assessing the culture of the community, organizers need to identify the power base within the community and figure out what it takes to get the power base to act. The political reality of community organization is that no matter how hard organizers may work, the power base may prevent a resolution of the problem or issue. Community problems are complex, and the reality is that someone usually benefits if a problem remains unsolved (Archer & Fleshman, 1985). Do not be naive concerning a community's power base and political influences.

Determining Priorities and Setting Goals

Once the needs of the community have been assessed, the community group is ready to develop its goals. The goal-setting process includes two phases. The first phase consists of identifying the priorities of the group—what the group wants to accomplish. The priorities should be determined through consensus rather than through an individual or small group decision. The second phase consists of using the priority list to write the goals. To help ensure that the ideals of community organization take hold, the **stakeholders** (those in the community who have something to gain or lose from the community organization efforts) must be the ones to establish priorities and set goals. This may sound simple, but in fact it may be the most difficult part of community organization. Getting the stakeholders to agree on priorities takes a skilled group facilitator because there is sure to be more than one point of view.

When working with coalitions and task forces, one is likely to find that determining priorities and setting goals causes turf struggles. Even though individuals or representatives of their organizations have come together to solve a problem, many people will still be concerned with finding specific solutions to the problems faced by their organization. For example, in the case of drug abuse in the community, consensus may indicate that the majority of people believe the problem lies in the educational system, but people who work in the treatment centers may believe the problem lies in the treatment of drug abuse. The facilitator will need special skills to keep these treatment center people involved after the priority-setting process does not identify their concern as a problem the group will attack. One means of dealing with this is to have subgoals, objectives that can be worked on by special interest subcommittees. Such an arrangement will allow the subcommittee to have a feeling of **ownership** in the process of solving the problem.

Arriving at a Solution and Selecting Intervention Activities

To achieve the goals that it has set, the group will need to identify alternative solutions and—again through consensus—choose a course of action. Most problems can be solved in any of several ways, however, each alternative has advantages and disadvantages. The group should examine the alternatives in terms of probable outcomes, acceptability to the community, probable long- and short-term effects on the community, and the cost of resources to solve the problem (Archer & Fleshman, 1985). Most of the interventions discussed in Chapter 8 are means by which the group can attack the problem.

Much of the work to identify the appropriate solution(s) can be accomplished through subcommittees. Subcommittees can complete specific tasks that will contribute to the larger plan of action. Their work should yield specific strategies that are culturally sensitive and appropriate to community needs. The plan of action is usually written in a proposal format and will be given final approval at a meeting of the full committee. It is important to take care in putting together this proposal; as many as possible of the ideas of the various subcommittees should be included. This will help to ensure approval of the entire plan. In the end, the real test of the course of action selected is whether it can provide whatever it is the people are seeking (Brager et al., 1987).

Final Steps in the Community Organization Process

The final four steps in a community organization process include implementing the plan, evaluating the outcomes of the plan of action, maintaining the outcomes in the community, and if necessary "looping" back to the appropriate point in the process to modify the steps and restructure the work plan. However, it may not be possible to succeed by handling the problem in a different way; some problems cannot be solved. Once the work of the group has been completed (that is, either the problem has been solved or it has been declared insoluble) the group can either disband or reorganize to take on another problem.

PLANNED APPROACH TO COMMUNITY HEALTH (PATCH)

What we have presented so far in this chapter is a general description of the process of organizing a community. However, there are some models for the community organization process that have been developed to guide community organizers. One model that has received considerable use and attention in the area of health promotion is the Planned Approach to Community Health, better known by its acronym, **PATCH** (Kreuter, Nelson, Stoddard, & Watkins, 1985). The concept of PATCH emerged in 1983 as the response of the Centers for Disease Control and Prevention (CDC) to the shift in the federal policy regarding the distribution of money to states via categorical (block) grants (Kreuter, 1992). PATCH was designed using the PRECEDE model and was created "to strengthen state and local health departments' capacities to plan, implement, and evaluate community-based health promotion activities targeted toward priority health problems" (Kreuter, 1992, p. 135). Since its development, PATCH has proved to be a useful process with a good "track record for facilitating collaborative, community-based programs" (Speers, 1992, p. 132). The use of PATCH also led to the inspiration for PROCEED (Green & Kreuter, 1992). (See the *Journal of Health Education*, April 1992, for accounts of some of the success stories.) The essential elements of PATCH include community organization with local support, participation, and leadership; community members using local health data to determine the health problems, prioritize the health problems, and set goals and objectives; carrying out interventions; and evaluating the results (Speers, 1992). PATCH is a team approach in which the people of the community make the decisions (via a consensus process) and do the work, with technical assistance from the state and local health departments and the Centers for Disease Control and Prevention. These team members not only facilitate the necessary work but also provide financial support for the project.

SUMMARY

Community organization refers to various methods of intervention whereby individuals, groups, and organizations engage in planned collective action to deal with social problems. The literature on community organization is not distinct; it is often intertwined with such terms as *citizen participation, community empowerment, community participation, grass-roots participation, macro practice,* and *community development.* The process of community organization has been used for many years in the area of social work, but its history in the area of health promotion is much more recent. Within this chapter a generic process for community organization was presented, which should be an adequate introduction to the process. Finally, a brief overview of the PATCH model was presented.

QUESTIONS

1. What is meant by the term *community?*
2. How does community organization relate to community empowerment?
3. Community organization originated out of what discipline?
4. What is the underlying concept of community organization?
5. What are some of the assumptions under which planners work when organizing a community?
6. What are the basic steps in the community organization process?
7. What is meant by the term *gatekeepers?*
8. What does the acronym PATCH stand for? What are the major components of this process?

ACTIVITIES

1. Assume that a core group of individuals have come together to deal with the problem of a high rate of teenage pregnancy in the community. Please identify (by job title/function) others who you think should be invited to be part of the larger group. In addition, provide a one-sentence rationale for inviting each. Assume that this community is large enough to have most social service organizations.

2. Provide a list of at least 10 different community agencies that should be invited to make up an antismoking coalition in your home town. Provide a one-sentence rationale for including each.
3. Assume that you want to make entry into a community with which you are not familiar, in order to help to organize the community. Describe such a community, and then write a two-page paper to tell what steps you would take to gain entrance into the community.
4. If you wanted to find out more about your community's resources regarding exercise programs, with whom would you network? Provide a list of at least five contacts, and provide a one-sentence rationale for why you selected each.
5. Ask your professor if he or she is aware of any community organization efforts in a local community. If such a program exists, make an appointment along with three of your classmates to interview the community organization leader. Ask the leader to respond to the following questions:
   a. What is the problem being tackled?
   b. Who identified the initial problem?
   c. Who makes up the core group? How large is it?
   d. Did the group complete a needs assessment or community resource assessment?
   e. What type of intervention is being used?
   f. Will the problem be solved?
   g. What type of community organization model was used?

10

Identification and Allocation of Resources

After reading this chapter and answering the questions at the end, you should be able to:

- Define *resources.*
- List the common resources used in most health promotion programs.
- Identify the tasks to be carried out by program personnel.
- Explain the difference between internal and external resources.
- List the agencies/organizations that offer "canned" health promotion programs.
- Identify questions to ask vendors when they are selling their programs.
- List and explain common means of financing health promotion programs.
- Define *budget.*
- Identify and explain the major components of a grant proposal.

Key Terms

- canned program
- curriculum
- external resources
- flex time
- grant money
- grantsmanship
- hard money
- in-house materials
- internal resources
- ownership
- peer education
- profit margin
- proposal
- request for proposals (RFP)
- resources
- soft money
- speaker's bureau
- vendors

For a program to reach the identified goals and objectives, it must be supported with the appropriate **resources**. Resources include all the people and things needed to carry out the desired program. The quantity or amount of resources needed to plan, implement, and evaluate a program depends upon the scope and nature of the program. Most resources carry a "price tag," which planners must take into account. Thus, planners face the task of securing the financial resources necessary to carry out a program. However, several different resources are provided by organizations, mostly voluntary or governmental health organizations, that are free or inexpensive. This chapter identifies, describes, and suggests sources for obtaining the resources commonly needed in planning, implementing, and evaluating health promotion programs.

PERSONNEL

The key resource of any program is the individuals needed to carry out the program. Instead of trying to identify all the individuals necessary to ensure the program's success (because many times the same person is responsible for several different program components), planners should focus on the tasks that need to be completed by the program personnel. These tasks include planning, identifying resources, advertising, marketing, conducting the program, evaluating the program, making arrangements for space and program materials, handling clerical work, and keeping records (for program sign-up, collection of fees, attendance, and budgeting).

In some cases, the program participants themselves constitute a program resource. In the case of a worksite health promotion program, planners will need to find out whether the employees will participate on company time, on their own time before or after work hours, on a combination of company time and employee time, or on their own anytime during the work day as long as they put in their regular number of work hours. (This last option is known as **flex time**.) The current trend in worksite health promotion programs is to ask the employees to participate at least partially on their own time. The reasoning behind this trend is that this investment by the participant helps to promote a sense of program **ownership** ("I have put something into this program, and therefore I am going to support it") and thus build loyalty among participants.

When identifying the personnel needed to conduct a program, planners have three basic options. One, referred to as **internal resources,** uses individuals from within the planning agency/organization or people from within the target population to supply the needed labor. For example, if a local health department was planning a health promotion program in a community, the employees of the health department might handle the planning, implementation, and evaluation of the program. If that same health department was planning a health promotion program for the faculty and staff of a school district, there would likely be many school employees (school nurse, health educator, physical education instructor, home economics teacher) who have the expertise (knowledge and skills) to carry out much of the program. If the department was planning a worksite program, there would probably be quite a few employees who would be qualified to conduct at least a portion of the program (for example, an employee who is certified to teach first aid or cardiopulmonary resuscitation).

Another internal resource that health promotion planners are using successfully in a variety of settings, especially in schools (from kindergarten to college), is **peer education.** The process is simple: Individuals who have specific knowledge, skills, or understanding of a concept help to educate their peers. For example, college students may work with other college students to help educate them about the dangers of drinking and driving. The major advantages of peer education are its low cost and the credibility of the instructor. Children, for example, are greatly influenced by their peers.

A second source of personnel for a program is to bring in individuals from outside the planning agency/organization or the target population to conduct part or all of the program. Such individuals are considered **external resources.** There are now many companies that offer or sell programs, services, or consulting to groups wanting health promotion programs. These companies are referred to as **vendors.** Some vendors are for-profit groups, such as hospitals, consulting agencies, health promotion companies, or related businesses, whereas others are nonprofit organizations, such as voluntary health agencies, YMCAs, YWCAs, governmental health agencies, universities/colleges, extension services, or professional organizations. Because of the recent growth of interest in health promotion programs, the quality of vendors can vary greatly. Planners should screen vendors carefully before using their services. Harris, McKenzie, and Zuti (1986) provide a checklist for choosing an appropriate vendor (see Appendix F).

An often untapped source of personnel for health promotion programs is experts available through **speaker's bureaus.** Most local offices of voluntary health agencies and other health-related organizations maintain speaker's bureaus. The services of these experts are usually available at little or no cost to groups. With

TABLE 10.1 Advantages and Disadvantages of Using Internal and External Personnel

	Advantages	Disadvantages
Internal program personnel	1. Reduce costs 2. Internal arrangements can be made to free needed personnel from their work schedules. 3. More control over those involved.	1. Limited by the interest of those on staff. 2. May have to train personnel or be limited by the expertise of those on staff. 3. Can spend more time developing the program than implementing it, thus reaching fewer people.
External program personnel	1. Known expertise. 2. The responsibility for conducting the program becomes the work of another. 3. Can request product (program) guarantees. 4. External personnel sometimes more respected than internal personnel.	1. Often more costly than using internal resources. 2. Subject to the limitations of any given vendor. 3. Sometimes less control over the program.

some inquiry and a little networking, it is not difficult for planners to identify organizations that have individuals available to speak on a variety of health-related topics, or hospitals willing to send their medical experts into the community to share their knowledge. The speaker's bureau is a win–win concept for both the group offering the service and the one receiving it. Groups that take advantage of a speaker's bureau gain access to expert information, but those delivering the information gain in terms of public relations and recognition.

There are advantages and disadvantages connected with using either internal or external personnel to conduct health promotion programs. Table 10.1 lists the pros and cons of each.

The third option for obtaining personnel to carry out a program is a combination of internal and external resources. This option is the one most commonly used because it allows the program planners to make use of the advantages of the first two options and avoid many of the disadvantages.

CURRICULA AND OTHER INSTRUCTIONAL RESOURCES

When it comes to selecting the **curriculum** and other instructional materials that will be used to present the content of the program, planners can proceed in three ways: (1) by developing their own materials (in-house) or having someone else develop custom materials for them; (2) by purchasing or obtaining "canned" programs from outside vendors; or (3) by using a combination of in-house and canned materials. Each choice has both advantages and disadvantages.

Developing **in-house materials** or having someone else develop custom materials has the major advantage of allowing the developers to create materials that match very closely the needs of the target population. The more "unique" the target population is, the more imprtant this approach may be. However, a serious drawback is the time, money, and effort necessary to develop an original curriculum and other instructional materials. The exact amount of time necessary would obviously depend on the scope of the program and the expertise of those doing the work. No matter who does the work, however, the commitment of time and resources is sure to be considerable. In putting together an in-house program, planners should be aware of several different sources from which they can obtain free or inexpensive materials to supplement the ones they develop. For example, most voluntary and official health agencies have up-to-date pamphlets on a variety of subjects that they are willing and eager to give away in quantity. Also, most communities have a public library with a film/video section that includes some health films/videos. If the public library does not carry health films/videos, almost all local and state health departments offer such a service. Planners who are unsure about what sources of information are available in their community can begin by checking the Yellow Pages of the local telephone directory. Appendix G provides a partial listing of organizations and the types of information available from each.

Purchasing or obtaining canned programs from vendors has become very popular in recent years because of the time and money needed to create programs. A **canned program** is one that has been developed by an outside group and includes the basic components and materials necessary to implement a program. Because some vendors are for-profit groups whereas others are nonprofit organizations, the cost of these programs can range from nothing at all to thousands of dollars.

Most canned programs have five major components:

1. A participant's manual (printed material that is easy to follow and read and is handy for participants).
2. An instructor's manual (a much more comprehensive document than the participant's manual, which includes the program content, background information, and lesson and unit plans with ideas for presenting the material).
3. Audiovisual materials that help present the program content (usually including films, video and audio tapes, overhead transparencies, charts, or posters).
4. Training for the instructors (a concentrated experience that prepares individuals to become instructors).
5. Marketing (the "wrapping" that makes the program attractive to both the participants and the program planners who will purchase it to market to the participants).

The advantages and disadvantages of these canned programs are just the opposite of those for materials developed in-house. No time is spent on development; however, the program may not fit the needs or the demographics of the target population. For example, using the same canned smoking cessation program with middle-aged adults who realize the long-term hazards of cigarettes and with teenagers who are required to attend a smoking cessation program for disciplinary reasons may not be advisable. Most adults who enter smoking cessation programs are there because they do not want to smoke. Obviously this is not the case with teenagers who have been caught smoking. The approaches taken with these two programs would have to be very different if both are to be successful. Another example of when use of a canned curriculum program would not be advisable is use of a program that was designed for upper-middle-class suburban adults in a program for low-income inner-city populations. The lifestyles of the two groups are just too different for the same curriculum to be appropriate in both situations. Because of the possible mismatch between the needs and peculiarities (i.e., age, culture, ethnicity, norms, race, sex, socioeconomic status) of a particular target population, planners are urged to move with caution when deciding on the use of a canned program. Make sure there is a good fit.

Appendix H provides a selected list of canned programs that are currently available to program planners.

Canned programs often come attractively packaged and seemingly complete, but this does not mean that they are well conceived and effective programs. Before adopting canned programs for use, planners should consider the following questions:

1. Is the program based on sound theory and tested models? As noted in an earlier chapter, all programs should be based on sound theory and tested models.
2. Does the program include a long-term behavior modification component? There are no "quick fixes" with regard to health behavior change. If behavior modification is used, it should be based on sound health behavior practice over an appropriate time frame.
3. Is the program educational? Not only should the program be based on sound psychological and sociological theory, it should also be based on valid educational theory.
4. Is the program motivational? Health behavior change is not easy to accomplish, and so all programs need to include activities that motivate people to get and stay involved.
5. Is the program enjoyable? Planned programs should be enjoyable. Some people like hard work, but it is difficult to sustain hard work for a long time without some enjoyment.
6. Can the program be modified to meet the specific needs and peculiarities of the target population? As mentioned earlier, not all populations have the same needs and ways of approaching a problem.

SPACE

Another major resource needed for most health promotion programs is sufficient space—a place where the program can be held. Depending on the type of program and the intended audience, space may or may not be readily available. For example, an employer may make space available for a worksite program, or a school system may furnish space for a school program. If space is a problem, planners may locate inexpensive space in local schools, colleges, and universities, and in "community service rooms" (rooms that are available free of charge to community groups as a community service) of local businesses. In addition, planners may find educational institutions and local businesses that are willing to cosponsor programs and thus contribute the space necessary to conduct the program. It may also be possible to obtain space by trading for it. For instance, a planner might trade expertise, such as serving as consultant for a program, in return for the use of suitable space. Or it might be possible to trade one space for another, such as trading the use of classrooms for time in the local YMCA/YWCA pool.

EQUIPMENT AND SUPPLIES

Some programs may require a great deal of equipment and supplies. For example, first aid and safety programs need items such as CPR mannequins, splints, blankets, bandages, dressings, and video equipment. Other programs, such as a stress management program, may need only paper and pencils. Whatever the kinds and amounts of equipment and supplies required, planners must give advance thought to their needs so as to:

1. Determine the necessary equipment and supplies to facilitate the program.
2. Identify the sources where the equipment and supplies can be obtained.
3. Find a way to pay for the needed equipment and supplies.

FINANCIAL RESOURCES

To hire the individuals needed to plan, implement, and evaluate a health promotion program and to pay for the other resources required, planners must obtain appropriate financial support. Most programs are limited by the financial support available. In fact, few programs are financed at such a level that planners would say they have all the money they need. Because of this, the planners are often faced with making decisions about how to allocate the funds that are available. Some typical questions that planners generally must address are the following:

1. Is it better to run an adequately financed program for a few people or to run a poorly financed program for more people?

2. If funds are limited, where is the first place we should cut?
3. Should we start a program knowing that we will be short of funds, or should we wait until we have appropriate funding before we begin?
4. Is it better to have fewer instructors or to make do with fewer supplies?

Programs can be financed in several different ways. Some sources of financial support are very traditional, while others may be limited only by the creativity and imagination of those involved. We present here several established ways of financing programs.

Participant Fee

This method of financing a program requires the participants to pay for the cost of the program. Depending on whether or not the program is offered on a profit-making basis, this fee may be equal to expenses or may include a profit margin. Participant fees not only are a means by which programs can be financed, but also help to motivate participants to stay involved in a program. If people pay to participate in a program, then they may be more likely to continue to participate because they have made an investment—that is, a commitment. This concept has also been referred to as ownership. Many participants who pay a fee feel like they are part "owners" of the program. However, it should be noted that not everyone shares in the ownership concept. There are some participants who still would prefer a free or almost free program that has been paid for by others—a fringe benefit, if you will. An example of the ownership and cost issue is the participant fees associated with smoking cessation programs. If planners were looking for vendors of smoking cessation programs, they would find that the costs of such programs range from zero (i.e., American Cancer Society's FreshStart program) to modest (i.e., American Lung Association's Freedom from Smoking program) to expensive (i.e., those offered by private health promotion companies).

Third-Party Support

Most individuals are familiar with insurance companies acting as third-party payers to cover the costs of health care. Although this is not a common means of paying for health promotion programs, it is sometimes used. By third-party, we mean that someone other than participants (the first party) or program planners (the second party) is paying for the program. Third-party payers that may cover the cost of health promotion programs are:

1. Employers that pick up the cost for employees, as is often the case in worksite health promotion programs.
2. Agencies other than the groups sponsoring the program, for example, when local service or civic groups "adopt" a pet program.
3. A professional association or union that financially supports a program.

The money used by third-party payers can be generated from a special fund-raising event, from sale of concessions, or with money saved from reduced health care costs, absenteeism, or the remodeling of employee benefit plans.

Cost Sharing

A third means of financing a program is a combination of participant fee and third-party support. It is not unusual to have an employer pay 50% to 80% of a program's costs and let the employee pay the remaining 20% to 50%. Such an arrangement has the advantages of both ownership and a fringe benefit.

Organizational Sponsorship

Many times the sponsoring organization (health department, hospital, or voluntary agency) bears the cost of the program as a part of its programming or operating budget. For example, the American Cancer Society offers its smoking cessation program free of charge. The program is paid for with the society's program-planning funds.

Grants and Gifts

Another means of financing health promotion programs is through gifts and grants from other agencies, foundations, groups, and individuals. This source of money is often referred to as **grant money**, external money, or **soft money**. The term *soft money* refers to the fact that grants and gifts are usually given for a specific period of time and at some point will be taken away. This is in contrast to **hard money**, which is an ongoing source of funds that is part of the operating budget of an organization from year to year.

Grant money is becoming more important to program planners because of limited resources dedicated to health promotion programming. It thus becomes necessary for program planners to develop adequate **grantsmanship** skills. These skills include (1) discovering where the grant money is located; (2) finding out how to get (apply for) the money; and (3) writing a proposal requesting the money.

Locating Grant Money

Those agencies, foundations, groups, and individuals that have money to give away can be found at three different levels—local, state, and national. Usually the organizations that have money to give away are businesses, foundations, service groups (such as Lion's Club and Jaycees), voluntary groups (such as United Way and American Heart Association), and other local groups, such as foundation specific to the locality. At the state and local levels, the majority of grant money comes from foundations and governmental agencies.

To find out what funding agencies are available in a specific area requires some of the skills of a detective. Planners can check the Chamber of Commerce directories, call the Better Business Bureau, or look in the Yellow Pages. They can go to the library and read through a directory of foundations, *Directory of Research Grants 1995* (1995), *National Guide to Foundation Funding in Health* (Clinton, 1988), or *Foundation Grants to Individuals* (Mills, 1993). They may ask those who are familiar with the area, or just contact groups they think would be likely granters, in order to find out where money is available in their community. Planners should also be alert for **requests for proposals,** known as RFPs. Many times some funding agency would like to have a project conducted for it, so the group will issue an RFP. If you feel qualified to do the work, you can submit a proposal.

Submitting Grant Proposals

Most funding agencies have specific guidelines outlining who is qualified to submit a proposal (perhaps only nonprofit groups can apply, or only practitioners who hold certain certifications) and the format for making an application. Those seeking money can request or apply for the money by writing a proposal. A **proposal** can be thought of as a written document that represents a request for money. A good proposal is one that is well written and explains how the needs of the funding agency can be met by the group wishing to receive the money. To increase your chances of writing a good proposal, we recommend that you call the funding agency first and speak with the grant officer to find out specifically what he or she is looking for and the format desired.

Because there is a great deal of competition for grant money, it is more than likely that proposals will be read by a busy, impatient, skeptical person who has no reason to give any one proposal special consideration and who is faced with many more requests than he or she can grant, or even read thoroughly. Such a reader wants to find out quickly and easily the answers to these questions:

1. What do you want to do, how much will it cost, and how much time will it take?
2. How does the proposed project relate to the sponsor's interests?
3. What will be gained if this project is carried out?
4. What has already been done in the area of the project?
5. How do you plan to do it?
6. How will the results be evaluated?
7. Why should you, rather than someone else, conduct this project?

As noted, funding agencies request proposals in a variety of different forms. However, there are several components that are contained in most proposals no matter what the funding agency. Table 10.2 presents these components.

A Combination of Sources

It should be obvious that program planners should not be limited to any single source for financing a health promotion program. In fact, it is more than likely that

TABLE 10.2 The Components of a Grant Proposal

1. **Title (or cover) page.** When writing title, be concise and explicit; avoid words that add nothing.
2. **Abstract or executive summary.** May be the most important part of the proposal. Should be written last and be about 200 words long.
3. **Table of contents.** May or may not be needed, depending on the length of the proposal. It is a convenience for the reader.
4. **Introduction.** Should begin with a capsule statement, be comprehensible to the informed layperson, and include the statement of the problem, significance of the program, and purpose of the program.
5. **Background.** Should include the proposer's previous related work and the related literature.
6. **Description of proposed program.** Should include objectives, description of intervention, evaluation plan, and time frame.
7. **Description of relevant institutional/agency resources.**
8. **List of references.** Should include references cited in the proposal.
9. **Personnel section.** Should include the résumés of those who are to work with the program.
10. **Budget.** hould include budget needs for personnel (salaries and wages), equipment, materials and supplies, travel, services, other needed items, and indirect costs.

most programs will be funded via a variety of sources—that is, any combination of the sources listed previously.

Preparing a Budget

Simply put, "a budget is a plan" (Finkler, 1992, p. 1). It is a plan that is presented in financial terms using quantitative units such as dollars, pounds, hours, and manpower (Shim & Siegel, 1994). A budget represents the decision makers' intentions and expectations by allocating funds to achieve desired outcomes (program goals and objectives) (Finkler, 1992; Shim & Siegel, 1994). In financial terms, the budget compares the expected income to the expected expenses in order to estimate the financial results of the program (Finkler, 1992).

A budget can be prepared for any length of time. When programs are planned, budgets are usually created for the entire length of the program. However, when a program is projected to last longer than a year, the overall program budget is typically broken down into twelve-month periods.

The purpose of a program has a lot to say about the type of budget created. From a financial standpoint, programs can make money (a profit), lose money, or break even. If a program must make money, the income will have to be greater than the expenses, and the intended profit **(profit margin)** will need to be included in the budgeting process. No matter what the desired bottom line is in a budget, the

Income		Amount	
Contribution from sponsors		______	
Gifts		______	
Grants		______	
Participant fee		______	
Sale of curriculum materials		______	
	Total income	______	
Expenses			
Curriculum materials		______	
Equipment		______	
Marketing		______	
Print advertising		______	
Other media		______	
Personnel		______	
For planning		______	
Program facilitators		______	
Clerical		______	
Evaluator(s)		______	
Participants		______	
Postage		______	
Space		______	
Supplies		______	
Travel		______	
	Total expenses	______	
	Balance		______

FIGURE 10.1 Sample Budget Sheet

budget should be put together in sufficient detail that all income and expenses are accounted for. Figure 10.1 presents a sample budget sheet that lists some line items that are typically included in a health promotion program budget.

SUMMARY

This chapter identified and discussed the most often used resources for health promotion programs: personnel, curriculum and other instructional materials, space, equipment and supplies, and funding. In addition, typical questions were covered regarding how to secure and allocate resources and how to obtain funding.

QUESTIONS

1. What are the major categories of resources that planners need to consider when planning a health promotion program?
2. List and explain the different means by which health promotion programs can be funded.
3. Define the terms *ownership, flex time, vendor,* and *canned programs.*
4. What are the advantages and disadvantages of using internal resources? External resources?
5. How might program planners obtain free or inexpensive space for a program?
6. What are some key questions that planners should ask vendors when they try to sell their product?
7. What is meant by the term *profit margin?*

ACTIVITIES

1. Identify and describe the resources you anticipate needing to carry out a program you are planning. Be sure to answer the questions below that apply to your program.
   a. What personnel will be needed to carry out the program? List the individuals and the duties to be carried out.
   b. What curriculum will you use in your program? Why did you select it?
   c. What kind of space allocation will your program require? How will you obtain the space? How much will it cost?
   d. What equipment and supplies do you anticipate using? How will you obtain them?
   e. How do you anticipate paying for the program? Why did you select this method?
2. Visit the local office of a voluntary agency and find out what type of resources it makes available to individuals planning health promotion programs. Ask for a sample of the materials. Also, ask if the agency offers any canned programs. If it does, find out as much as you can about the programs and ask for any available descriptive literature.
3. Collect information on a single type of canned health promotion program (for example, smoking cessation or stress management) from vendors. Then compare the strengths and weaknesses of the programs.

4. Through the process of networking and using the local telephone book, find where in your community there is free or inexpensive space available for health promotion programs.
5. Call three different voluntary agencies and one hospital in your community and find out if they have a speaker's bureau. If they do, find out how to use the bureaus and what topics the speakers can address.
6. Prepare a mock grant proposal for a program you are planning. Make sure it includes all the components noted in Table 10.2.
7. Outline the major sources of income and expenses that would be associated with the program you are planning by preparing a budget sheet.

11

Marketing: Getting and Keeping People Involved in a Program

After reading this chapter and answering the questions at the end, you should be able to:

- Define *market, marketing, social marketing,* and *target marketing.*
- Explain the diffusion theory.
- Explain how the diffusion theory can be used in marketing a health promotion program.
- Identify the functions involved in the marketing process as outlined by Syre and Wilson (1990).
- Explain the relationship between a needs assessment and a marketing program.
- Explain the four Ps of marketing.
- Define *marketing mix.*
- Name techniques for motivating program participants to continue in a program.

Key Terms

- audience segmentation
- contingencies
- diffusion theory
- early adopters
- early majority
- external advertising
- incentives
- innovators
- intangible
- internal advertising
- laggards
- late majority
- market
- marketing
- marketing mix
- market segmentation
- placement
- position the product
- price
- product
- promotion
- social marketing
- social support
- tangible
- target marketing

After putting a great deal of work and energy into planning a health promotion program, planners naturally hope that the target population will want to participate in it. They also hope that, once involved in the program, the participants will want to continue with the program for its duration. Hoping is not enough, however. Planners must not just hope these things will occur, but work to make sure they occur. Planners need to have skills in marketing and psychology in order to get the target population involved and keep them involved. Only when the participants continue the behavior learned in a health promotion program over a long period of time can the health goals of both the individual and the program be met.

MARKET AND MARKETING

For the purposes of program planning, the people in the target population make up the market. Kotler and Clarke (1987, p. 108) have defined **market** as "the set of all people who have an actual or potential interest in a product or service." A key to getting and keeping these people involved in a health promotion program is to be able to market the program effectively. The process of **marketing** operates on the underlying concept of the exchange theory. "Marketing is the planned attempt to influence the characteristics of voluntary exchange transactions—exchanges of costs and benefits by buyers and sellers or providers and consumers. Marketing is considerably different from selling in that selling concentrates on the needs of the producer (to sell more products), whereas marketing, which may have the same ultimate objective, concentrates necessarily on the needs of the buyer or the public" (Pickett & Hanlon, 1990, p. 231). "Strip away all the fancy language, and market-

TABLE 11.1 Marketing a Tangible versus an Intangible

Concern	Tangible	Intangible
Success	Increase sales 3–5%	Great enough to be cost-effective
Changes	One-time sales	Lasting a lifetime
Target population	MosNespond	Least likely to respond

ing comes down to offering benefits that an identified group of potential customers will pay a price for and be satisfied with" (Novelli, 1988, p. 7).

Applying the definition of marketing to health promotion suggests that program planners would like to exchange costs and benefits with those in the target population. That is to say, program planners would like to exchange the benefits of participation in health promotion programs (the objectives or outcomes of the programs they planned), such as "a longer healthier life, looking and feeling better, and having fewer but healthier children" (Novelli, 1988, p. 6) for the costs of the program, which come from the participants, such as time, money, and effort.

For this exchange to take place, program planners must have an understanding of marketing principles. Unfortunately, many health promotion planners have had to learn the hard way—by planning a program and then not have anyone sign up to participate in it. The principles of marketing are not difficult to learn, but their application can be challenging. Applying marketing principles to health promotion programs is not as easy as applying them to the latest model of a car or a new line of clothing. Health promotion programs are social programs; as such, they do not have material objects to market, but instead must market awareness, knowledge, skills, and behavior. The marketing of health promotion programs falls into a special type of marketing called social marketing.

Lefebvre and Flora (1988, p. 300) define **social marketing** this way: "Social marketing concepts and methods borrow heavily from traditional marketing literature. However, social marketing is distinguished by its emphasis on so-called 'non-tangible' products—ideas, attitudes, lifestyle changes—as opposed to the more tangible products and services that are the focus of marketing in business, health-care, and nonprofit service sectors." They continue, "For example, how does one buy a 'healthier life'? The challenge is to begin to make these 'intangibles' tangible in a way that appeals to the target audience" (Lefebvre & Flora, 1988, p. 306).

Table 11.1 compares the marketing of a **tangible** (product) and an **intangible** (a program that will improve the quality of life).

MARKETING AND THE DIFFUSION THEORY

One analytical tool that has been most useful in understanding the importance of marketing principles is the **diffusion theory** (Rogers, 1962). The theory provides an explanation for the diffusion of innovations (something new) in populations; stated another way, it provides an explanation for the pattern of adoption of the innovations. If we think of a health promotion program as an innovation, the theory describes a pattern the target population will follow in adopting the program. The pattern of adoption can be represented by the normal bell-shaped curve (Rogers, 1983) (Figure 11.1). Therefore, those individuals who fall in the portion of the curve to the left of minus 2 standard deviations from the mean (this would be between 2% and 3% of the target population) would probably become involved in the program just because they had heard about it and wanted to be first. These people are called **innovators**. They are venturesome, independent, risky, and daring. They want to be the first to do things, and they may not be respected by others in the social system.

The second group of people to become involved are those represented on the curve between minus 2 and minus 1 standard deviations. This group would include about 14% of the target population; they are called **early adopters**. These people are very interested in the innovation, but they are not the first to sign up. They wait until the innovators are already involved to make sure the innovation is useful. Early adopters are respected by others in the social system and looked at as opinion leaders.

FIGURE 11.1 Bell-Shaped Curve and Adopter Categories

Source: Adapted from *Diffusion of Innovations,* 3rd ed. (p. 247), by E. M. Rogers, 1983, New York: Free Press.

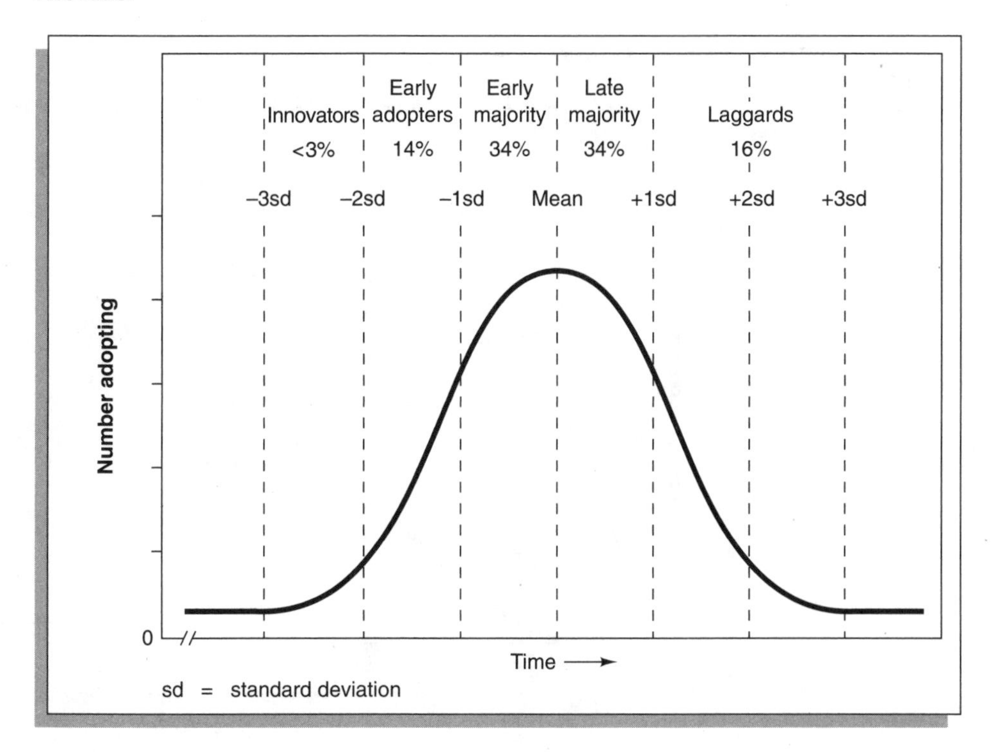

The next two groups are the **early majority** and the **late majority**. They fall between minus 1 standard deviation and the mean and between the mean and plus 1 standard deviation on the curve, respectively. Each of these groups comprises about 34% of the target population. Those in the early majority may be interested in the health promotion program, but they will need external motivation to become involved. Those in the early majority will deliberate for some time before making a decision. It will take more work to get the late majority involved, for they are skeptical and will not adopt an innovation until most people in the social system have done so. Planners may be able to get them involved through a peer or mentoring program, or through constant exposure about the innovation.

The last group, the **laggards** (16%), are represented by the part of the curve greater than plus 1 standard deviation. They are not very interested in innovation and would be the last to become involved in new health promotion programs. Some would say that this group will not become involved in health promotion programs at all. They are very traditional and are suspicious of innovations. Laggards tend to have limited communication networks, so they really do not know much about new things.

As time passes, the number of adopters of an innovation increases. Figure 11.2 presents an *s*-shaped curve showing the cumulative prevalence of adopters at successive points in time.

The real plus of using the diffusion theory when trying to market a health promotion program is that "the distinguishing characteristics of the people who fall into each

FIGURE 11.2 S-Shaped Curve and Cumulative Adoption

Source: Adapted from *Diffusion of Innovations*, 3rd ed. (p. 95), by E. M. Rogers, 1983, New York: Free Press.

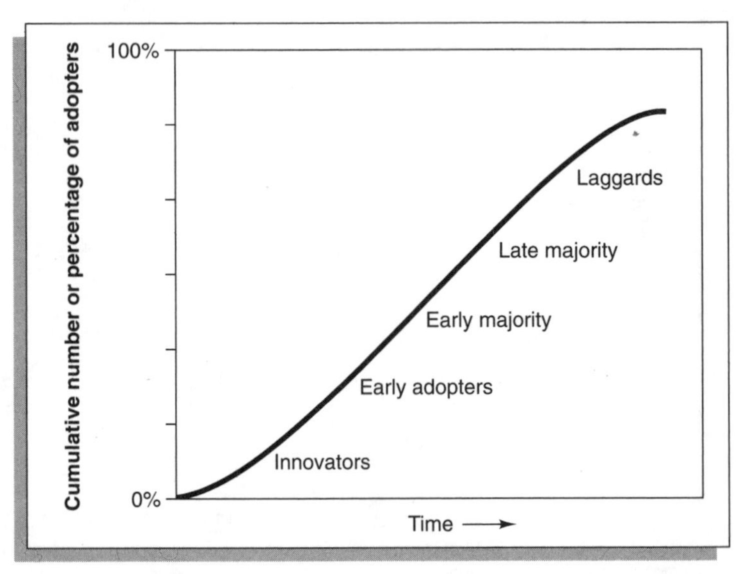

category of adopters from 'innovators' to 'early adopters' to middle majority categories to 'late adopters' [laggards] tend to be consistent across a wide range of innovations" (Green, 1989, March). Therefore, different marketing techniques can be used depending on the type of people the program planners are trying to attract to a program. For example, smoking cessation programs have been around for many years. In the last twenty-five years, the percentage of adult smokers in the United States has dropped from just over 50% to less than 26%. Thus, taking into account that there will always be some new smokers, one could safely assume that the majority of smokers in the United States today are probably not innovators, early adopters, or early majority, at least with regard to smoking cessation programs. Instead, they are likely to be those who would be much more difficult to reach—late majority and laggards. Therefore, according to the diffusion theory, the marketing techniques that were used to get people to stop smoking right after former U.S. Surgeon General Terry's report in 1964, probably would be less effective if used today.

Table 11.2 on page 190 lists some generalizations drawn from the work of various researchers on innovations and reported in Rogers (1983). These generalizations could have an application to the innovation of health promotion programs.

The application of the diffusion theory to health promotion programs is quite common now. To learn more about the concept and its application to health promotion programs, you should review some other references to see how they have applied the concept in a variety of health promotion and health education settings (Anderson & Portnoy, 1989; Basch, 1984; Basch & Sliepcevich, 1983; Dishman, 1988; Greer, 1977; Kolbe & Iverson, 1981; Monahan & Scheirer, 1988; Orlaldi, 1986; Parcel, Erickson, Lovato, Gottlieb, Brink, & Green, 1989; Steckler, Goodman, McLeroy, Davis, & Koch, 1992; USDHHS, 1987; Wolfe, Slack, & Rose-Hearn, 1993).

One of the more interesting uses of the diffusion theory has been its use to "conceptualize the transference of health promotion programs from one locale to another" (Steckler et al., 1992). Steckler et al. (1992) developed a series of six questionnaires to measure the extent to which health promotion programs are successfully disseminated. Program planners should refer to this work if they are interested in trying to measure diffusion.

THE MARKETING PROCESS AND HEALTH PROMOTION PROGRAMS

If everyone in a given population were an innovator or early adopter there would be no need for marketing plans. Since that is not the case, there is a need for program planners to understand the marketing process and be able to apply its principles.

Syre and Wilson (1990) have identified five distinct functions of the marketing process as they relate to the health care field. These include:

1. Using marketing research to determine the needs and desires of the present and prospective clients from the target population.
2. Developing a product that satisfies the needs and desires of the clients.

TABLE 11.2 Generalizations about Selected Variables and Innovation

Socioeconomic Characteristics

1. Earlier adopters have more years of education than later adopters have.
2. Earlier adopters are more likely to be literate than are later adopters.
3. Earlier adopters have higher social status than do later adopters.
4. Earlier adopters have a greater degree of upward social mobility than do later adopters.
5. Earlier adopters are more likely to have a commercial (rather than a subsistence) economic orientation than are later adopters.

Personality Variables

1. Earlier adopters have a greater ability to deal with abstractions than do later adopters.
2. Earlier adopters have a more favorable attitude toward change than later adopters have.
3. Earlier adopters are more able to cope with uncertainty and risk than are later adopters.
4. Earlier adopters have a more favorable attitude toward education than do later adopters.
5. Earlier adopters have a more favorable attitude toward science than do later adopters.
6. Earlier adopters have higher levels of achievement motivation than do later adopters.
7. Earlier adopters have higher aspirations (for education, occupations, and so on) than later adopters have.

Communication Behavior

1. Earlier adopters have more social participation than do later adopters.
2. Earlier adopters are more highly interconnected in the social system than are later adopters.
3. Earlier adopters are more cosmopolitan than later adopters are.
4. Earlier adopters have more change agent contact than do later adopters.
5. Earlier adopters have greater exposure to mass media communication channels than do later adopters.
6. Earlier adopters have greater exposure to interpersonal communication channels than later adopters have.
7. Earlier adopters have a higher degree of opinion leadership than later adopters have.
8. Earlier adopters are more likely to belong to highly interconnected systems than are later adopters.

Source: Adapted from *Diffusion of Innovations,* 3rd ed. (pp. 251–259), by E. M. Rogers, 1983, New York: Free Press.

3. Developing informative and persuasive communication flows between those offering the program and the clients.
4. Ensuring that the product is provided in the appropriate form, at the right time and place, and at the best price.
5. Keeping the clients satisfied and loyal after the exchange has taken place.

Next, we will discuss each of these functions.

Using Marketing Research to Determine Needs and Desires

Stated another way, this particular function involves conducting a marketing needs assessment. Since the needs assessment process was discussed in detail in Chapter 4, we will not repeat the discussion here. However, we would like to point out that when conducting a needs assessment, if appropriate, planners might include marketing questions. If planners collect primary data as a part of the needs assessment process, they could easily include questions that would later prove helpful in marketing the program. Examples of such questions would be:

1. What type of health promotion programs would you participate in if they were offered in the community?
2. Where would you like the program offered?
3. On what days of the week would you like the program offered?
4. At what time of the day would you like the program offered?
5. How much would you be willing to pay to attend the program?
6. What might be the best way to notify you of future programs?
7. Do you think other members of your family would like to attend these programs? If yes, which members?

Developing a Product That Satisfies the Needs and Desires of the Clients

The steps involved in developing a high-quality, marketable product (health promotion program) were discussed in earlier chapters. One key to developing a marketable product is knowing as much as possible about the target population. The more they know about a population, the better program planners can describe the population. By describing the population, planners are then able to divide the population based upon certain characteristics, a process called **audience segmentation** or **market segmentation**. Figure 11.3 on page 192 shows the concept of market segmentation, identifying black teenagers for a dietary excess intervention. "Audience segmentation has two major goals: (1) define homogeneous subgroups for message and product design purposes, and (2) identify segments that will target distribution and communication channel strategies" (Lefebvre & Flora, 1988, p. 303). Segmentation permits planners to develop programs that will meet the specific needs and desires of the target population, thus greatly increasing the chances for an exchange between the two parties. For example, there are certain employee segments that are more likely than others to read health newsletters distributed by their company (Davis, 1990; Golaszewski, Yen, Clearie, Lynch, & Vickery, 1989, September; Miller & Golaszewski, 1992). Segmentation is especially useful when trying to reach "high-risk" and "hard-to-reach" groups. This type of marketing is referred to as **target marketing** and allows program planners to strongly **position the product** (health promotion program) in the community by focusing on the needs and wants of a particular group. Figure 11.4 outlines the steps in market segmentation and target marketing.

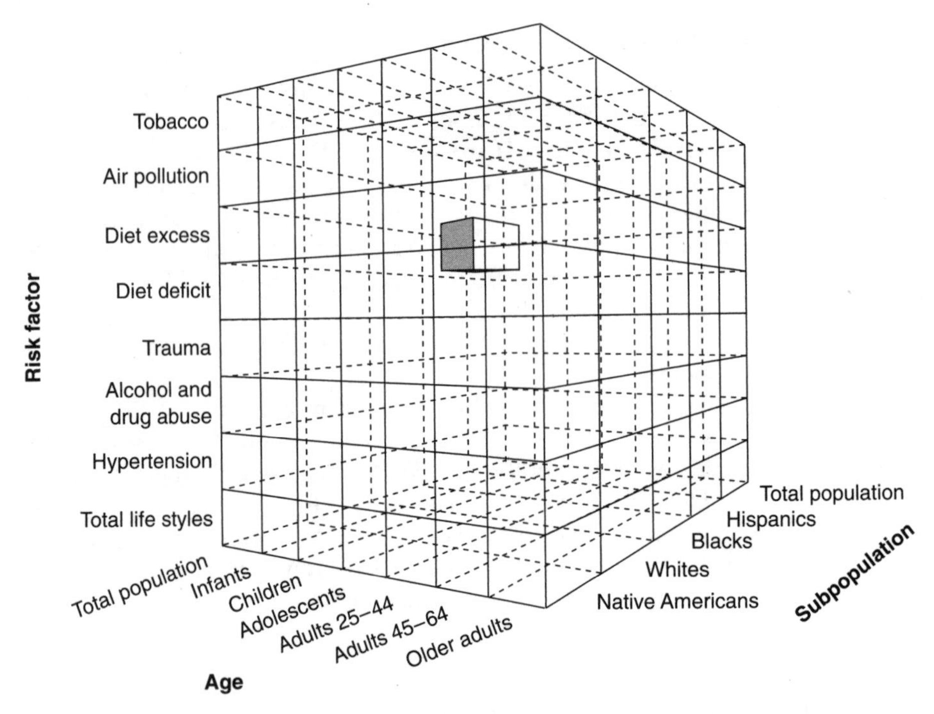

FIGURE 11.3 Example of Market Segmentation, Identifying Black Teenagers for a Dietary Excess Intervention

Source: From *Integration of Risk Factor Interventions* (p. 41), by U.S. Dept. of Health and Human Services, Public Health Service, Office of Disease Prevention and Health Promotion, 1986a, Washington, DC: U.S. Government Printing Office.

Planners can carry out the segmentation of groups of people before surveying them (a priori) by examining demographic variables, such as age, gender, income, marital status, occupation, religion, ethnicity, and socioeconomic status, or on the basis of a relevant model or theory. Or planners can conduct segmentation after surveying (a posteriori) the target population and collecting data, such as psychographics (attitudes, values, and lifestyle), risk factors, health history, or personal health behaviors. For example, the National Cancer Institute (NCI) used attitudes and lifestyle to identify different segments of the target population for communications about cancer. They found that one group, which they called the naive optimists, were generally optimistic, self-involved, and complacent about their health. They did not make any effort to stay healthy or seek health information and did not worry about their health. This group of people was young with high incomes and made up about 12% of the population (Freimuth & Mettger, 1990). Segmentation is thus most helpful in developing a market plan for this group of people.

Kotler and Clarke (1987, p. 236) have indicated that "there is no one, or right, way to segment a market." Demographic segmentation has been the most common

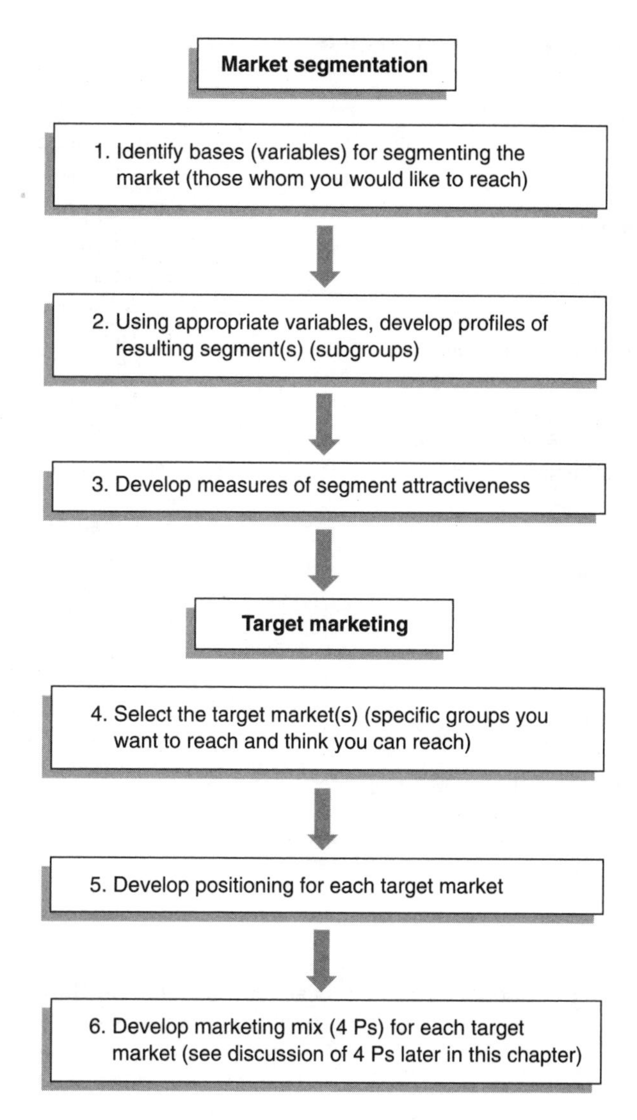

FIGURE 11.4 Steps in Segmenting and Targeting the Market

Source: Adapted from *Strategic Marketing for Nonprofit Organizations*, 4th ed. (p. 168), by P. Kotler & A. R. Andreasen, 1991, Englewood Cliffs, NJ: Prentice-Hall. Reprinted by permission of Prentice-Hall, Inc., Englewood Cliffs, NJ 07632.

means of segmentation in commercial marketing (Hertoz, Finnegan, Rooney, Viswanath, & Potter, 1993). However, it may not be the most efficient for social marketing. Program planners will need to experiment with the various variables to determine what works best for them. Table 11.3 includes many of the major seg-

TABLE 11.3 Segmentation and Variables

1. Geographic segmentation
   a. Nations
   b. States
   c. Regions
   d. Service areas
   e. Counties
   f. Cities, towns, villages
   g. Neighborhoods
2. Demographic segmentation
   a. Age
   b. Stage of life cycle
   c. Disease or diagnostic category
      - Health history
      - Risk factors
   d. Gender
   e. Health insurance
   f. Income
   g. Education
   h. Religion
   i. Race/ethnicity
3. Psychographic segmentation
   a. Social class
      - Upper upper (less than 1% of population)
      - Lower upper (2%)
      - Upper middle (12%)
      - Lower middle (30%)
      - Upper lower (35%)
      - Lower lower (20%)
   b. Lifestyle
   c. Attitudes
   d. Values
   e. Personality
      - Self-image
      - Self-concept
4. Behavioristic segmentation
   a. Purchase occasion
   b. Benefits sought
   c. User status
   d. Usage rate
   e. Loyalty status
   f. Stages of buyer readiness
   g. Health behavior
5. Multivariable segmentation (i.e., males age 42 living in Indiana)
6. Constructs of behavior theories and models

menting variables identified by several different authors (Hertoz et al., 1993; Kotler & Clark, 1987; Romer & Kim, 1995; Williams & Flora, 1995).

Developing Informative and Persuasive Communication Flows and Ensuring That the Product Is Provided in an Appropriate Manner

The third and fourth marketing functions outlined by Syre and Wilson (1990) can best be explained by McCarthy's (1978) four Ps—product, price, placement, and promotion. The particular blend of these four marketing variables that planners use to achieve their objective(s) in the target market is referred to as the **marketing mix** (Kotler & Andreasen, 1991; Kotler & Clarke, 1987; Wilson & Olds, 1991).

Product

Product refers to the actual program you are planning: The program is your product. A goal for all planners is to develop the best product possible with the resources available.

Price

"Prices can be thought of in a variety of ways; in addition to economic reasons, there are social, behavioral, psychological, temporal, structural, geographic, and physical reasons for exchanging or not exchanging" (Lefebvre & Flora, 1988, p. 307). From an economic standpoint, **price** refers to charging the appropriate amount for the product (program) being provided. As was mentioned in Chapter 10, there are many ways to finance a program. If you are "selling" participation in the program, then the price must match the participants' ability to pay. When considering the amount to be charged for a product (program), planners should determine the following:

1. Who are the clients?
2. What is their ability to pay?
3. Are copayers involved?
4. Is the program covered under an insurance program?
5. What is the mission of the planner's agency?
6. What are competitors charging?
7. What is the demand for the program?

The price of a program and who pays for it help determine how a program should be marketed. Whether or not the program is intended to make a profit will have a great impact on the price. Does the program have to make money? Break even? Or can it lose money? It is a real art not to overprice or underprice the program. Demand and location (placement) will also influence price. If a program is in high demand, obviously the price can be higher than if it is not. For example, a stress management program in a large metropolitan area may be able to command a higher price than one located in a small rural area.

Not only do the demand and the location influence the amount one might charge for a program, but so can the psychological mindset of those in the target population. There are some individuals who would not participate in a free or inexpensive program because "how could such a program be any good?" Some people believe you have to put out a lot of money to get anything of worth. Also, sometimes when programs are offered free of charge, people may be less likely to attend regularly because they have not "invested" financially in the program. On the other hand, there are some people, who if given the choice of a free program versus one with a cost, will always take the free program even if they are financially able to pay. Being able to segment the target population with regard to these economic issues can help in setting the right price.

In addition to the economic price of a program, there are also noneconomic prices, such as physical and social prices. A physical price is one that physically hurts the participant, while a social price is one that affects the participant in a social setting. Bensley (1989, p. 20) gives some examples of physical and social prices by stating that "sacrifice may include physical withdrawal symptoms, or even a social price which is particularly high among young people when they resist the pressures from their peer group."

Placement

The third P of marketing is **placement**, which can be thought of as distribution. Where is the best place to offer the program? How large is the service area? How many distribution points should there be? A good example of the importance of placement is worksite health promotion programs. The advantages of providing health promotion programs in this setting include:

1. Access to a large portion of the adult population.
2. An effective internal communication channel to employees.
3. Stable social support.
4. Opportunity to create environments that support healthy behaviors.
5. Convenient access for employees (O'Donnell, 1992; O'Donnell & Ainsworth, 1984; Sciacca et al., 1993; Sloan, Gruman, & Allegrante, 1987).

In placing a program, it is also important to avoid areas where people do not normally go or places where they would not feel comfortable or safe.

Two other good examples concerning program placement can be found in the literature. Scandrett (1994) presents a case for the church as a place to deliver programs in the Black community, and Sutherland, Harris, Kissinger, Barber, and Lewis (1994) suggest the beauty shop as a place to deliver health information.

The timing of a program is closely associated with its placement. When is the program best offered? If a worksite program was offered in the evenings, so that the workers had to return to the worksite after dinner, that probably would not be much different from driving across town from work to attend a program. Offering a program right after a shift or on a lunch hour would be much more appealing to most workers. Obviously, planners should be concerned about placing their program in a desirable locale (where they are wanted and needed) at the best possible time.

Promotion

The fourth P of marketing is **promotion**. This deals with both the oral and written communication that program planners use to attract those in the target population to become involved in a program. This means taking the necessary steps to make people aware that you have a product (program) in which they would be interested. Such communication should be both informative and persuasive. The choice of a title for a program is an important element in its promotion, since the title can make a difference in whether or not someone from the target population will be interested in a program. Creating a title is part of the marketing process used to develop informative and persuasive communication flows between the providers of a program and those in the target population. More likely than not, a program title will be the first contact that someone in the target population will have with the product (health promotion program). A title to a program is analogous to the headline of a newspaper article. When most of us read a newspaper, we do not read every article; rather, we skim the headlines of the articles and then read those articles that appeal to us. It is the headlines that grab our attention. The same concept applies in advertising a product. "A good headline ought to compel members of the target audience to read the rest of the message" (Granat, 1994, p. 58). Or, in the case of a health promotion program, create enough interest that those in the target audience want to find out more about the program. Which of these program titles do you think would attract more attention, "Alcohol and You" or "Not Knowing Your Company's Drug Policy Can Cost You Your Job"?

In addition to creative titles, acronyms are useful in bringing attention to a program. For example, Foldcraft, a company in Minnesota, uses the acronym H.E.A.L.T.H. as the name of its health program. It stands for "Hey everyone always learns the hardway." Program titles and acronyms seem to be limited only by the planners' creativity. See Table 11.4 on page 198 for additional examples of program titles and acronyms.

Promotion can be thought of as advertising the program. As with product development, planners should consider the segmentation of the target population when promoting the program. For example, advertising for a program to reach high-risk new mothers would be very different from that for one intended for all new mothers. Depending on the type of program planned and the setting for the program, the techniques of advertising the program will vary. If the program is being promoted through **internal advertising**—that is within an organization, say for the employees of a business or for the faculty and staff of a school—promotion might include such elements as posters, bulletin boards, brochures, displays, table tents, newsletters, envelope stuffers, and announcements made through groups that represent the target population, such as unions or professional organizations. If the program is being promoted through **external advertising**—that is, not within an organization but in a community at large—some of the same techniques can be used. Posters, bulletin boards, brochures, and displays are also useful when trying to attract members of a larger community. Other useful techniques for external advertising might include:

1. Advertising through the mass media (newspapers, television, and radio).
2. Direct contact with specific groups that might be at high risk and in need of the programs (contacting recent heart attack patients about a program on the need to eat in a "heart healthy" way).
3. Contact with specific professionals who would be in a position to make referrals to your program.

TABLE 11.4 Example Program Names and Acronyms

Title (topic)	Acronym (if appropriate)	Organization/Company
Freedom from Smoking (smoking)		American Lung Association
FreshStart (smoking)		American Cancer Society
Heart at Work (cardiovascular health)		American Heart Association
Hey everyone always learns the hardway	H.E.A.L.T.H.	Foldcraft (Minnesota)
Live for Life (general health)		Johnson & Johnson
Live Well—Be Well (general health)		Quaker Oats
Time Out for Life (general health)		Colonial Life and Accident Insurance Company
Total Life Concept (general health)	TLC	AT&T
United Way at Work (general health)		United Way
Lifestyle Improvements for Everyone (general health)	LIFE	Physicians' Health Plan (Ft. Wayne, IN)
Life after Work Program (general health)		Physicians' Health Plan (Ft. Wayne, IN)
Start Smart (prenatal care)		Key Care Health Resources (Indianapolis, IN)
StayWell (general health)		Control Data
Work Well (general health)		Washtenaw County (MI) government

Of these techniques, the first, advertising through the mass media, requires a special set of skills in order to be used effectively. High on the list of these skills is the ability to interact with media representatives (newspaper reporters and television or radio journalists, and advertising staff). Before a program is ready to be marketed, planners should meet with the advertising staff, the health editor and/or writers, and the health/consumer reporters. These people can provide insight into the type of advertising to be used. They know what attracts their readers, listeners, and watchers to an advertisement. They can also provide additional insight into how to prepare news releases and stage newsworthy activities that can lead to stories and articles in the media. Such stories can be thought of as free advertising, since the space or time is not paid for.

Other techniques that can be useful in promoting a program either internally or externally are:

1. Providing incentives for people to become involved, such as free tee shirts, extra vacation time, a free introductory offer, free health appraisal, flex time, or money.
2. Gaining the endorsement of key people in an organization (those who are admired, a supervisor or the boss) or a famous person or someone well known in the community.
3. Distributing mailbox or door-to-door stuffers.
4. Making a personal contact with an individual, such as a friend or a superior or boss who is already involved.
5. Setting up a mentoring program where someone already in the program works with a beginner.
6. A special kick-off, countdown, ribbon-cutting, or health party to get a program started.

Keeping the Clients Satisfied and Loyal

Keeping clients satisfied and loyal involves two key concepts. The first is that satisfied and loyal clients can add much to future marketing efforts by providing word-of-mouth advertising. They can provide a lot of favorable advertising, free of charge. Second, and more important, is the value of keeping the target population involved in the health-enhancing behavior that they began as a result of being involved in the health promotion program. Becoming involved in a program is important, but maintaining a health-enhancing behavior is a more important objective. There is strong evidence that people are not very likely to maintain health behavior change over a long period of time. The problem of recidivism to past behaviors, such as substance abuse, has been known for quite a while (Hunt, Barnett, & Branch, 1971). More recently, however, researchers have warned health education and health promotion program planners of recidivism and dropout problems associated with exercise (Dishman, Sallis, & Orenstein, 1985; Horne, 1975), weight loss (Stunkard & Braunwell, 1980), and smoking cessation (Leventhal & Cleary, 1980; Marlatt & Gordon, 1980). (A detailed discussion of relapse can be found in Chapter 7.)

Why do people behave the way they do? Why do some people begin and continue with health promotion programs, whereas others make a strong start but drop out, and still others never begin? Research has shown that the reasons are many and varied. Participation in health promotion programs may be influenced by a variety of factors, including demographic, behavioral, and psychosocial variables, and program structure. "Lack of time, failure to recognize significance of participation, inconvenience to the participant, failure to achieve personal goals, and lack of enjoyment of participation are some of the reasons why individuals drop out of wellness [health promotion] programs" (Bensley, 1991, p. 89). Proper motivation is one way of preventing dropouts.

Motivation

A key element for initial involvement and continued participation in a health promotion program seems to be motivation, which has been described as a concept that is both simple and complex. "The concept of motivation . . . is simple because the behavior of individuals is goal-directed and either externally or internally induced. It is complex because the mechanism which induces behavior consists of the individual's needs, wants, and desires and these are shaped, affected, and satisfied in many different ways" (Rakich, Longest, & O'Donovan, 1977, p. 262). Feldman (1983) has suggested a variety of ways in which participants may be motivated to adopt a new health behavior. These means are seldom independent of each other, but from a planning standpoint they are usually viewed separately. In our opinion, the key to motivation is matching the means of motivating with those things that seem to reinforce the individual program participants. What motivates one individual may not be the least bit motivating to another individual, and vice versa.

Two approaches are commonly used. The first is to include questions about motivation as part of any needs assessment conducted in program planning. For example, if the planners are surveying a target population regarding their needs, they could include questions on reinforcers, such as "What incentives would entice you to participate in the exercise program?" or "What would it take to get you to participate in this program?" or "What would it take to keep you involved in a program?" The responses to these questions should provide some direction concerning the type of reinforcers that would be most useful for the target audience. The second is the "shotgun" approach based upon a planner's previous experience or the experience reported by others. Using the "shotgun" approach, a program planner would offer a variety of reinforcers to meet the needs of a large percentage of the program's target population. We recommend the former approach in most cases, but sometimes motivation is not considered when a needs assessment is completed. In such a case, the latter approach is used. The remaining portions of this chapter provide ideas for motivating program participants.

Using Contracts to Motivate. A contract is an agreement between two or more parties that outlines the future behavior of those parties. Contracts are a common part of everyday living. We enter into contracts when we sign a lease for an apartment or a residence hall agreement, take out an insurance policy, borrow money, or buy something over a period of time. The same concept can be applied to getting and keeping people motivated in health promotion programs. Each program participant would enter into a contract with another person (the program facilitator, a significant other, or a fellow participant) and then work toward an objective or agreement specified in the contract. The contract would also specify contingencies—that is, what happens as a result of the contract's either being met or not being met.

For an exercise program, this system might work as follows. The program participant and program facilitator would draw up a contract based upon the participant's present status in the program (exercising for twenty minutes once a week) and upon what would be a reasonable goal for the near future—say, eight weeks.

Thus the contract might state that the participant will exercise for twenty minutes twice a week for the first week, twenty minutes three times a week for the second week, and so forth, thus building up gradually to the final goal of exercising for fifty minutes three or four times a week at the end of eight weeks. The outcome should focus on a behavior that can be maintained at the end of the contract period. For a weight loss program, the goal might be written as eliminating snacking in the evening, increasing fruits and vegetables in the diet to five servings per day, and walking for twenty minutes three times a week. These are behaviors that can reasonably be maintained after the weight loss.

The parties to the contract then decide upon what the contingencies will be. Thus the participant might offer to make a contribution to some local charity or state that she will continue in the program for another eight weeks if she does not meet the contract goal. The facilitator might promise the participant a program tee shirt if she fulfills the contract during the specified eight-week period. Other ideas for contingencies might include granting a kickback on fees for completing a certain percentage of the classes, or earning points towards products or services. No matter what the contingencies are, it seems to help if the contract is completed in writing. A sample contract is presented in Appendix I.

Using Social Support to Motivate. It has long been recognized that whatever the behavior may be, it is almost always easier to do if people have the support of those around them. Long-standing examples of the concept of **social support** in the area of health education and health promotion are programs like Weight Watchers and Alcoholics Anonymous. They are based upon the support of others who are experiencing the same behavior change. One of the key reasons why worksite health promotion programs are so effective is that the working environment lends itself to social support. Being around other individuals who are engaging in the same behavior change provides a good support system.

Another means of helping program participants develop the necessary support system might be to pair them with other participants in a "buddy" arrangement. People find it harder to let others down than to disappoint themselves. Another technique that is being used increasingly is to incorporate the help of family members or significant others to provide the needed motivation. It is easier for someone to quit smoking if all members in the household try quitting at the same time, than to "go it alone" while others in the household continue to smoke.

Using Media to Motivate. Another technique for keeping people motivated to continue in a health promotion program is to recognize them publicly through some medium available to those in the program. Examples of such media include organization newsletters or newspapers, community newspapers, local television and radio stations, bulletin boards at the location where the program is being offered or public bulletin boards elsewhere, and letters sent to the significant others of the participants (family members, job superiors, and so forth) noting the participants' progress in the program.

It is important for program planners to exercise caution when recognizing people through the different types of media. Not everyone likes to see their name publicized. Before you publicly acknowledge individual participants, make sure they do not mind if you do so.

Using Incentives to Motivate. In Chapter 8, **incentives** were discussed as an intervention strategy, but they are also useful in keeping people involved in programs (Jason, Jayaraj, Blitz, Michaels, & Klett, 1990). Dunbar, Marshall, and Howell (1979) state that reinforcement may be any consequence that would increase the probability of a behavior's being repeated. Wilson (1990, p. 33) defined incentive as "some reward for achieving a level of performance or goal." It has been reported (Frederiksen, 1984) that incentives seem to be most effective if they are provided in small quantities, are frequent in nature, are tailored to those in the target population, address behaviors over which the individual has control, and do not conflict with any organizational policies.

To give program planners some ideas for appropriate incentives, we offer the following list. The ideas included in it have been reported in the literature; shared with us by current practitioners or students; or created by McKenzie, Luebke, and Romas (1992). No attempt has been made to identify which incentives would be best used to entice people to enroll in a program, and which ones would be best to keep people participating after they are enrolled. Thus the list could be used to encourage individuals to start a program, to induce them to continue participating in a program, or to help them meet an individual, group, or program goal. The incentives listed have been categorized into two types of reinforcers defined by Feldman (1983)—social reinforcers and material reinforcers—and a third category of miscellaneous reinforcers.

I. Social reinforcers (Feldman, 1983; Shepard, 1985)
   1. Special attention or recognition from instructors, peers, classmates, coworkers, or chief executive officers
   2. Praise/verbal reinforcement
   3. Public and other recognition (name in newsletter, name on bulletin board)
   4. Encouragement
   5. Friendship
   6. Inclusion of family members in the program
   7. Personal letter to those reaching goals (Bensley, 1991)

II. Material reinforcers
   1. Inexpensive "token" incentives
      a. Tee shirts, hats, caps, visors, warm-up jackets, calendars, key chains, flashlights, pens, windshield scrapers, wallets, tape measures, vacuum bottles, mugs, home fire extinguishers, smoke de-

tectors, and auto safety kits (Cinelli, Rose-Colley, & Hayes, 1988; Kendall, 1984)

b. Certificates
c. Pins, buttons, patches, decals that can be worn, and plaques or markers that can be displayed in the work area
d. Towels, lockers
e. Preferred or free parking

2. Program cost sharing between employer and employee
   a. Cost of registering for a program (Pollock, Foster, Salisburg, & Smith, 1982)
   b. Membership at a fitness center/club
   c. Sliding-scale fee based upon the ability to pay
   d. Refund of part or all of the program fee upon participant's completion
3. Health insurance
   a. Sharing between employer and employee of the money saved on health insurance from one year to the next (Toufexis, 1985)
   b. Alteration of the fringe benefit package to reward good health practices
   c. Employer picking up more of the insurance costs to reward good health practices (Toufexis, 1985)
   d. Provision of a fund for each employee to pay for the person's health care costs during the year, with any unused money from this account given to the employee at the end of the year (Hosokawa, 1984; Toufexis,1985)
   e. Lower premiums for employees with fewer health risks (non-smoker or exerciser) (Hosokawa, 1984)
4. Monetary items
   a. Tokens, Monopoly-style dollars, stamps, coupons, or points that are redeemable at a company store, at retail stores, or for catalog shopping for prizes or merchandise (Kendall, 1984; Piniat, 1984; Toufexis, 1985)
   b. Drawings, lotteries, and raffles open to those who have participated or met a goal (Cinelli et al., 1988; Toufexis, 1985; Health Insurance Association of America, 1983)
   c. Bonus, extra pay, or just plain pay for completion of contract, participation, not smoking on the job, or quitting (DiBlase, 1985; Toufexis, 1985)
   d. Financial rewards for both individuals and groups who have fewer and/or no work accidents during the year (DiBlase, 1985)
   e. "Well pay" for unused sick days (DiBlase, 1985)
   f. Gift certificates, from a small one such as a free ice cream cone to something of greater value, such as a U.S. savings bond (Kendall, 1984)

5. Work hours
   a. Flex time (flexible work hours) in order to participate
   b. Released time to participate
   c. Time off (Cinelli et al., 1988)
6. Contracts
   a. Contract (competition) with a buddy
   b. Contract with instructor to reach a specific goal, with a material incentive provided by instructor
   c. Forfeiture of money or time to charity for not fulfilling a contract (Bloomquist, 1981)
   d. Contract with instructor in which money is withheld (via payroll deduction) while the person is enrolled in the program, so that if goal is met, the money is refunded; if not, it is forfeited (Bensley, 1991; Forster, Jeffery, Sullivan, & Snell, 1985)

III. Miscellaneous
1. Special medical examinations and screenings for those who participate
2. Special events, such as contests or luncheons (Kendall, 1984; Patton et al., 1986)
3. Providing special "space" like a table in the lunch room for those on a special diet (Bensley, 1991)

Finally, we offer this advice for program planners who choose to use incentives:

1. Make sure everyone can receive one, whatever the incentive may be (Kendall, 1984).
2. Make the incentives useful and meaningful (Kendall, 1984).
3. Ensure that the ground rules are fair, understandable, and followed by everyone (Kendall, 1984).
4. Make a big deal of awarding the incentive.
5. Use incentives that are consistent with health promotion philosophies. For example, avoid incentives of alcoholic beverages, high-fat or high-sugar foods, or other mixed-message prizes.

Competition as a Means of Motivating. Wilson (1990, p. 33) has reported that competitions have been a useful means of "introducing and promoting health promotion programs and achieving significant initial participation rates." A *competition* can be described as a contest between two teams (groups) or individuals in which the object is to try to outperform the other competitor. In a health promotion context, this could mean competing to lose the most pounds, smoke fewer cigarettes, walk the most miles, swim the most laps, or plan the most nutritious meals. Competitions are a good method of introducing a health promotion program, but they are probably not useful as an ongoing recruitment tool (Wilson, 1990).

Final Comment on Marketing

Planners who intend to use a canned program should be sure to ask the vendor if there is a marketing plan that goes along with the program. The good programs will usually include some useful marketing strategies, if not an entire plan. A word of caution about the marketing materials: Like the canned programs themselves, they are usually aimed at a general target population, not one that has been segmented. Therefore, they may have to be adapted to meet local needs.

SUMMARY

An important aspect of any health promotion program is being able to attract participants initially and to keep them involved once they have begun the program. An understanding of the diffusion theory is helpful in determining strategies for marketing a program. The actual marketing mix for a program should take into account the four Ps of marketing: product, price, placement, and promotion. Special attention should be given to segmenting the target population. Once people are enrolled in a program, they need to be motivated to remain involved. Strategies of contracts, social support, media recognition, incentives, and competition can be most helpful in motivating people to continue their participation in a program.

QUESTIONS

1. Define the following terms: *market, marketing, social marketing, target marketing.*
2. What is the relationship between marketing and needs assessment?
3. How does the diffusion theory relate to marketing a program?
4. What are the five different groups of people described in the diffusion theory? When would each group most likely join a health promotion program?
5. What is the difference between marketing a tangible product and an intangible product?
6. What are the four Ps of marketing? Explain each one.
7. What is meant by *marketing mix?*
8. What are five techniques for motivating people to stay involved in a health promotion program?

ACTIVITIES

1. Respond to the following statements/questions with regard to a program you are planning.
   a. Describe your product.
   b. Describe your segmented population.

   c. How much will you charge for the program? Explain the rationale on which you based your decision. What other "prices" do you see for this program?
   d. Where will you place your program (location, days, and time)? Why are you placing it this way?
   e. How will you promote your program? How, when, where will you advertise?
2. Create a marketing plan for a health promotion program you are developing or another program described by your professor. Use the outline below [a modification of the work of Kotler and Clarke (1987) and Syre and Wilson (1990)] for presenting your plan.
   I. Executive summary or abstract of the plan (written as a paragraph)
      A. Product (program) to be offered (describes the program and who it is for)
      B. Summary of main marketing goals (what will be accomplished by marketing the program)
      C. Summary of recommendations of marketing plan (how the program will be marketed)
      D. Budget summary (including both expected income and expenses)
   II. Situational analysis
      A. Needs and desires assessment (including marketing questions: What did you find to be the needs and desires of the target group? What questions did you use to find this out?)
      B. Program strengths and weaknesses
      C. Competition from other programs (including their strengths and weaknesses: What other programs will you be competing against for those in the target group? What are their strengths and weaknesses?)
   III. Marketing objectives
      A. Target market (Whom do you hope to reach?)
      B. Market share expected (What percentage of the market do you want to use your product?)
      C. Outcomes expected from the program (What will happen because of the marketing process?)
   IV. Marketing strategies/mix
      A. Price (What must those in the market give up to be involved in your program? Consider economic, physical, and social prices.)
      B. Placement (Where will the program be offered?)
      C. Promotion (communication channels)
         1. Oral (electronic media, word of mouth)
         2. Written

V. Time line (When and in what sequence will the marketing events take place?)
VI. Exhibits supporting the plan (brochures, flyers, table tents, PSAs, and ads)

3. Create a one-page advertisement that could be used as a table tent, a newspaper ad, or a poster for your program.
4. Give an example of how you could use each of the four methods described in the chapter for motivating program participants to stay in a program.

12

Implementation: Strategies and Associated Concerns

After reading this chapter and answering the questions at the end, you should be able to:

- Define *implementation.*
- Identify several different strategies for implementing health promotion programs.
- List the concerns that need to be addressed before implementation can take place.

Key Terms

acts
beneficence
commission
implementation
informed consent
liability
logistics
nonmaleficence
omission
phased in
pilot testing
prudent

Once a program has been planned and marketed, it must then be implemented. Ross and Mico (1980, p. 225) have stated that **implementation** "consists of initiating the activity, providing assistance to it and to its participants, problem-solving issues that may arise, and reporting on progress." To accomplish all of this, program planners must select the most appropriate implementation strategy and see that any special concerns associated with implementation are handled properly.

STRATEGIES FOR IMPLEMENTATION

Planners decide on the best way to implement the program they have planned based upon the resources available and the setting for which the program is intended. Two models for implementing a program are presented here. The first combines some of our ideas with those of Parkinson and Associates (1982). The second model was developed by Borg and Gall (1989) for research and development projects. Both models are flexible and can be modified to meet the circumstances of different programs.

First Implementation Model

Parkinson and Associates (1982) have suggested three major ways of implementing a program: by using a piloting process; by phasing it in, in small segments; or by initiating the total program all at once. We think these three strategies are best explained by using an inverted triangle, as shown in Figure 12.1. The triangle rep-

FIGURE 12.1 Implementation Strategies

Advantages	Strategy	Disadvantages
• More people involved • Evaluation more meaningful with larger group	**Total Program**	• Big commitment • No chance to test program
• Easier to cope with workload • Gradual investment	**Phased-in**	• Fewer people involved
• Opportunity to test program • Close control of program	**Pilot**	• Very few involved • Not meeting all needs • Hard to generalize about results

resents the number of people from the target population who would be involved in the program based upon the implementation strategy chosen. The wider portion of the triangle at the top would indicate offering the program to a larger number of people than is represented by the point of the triangle at the bottom.

We see these three different implementation strategies as an implementation hierarchy. It is our opinion that all programs should go through all three of the strategies, starting with piloting, then phasing in, and finally implementing the total program.

Pilot Testing

Pilot testing (or piloting or field testing) the program is a crucial step. Even though planners work hard to bring a program to the point of implementation, it is important to try to identify any problems with the program that might exist. Pilot testing allows planners to work out any bugs before the program is offered to a larger segment of the target population, and also to validate the work that has been completed up to this point. For the most meaningful results, a newly developed program should be piloted in a similar setting and with people like those who are eventually to use the program. Use of any other group may fail to identify problems or concerns that would be specific to the target population. As an example of the piloting process, take the case of a hospital developing a worksite health promotion program. It would be best if the program was piloted on a worksite group before it was marketed to worksites in the community. The hospital could look for a company that might want to serve as a pilot group, or it might use its own employees.

As part of piloting the program, planners should check to make sure that:

1. The intervention activities work as planned.
2. Adequate program logistics have been worked out.
3. The program participants are asked to evaluate the program.

It is important to have the program participants critique such aspects of the program as content, approaches used, instructor's effectiveness, space, accommodations, and other resources used. Such feedback will give planners insight into how to revise the program. If many changes are made in the program as a result of piloting, planners may want to pilot it again before moving ahead. This evaluation process during the piloting phase is part of process or formative evaluations and will be discussed further in Chapter 13.

Phasing In

Once a program has been piloted and revised, we believe the program should be **phased in** rather than implemented in its entirety. This is especially true when there is a very large target population. Phasing in allows the planners to have more control over the program and helps to protect planners and facilitators from getting in over their heads.

There are several ways in which to phase in a program:

1. By different program offerings.
2. By a limit on the number of participants.
3. By choice of location.
4. By participant ability.

Say a comprehensive health promotion program was being planned for Blue Earth County, Minnesota. To phase in the program by different offerings, planners might offer stress management classes the first six months. During the next six-month period, they could again offer stress management but also add smoking cessation programs. This process would continue until all offerings are included.

If the program was to be phased in by limiting the number of participants, planners might limit the first month's enrollment to twenty-five participants, expand it to thirty-five the second month, to forty-five the third month, and so on until all who wanted to participate were included. To phase in the program by location, it might initially be offered only to those living in the southwest portion of the county. The second year, it might expand to include those in the southeast, and continue in the same manner until all were included. A program planned for a college town might be offered first on campus, then off campus to the general public. A program phased in by participant ability might start with a beginning group of exercisers, then add an intermediate group, and finally include an advanced group.

Total Implementation

We believe that implementing the total program all at once is the wrong way to proceed. It is our opinion that planners should work toward total implementation through the piloting and phasing-in processes. The only exception to this might be "one-shot" programs, such as programs designed around a single lecture. Another possible exception would be screening programs, but even then piloting would probably help.

Second Implementation Model (Borg and Gall)

The second model for implementation provides program planners with another way of approaching implementation. Borg and Gall (1989) have presented a ten-step research and development cycle, of which the last seven steps can be used as an implementation model for health promotion programs. Table 12.1 lists the major steps in the model.

The implementation portion of the model begins with the fourth step in the process—the preliminary field test. This step is performed "to obtain an initial qualitative evaluation" (Borg & Gall, 1989, p. 790). The preliminary test would include implementation of the program as it has been developed to date, followed by the collection of feedback from both those who receive the program (target population) and those who facilitate it. These individuals would be asked questions like,

TABLE 12.1 Major Steps of Borg and Gall's Research and Development Cycle Applied to Creating a Health Promotion Program

1. Research and information collecting—includes needs assessment, review of the literature, small-scale research studies, and preparation of report on the state of the art.
2. Planning—includes defining skills to be learned, stating and sequencing the objectives, identifying learning activities, and small-scale feasibility testing.
3. Development of preliminary form of program—includes preparation of instructional materials, procedures, and evaluation instruments.
4. Preliminary field testing—program given to just a few individuals from the target population. Interview, observational, and questionnaire data collected and analyzed.
5. Main program revision—based on results of preliminary field test.
6. Main field testing—program given to approximately twice as many as in preliminary field test. Pre- and postprogram quantitative data on participants collected; results examined with respect to program objectives and compared to control/comparison group, when possible.
7. Operational program revision—based on results of the main field test.
8. Operational field testing—program given to approximately twice as many as in main field test. Interview, observational, and questionnaire data collected and analyzed.
9. Final program revision—based on results of the operational field test.
10. Dissemination and implementation—program shared with others and implemented where appropriate.

Source: Adapted from *Educational Research: An Introduction,* 5th ed. (pp. 784–785), by W. R. Borg and M. D. Gall, 1989, New York: Longman.

"What do you like about the program? What do you dislike? If given a chance to do so, what would you change about the program?" Only a very small number from the target population would participate in this test. The fifth step deals with the revision of the program based on information gained from the preliminary testing. All aspects of the program would be reviewed and revised as appropriate. The revised program would then be tested again with a slightly larger group from the target population. This second testing of the program makes up step 6 and is called the main field test. The purpose of the main field test is to determine whether the program under development meets the program objectives set forth in the earlier stages of planning. If it was found that the program did not meet the objectives, it would be revised accordingly and the main field test would be repeated. In practice, if the program did not meet the objectives during this second main field test, it would more than likely be abandoned. However, if it met the objectives, minor adjustments would be made (step 7), and the program would be readied for the eighth step—operational field testing (Borg & Gall, 1989). The operational field test should very much resemble the final implementation. One could think of this step as the final "dress rehearsal."

The purpose of the first eight steps is to determine whether the program is fully ready for implementation without the presence of the program planner. In order to be fully ready for use, the program must be completely and thoroughly tested in every respect. In step 9, the final program is revised based on the operational test. The tenth step would include dissemination and final implementation. This includes distributing the program to those who are to use it and helping them to use it properly (Borg & Gall, 1989).

Remember, Borg and Gall's model was originally presented as a research and development cycle, not as an implementation model. We have found, however, that the last seven steps of the cycle make up a well-conceived and thorough implementation model. Some might say this model is too thorough because it requires so much testing before implementation and does not take into account the frequent lack of time and money for program development. We suggest, however, that planners should modify the model as needed to meet specific needs and available resources.

First Day of Implementation

No matter what implementation model or strategy the planners choose, there will be a "first day" for the program. The first day of the program is just an extension of the fourth P of marketing, promotion (see Chapter 11). The purpose of promotion is to make the target population aware of the health concern that is the focus of the program. This leads to the initiation of the program. The first day of the program might include some special event, such as a ribbon cutting, appearance by a celebrity, or some other event that starts off the program on a positive note. Celebrities need not be individuals with national or international recognition, but may be individuals like the chief executive officer (CEO) of the company, a foreman, a visible person in the community (i.e., the mayor or a coach), or a common person who has been affected by the health problem. Consideration should be given to obtaining news coverage (print and/or broadcast) for the first day to further publicize the program.

Dealing with Problems

With the program up and running, the task of the planners is to deal with problems that might arise and to do so in a constructive manner (Ross & Mico, 1980). Even if a program has been piloted, problems can still arise. The problems that could be encountered can range from petty concerns to matters of life and death. Problems might involve **logistics** (room size, meeting time, or room temperature), participant dissatisfaction, or a personal or medical emergency. Whatever the problem, it should be worked out as much as possible to the satisfaction of all concerned. If there is a question of whether to accommodate a program participant or the program personnel, 99% of the time the participants should be satisfied. They are the life blood of all programs. As a part of this implementation step, it might be a good idea to conduct a one-month evaluation asking questions similar to the ones asked in the piloting evaluation.

FIGURE 12.2 Sample Planning and Implementation Timetable

Tasks Year 1	Months											
	J	F	M	A	M	J	J	A	S	O	N	D
Develop program rationale	✓	✓										
Conduct needs assessment			✓									
Develop goals and objectives				✓								
Create intervention					✓							
Conduct formative evaluation						✓						
Assemble necessary resources						✓						
Market program						✓	✓					
Pilot test program								✓				
Refine program									✓			
Phase in program #1										✓		
Phase in program #2											✓	
Phase in program #3												✓

Tasks Year 2	Months											
	J	F	M	A	M	J	J	A	S	O	N	D
Phase in program #4	✓											
Total implementation		✓	✓	✓	✓	✓	✓	✓	✓	✓	✓	✓
Summative evaluation			✓									
Prepare evaluation report				✓								
Distribute report					✓							
Continue with follow-up for long-term evaluation						✓	✓	✓	✓	✓	✓	✓

Reporting and Documenting

Planners need to give attention to reporting or documenting the ongoing progress of the program to interested others (Ross & Mico, 1980). Planners should keep others informed about the progress of the program for several different reasons, including: (1) accountability; (2) public relations; (3) motivation of present participants; and (4) recruitment of new participants. The exact nature of the reporting or documenting will vary, but it is important for planners to keep all stakeholders informed.

Implementation Timetable

To provide some guidance in implementing a program, it is helpful to compile a tentative timetable for implementation. It might even be useful to include the entire planning process. Figure 12.2 presents an example of a planning and implementation timetable using a Gantt chart.

CONCERNS ASSOCIATED WITH PLANNING

There are many matters of detail to be considered before the implementation actually takes place. The exact order in which they are considered is not as important as just making sure that they have been taken care of. Therefore, we list and describe these items in no specific order.

Legal Concerns

Liability is on the mind of many professionals today because of the concern over lawsuits. With this in mind, all personnel connected with the planned health promotion program, no matter how small the risk of injury to the participants (physical or mental), should make sure that they are adequately covered by liability insurance. In addition, program personnel should have an understanding of informed consent, negligence, and approval of appropriate professional groups (see Chapter 8 for information about guidelines from professional groups).

Informed Consent

Individuals should not be allowed to participate in any health promotion program without giving their **informed consent.** As a part of the process of obtaining informed consent from participants, program facilitators should:

1. Explain the nature and purpose(s) of the program.
2. Inform program participants of any inherent risks or dangers associated with participation and any possible discomfort they may experience.
3. Explain the expected benefits of participation.

4. Inform participants of alternative programs (procedures) that will accomplish the same thing.
5. Indicate to the participants that they are free to discontinue participation at any time.

In addition, planners must ask if the participants "have any questions, answer any such questions, and make it clear they should ask any questions they may have at any time during the program. Informed consent forms should be signed by participants before they enter the program" (Patton et al., 1986, p. 236).

Program planners must be aware that informed consent forms (or waiver of liability or release of liability, as some refer to them) do not protect them from being sued. There is no such thing as a waiver of liability. If you are negligent, you can be found liable. However, informed consent forms do make participants aware of special concerns. Further, because people must sign the forms, they may not consider legal action even if they have a case, feeling that they were duly warned. Appendix J provides a sample consent form.

Negligence

Negligence is failing to act in a **prudent** (reasonable) manner. If there is a question whether someone should or should not do something, it is generally best to err on the side of safety. Negligence can arise from two types of **acts—omission** and **commission**. An act of *omission* is not doing something when you should, such as failing to warn program participants of the inherent danger in participation. An act of *commission* is doing something you should not be doing, such as leading an aerobic dance program when you are not trained to do so.

Reducing the Risk of Liability

The real key to avoiding liability is to reduce your risk by planning ahead. Patton et al. (1986, p. 236) offer the following tips for reducing legal problems in exercise programs; however, similar advice would apply to all types of health promotion programs. We have added the words in brackets.

1. Be aware of legal liabilities.
2. Select certified instructors [in the activity and emergency care procedures] to lead classes and supervise exercise equipment [and for that matter all types of equipment].
3. Use good judgment in setting up programs and provide written guidelines for medical emergency procedures.
4. Inform participants about the risks and danger of exercise [or other activities] and require written informed consent.
5. Require that participants obtain medical clearance before entering an exercise program [or other strenuous programs].
6. Instruct staff not to "practice medicine," but instead to limit their advice to their own area of expertise.

7. Provide a safe environment by following building codes and regular maintenance schedule for equipment.
8. Purchase adequate liability insurance for all staff.

Medical Concerns

Does the program put the participants at any special medical risk so that they would need medical clearance (for example, cardiovascular exercise programs)? If so, the necessary steps need to be taken so that the participants can provide proof of clearance. Appendix K presents an example of a medical clearance form.

Program Safety

The necessary steps must be taken to ensure the health and safety of those participating in the program and all staff members. Providing a safe environment includes finding a safe program location (e.g., low-crime area), ensuring that classrooms and laboratories are free of hazards, providing qualified facilitators, supplying first-aid equipment, and developing an emergency care plan. Table 12.2

TABLE 12.2 Checklist of Items to Consider when Developing an Emergency Care Plan

_____	1.	Duties of program staff in an emergency situation are defined.
_____	2.	Program staff are trained (CPR and first aid) to handle emergencies.
_____	3.	Program participants are instructed what to do in an emergency situation (e.g., medical, natural disaster).
_____	4.	Participants with high-risk health problems are known to program staff.
_____	5.	Emergency care supplies and equipment are available.
_____	6.	Program staff has access to a telephone.
_____	7.	Standing orders are available for common emergency problems.
_____	8.	There is a plan for notifying those needed in an emergency situation.
_____	9.	Responsibility for transportation of ill/injured is defined.
_____	10.	Accident report form procedures are defined.
_____	11.	Universal precautions are outlined and followed.
_____	12.	Responsibility for financial charges incurred in the emergency care process are defined.
_____	13.	The emergency care plan has been approved by the appropriate personnel.
_____	14.	The emergency care plan is reviewed and updated on a regular basis.

provides a checklist of items that should be considered when creating an appropriate emergency care plan.

Program Registration and Fee Collection

If the program you are planning requires people to sign up and/or pay fees, you will need to establish registration procedures. Program registration and fee collection may take place before the program (preregistration), by mail, in person, via an indirect method like payroll deduction, or at the first session. Planners should also give thought to the type of payment that will be accepted (cash, credit card, or check).

Procedures for Recordkeeping

Almost every program requires that some records be kept. Items such as information collected at registration, medical information, data on participant progress, and evaluations must be accounted for. In addition, planners must decide whether participant files will be kept in a traditional way, with paper and pencil, or using some type of computer program. It is not unusual today to find participants in health promotion programs "logging in" and out on computers for purposes of keeping records of attendance and daily activities.

Program Logistics

Before implementation, program planners need to make sure that arrangements are made for a number of small but important program details. These are often referred to as program logistics. *Logistics* have been defined as the procurement, maintenance, and transportation of materials, facilities, and personnel (Woolf, 1979). Reserving space where the program is to be held, making sure audiovisual equipment is available when requested, and ordering the correct number of participant education packets are examples of program logistics that are important to the success of the program.

Moral and Ethical Concerns

There are times when certain behavior is legal but not moral or ethical. Program planning and evaluation provide the health educator with almost daily opportunities to make decisions that affect other people. There are times when these decisions are easy to make, and other times when there is a question of what is the right or wrong decision. In other words, because of the nature of health promotion, program planners are confronted with many moral and ethical decisions.

One might ask, Who is to judge what is right and wrong? Most often these decisions are compared to a standard of practice that has been defined by other professionals in the same field. For health promotion planners, the standard of practice is outlined in the Code of Ethics for Health Educators developed by the

TABLE 12.3 Hierarchy of Autonomy

A. Facilitation—assist in achieving objectives set by a target group. Examples: putting safety belts in cars or teaching people the skills necessary to perform CPR.
B. Persuasion—argue and reason. Examples: tell people about the importance of wearing safety belts or taking blood pressure medicine.
C. Manipulation—modify the environment around a person or the psychic disposition of the person. Example: automatic safety belts.
D. Coercion—threat of deprivation. Example: safety belt or motorcycle helmet laws and fine.

Association for the Advancement of Health Education (see Appendix L). However, even a code of ethics cannot spell out all the rights and wrongs of the many decisions that must be made. The interpretation of the code still creates some gray areas. Although the purpose of this section is not to say what is right or wrong, we do want to alert health promotion planners to some of the more common ethical issues that they will face.

The first is respect. Even though one may not agree with the values, behavior, and goals of others, it is important to respect them. The program planner's role is not to judge but to facilitate. Fennell and Beyrer (1989) have written a thought-provoking article on some ethical issues concerning AIDS and the health educator.

Autonomy is another issue with which program planners must deal. Should letting people voluntarily adopt health behavior be the guiding principle? Or is there a place for manipulation and coercion in health promotion? Table 12.3 presents a hierarchy of autonomy.

A third issue concerns informed consent. Although this was discussed earlier with regard to legal concerns, it is often also an ethical concern. Program planners are faced with questions such as these: Even though the benefits outnumber the risks, do we scare people away by telling them the risks? Is it okay to withhold information if it could affect the results of an evaluation?

Program planners also have to consider the concept of **nonmaleficence**—not causing harm or not doing evil. For example, is it permissible to use an aversive behavior technique to get someone to stop smoking? Which is worse, smoking cigarettes or receiving some physical punishment for doing so?

The concept of **beneficence**—that is, bringing about or doing good—can also be related to ethical issues. Can there be any question whether it is right to do good? If the good comes at the expense of another, then it raises ethical concerns.

Justice and fairness are also involved in ethical issues. For example, the question of fairness might arise in pricing a program. The program needs to show a profit, but the clients cannot afford the price that would be necessary to achieve a profit. (Legal concerns can enter into this area, too.) Issues of sexism and racism also involve concepts of justice and fairness.

Finally, the concepts of confidentiality and privacy are involved in ethical issues. Should a program planner be barred from releasing information about a person without his or her consent, even though it will benefit that person? Consider a high school sophomore who approaches the health teacher with confidential information that she is pregnant. Should the health teacher tell anyone else, such as the girl's parents?

The opportunities for dealing with ethical issues are many, and program planners need to be prepared to handle them.

Procedural Manual and/or Participant's Manual

Depending on the complexity of a program, there may be a need to develop manuals, or to purchase them from a vendor. Manuals may outline procedures for program facilitators; some refer to these as training manuals. Manuals may also provide the participants with detailed information. Developing either type of manual in-house would be a major task; therefore, adequate resources and time need to be given to developing manuals.

Training for Facilitators

If a program that is being planned needs a specially qualified person (certified or licensed) to facilitate it, every effort should be made to secure such a person. This may mean having to hire a vendor to provide such a service. If funds to hire one are not available, others will need to be trained appropriately. This may mean running your own training program, or sending people to other training classes to become qualified facilitators.

SUMMARY

Much work goes into developing a program before it is ready for implementation. The process used to implement a program may have much to say about its success. This chapter presents two models for program implementation. The first, a modification of the Parkinson and Associates (1982) model, includes three commonly used strategies—piloting, phasing in, and total implementation. The second, Borg and Gall's (1989) research and development cycle, can be modified to provide a thorough implementation strategy. Also presented in this chapter are matters that need to be considered and planned for prior to implementation.

QUESTIONS

1. What is meant by the term *implementation?*
2. What are three strategies from the modified model of Parkinson and Associates (1982) for implementing health promotion?
3. Why are the final seven steps of Borg and Gall's (1989) research and development cycle considered a thorough implementation model?

4. Name the fourth P of marketing and explain how it leads into implementation.
5. What are the legal concerns planners need to be aware of when implementing a program?
6. What is logistics and why is it important to program planners?
7. What is the difference between an act of omission and an act of commission?
8. What role does autonomy play in the ethical decisions a program planner must make?

ACTIVITIES

1. Explain how you would implement a program you are planning using a pilot study, phasing in, and total implementation. Also explain what you plan to do to "kick off" the program.
2. Explain how you would implement a program you are planning using the final seven steps of the Borg and Gall (1989) research and development cycle.
3. Develop an informed consent form that outlines the risks inherent in a program you are planning. Make sure the form includes a place for signatures of the participant and a witness and the date.
4. In a one-page paper, identify what you see as the biggest ethical concern of health promotion programming, and explain your choice.

13

Evaluation: An Overview

After reading this chapter and answering the questions at the end, you should be able to:

- Compare and contrast the various types of evaluation.
- Identify some of the problems that may hinder an effective evaluation.
- List reasons why evaluation should be included in all programs.
- Explain the difference between internal and external evaluation.
- Describe several considerations in planning and conducting an evaluation.

Key Terms

baseline data
evaluation
external evaluation
formative evaluation
impact evaluation
internal evaluation
process evaluation
outcome evaluation
summative evaluation

Whether they realize it or not, program planners are constantly evaluating their health promotion efforts by asking questions such as: Did the program have an impact? How many people stopped smoking? Were the participants satisfied with the program? Properly conducted, an evaluation can provide objective answers to these types of questions; however, the usefulness of an evaluation can be limited by a variety of biases and/or inadequate design.

Evaluation is critical for all health promotion programs. It is important to have accurate information to determine the impact of programs and to make decisions about their future. For example, evaluation can help a program planner determine whether participants were satisfied with a weight loss program, whether a smoking cessation workshop actually changed smoking behavior, or whether an exercise program should continue or not. Without adequate evaluation, accurate information is not gained, and decisions are based on speculation.

In order to generate useful and meaningful data about programs, the evaluation must be designed early in the process of program planning. As mentioned in an earlier chapter, evaluation begins when the program goals and objectives are being developed. Evaluation can help not only to determine whether program goals and objectives are met, but also to answer questions about the program as it is being implemented. If the evaluation is not designed until the program has ended, the information cannot be used to improve the program as it progresses. For example, low enrollment in a stress management workshop might reflect an inadequate setting, inconvenient hours, or lack of publicity. All of these problems could be reduced or eliminated if evaluation was conducted in the planning stage.

The process of designing an evaluation should be a collaborative effort of program stakeholders (those individuals who have a vested interest in the program). Evaluation results must be relevant to the stakeholders in order to be used most effectively. For example, program planners, administrators, program facilitators, and the representatives from the funding source all have specific questions they would like answered regarding the program's development and outcome. Program planners may want to know if the program met the needs of the target population; program administrators may want to know if the program is making any money; program facilitators may want to know if participants changed their behavior as a result of the program; and representatives from the funding source may be interested in knowing if the program was cost-effective. These questions can all be answered if the evaluation is properly planned and implemented.

While evaluation is a necessary component of health promotion programs, program planners may find it threatening. If evaluation is seen as a way to judge a program or determine its worth, the program planner may feel that negative results from evaluations may eliminate a program, staff positions, or even an entire department.

Sarvela and McDermott (1993) describe additional situations in which evaluations may be political. Results may be intentionally skewed by reporting only successes and not weaknesses to decision makers in order to prevent the elimination of a program. Management may use evaluation as a way to eliminate a program that is not generating revenue.

Even when results are reported fairly, political ramifications may occur—reviewing an unpopular but highly visible program, complying with governmental regulations, or the evaluator's desire to publish the results. Sarvela and McDermott (1993) also indicate that an evaluation can be a political "hot potato." For example, if objective results lead to the recommendation that a drug abuse program serving poor, pregnant minority women be eliminated, what are the implications for the agency with regard to morale, racial harmony, and trust in governmental agencies?

Since evaluations may also have ethical considerations for the individuals involved, most colleges, universities, and school systems have boards to review the evaluation design. These groups are sometimes referred to as institutional review boards or human subject review committees. The purpose of these boards is to safeguard the rights, privacy, health, and well-being of the participants.

BASIC TERMINOLOGY

A variety of definitions of the term *evaluation* have been written; most include the concept of determining the value or worth of the object of interest (the health promotion program) against a standard of acceptability. Table 13.1 lists commonly used standards of acceptability for evaluating health promotion programs.

When determining the value of a program, planners can use several types of evaluation. The type of evaluation reflects whether the results are needed to improve a program before or during implementation, to assess the effectiveness of a program, or to determine whether the program met the goals and objectives.

Evaluations generally use one of two sets of evaluation terms. Some authors use the terms *process, impact,* and *outcome* to identify types of evaluation used to determine the value of a program. Other authors use the terms *formative* and *summa-*

TABLE 13.1 Standards of Acceptability

Standard of Acceptability	Examples
Mandate (policies, statutes, laws) of regulating agencies	Percent of children immunized for school; percent of target population wearing safety belts
Target population health status	Rates of morbidity and mortality compared to state and national norms
Values expressed in the local community	Type of school curriculum expected
Standards advocated by professional organizations	Passing scores, certification, or registration examinations
Norms established via research	Treadmill tests or percent body fat
Norms established by evaluation of previous programs	Smoking cessation rates
Comparison or control groups	Used in experimental or quasi-experimental studies

tive to describe the evaluation that occurs during the program and after the program, respectively.

- **Process evaluation:** Provides documentation during program implementation to make adjustments for improvement of the program, for example, getting reactions from participants about the times programs are offered or about speakers in a workshop. This could be accomplished with a short questionnaire or with information gained from a focus group.
- **Impact evaluation:** Assesses the overall effectiveness of a program in producing favorable knowledge, attitudes, behaviors, health status, and/or skills in the target population; indicates immediate effects, such as a change in behavior or an increase in knowledge. For example, how many people stopped smoking? How many people can perform CPR? How much do people know about AIDS?
- **Outcome evaluation:** Determines whether the program met the stated long-term goals and objectives, such as a reduction in morbidity or mortality rates of the target population or an improvement in quality of life.
- **Formative evaluation:** Provides immediate feedback during program planning and implementation to improve and refine the program. It is more comprehensive than process evaluation, since information is collected from a variety of sources (such as program participants or program providers) both before and during program implementation.
- **Summative evaluation:** Determines achievements, such as numbers of individuals who changed their behavior or whether other program objectives were reached. It is conducted at the end of the program.

Even though the sets of terms are used to describe evaluation activities, there is some overlap among the terms. Process evaluation occurs during the program and is a form of formative evaluation. Impact and outcome evaluation occur at the completion of the program and are considered forms of summative evaluation. Both sets of evaluation (process, impact, and outcome; formative and summative) take into account the need to conduct evaluation before and/or during the program, and at the end of the program. All types of evaluation should be in place before or during program implementation.

PURPOSE FOR EVALUATION

Basically, there are two reasons for evaluating a program: to improve it or to determine its effectiveness (Fink & Kosecoff, 1978). The types of evaluation are distinguished by how the information is going to be used. The information may be used by program planners during the implementation of a program to make improvements in services (process evaluation). It may be used to see if certain immediate outcomes, such as knowledge, attitude, skills, and behavior change, have occurred (impact evaluation). It may be used at the end of a program to determine whether long-term goals and objectives have been met (outcome evaluation). Within this general rationale for evaluation, several additional reasons can be found for evaluating a program:

1. *To demonstrate the worth of a program.* An evaluation can help to determine whether the program is moving in the right direction, is justifying past or projected expenditure, is providing a positive change in conditions or behavior, or is cost effective. Evaluation can document whether the health needs of the target population have been met. Information about the worth of a program can be used to make decisions about the fate of the program.
2. *To compare different types of programs.* Different types of programs, methods, or approaches can be compared to determine which are the most effective in meeting initial goals. For example, if the goal is to reduce the number of smokers in a corporation, smoking rates of those who completed a smoking cessation workshop could be compared to the rates of those who completed a self-directed program. An evaluation can also test innovative ideas to determine whether the effort should be duplicated. A cost-benefit or cost-effectiveness analysis could be completed to compare the economic aspects of different programs.
3. *To meet requirements of the funding source.* Many times the funding source requires an evaluation to determine whether the goals and objectives of a program have been met, to document that the program is cost-effective, to make decisions about the fate of the program (whether it should be continued, duplicated, expanded, or discontinued), or to determine whether mandates of regulatory agencies have been met, as in the case of immunizations or environmental standards.
4. *To provide information about the program.* When information is provided to the media, the evaluation results often increase the program's visibility and public support; it may be possible to use the results as a marketing technique to "sell" the program. Information about the program can also be provided to select groups, such as the program staff, participants, and potential participants. Providing information to professional colleagues can increase the knowledge base and avoid duplication of efforts when designing and implementing health promotion programs in the future.

THE PROCESS FOR EVALUATION

The process of evaluating a program or activity begins with the initial program planning. Those involved in developing new programs need to be aware of the importance of a well-defined evaluation plan. The evaluation process consists of several steps. The following list provides guidelines for planning and conducting an evaluation.

Planning

- Review the program goals and objectives.
- Meet with the stakeholders to determine what general questions should be answered.
- Determine whether the necessary resources are available to conduct the evaluation; budget for additional costs.
- Hire an evaluator, if needed.
- Develop the evaluation design.
- Decide which evaluation instrument(s) will be used and, if needed, who will develop the instrument.
- Determine whether the evaluation questions reflect the goals and objectives of the program.
- Determine whether the questions of various groups are considered, such as the program administrators, facilitators, planners, participants, and funding source.
- Determine when the evaluation will be conducted; develop a time line.

Data Collection

- Decide how the information will be collected: survey, records and documents, telephone interview, personal interview, observation.
- Determine who will collect the data.
- Plan and administer a pilot test.
- Review the results of the pilot test to refine the data collection instrument or the collection procedures.
- Determine who will be included in the evaluation—for example, all program participants, or a random sample of participants.
- Conduct the data collection.

Data Analysis

- Determine how the data will be analyzed.
- Determine who will analyze the data.
- Conduct the analysis, and allow for several interpretations of the data.

Reporting

- Determine who will receive the results.
- Choose who will report the findings.
- Determine how (in what form) the results will be disseminated.
- Discuss how the findings of the process or formative evaluation will affect the program.
- Decide when the results of the impact, outcome, or summative evaluation will be made available.
- Disseminate the findings.

Application

- Determine how the results can be implemented.

PRACTICAL PROBLEMS IN EVALUATION

Certain problems may exist that may impede an effective evaluation. Solomon (1987, pp. 366–68) identifies seven types of problems that can hinder an effective evaluation:

1. The planner failed to build evaluation into program planning.
2. Adequate procedures cost time and resources.
3. Changes in adults come slowly.
4. Some changes do not last.
5. It is often difficult to distinguish between cause and effect.
6. Conflict can arise between professional standards and "do it yourself" attitudes.
7. Sometimes people's motives get in the way.

Examples of these problems in health promotion programs include not collecting initial information from participants because evaluation plans were not in place, failure to budget for the cost of the evaluation (e.g., printing questionnaires, additional staff, postage), or conducting the evaluation before a change can occur (e.g., changes in cholesterol level) or too long after program completion (e.g., long-term effects of a weight loss program). Those without evaluation expertise may conduct an evaluation without a sound design, such as not using random sampling to select participants. Program managers, who have a motivation to make their programs look cost effective, may minimize costs and exaggerate program benefits.

Awareness of these problems and development of strategies to deal with them may improve the accuracy of program evaluation. We discuss many approaches that can help minimize these problems, such as including evaluation in the early stages of program planning, determining who will conduct the evaluation, carefully considering the evaluation design, increasing objectivity, and developing a plan to use the evaluation results.

EVALUATION IN THE PROGRAM-PLANNING STAGES

As we discussed in Chapter 6, the evaluation design must reflect the goals and objectives of the program. The results of the evaluation will determine whether the goals and objectives were met. To be most effective, the evaluation must be planned in the early stages of program development and must be in place before the program begins.

Results from evaluations conducted early in the program-planning process can assist in improving the program. Having a plan in place to conduct an evaluation before the end of a program will make collecting information regarding program outcomes much easier and more accurate.

We will discuss how evaluation plans can be included in program planning by using the examples of formative and summative evaluations. The formative evaluation should provide feedback to the program administrator, with program monitoring beginning in the early stages. Collecting information and communicating it to the administrator quickly allows for the program to be modified and improved.

Data reflecting the initial status or interests of the participants **(baseline data)** or data from a needs assessment can be used for comparison to the early data collected from program participants. Additional information from the formative evaluation may indicate that the necessary staff have been hired, the program sites are available, brochures have been printed, participants are satisfied with the times the programs are offered, and classes are offered with the needs of the prospective participants in mind.

Early data regarding the program should be analyzed quickly to make any necessary adjustments to the program. This type of evaluation can improve both new and existing programs. Information from the formative evaluation can be useful in answering questions, such as whether the programs are provided at convenient locations for the community members, whether the necessary materials arrived on time, and whether people are attending the workshops at all the various times they are offered.

By developing the summative evaluation plan at the beginning of the program, planners can ensure that the results will be less biased. Early development of the summative evaluation plan ensures that the questions answered reflect the original objectives and goals of the program. This type of evaluation can provide answers to many questions, such as whether the group approach or the individual approach was more effective in reducing tobacco use among the participants in a smoking cessation program, whether the participants in a weight loss program lost weight and kept the weight off, and how many people in the target population participated in a given program.

WHO WILL CONDUCT THE EVALUATION?

At the beginning of the program, planners must determine who will conduct the evaluation. The program evaluator must be as objective as possible, and should have nothing to gain from the results of the evaluation. The evaluator may be someone associated with the program or someone from outside.

If someone trained in evaluation who is personally involved with the program conducts the evaluation, it is called an **internal evaluation**. An internal evaluator would have the advantage of being closer to the program staff and activities, making it easier to collect the relevant information. Conducting an internal evaluation is also less expensive than hiring additional personnel to conduct the evaluation. The major drawback, however, is the possibility of evaluator bias or conflict of interest. Someone closely involved with the program has an investment in the outcome of the evaluation and may not be completely objective. After all, a positive evaluation of the program may result in future funding that would secure the positions of the staff members.

An **external evaluation** is one conducted by someone who is not connected with the program. This type of evaluator is somewhat isolated, lacking the knowledge and experience of the program that the internal evaluator possesses. This type of evaluation is also more expensive, since an additional person must be hired to carry out the work. However, this type of evaluation can provide a more objective outlook and a fresh perspective, and it helps ensure an unbiased outcome evaluation.

Whether an internal or external evaluator conducts the program evaluation, the main goal is to choose someone with credibility and objectivity. The evaluator must have a clear role in the evaluation design, accurately reporting the results regardless of the findings.

EVALUATION RESULTS

The question of who will receive the evaluation results is also an important consideration. The evaluation can be conducted from several vantage points, depending on whether the results will be presented to the program administrator, the funding source, the organization, or the public. These stakeholders may all have different sets of questions they would like answered. The evaluation results must be disseminated to groups interested in the program. Different aspects of the evaluation can be stressed, depending on the group's particular needs and interests. A program administrator may be interested in which approach was more successful, the funding source may want to know if all objectives were reached, and a community member may want to know if participants felt the program was beneficial.

The planning process of the evaluation should include a determination of how the results will be used. It is especially important in process and formative evaluation to implement the findings rapidly to improve the program. However, an action plan is needed in summative, impact, and outcome evaluation to ensure that the results are not filed away, but are used in the provision of future health promotion programs.

SUMMARY

Evaluation can be thought of as a way to make sound decisions regarding the worth or effectiveness of health promotion programs, to compare different types of programs, to meet requirements of funding sources, or to provide information about programs. The evaluation process takes place before, during, and after program implementation. If the evaluation is well designed and conducted, the findings can be extremely beneficial to the program stakeholders.

QUESTIONS

1. Give an example of a question that could be answered in a process evaluation, impact evaluation, and outcome evaluation.
2. What are some of the general reasons for evaluating a program?
3. Why can an evaluation be viewed as political?
4. What types of problems can block an effective evaluation?
5. What different types of information could an evaluation provide for the various stakeholders (program planners, the funding source, the administrators, and the participants)?
6. Why is it important to begin the evaluation process in the program-planning stages?
7. Explain how feedback from an evaluation can be used in program planning.
8. What are some of the steps in evaluation planning, data collection, data analysis, and reporting?
9. In what type of situation would an internal evaluation be more appropriate than an external evaluation?

ACTIVITIES

1. Describe how process, impact, and outcome evaluation could be used in a stress management program for college students. Describe how formative and summative evaluation could be used.
2. Write a rationale to a funding source for hiring an external evaluator.
3. Review the evaluation component from a health promotion program in your community and/or discuss an evaluation plan with a program planner or evaluator. Look for the planning process used, the rationale for the data collection method, and how the findings were reported.
4. Assume you are responsible for selecting an evaluator for a health promotion program you are planning. Would you select an internal or an external evaluator? Explain your rationale. If you select an external evaluator, where do you think you could find such a person?

14

Evaluation Models and Designs

After reading this chapter and answering the questions at the end, you should be able to:

- Define the term *model,* and discuss the rationale for the use of a model in evaluation.
- Describe the various evaluation models outlined.
- List some considerations in selecting an evaluation design.
- Compare and contrast quantitative and qualitative approaches to evaluation.
- Differentiate among experimental, control, and comparison groups.
- Compare and contrast the major types of evaluation design.
- Identify the threats to internal and external validity and explain how evaluation design can increase control.

Key Terms

- behavioral objectives model
- blind
- comparison group
- control group
- cost-benefit analysis
- cost-effectiveness analysis
- cost-identification analysis
- cost-utility analysis
- decision-making model
- deductive
- double blind
- evaluation design
- evaluation model
- experimental design
- experimental group
- external validity
- generalizability
- goal-attainment model
- goal-based model
- goal-free model
- inductive
- internal validity
- measurement
- nonexperimental design
- posttest
- pretest
- qualitative approach
- quantitative approach
- quasi-experimental design
- systems analysis model
- triple blind

This chapter is about evaluation models and designs. An **evaluation model** can be thought of as a framework or plan that can be used to conduct an evaluation. Washington (1987) indicates that each evaluation model represents a certain way of thinking, which defines what evaluation questions should be asked. For example, the evaluation questions may focus on the goals and objectives of the program, the effects of the intervention, the cost-benefit ratio of the program, and the behavior of the participants.

An **evaluation design** is more specific than an evaluation model. It is used to organize the evaluation and to provide for planned, systematic data collection, analysis, and reporting. A well-planned evaluation design helps ensure that the conclusions drawn about the program will be as accurate as possible. The design is developed during the early stages of program planning and has program goals and objectives as its focus. Program planners must give consideration to the audience and/or stakeholders who will read the results of the evaluation; the design must produce information that will answer their evaluation questions.

EVALUATION MODELS/APPROACHES

In setting up the program evaluation, evaluators have a variety of models/approaches from which to select. A single model/approach need not be selected. In fact, Popham (1988) has suggested an eclectic approach. He believes that models can rarely be used in their pure form, so that choosing parts of models or categories may be more beneficial to the evaluator.

House (1980) has done a nice job of categorizing the different evaluation models/approaches. A brief description of each is presented below.

- *Systems analysis* uses output measures, such as test scores, to determine if the program has demonstrated the desired change. It also determines whether funds have been efficiently used, as in cost analyses.
- *Behavioral objectives*, or goal-based evaluation, uses the program goals and collects evidence to determine whether the goals have been reached.
- *Decision making* focuses on the decision to be made and presents evidence about the effectiveness of the program to the decision maker (manager or administrator).
- *Goal-free evaluation* does not base the evaluation on program goals; instead, the evaluator searches for all outcomes, often finding unintended side effects.
- *Art criticism* uses the judgment of an expert in the area to increase awareness and appreciation of the program in order to lead to improved standards and better performance.
- *Professional (accreditation) review* uses professionals to judge the work of other professionals; the source of standards and criteria is the professionals conducting the review.
- *Quasi-legal evaluation* uses a panel to hear evidence considering the arguments for and against the program; a quasi-legal procedure is used for both evaluating and policy making.
- *Case study* uses techniques such as interviews and observations to examine how people view the program.

Because some of these evaluation models/approaches are used more than others by health educators, we felt it was important to provide a more detailed discussion of those that were more often used.

Systems Analysis Model

A **systems analysis model** of evaluation is based upon efficiency—determining which are the most effective programs. It focuses on the organization, determining whether appropriate resources are devoted to goal activities (and to nongoal activities, such as staff training or maintenance of the system). This model is centrally concerned with the measurement of general goals, but it does not focus on the achievement of a specific goal. This is due to the recognition that organizations function at different levels with various goals at each level.

Economic evaluations are typical strategies used in the systems analysis model. Control over rising health care costs has forced many administrators and planners to be concerned about the cost of health promotion programs. Using cost analyses, decisions can be made regarding which programs are most effective within a certain budget. In order to be able to perform cost analyses, evaluators need to be able to measure both the costs and the outcomes associated with a program.

Some costs may be quite easy to determine, such as those for staff, books, and medical equipment. Other costs are more difficult to determine, such as those associated with years of productive life lost due to accidental death, loss of productivity due to absenteeism, and cost of pain and suffering.

Outcomes can be determined by a number of factors, including health care costs saved due to health promotion programs, years of life saved, number of smokers who quit, reduced absenteeism, and number of pounds lost.

Several different types of cost analysis can be used (Sarvela & McDermott, 1993). **Cost-identification analysis** is used to compare different interventions available for a program, often to determine which intervention would be the least expensive. With this type of analysis, planners identify the different items (i.e., personnel, facilities, curriculum, etc.) associated with a given intervention, determine a cost for each item, total the costs for that intervention, and then compare the total costs associated with each of several interventions. For example, if a health department was interested in providing a tobacco control program for a school district, it could conduct a cost identification analysis on three different interventions; (1) teacher led, (2) peer education, and (3) voluntary agency provided. Costs for each of these interventions, such as staff time, staff benefits, curriculum materials, and volunteer training, would be identified, compared, and analyzed.

Cost-benefit analysis looks at how resources can best be used. It will yield the dollar benefit received from the dollars invested in the program. **Cost-effectiveness analysis** is used to quantify the effects of a program in monetary terms. Cost-effectiveness analysis is more appropriate for health promotion programs than cost-benefit analysis, because a dollar value does not have to be placed on the outcomes of the program. Instead, a cost-effectiveness analysis will indicate how much it costs to produce a certain effect. For example, based on the cost of a program, the effect of years of life saved, number of smokers who stop smoking, or morbidity or mortality rates can be determined. A thorough explanation of both cost-benefit and cost-effectiveness analysis is presented in Appendix M in an article written by McKenzie (1986).

A fourth type of cost analysis that is used with health promotion programs is **cost-utility analysis.** This approach is different from the others in that the values of the outcomes of a program are determined by their subjective value to the stakeholders rather than their monetary cost. For example, an administrator may select a more expensive intervention for a program just because of the good public relations (i.e., the subjective value in the administrator's eye) for the organization. Or, an administrator may survey those in the target population to determine what outcomes they value from a program. Then, based on these data, the administrator selects the appropriate intervention.

Two advantages of the systems analysis model are that the findings are objective and that the findings can convince decision makers that a program is effective in improving health status. A disadvantage, however, is that this is only one part of the data to be considered when making program decisions: information from program participants is not included. The fate of a program should not be based on cost-benefit or cost-effectiveness analysis alone.

Behavioral Objectives/Goal-Attainment/Goal-Based Model

One of the most commonly used types of evaluation models is the **behavioral objectives model**, which focuses on the stated goals of the program. Models using this type of goal-directed focus are also known as **goal-attainment models** or **goal-based models**. Data are collected to determine whether the predetermined goals have been met. Success or failure is measured by the relationship between the outcome of the program and the stated goals. This type of model is based on behavior, and the dependent variable is defined in terms of behaviors the program participant should be able to demonstrate at the end of the intervention.

In the behavioral objective model, the program goals serve as the standards for evaluation. This type of evaluation was first used in education, to assess student behaviors. Competency testing is an example of goal-attainment evaluation, determining whether a student is able to pass an exam or advance to the next grade. Goal attainment was later used in other fields, and more emphasis was placed on how objectives are to be measured. This model is also found in business, where or-

FIGURE 14.1 The Evaluation Process

Source: From *Evaluation Research* (p. 34), by E. A. Suchman, 1967, New York: Russell Sage Foundation. Reprinted by permission of the Russell Sage Foundation.

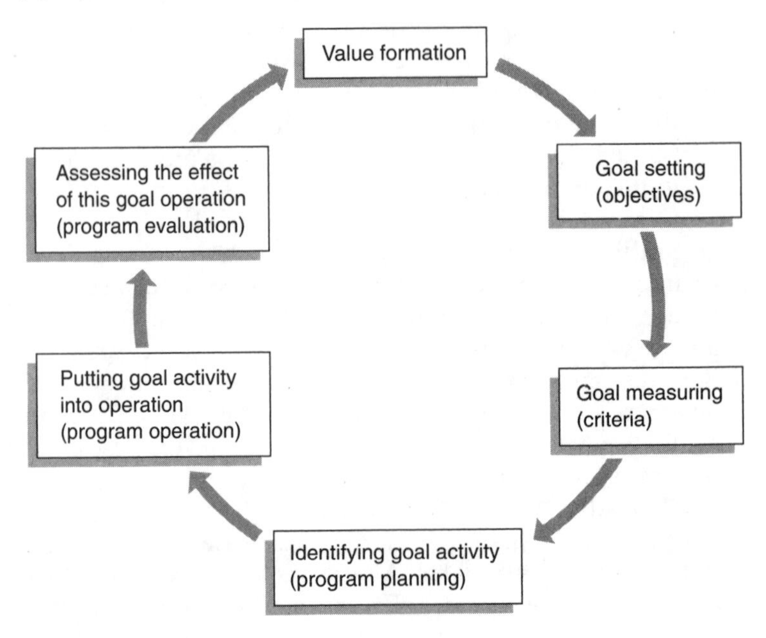

ganizations use "management by objectives" to determine how well they are meeting their objectives.

This model was used in public health by Suchman (1967), who identified the evaluation process as circular (see Figure 14.1). Evaluation starts with a value; the goal is derived from this value, and objectives are set. The following steps include determining criteria to measure the goal, identifying the goal activity (program planning), and putting the goal activity into operation (program operation). The assessment step evaluates the extent to which the objectives have been met. Using this information, a judgment is made about the goal activity, which leads back to the initial value. At this point, the value may be changed, reaffirmed, or reassessed.

Washington (1987, pp. 373–374) has identified five steps in measuring goal attainment. These steps include:

1. Specification of the goal to be measured.
2. Specification of the sequential set of performances that, if observed, would indicate that the goal has been achieved.
3. Identification of the performances that are critical to the achievement of the goal.
4. Description of the "indicator behavior" of each performance episode.
5. Collective testing to find whether each "indicator behavior" is associated with each other.

Within the general goal statement is the outcome behavior of the individual. The goal should be operationally defined—that is, it should consist of measurable objectives—and those objectives most critical in achieving the goal should be identified. An indicator of a performance episode refers to a measurable, observable behavior, based on normative criteria. Measurement should be standardized in order to compare outcomes from one behavior to another. (See Chapter 6 for a discussion of writing goals and objectives.)

A strength of the behavioral objective model is its objectivity. The values of the evaluator do not interfere with the outcome of the evaluation. Another strength is that the goal is predetermined: The evaluation is based on whether or not the goal was met, not on whether it was appropriate. The goal can be expressed as measurable objectives, making it easier to determine whether the goal was met.

A possible limitation of this model is how the goal is set, since the outcome of the evaluation is determined by the specification of the goal. The goal reflects the values or interests of the funding source, program staff, or consumers. Who sets the goal is an important factor, and consideration must be given to whose interests the goal represents.

Another limitation of this model is that only those items included in the objectives are evaluated. There may be other very positive outcomes of a program, but they will not be identified or evaluated because they were not included in the objectives. An example would be to include only behavior change in the objectives of a program; any other positive changes, such as in attitudes or knowledge, would be overlooked in the evaluation.

Decision-Making Model

According to Stufflebeam et al. (1971), the developer of the **decision-making model**, there are three steps to the evaluation process: delineating (focusing of information), obtaining (collecting, organizing, and analyzing information), and providing (synthesizing information so it will be useful). The decision maker, usually a manager or administrator, wants and needs information to help answer relevant questions regarding a program.

The four types of evaluation in this model include context, input, process, and product (CIPP), with each providing information to the decision maker. Context evaluation describes the conditions in the environment, identifies unmet needs and unused opportunities, and determines why these occur. The purpose of input evaluation is to determine how to use resources to meet program goals. Process evaluation provides feedback to those responsible for program implementation. The purpose of product evaluation is to measure and interpret attainments during and after the program (Stufflebeam et al., 1971). It is the decision maker, not the evaluator, who uses this information to determine the worth of the program.

The main advantage to this type of model is the increased likelihood that the information will actually be used by the decision makers. The information most relevant to them will be obtained by this type of evaluation. The advantage for the evaluator is that the evaluation is focused, with criteria already determined. A limitation of the decision-making model is that the amount of input from administrators may reduce the objectivity of the evaluation.

Goal-Free Model

The **goal-free model** of evaluation was developed in response to the limitations of the goal-attainment model. Scriven (1973), who developed the goal-free model, believed that evaluation should not be based on goals in order to enable the evaluator to remain unbiased. The evaluator must search for all outcomes, including unintended positive or negative side effects. Thus, the evaluator does not base the evaluation on reaching goals and remains unaware of the program goals.

Ideally, the evaluator suspends judgment concerning what the program is intended to accomplish and focuses on what actually happens. However, Popham (1988) sees this approach as oriented toward the output of the program and as a judgmental approach, since the evaluator is required to present a judgment regarding the program to the decision makers.

The techniques that the evaluator uses include examining pre-intervention test results, reading expert reviews, visiting program sites, reviewing the literature, examining similar programs, interviewing staff and clients, and examining materials. The techniques are generally qualitative methods, but quantitative methods can also be used.

The goal-free model is not often used in evaluation. It is difficult for evaluators to determine what to evaluate when program objectives are not to be used. One concern is that evaluators will substitute their own goals, since there is a lack of

TABLE 14.1 Comparison of the Goal-Attainment and Goal-Free Models

Goal-Attainment Model	Goal-Free Model
Have the objectives been reached?	What is the outcome of the program?
Has the program met the needs of the target population?	Who has been reached by the program?
How can the objectives be reached?	How is the program operating?
Are the needs of the program administrators and funding source being met?	What has been provided?

clear methodology as to how to approach the model. The goal-free evaluation model may be most useful in combination with other models.

On the other hand, this model has certain advantages. One is that it avoids classifying side effects and unanticipated effects as being of secondary interest, since these may be crucial to setting new priorities in a program. A classic example of this model was an evaluation of an educational program for coronary care patients. The results of the evaluation indicated no increase in knowledge, which was the program goal. However, an unanticipated side effect was reduction in patients' anxiety during exercise. Without the use of goal-free evaluation, this benefit of the program might not have been discovered.

The main differences between the goal-attainment and goal-free models are presented in Table 14.1. The types of questions asked in each model reflect the difference in focus of the evaluation.

SELECTING AN EVALUATION DESIGN

When planning an evaluation, careful consideration should be given to the evaluation design, since the design is critical to the outcome of the evaluation. There are few perfect evaluation designs because no situation is ideal and there are always constraining factors, such as limited resources. Planners should give much thought to selecting the best design for each situation. The following questions may be helpful in the selection of a design:

- How much time do you have to conduct the evaluation?
- What financial resources are available?
- How many participants can be included in the evaluation?
- Are you more interested in qualitative or quantitative data?
- Do you have data analysis skills or access to computers and statistical consultants?
- In what ways can validity be increased?
- Is it important to be able to generalize your findings to other populations?
- Are the stakeholders concerned with validity and reliability?

- Do you have the ability to randomize participants into experimental and control groups?
- Do you have access to a comparison group?

Dignan (1986) presents four steps in choosing an evaluation design. These four steps are outlined in Figure 14.2. The first step is to orient oneself to the situation. The evaluator must identify resources (time, personnel), constraints, and hidden agendas (unspoken goals). During this step, the evaluator must determine what is to be expected from the program and what can be observed.

The second step involves defining the problem—determining what is to be evaluated. During this step, definitions are needed for independent variables (what the sponsors think makes the difference), dependent variables (what will show the difference), and confounding variables (what the evaluator thinks could explain additional differences).

The third step involves making a decision about the design, that is, whether to use a qualitative or quantitative approach or both. The **quantitative approach** is **deductive** in nature (applying a generally accepted principle to an individual case), so that the evaluation produces hard data, such as counts, ratings, scores, or classifica-

FIGURE 14.2 Steps in Selecting an Evaluation Design

Source: From M. B. Dignan, *Measurement and Evaluation of Health Education,* 2nd ed., 1986 (p. 93). Courtesy of Charles C Thomas Publisher, Springfield, IL.

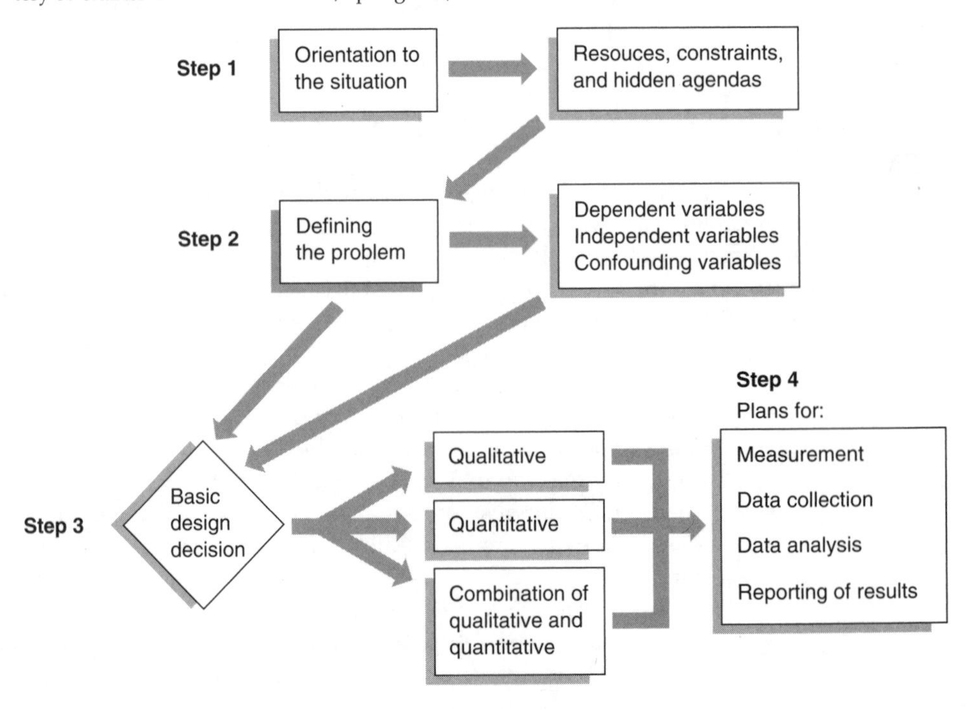

tions. Examples of quantitative data would be the number of participants in a stress management program, the ratings on a participant satisfaction survey, and the pretest scores on a nutrition knowledge test. This approach is suited to programs that are well defined and compares outcomes of programs with those of other groups or the general population. It is the method most often used in evaluation designs.

The **qualitative approach** is an **inductive** method (individual cases are studied to formulate a general principle) and produces soft data, such as descriptions. The methods most often used to collect qualitative data are interviews, case studies, focus groups, and observations. This is a good method to use for programs that emphasize individual outcomes or in cases where other descriptive information from participants is needed.

Patton (1988) offers a checklist to determine whether qualitative data might be appropriate in a particular program evaluation. Collecting qualitative data may be a good strategy if there is a need to describe individual outcomes, to understand the dynamics and process of the programs, to obtain in-depth information on certain clients or sites, or to focus on the diversity of program clients or sites; it is also helpful in gathering information to improve the program during formative evaluation.

Rather than choose one approach, it may be advantageous to combine quantitative and qualitative methods. For example, combining ratings or scores of program participants with interviews of a few selected participants can strengthen the evaluation. Supplementing the hard data with anecdotal information further describes the results.

The fourth step includes choosing how to measure the dependent variable, deciding how to collect the data (these components were discussed in Chapter 5), and how the data will be analyzed, and determining how the results will be reported. (These components are discussed in Chapter 15.)

EXPERIMENTAL AND CONTROL GROUPS

The group of individuals participating in the program that is to be evaluated is known, as in other types of research studies, as the **experimental group**. The evaluation is designed to determine what effects the program has on these individuals. To make sure that the effects are caused by the program and not by some other factor, a **control group** should be used. The control group should be as similar to the experimental group as possible, but the members of this group do not receive the program (intervention or treatment) that is to be evaluated.

Without the use of a properly selected control group, the apparent effect of the program could actually be due to a variety of factors, such as differences in participants' educational background, environment, or experience. By using a control group, the evaluator can show that the results or outcomes are due to the program and not to those other variables. In an ideal situation, participants should be randomly selected, then randomly assigned to one of two groups, and finally it should be randomly determined which group would become the experimental group and which the control group. Theoretically, this would evenly distribute the characteristics of the participants. This technique increases the credibility of the evaluation by controlling for extraneous events and factors.

It is not always possible or ethical to assign participants to a control group, especially if doing so would mean that they would be denied a necessary program or service. For example, a health promotion program could be designed for individuals with hypertension. Individuals diagnosed with hypertension could be referred by a physician into a health promotion class focused on reducing the risk factors associated with this disease. Denying some individuals access to the program in order to form a control group would clearly be unethical.

One way to deal with this problem is to provide the control group with an alternative program, or to offer the regular program to the group at a later time (if a delay is not potentially harmful). Another alternative is to compare two programs: offer an innovative program to some participants, and continue the conventional program for others. Wagner and Guild (1989) see the advantage of this strategy as providing service to all participants (which fulfills a moral obligation) and still providing a comparison to assess the effectiveness of the innovative program.

Since the main purpose of social programs is to help clients, the client's viewpoint should be the primary one. It is important to keep this in mind when considering ethical issues in the use of control groups. Conner (1980) identifies four underlying premises for the use of control groups in social program evaluation:

1. All individuals have a right to status quo services.
2. All individuals involved in the evaluation are informed about the purpose of the study and the use of a control group.
3. Individuals have a right to new services, and random selection gives everyone a chance to participate.
4. Individuals should not be subjected to ineffective or harmful programs.

The ethical issues that must be considered involve the potential denial of a service and allocation of scarce resources. When randomization is not feasible, planners should consider an equitable process of providing services for individuals while maintaining control over the evaluation design.

When participants cannot be randomly assigned to an experimental or control group, a nonequivalent control group may be selected. This is known as a **comparison group**. It is important to find a group that is as similar as possible to the experimental group, such as two classrooms of students with similar characteristics or residents in two comparable cities. Factors to consider include participants' age, gender, education, location, socioeconomic status, and experience, as well as any other variable that might have an impact on program results.

EVALUATION DESIGNS

Measurements used in evaluation designs can be collected at three different times: after the program; both before and after the program; and several times before,

TABLE 14.2 Evaluation Designs

Design								
I. Experimental design								
1. Pretest-posttest design								
—Experimental group	(R)	O	X	O				
—Control group	(R)	O		O				
2. Posttest-only design								
—Experimental group	(R)		X	O				
—Control group	(R)			O				
3. Time series design								
—Experimental group	(R)	O	O	O	X	O	O	O
—Control group	(R)	O	O	O		O	O	O
II. Quasi-experimental design								
1. Pretest-posttest design								
—Experimental group		O	X	O				
—Comparison group		O		O				
2. Time series design								
—Experimental group		O	O	O	X	O	O	O
—Comparison group		O	O	O		O	O	O
III. Nonexperimental design								
1. Pretest-posttest design								
—Experimental group		O	X	O				
2. Time series design								
—Experimental group		O	O	O	X	O	O	O

Key: (R) = Random assignment
O = Measurement
X = Program

during, and after the program. **Measurement** is defined by Green and Lewis (1986) as the method or procedure of assigning numbers to objects, events, and people. How such information is obtained has been discussed in Chapter 5.

Table 14.2 presents evaluation designs commonly used in health promotion. In the table, the letter *O* refers to measurement (or data collection), such as surveys, tests, interviews, observations, or other methods of gaining information. Measurement before the program begins is known as the **pretest**, and measurement after the completion of the program is known as the **posttest**. The letter *X* represents the program (or intervention); the relative positions of the two letters in the table indicate when measurements are made in relation to when the program is provided. The table also shows which groups receive the program and when participants are randomly assigned to groups [*(R)*].

Windsor, Baranowski, Clark, and Cutter (1994) differentiate among three types of evaluation designs: experimental, quasi-experimental, and nonexperimental.

Experimental design offers the greatest control over the various factors that may influence the results. It involves random assignment to experimental and control groups with measurement of both groups. It produces the most interpretable and defensible evidence of effectiveness. **Quasi-experimental design** results in interpretable and supportive evidence of program effectiveness, but usually cannot control for all factors that affect the validity of the results. There is no random assignment to the groups, and comparisons are made on experimental and comparison groups. **Nonexperimental design,** without the use of a comparison or control group, has little control over the factors that affect the validity of the results.

The most powerful design is the experimental design, in which participants are randomly assigned to the experimental and control groups. The difference between I.1 and I.2 in Table 14.2 is the use of a pretest to measure the participants before the program begins. Use of a pretest would help assure that the groups are similar. Random assignment should equally distribute any of the variables (such as age, gender, and race) between the different groups. Potential disadvantages of the experimental design are that it requires a relatively large group of participants and that the intervention may be delayed for those in the control group.

A design more commonly found in evaluations of health promotion programs is the quasi-experimental pretest-posttest design using a comparison group (II.1 in Table 14.2). This design is often used when a control group cannot be formed by random assignment. In such a case, a comparison group (a nonequivalent control group) is identified, and both groups are measured before and after the program. For example, a program on fire safety for two fifth-grade classrooms could be evaluated by using a pre/post knowledge test. Two fifth-grade classrooms not receiving the program could serve as the comparison group. Similar pretest scores between the comparison and experimental groups would indicate that the groups were equal at the beginning of the program. However, without random assignment, it would be impossible to be sure that other variables (a unit on fire safety in a 4-H group, distribution of smoke detectors, information from parents) did not influence the results.

Sometimes participants cannot be assigned to a control group and no comparison group can be identified. In such cases, a nonexperimental pretest-posttest design (III.1 in Table 14.2) can be used, but the results are of limited significance, since changes could be due to the program or to some other event. An example of this type of nonexperimental design would be the incidence of safety belt use after a community program on that topic. An increase in use might mean that the program successfully motivated individuals to use safety belts; however, it could also reveal the impact of increased enforcement of the mandatory safety belt law, of a traffic fatality in the community, or a safety article in the local newspaper.

A time series evaluation design (I.3, II.2, III.2 in Table 14.2) can be used to examine differences in program effects over time. Random assignment to groups (I.3) offers the most control over factors influencing the validity of the results. The use of a comparison group (II.2) offers some control; without a control group or comparison group (III.2), it is possible to determine changes in the participants over time, but one cannot be sure that the changes were due to the program.

TABLE 14.3 Staggered Treatment Design

Experimental group 1	(R)	X	O		O		O		O
Experimental group 2	(R)		O	X	O		O		O
Experimental group 3	(R)				O	X	O		O
Experimental group 4	(R)							X	O

Key: (R) = Random assignment
O = Measurement
X = Program

In the time series design, several measurements are taken over time both before and after the program is implemented. This process helps to identify other factors that may account for a change between the pretest and posttest measurements and is especially appropriate for measuring delayed effects of a program. A time series design could be used in a weight loss program to indicate the amount of weight loss over time and the ability to maintain a desired weight.

When more than one experimental group is part of the evaluation, these can be included in the designs we have discussed. This design could be used to evaluate several types of programs, for example, to compare the effect of lectures, workshop, and self-study. Measurements could be collected from all groups at the same points in time, and programs could occur simultaneously.

Another design that may be used is the staggered treatment design (Table 14.3). It is used to determine the effects of a program over time by including several measurements after the end of the program. It also indicates the effects of testing, since not all groups in this design receive a pretest. The staggered treatment design can also be used in quasi-experimental and nonexperimental designs, although with the limitations of not using a control group or comparison group.

INTERNAL VALIDITY

The **internal validity** of evaluation is the degree to which the program caused the change that was measured. Many factors can threaten internal validity, either singly or in combination, making it difficult to determine if the outcome was brought about by the program or some other cause. Cook and Campbell (1979) have identified some of the threats to internal validity, which we summarize here.

- *History* occurs when an event happens between the pretest and posttest that is not part of the health promotion program. An example of history as a threat to internal validity is having a national antismoking campaign coincide with a local smoking cessation program.
- *Maturation* occurs when the participants in the program show pretest-to-posttest differences due to growing older, wiser, or stronger. For example, in tests of muscular strength in an exercise program for junior high stu-

dents, an increase in strength could be the result of muscular development and not the effect of the program.

- *Testing* occurs when the participants become familiar with the test format due to repeated testing. This is why it is helpful to use a different form of the same test for pretest and posttest comparisons.
- *Instrumentation* occurs when there is a change in the measuring between pretest and posttest, such as the observers becoming more familiar with or skilled in the use of the testing format over time.
- *Statistical regression* is when extremely high or low scores (which are not necessarily accurate) on the pretest are closer to the mean or average scores on the posttest.
- *Selection* reflects differences in the experimental and comparison groups, generally due to lack of randomization. Selection can also interact with other threats to validity, such as history, maturation, or instrumentation, which may appear to be program effects.
- *Mortality* refers to participants who drop out of the program between the pretest and posttest. For example, if most of the participants who drop out of a weight loss program are those with the least (or the most) weight to lose, the group composition is different at the posttest.
- *Diffusion or imitation of treatments* results when participants in the control group interact and learn from the experimental group. Students randomly assigned to an innovative drug prevention program in their school (experimental group) may discuss the program with students who are not in the program (control group), biasing the results.
- *Compensatory equalization of treatments* occurs when the program or services are not available to the control group and there is an unwillingness to tolerate the inequality. For instance, the control group from the previous example (students not enrolled in the innovative drug prevention program) may complain since they are not able to participate.
- *Compensatory rivalry* is when the control group is seen as the underdog and is motivated to work harder.
- *Resentful demoralization of respondents receiving less desirable treatments* occurs among participants receiving the less desirable treatments compared to other groups, and the resentment may affect the outcome. For example, an evaluation to compare two different smoking cessation programs may assign one group (control) to the regular smoking cessation program and another group (experimental) to the regular program plus an exercise class. If the participants in the control group become aware that they are not receiving the additional exercise class, they may resent the omission, and this may be reflected in their smoking behavior and attitude toward the regular program.

The major way in which threats to internal validity can be controlled is through randomization. By random selection of participants, random assignment to groups, and random assignment of types of treatment or no treatment to groups, any differences between pretest and posttest can be interpreted as a result of the program. When random assignment to groups is not possible and quasi-experimental designs are used, the evaluator must make all threats to internal validity explicit and then rule them out one by one.

EXTERNAL VALIDITY

The other type of validity that should be considered is **external validity**, or the extent to which the program can be expected to produce similar effects in other populations. This is also known as **generalizability**. The more a program is tailored to a particular population, the greater the threat to external validity, and the less likely it is that the program can be generalized to another group.

As with internal validity, several factors can threaten external validity. They are sometimes known as reactive effects, since they cause individuals to react in a certain way. We list here several types of threats to external validity.

- *Social desirability* occurs when the individual gives a particular response to try to please or impress the evaluator. An example would be a child who tells the teacher she brushes her teeth every day, regardless of her actual behavior.
- *Expectancy effect* is when attitudes projected onto individuals cause them to act in a certain way. For example, in a drug abuse treatment program, the facilitator may feel that a certain individual will not benefit from the treatment; projecting this attitude may cause the individual to behave in self-defeating ways.
- *Hawthorne effect* refers to a behavior change because of the special status of those being tested. This effect was first identified in an evaluation of lighting conditions at an electric plant; workers increased their productivity when the level of lighting was raised, as well as when it was lowered. The change in behavior seemed to be due to the attention given to them during the evaluation process.
- *Placebo effect* causes a change in behavior due to the participants' belief in the treatment.

Cook and Campbell (1979) discuss the threats to external validity in terms of statistical interaction effects. These include interaction of selection and treatment (the findings from a program requiring a large time commitment may not be generalizable to individuals who do not have much free time); interaction of setting and treatment (evaluation results from a program conducted on campus may not be generalizable to the worksite); and interaction of history and treatment (results from a program conducted on a historically significant day may not be generalizable to other days).

Conducting the program several times in a variety of settings, with a variety of participants, can reduce the threats to external validity. Threats to external validity can also be counteracted by making a greater effort to treat all subjects identically. In a **blind** study, the participants do not know what group (control or type of experimental group) they are in. In a **double blind** study, the type of group participants are in is not known by either the participants or the program planners. In a **triple blind** study, this information is not available to the participants, planners, or evaluators.

It is important to select an evaluation design that provides both internal and external validity. This may be difficult, since lowering the threat to one type of validity may increase the threat to the other. For example, tighter evaluation controls make it more difficult to generalize the results to other situations. There must be enough control over the evaluation to allow evaluators to interpret the findings while sufficient flexibility in the program is maintained to permit the results to be generalized to similar settings.

SUMMARY

This chapter focuses on evaluation models and designs. House's (1980) taxonomy of evaluation models/approaches was presented. Each of the eight models could serve as a framework for an evaluation. No one model is useful in all situations. Therefore, it was recommended that evaluators select a model or parts of models to structure the evaluation based on the needs of the stakeholders involved with each program.

The specifics of evaluation design should be considered early in the planning process. Planners need to identify what measurements will be taken, and when and how. In doing so, a design should be selected that controls for both internal and external validity.

QUESTIONS

1. Why is a model used in evaluation?
2. List the eight major evaluation approaches in the taxonomy by House (1980). Discuss the major audiences and some of the evaluation questions that could be answered.
3. What are the major features of the behavioral objective, goal-free, decision-making, and systems analysis models? What are the strengths and limitations of each of these models?
4. What is the difference between cost-benefit analysis and cost-effectiveness analysis? Which is more appropriate for use in health promotion programs?
5. What is the difference between quantitative and qualitative evaluation? When would one approach be more appropriate than the other? How could they be combined in an evaluation design?

6. What are the advantages of using a control group? What types of evaluation design do not use control groups? What is the difference between a control group and a comparison group?
7. What are the strengths and weaknesses of the various evaluation designs?
8. What is the difference between internal validity and external validity?
9. What are some considerations in the selection of an evaluation design presented in this chapter? What considerations can you add to this list?

ACTIVITIES

1. Identify which model or models you would use in developing an evaluation for a program you are planning. Provide a rationale for your decision.
2. Look at an evaluation of a health promotion program that has been conducted in your community. Identify the evaluation model(s) it most closely follows. Discuss your view with the program evaluator.
3. Talk with a program administrator or other decision makers about their view of evaluation; discuss the advantages and disadvantages of the major models from their perspective. For example, who should make the decision about how the evaluation results are used? What are the questions they would like answered? Conduct the same activity using program participants instead of administrators. How does the view of the participants differ from the view of administrators?
4. Develop an evaluation design for a program you are planning. Explain why you chose this design, and list the strengths and weaknesses of the design.
5. If you were hired to evaluated a safety belt program in a community, what evaluation design would you use and why? Assume you have all the resources you need to conduct the evaluation.
6. Explain what evaluation design you would use in evaluating the difference between two teaching techniques. Why would you choose this design?

15

Data Analysis and Reporting

After reading this chapter and answering the questions at the end, you should be able to:

- List examples of univariate, bivariate, and multivariate analysis and explain how they could be used in evaluation.
- Differentiate between descriptive and inferential statistics.
- Explain the difference between the null hypothesis and the alternative hypothesis in significance testing.
- Define *level of significance, Type I error,* and *Type II error.*
- Define *independent variable* and *dependent variable.*
- Describe how statistical results can be interpreted.
- Describe the format for the evaluation report, guidelines for presenting data, and ways to enhance the report.
- Discuss ways to increase the utilization of the evaluation findings.

Key Terms

alpha level
alternative hypothesis
analysis of variance (ANOVA)
bivariate data analysis
chi square
correlation
dependent variable
descriptive data analysis
independent variable
inferential data analysis
level of significance
mean
measures of central tendency
measures of spread or variation
median
mode
multiple regression
multivariate data analysis
null hypothesis
practical significance
program significance
statistical significance
Type I error
Type II error
univariate data analysis
variables

Like all other aspects of evaluation, the types of data analysis to be used in the evaluation should be determined in the program-planning stage. Basically, the analysis determines whether the outcome was different from what was expected. The evaluator then draws conclusions and prepares reports and/or presentations. The types of analysis to be used and how the information is presented are determined by the evaluation questions and the needs of the stakeholders.

In this chapter, we describe different types of analyses commonly used in evaluating health promotion programs. To present them in detail or to include all possible techniques is beyond the scope of this text. Readers needing more information are referred to statistics textbooks, research methods and statistics courses, or statistical consultants.

Evaluations that suffer from major methodological problems are not likely to inspire confidence. A common problem is inadequate documentation of methods, results, and data analysis. The evaluation itself should be well designed; the report should contain a complete description of the program, objective interpretation of facts, information about the evaluation design and statistical analysis, and a discussion of features of the study that may have influenced the findings. In order to add accurate findings to the knowledge base of the profession, appropriate evaluation standards should be adopted to serve as guidelines for reporting and reviewing evaluation research (Moskowitz, 1989).

ORGANIZATION OF DATA

Once evaluators have collected the data, they must compile and analyze the information collected in order to interpret the findings. The data must be cleaned, reduced, coded, and pulled into a usable form. Information from surveys and observation sheets, for example, must be coded and entered into the computer to be compiled and analyzed. This is done with both quantitative and qualitative data.

TYPES OF ANALYSES

Statistical analysis techniques can be used to describe data, generate hypotheses, or test hypotheses. Techniques that summarize and describe characteristics of a group or make comparisons of characteristics between groups are known as descriptive statistics. Inferential statistics are used to make generalizations or inferences about a population based on findings from a sample.

Variables are characteristics, such as age, level of knowledge, or type of educational program. **Independent variables** are controlled by the evaluator; an example is the type of fitness program chosen (high-impact aerobics or stretching and toning). This choice results in an outcome, known as the **dependent variable.** Examples of dependent variables include scores on an alcohol knowledge test, fitness level, or attitude toward safety. When one variable is analyzed, this is called **univariate data analysis**. Analysis of two or more than two variables is called **bivariate and multivariate data analysis**, respectfully.

TABLE 15.1 Types of Evaluation Questions Answered Using Univariate, Bivariate, and Multivariate Data Analysis

Univariate Analysis	Bivariate Analysis	Multivariate Analysis
What was the average score on the cholesterol knowledge test?	Is there a difference in smoking behavior between the individuals in the experimental and control groups after the healthy lifestyle program?	Can the risk of heart disease be predicted using smoking, exercise, diet, and heredity?
How many participants at the worksite attended the healthy lifestyle presentation?	Is peer education, classroom instruction, or media presentations more effective in increasing knowledge about the effects of drug abuse?	Can mortality risk among motorcycle drivers be predicted from helmet use, time of day, weather conditions, and speed?
What percentage of the participants in the corporate fitness program met their target goal?	Do students' attitudes about bicycle helmets differ in rural and urban settings?	

The choice of a type of analysis is based on the evaluation questions, the type of data collected, and the audience who will receive the results (Newcomer, 1994). For some types of evaluation, descriptive data are all that is needed, and techniques are chosen to determine frequencies or relationships between variables. Other evaluation questions focus on testing a hypothesis about relationships between variables, and in such cases more elaborate statistical techniques are needed. Table 15.1 lists the types of evaluation questions that can be answered by using different types of data analyses.

The level of measurement (i.e., nominal, ordinal, interval, or ratio, discussed in Chapter 5) is an important factor in selecting the type of data analysis. For the most part, analytical techniques have been developed for use with selected levels of measurement. In other words, not all analytical techniques can be used with all levels of measurement. For example, multiple regression analysis is a technique that has been reserved for use with interval and ratio data. Newcomer (1994) has created a very useful summary (see Table 15.2 on page 254) to assist evaluators in selecting appropriate statistical techniques.

The issue of who will be the recipients of the final evaluation report should also be considered when selecting the type of analysis. Evaluators want to be able to present the evaluation results in a form that can be understood by the stakeholders. With regard to this issue, it is probably best to err on the side of too simple an analysis rather than one that is too complex.

Finally, regardless of the type of analysis selected for an evaluation, the method should be chosen early in the evaluation process and should be in place before the data are collected.

Univariate Data Analyses

Univariate data analysis examines one variable at a time. It is common for univariate analysis to be descriptive in nature. **Descriptive data analyses** are used to describe, classify, and summarize data. Summary counts (frequencies) are totals, and are the easiest type of data to collect and report. Summary counts could be used in formative evaluation, to count the number of participants in blood pressure screening programs at various sites. The information would assist the program planners in publicizing sites with low attendance or adding additional personnel to busy sites. Other examples of frequencies, or summary counts, are the number of participants in a workshop, those who scored over 80% on a knowledge posttest, or number of individuals wearing a safety belt.

Measures of central tendency are other forms of univariate data analyses. The **mean** is the arithmetic average of all the scores. The **median** is the midpoint of all the scores, dividing scores ranked by size into equal halves. The **mode** is the score that occurs most frequently. These are all useful in describing the results, and reporting all three measures of central tendency will be especially helpful if extreme scores are found.

Measure of spread or variation refers to how spread out the scores are. Range is the difference between the highest and lowest scores. For example, if the high

TABLE 15.2 Selecting Statistical Techniques

Purpose of the Analysis	How the Variables Are Measured	Appropriate Technique	Appropriate Test for Statistical Significance	Appropriate Measure of Magnitude
To compare a sample distribution to a population distribution	Nominal/ordinal	Frequency counts	Chi-square	NA*
	Interval	Means/medians Standard deviations/ Interquartile range	Chi-square	NA
To analyze a relationship between two variables	Nominal/ordinal	Contingency tables	Chi-square	Percentage difference
	Interval	Contingency tables/test of differences of means	Chi-square or t	Difference in means
To reduce data through identifying factors that explain variation in a set of measures	Nominal/ordinal	NA	NA	NA
	Interval	Factor analysis	t	Pearson's correlations
To sort units into similar clusters or groupings	Nominal/ordinal	NA	NA	NA
	Interval	Cluster or discriminant analysis	t	Equivalent of R-square
To predict or estimate program impact	Nominal/ordinal	Loglinear regression	t and F	R-square, beta weights
	Interval	Regression	t and F	
To describe or predict a trend in a series of data collected over time	Nominal/ordinal	Regression	t and F	R-square, beta weights
	Interval	Regression	t and F	Same as above

Source: From "Using Statistics Appropriately," by K. E. Newcomer, in *Handbook of Practical Program Evaluation* (p. 397), by J. S. Wholey, H. P. Hatry, & K. E. Newcomer (Eds.), 1994, San Francisco: Jossey-Bass. Copyright 1994 by Jossey-Bass, Inc., Publishers. Used with permission.

Note: *NA = not applicable

score is 100 and the low score is 60, the range is 40. **Measures of spread or variation**, such as range, standard deviation, or variance, can be used to determine whether scores from groups are similar or spread apart.

Bivariate Data Analyses

Bivariate data analyses analyze the relationship between two variables. Measures of relationship, or **correlation**, are used to establish a relationship between two variables. Correlation is expressed as a value between +1 (positive correlation) and -1 (negative correlation), with 0 indicating no relationship between the variables. Correlation between variables only indicates a relationship; this technique does not establish cause and effect. An example of the use of correlation would be to determine the relationship between safety belt use and age of the driver. If older people were found to wear their safety belts more often than young people, that would constitute a positive correlation between age and belt use. If younger people wore their safety belts more often, it would be a negative correlation. If age made no difference in who wore the belts more often, the correlation would be 0.

Analysis of variance (ANOVA) is a statistical test used to compare the difference in means of two or more groups. It does not prove that there is a difference between groups; it only allows the evaluator to reject or retain the null hypothesis, then make inferences about the population.

Chi square is a statistical technique to test hypotheses about frequencies in various categories. This technique uses categories that can be distinguished from one another but are not hierarchical. This type of analysis could be used to analyze attitudes toward the use of bicycle helmets (strongly agree, agree, neutral, disagree, and strongly disagree) between children in three different grade levels.

Inferential data analyses use statistical tests to draw tentative conclusions about the relationship between variables; conclusions are drawn in the form of probability statements, not absolute proof. The evaluation question is stated in the form of hypotheses. The **null hypothesis** holds that there is no observed difference between the variables. The **alternative hypothesis** says that there is a difference between the variables. For example, a null hypothesis states that there is no difference between the experimental and control groups in knowledge about cancer risk factors. The alternative hypothesis states that there is a difference.

Statistical tests are used to determine whether the null hypothesis can be rejected (meaning that a relationship between the variables probably does exist) or whether it should be retained (indicating that any apparent relationship between variables is due to chance). There is the possibility that the null hypothesis can be rejected when it is, in fact, true; this is known as a **Type I error**. There is also the possibility of failing to reject the null hypothesis when it is, in fact, not true; this is a **Type II error**. The probability of making a Type I error is reflected in the alpha level. The **alpha level**, or **level of significance**, is established before the statistical tests are run and is generally set at .05 or .01. This indicates that the decision to reject the null hypothesis is incorrect 5% (or 1%) of the time; that is, there is a 5% probability (or 1% probability) that the outcome occurred by chance alone.

When a smaller alpha level is used (.01 or .001), the possibility of making a Type I error is reduced; at the same time, however, the possibility of a Type II error increases. An example of a Type I error is the adoption of a new program due to higher scores on a knowledge test, when in reality increases in knowledge occurred by chance and the new program is not more effective than the existing program. An example of a Type II error is not adopting the new program when it is, in reality, more effective.

Multivariate Data Analyses

Multivariate data analyses are used to determine the relationships between more than two variables. One type of multivariate statistic is **multiple regression.** It is used to make a prediction from several variables. For example, the risk of heart disease may be predicted from the following variables: smoking, exercise, diet, and family history.

Applications of Data Analyses

Up to this point in time, we have presented many evaluation concepts—so many, in fact, that you might find it difficult to keep them all clear in your mind and then apply them. Therefore, we thought it might be useful if we presented a few examples so that you can see how to move from a program goal to an intervention to an evaluation design to data analysis. To illustrate these concepts, we have selected a couple of statistics that are commonly used with health promotion programs: chi-square and *t*-tests.

Case #1

Program goal: Reduce the prevalence of smoking in the target population
Target population: The seventy smoking employees of Company XYZ
Intervention (independent variable): Two different smoking cessation programs
Variable of interest (dependent variable): Smoking cessation after one year
Evaluation design: R A X_1 O_1
R B X_2 O_1

where:

R = random assignment
A = group A
B = group B
X_1 = method 1
X_2 = method 2
O_1 = self-reported smoking behavior

Data collected: Nominal data; quit yes or no

	Smoking Employees	
	Group A Method 1	Group B Method 2
Quit	24%	33%
Did not quit	76%	67%

Data analysis: A chi-square test of statistical significance can be used to test the null hypothesis that there is no difference in the success of the two groups.

Case #2

Program goal: Increase the AIDS knowledge of the target population
Target population: The 1,200 new freshmen at ABC University
Intervention (independent variable): A two-hour lecture-discussion program given during the freshmen orientation program
Variable of interest (dependent variable): AIDS knowledge
Evaluation design: O_1 X O_2

where:

O_1 = pretest scores
X = two-hour program at freshman orientation
O_2 = posttest scores

Data collection: Ratio data; scores on 100-point-scale test

	Test Results	
	Pretest	Posttest
Number of students	1,200	1,200
Mean score	69.0	78.5

Data analysis: A dependent *t*-test of statistical significance can be used to test the null hypothesis that there is no difference between the pre- and posttest means on the knowledge test.

Case #3

Program goal: To improve the testicular self-examination skills of the target population
Target population: All boys enrolled in the eighth grade at Jones Junior High School
Intervention (independent variable): Two-week unit on testicular cancer
Variable of interest (dependent variable): Score on testicular self-exam skills test
Evaluation design:

A O_1 X O_2
B O_1 O_2

where:

A = eighth grade boys at Jones Junior High School
B = eighth grade boys at Hastings Junior High School
O_1 = pretest scores
X = two-week unit on testicular cancer
O_2 = posttest scores

Data collected: Ratio data; scores on 100-point skills test

Test Results

	Jones Junior High (n = 142)	Hastings Junior High (n = 131)
Pre	62	63
Post	79	65

Data analysis: An independent *t*-test of statistical significance can be used to (1) test the null hypothesis that there is no difference in the pretest scores of the two groups, since the groups were not randomly assigned, and (2) test the null hypothesis that there is no differences in the posttest scores of the two groups.

INTERPRETING THE RESULTS

Once the results of the analyses are available, evaluators must interpret them to answer the evaluation questions. Utilization-focused evaluation suggests having a pre-evaluation session with the stakeholders to simulate interpreting the results of the data. The purpose of this session is to check on the evaluation design, train the stakeholders to interpret data, help stakeholders set realistic expectations, and build a commitment to use the findings, or else reveal the lack of commitment (Patton, 1986).

Evaluators should also seek input from the leaders of the group affected by the program to assist in the interpretation of the results and to develop recommendations. They should present the facts in a logical order, allowing for questions about the possible relationships among the findings. Various courses of action can then be discussed (Solomon, 1987).

Standards of acceptability should be established in the program-planning stage. These standards can be modified after a session with stakeholders, during instrument development, or before data collection. The role of evaluators as decision makers may vary in the different evaluation models. Even if evaluators are responsible for making decisions and recommendations, they should still seek input from stakeholders.

The interpretation of the results must distinguish between **program significance (practical significance)** and **statistical significance**. Programmatic significance measures the meaningfulness of a program regardless of statistical significance. Statistical significance is determined by statistical testing. It is possible—especially when a large number of people are included in the data collection—to have statistically significant results that indicate gains in performance but are not meaningful in terms of program goals. Statistical significance is similar to reliability in that they are both measures of precision. It is important to consider whether statistical significance justifies the development, implementation, and costs of a program (Fink and Kosecoff, 1978).

EVALUATION REPORTING

The results and interpretation of the data analyses, as well as a description of the evaluation process, are incorporated into the final report to be presented to the stakeholders. The report itself generally follows the format of a research report, including an introduction, methodology, results, conclusions, and discussion.

The number and type of reports needed are determined at the beginning of the evaluation based on the needs of the stakeholders. For a formative evaluation, reports are needed early and may be provided on a weekly or monthly basis. The formative evaluations may be formal or informal, ranging from scheduled presentations to informal telephone calls. They must be submitted on time in order to provide immediate feedback so that program modifications can be made. Generally, a report is submitted at the end of an evaluation and may be written and/or oral.

Evaluators must be able to communicate to all audiences when presenting the results of the evaluation. The reaction of each audience—participants, media, administrators, funding source—must be anticipated in order to prepare the necessary information. In some cases, technical information must be included; in other cases, anecdotal information may be appropriate. The evaluator must fit the report to the audience and also prepare for a negative response if the results of the evaluation are not favorable. This involves looking critically at the results and developing responses to anticipated reactions.

The format for communicating the evaluation results may include several methods, such as a technical report, journal article, news release, meeting, presentation, press conference, letter, or workshop. Generally, more than one method is selected in order to meet the needs of all stakeholders. For example, following an innovative worksite health promotion program, the evaluator might prepare a news release for the community, a letter to all staff who participated, a technical report for the funding source, and an executive summary for the administrators.

Designing the Written Report

As previously mentioned, the evaluation report follows a similar format to that used in a research report. The evaluation report generally includes the following sections:

- *Abstract or executive summary.* This is a summary of the total evaluation, including goals and objectives, methods, results, conclusions, and recom-

TABLE 15.3 What to Include in the Evaluation Process

Abstract/executive summary	Overview of the program and evaluation General results, conclusions, and recommendations
Introduction	Purpose of the evaluation Program and participant description (including staff, materials, activities, procedures, etc.) Goals and objectives Evaluation questions
Methods/procedures	Design of the evaluation Target population Instrument Sampling procedures Data collection procedures Pilot study results Validity and reliability Limitations Data analyses procedures
Results	Description of findings from data analyses Answers to evaluation questions Addresses any special concerns Explanation of findings Charts and graphs of findings
Conclusions/recommendations	Interpretation of results Conclusions about program effectiveness Program recommendations Determining if additional information is needed

mendations. It is a concise presentation of the evaluation, since it may be the only portion of the report that some of the stakeholders may read. Most abstracts/executive summaries range in length from 150 to 600 words.

- *Introduction.* This section of the report includes a complete description of the program and the evaluation. Goals and objectives of the program are listed, as are the evaluation questions to be answered.
- *Methods/procedures.* The methods/procedures section of the report includes information on the evaluation design, the target groups, the instruments used, and how the data were collected and analyzed.
- *Results.* This section is the main part of the report. It includes the findings from the evaluation, summarizing and simplifying the data and presenting them in a clear, concise format. Data are presented for every evaluation question.

- *Conclusions/recommendations.* This section uses the findings (presented in the previous section) to answer the evaluation questions. The results are interpreted to determine significance and explanations. Judgments and recommendations are included in this section; they may have been made by the evaluator and/or the administrator, depending on the evaluation model used.

Table 15.3 summarizes what is included in the evaluation report.

Presenting Data

The data that have been collected and analyzed are presented in the evaluation report. Graphs and tables may be used to illustrate certain findings, and these are often a central portion of the results section. The narrative should not repeat what is shown in the graphs and tables but should expand and enhance this information. If many tables are included, the main ones can be placed in the text of the report and the rest relegated to an appendix. Table 15.4 on page 262 lists guidelines to follow when presenting data in the evaluation report and/or presentation.

How and When to Present the Report

Evaluators must consider carefully the logistics of presenting the evaluation findings. They should discuss this with the decision makers involved in the evaluation. An evaluator may be in the position of presenting negative results, encountering distrust among staff members, or submitting a report that will never be read. We offer several suggestions for enhancing the evaluation report:

- Give key decision makers advance information on the findings; this increases the likelihood that the information will actually be used and prevents the decision makers from learning about the results from the media or another source.
- Maintain anonymity of individuals, institutions, and organizations; use sensitivity to avoid judging or labeling people in negative ways; maintain confidentiality of the final report according to the wishes of the administrators; maintain objectivity throughout the report (Windsor et al., 1994).
- Choose ways to report the evaluation findings so as to meet the needs of the stakeholders, and include information that is relevant to each group.

INCREASING UTILIZATION OF THE RESULTS

Far too often, an evaluation will be conducted and a report submitted to the decision makers, but the recommendations will not be implemented. This occurs for a variety of reasons. Decision makers may not use findings because they are conducting the evaluation only to fulfill the requirements of the funding source, to

TABLE 15.4 Guidelines for Presenting Data

1. Use graphic methods of presenting numerical data whenever possible.
2. Build the results and discussion section of the evaluation report—and perhaps other sections as well—around tables and figures. Prepare the tables and graphs first; then write text to explain them.
3. Make each table and figure self-explanatory. Use a clear, complete title, a key, label, footnotes, and so forth.
4. Discuss in the text the major information to be found in each table and figure.
5. Play with, and consider using, as many graphs as you have the time and ingenuity to prepare. Not only do they communicate clearly to your audiences, they also help you to see what is happening.
6. Since graphs tend to convey fewer details than numerical tables, consider providing both tables and graphs for the same data, where appropriate.
7. If you have used a mixed evaluation design with both quantitative and qualitative data collection procedures, use the direct quotations and descriptions from the qualitative results to add depth and clarity to information reported graphically.
8. When presenting complicated graphs to a live audience, give some instruction about how to read the graph and a few sample interpretations of simpler versions, then present the real data.
9. When a complete draft of the report has been completed, ask yourself the following questions:
   a. Do the figure titles give a comprehensive description of the figures? Could someone leafing through the report understand the graphs?
   b. Are both axes of every graph clearly labeled with a name?
   c. Is the interval size marked on all axes of graphs?
   d. Is the number of cases on which each summary statistic has been based indicated in each table or on each graph?
   e. Are the tables and figures labeled and numbered throughout the report?
   f. If the report is a lengthy one, does it include a list of tables and figures at the front following the table of contents?

Source: From L. L. Morris, C. T. Fitz-Gibbon, and M. E. Freeman, *How to Communicate Evaluation Findings* (pp. 75–76), Copyright © 1987 by Sage Publications, Inc. Reprinted by permission of Sage Publications, Inc.

serve their own self-interest, or to gain recognition for a successful program. Even decision makers who plan to use the evaluation results in their health promotion program may find that they are unable to state the evaluation question or that the final report contains language and concepts that are unfamiliar to them. Weiss (1984) sees the need to improve the quality both of evaluation research and of modes of disseminating the findings. Weiss (1984) developed the following guidelines to increase the chances that evaluation results will actually be used.

1. Plan the study with program stakeholders in mind and involve them in the planning process.

2. Continue to gather information about the program after the planning stage; a change in the program should result in a change in the evaluation.
3. Focus the evaluation on conditions about the program that the decision makers can change.
4. Write reports in a clear, simple manner and submit them on time. Use graphs and charts within the text, and include complicated statistical information in an appendix.
5. Base whether to make recommendations or not on how specific and clear cut the data are, how much is known about the program, and whether differences between programs are obvious. A joint interpretation between evaluator and decision maker may be best.
6. Disseminate the results to all stakeholders, using a variety of methods.
7. Integrate evaluation findings with other research and evaluation about the program area.
8. Provide high-quality research.

SUMMARY

Evaluation questions developed in the early program-planning stages can be answered once the data have been analyzed. Descriptive statistics can be used to summarize or describe the data, and inferential statistics can be used to generate or test hypotheses. Evaluators then interpret the findings and present the results to the stakeholders, via a formal or informal report.

QUESTIONS

1. What are some common problems with evaluations, and how can these problems be reduced or overcome?
2. What are some types of univariate data analyses used in evaluation? When would these be used?
3. How are bivariate and multivariate data analyses used in evaluation?
4. Explain the concepts of hypothesis testing, level of significance, Type I error, and Type II error.
5. What is the role of evaluators and decision makers in interpreting the results and making recommendations?
6. What is the difference between statistical significance and program significance?
7. What information is included in the written evaluation report? How is the information modified for various audiences?
8. What are some guidelines for presenting data in an evaluation report?
9. How can the evaluation report be enhanced?
10. How can the evaluator increase the likelihood of utilization of the evaluation findings?

ACTIVITIES

1. Obtain an actual report from a program evaluation. Look for the type of statistical test used, the level of significance, the independent and dependent variables, the interpretation of the findings, recommendations, and format for the report.
2. Discuss evaluation with a decision maker from a health agency. Find out what types of evaluation have been conducted, who has conducted them, what the findings have been, whether the findings were implemented, and how the information was reported.
3. Compare an evaluation report with a research report. What are the similarities and differences? How could you improve the report?
4. Using data that you have generated or data presented by your instructor, create one table and one graph.

APPENDIXES

APPENDIX A ☐ Model Alcohol Policy

INTER-ASSOCIATION TASK FORCE

Model Campus Alcohol Policy Guidelines

The Task Force recommends that a comprehensive campus policy on alcohol include a summary of state and city laws covering each of the following areas:

1. Drinking Age Laws pertaining to the possession, consumption, and sale of alcoholic beverages as well as penalties for violation of such laws.
2. Regulations of Sale Laws with special emphasis on Alcohol Beverage Control (ABC) Board's requirements for special permits or licenses by groups that charge admission or dues for events involving alcoholic beverages.
3. Open Container Laws governed by city or county ordinances or state statutes concerning the consumption of alcoholic beverages in outdoor areas or automobiles.
4. Other Laws pertinent to the jurisdiction (such as dram shop or implied consent laws).

College Regulations

In addition to legal responsibilities, The Task Force recommends that the following regulations be instituted as part of an alcohol policy on campus:

1. Locations where alcoholic beverages are permitted to be possessed, served, and consumed by persons of legal drinking age on the campus should be visibly marked. A specific listing of such places (e.g., in private rooms, designated common areas of residence halls, college unions, etc.) helps clarify questions that students, faculty, or staff might have about where alcoholic beverages are permitted on campus.
2. Locations where alcoholic beverages are permitted to be sold as opposed to merely served on campus (e.g., faculty lounge, college union, pub, etc.) should be delineated clearly.
3. Guidelines should be established regarding public and private social events that involve alcoholic beverages within the institution's jurisdiction. An event that is open to the public (i.e., where admission is charged or public announcement is made) should be registered with the appropriate campus office before the event. Such events should be conducted within the following guidelines:
   a. If the function includes the sale of alcoholic beverages, a permit should be obtained from the appropriate state office or ABC Board.
   b. Individuals sponsoring the event should implement precautionary measures to ensure that alcoholic beverages are not accessible or served to persons under the legal drinking age or to persons who appear intoxicated.
   c. At social functions where alcoholic beverages are provided by the sponsoring organization, direct access should be limited to a person(s) designated as the server(s).
   d. Consumption of alcoholic beverages should be permitted only within the approved area designated for the event.
   e. Nonalcoholic beverages must be available at the same place as the alcoholic beverages and featured as prominently as the alcoholic beverages.
   f. A reasonable portion of the budget for the event shall be designated for the purchase of food items.
   g. No social event shall include any form of "drinking contest" in its activities or promotion.
   h. Advertisements for any university event at which alcoholic beverages are served shall mention the availability of nonalcoholic beverages as prominently as alcohol. Alcohol should not be used as an inducement to participate in a campus event.
   i. Promotional materials including advertising for any university event shall not make reference to the amount of alcoholic beverages (such as number of beer kegs) available.
   j. Institutionally approved security personnel shall be present at all times during the event.
4. A specific statement concerning the use or nonuse of alcoholic beverages at membership

recruitment functions (e.g., fraternity/sorority rush, departmental clubs, and special interest groups) should be an integral part of a comprehensive campus alcohol policy.

5. A specific statement concerning the use or nonuse of alcoholic beverages in athletic facilities or at athletic events should be included as part of a comprehensive campus alcohol policy. Such a statement should apply equally to students, faculty, staff, alumni, and others attending the event.
6. Guidelines for any marketing, advertising, or promotion of alcoholic beverages on campus or at campus events involving alcohol should be stated as part of a comprehensive campus alcohol policy.
7. Procedures for adjudicating violations of the alcohol policy should be articulated. Such procedures should include an explicit statement of sanctions.

Source: Alcohol programs and policies on campus: NASPA monograph #7, ed. S. Sherwood, 1987, Washington, DC: National Association of Student Personnel Administrators. Reprinted by permission of National Association of Student Personnel Administrators.

APPENDIX B □ McSmeltzer Corporation Smoking Policy

McSMELTZER CORPORATION

Health Policy H-48
Effective January 1, 1997
Approved by the Board on August 4, 1996

Smoking Policy

It is the policy of the McSmeltzer Corporation that smoking will not be permitted on Corporation property (this includes the physical plant, the surrounding Corporation-owned grounds, and parking lots) and in Corporation vehicles (this includes vehicles owned by the Corporation and those leased vehicles that are being operated at Corporation expense). The policy applies to all employees, full- and part-time, and guests of the Corporation.

Violations of this policy will be dealt with according to the progressive discipline policy of the Corporation (see Policy A-5).

APPENDIX C □ Model Ordinance Eliminating Smoking in Workplaces and Enclosed Public Places (100% Smokefree)

SEC. 1000. Title

This article shall be known as the Smoking Pollution Control Ordinance.

SEC. 1001. Findings and Purpose

The City Council [Board of Supervisors] does hereby find that:

Numerous studies have found that tobacco smoke is a major contributor to indoor air pollution, and that breathing secondhand smoke is a cause of disease, including lung cancer, in nonsmokers. At special risk are children, elderly people, individuals with cardiovascular disease, and individuals with impaired respiratory function, including asthmatics and those with obstructive airway disease; and

Health hazards induced by breathing secondhand smoke include lung cancer, heart disease, respiratory infection, and decreased respiratory function, including bronchoconstriction and broncho-spasm.

Accordingly, the City Council [Board of Supervisors] finds and declares that the purposes of this ordinance are (1) to protect the public health and welfare by prohibiting smoking in public places and places of employment; and (2) to guarantee the right of nonsmokers to breathe smoke-free air, and to recognize that the need to breathe smoke-free air shall have priority over the desire to smoke.

SEC. 1002. Definitions

The following words and phrases, whenever used in this article, shall be construed as defined in this section:

1. "Bar" means an area which is devoted to the serving of alcoholic beverages for consumption by guests on the premises and in which the serving of food is only incidental to the consumption of such beverages. A "bar" for the purpose of this definition does not include any establishment where tobacco smoke can filter into any area where smoking is prohibited through a passageway, ventilation system, or any other means.
2. "Business" means any sole proprietorship, partnership, joint venture, corporation, or other business entity formed for profit-making purposes, including retail establishments where goods or services are sold as well as professional corporations and other entities where legal, medical, dental, engineering, architectural, or other professional services are delivered.
3. "Employee" means any person who is employed by any employer in the consideration for direct or indirect monetary wages or profit, and any person who volunteers his or her services for a nonprofit entity.
4. "Employer" means any person, partnership, corporation, including a municipal corporation, or nonprofit entity, who employs the services of one or more individual persons.
5. "Enclosed Area" means all space between a floor and ceiling which is enclosed on all sides by solid walls or windows (exclusive of door or passage ways) which extend from the floor to the ceiling, including all space therein screened by partitions which do not extend to the ceiling or are not solid, "office landscaping," or similar structures.
6. "Place of Employment" means any enclosed area under the control of a public or private employer which employees normally frequent during the course of employment, including, but not limited to, work areas, employee lounges and restrooms, conference and classrooms, employee cafeterias, and hallways. A private residence is not a "place of employment" unless it is used as a child care, adult day care, or health care facility.
7. "Public Place" means any enclosed area to which the public is invited or in which the public is permitted, including but not limited to, banks, educational facilities, health facilities, laundromats, public transportation facilities, reception areas, restaurants, retail food production and marketing establishments, retail service establishments, retail stores, theatres, and waiting rooms. A private residence is not a "public place."

8. "Restaurant" means any coffee shop, cafeteria, sandwich stand, private and public school cafeteria, and any other eating establishment which gives or offers for sale food to the public, guests, or employees, as well as kitchens in which food is prepared on the premises for serving elsewhere, including catering facilities, except that the term "restaurant" shall not include a cocktail lounge or tavern if said cocktail lounge or tavern is a "bar" as defined in Section 1002 (1).
9. "Retail Tobacco Store" means a retail store utilized primarily for the sale of tobacco products and accessories and in which the sale of other products is merely incidental.
10. "Service Line" means any indoor line at which one (1) or more persons are waiting for or receiving service of any kind, whether or not such service involves the exchange of money.
11. "Smoking" means inhaling, exhaling, burning, or carrying any lighted cigar, cigarette, weed, plant, or other combustible substance in any manner or in any form.
12. "Sports Arena" means sports pavilions, gymnasiums, health spas, boxing arenas, swimming polls, roller and ice rinks, bowling alleys, and other similar places where members of the general public assemble either to engage in physical exercise, participate in athletic competition, or witness sports events.

SEC. 1003. Application of Article to City-Owned Facilities

All enclosed facilities owned by the City of ______ shall be subject to the provisions of this article.

SEC. 1004. Prohibition of Smoking in Public Places

A. Smoking shall be prohibited in all enclosed public places within the City of ______, including, but not limited to, the following places:
    1. Elevators.
    2. Restrooms, lobbies, reception areas, hallways, and any other common-use areas.
    3. Buses, taxicabs, and other means of public transit under the authority of the City of ______, and ticket, boarding, and waiting areas of public transit depots.
    4. Service lines.
    5. Retail stores.
    6. All areas available to and customarily used by the general public in all businesses and nonprofit entities patronized by the public, including but not limited to, attorneys' offices and other offices, banks, laundromats, hotels, and motels.
    7. Restaurants.
    8. Public areas of aquariums, galleries, libraries, and museums when open to the public.
    9. Any facility which is primarily used for exhibiting any motion picture, stage, drama, lecture, musical recital, or other similar performance, except when smoking is part of a stage production.
    10. Sports arenas and convention halls.
    11. Every room, chamber, place of meeting or public assembly, including school buildings under the control of any board, council, commission, committee, including joint committees, or agencies of the City or any political subdivision of the State during such time as a public meeting is in progress, to the extent such place is subject to the jurisdiction of the city.
    12. Waiting rooms, hallways, wards, and semiprivate rooms of health facilities, including, but not limited to, hospitals, clinics, physical therapy facilities, doctors' offices, and dentists' offices.
    13. Lobbies, hallways, and other common areas in apartment buildings, condominiums, trailer parks, retirement facilities, nursing homes, and other multiple-unit residential facilities.
    14. Polling places.

B. Notwithstanding any other provision of this section, any owner, operator, manager, or other person who controls any establishment or facility may declare that entire establishment or facility as a nonsmoking establishment.

SEC. 1005. Prohibition of Smoking in Places of Employment

A. It shall be the responsibility of employers to provide a smoke-free workplace for all employees, but employers are not required to incur any expense to make structural or other physical modifications.

B. Within 90 days of the effective date of this article, each employer having an enclosed place of employment located within the city shall adopt, implement, make known, and maintain a written smoking policy which shall contain the following requirements:

Smoking shall be prohibited in all enclosed facilities within a place of employment without exception. This includes common work areas, auditoriums, classrooms, conference and meeting rooms, private offices, elevators, hallways, medical facilities, cafeterias, employee lounges, stairs, restrooms, vehicles, and all other enclosed facilities.

C. The smoking policy shall be communicated to all employees within three (3) weeks of its adoption.

D. All employers shall supply a written copy of the smoking policy upon request to any existing or prospective employee.

SEC. 1006. Reasonable Distance

Smoking shall occur at a reasonable distance outside any enclosed area where smoking is prohibited to ensure that tobacco smoke does not enter the area through entrances, windows, ventilation systems or any other means.

SEC. 1007. Where Smoking Not Regulated

A. Notwithstanding any other provision of this article to the contrary, the following areas shall not be subject to the smoking restrictions of this article:

1. Bars which meet the requirements of Section 1002 (1) of this article.
2. Private residences, except when used as a child care, adult day care, or health care facility.
3. Twenty-five percent (25%) of hotel and motel rooms rented to guests.
4. Retail tobacco stores.
5. Restaurants, hotel and motel conference or meeting rooms, and public and private assembly rooms while these places are being used for private functions.

B. Notwithstanding any other provision of this section, any owner, operator, manager, or other person who controls any establishment described in this section may declare that entire establishment as a nonsmoking establishment.

SEC. 1008. Posting of Signs

A. "No Smoking" signs or the international "No Smoking" symbol (consisting of a pictorial representation of a burning cigarette enclosed in a red circle with a red bar across it) shall be clearly, sufficiently, and conspicuously posted in every building or other area where smoking is prohibited by this article, by the owner, operator, manager, or other person having control of such building or other area.

B. Every restaurant shall have posted at every entrance a conspicuous sign clearly stating that smoking is prohibited.

C. All ashtrays and other smoking paraphernalia shall be removed from any area where smoking is prohibited by this article by the owner, operator, manager, or other person having control of such area.

SEC. 1009. Enforcement

A. Enforcement of this article shall be implemented by the Department of Health [or the City Manager].

B. Notice of the provisions set forth in this article shall be given to all applicants for a business license in the City of _________.

C. Any citizen who desires to register a complaint under this chapter may initiate enforcement with the Department of Health [or the City Manager].

D. The Fire Department or the Health Department shall require, while an establishment is undergoing otherwise mandated inspections, a "self-certification" from the owner, manager, operator, or other person having control of such establishment that all requirements of this article have been complied with.

E. Any owner, manager, operator, or employee of any establishment regulated by this article may inform persons violating this article of the appropriate provisions thereof.

F. Notwithstanding any other provision of this article, a private citizen may bring legal action to enforce this article.

SEC. 1010. Violations and Penalties

A. It shall be unlawful for any person who owns, manages, operates, or otherwise controls the use of any premises subject to regulation under this article to fail to comply with any of its provisions.

B. It shall be unlawful for any person to smoke in any area where smoking is prohibited by the provisions of this article.

C. Any person who violates any provision of this article shall be guilty of an infraction, punishable by:

1. A fine not exceeding one hundred dollars ($100) for a first violation.
2. A fine not exceeding two hundred dollars ($200) for a second violation of this article within one (1) year.
3. A fine not exceeding five hundred dollars ($500) for each additional violation of this article within one (1) year.

SEC. 1011. Nonretaliation

No person or employer shall discharge, refuse to hire, or in any manner retaliate against any employee or applicant for employment because such employee or applicant exercises any right to a smoke-free environment afforded by this article.

SEC. 1012. Public Education

The Department of Health [or City Manager] shall engage in a continuing program to explain and clarify the purposes and requirements of this ordinance to citizens affected by it, and to guide owners, operators, and managers in their compliance with it. Such program may include publication of a brochure for affected businesses and individuals explaining the provisions of this ordinance.

SEC. 1013. Other Applicable Laws

This article shall not be interpreted or construed to permit smoking where it is otherwise restricted by other applicable laws.

SEC. 1014. Severability

If any provision, clause, sentence, or paragraph of this article or the application thereof to any person or circumstances shall be held invalid, such invalidity shall not affect the other provisions of this article which can be given effect without the invalid provision or application, and to this end the provisions of this article are declared to be severable.

SEC. 1015. Effective Date

This article shall be effective thirty (30) days from and after the date of its adoption.

Source: Americans for Nonsmokers' Rights, 2530 San Pablo Avenue, Suite J, Berkeley, CA 94702, November 1994.

APPENDIX D ☐ Examples of PSAs from the Indiana State Department of Health

Mammograms for Mother's Day
Indiana State Department of Health
Television Public Service Announcement

Video	Audio/Narration
Susan Bayh (wife of Gov. Evan Bayh)	I'm Susan Bayh, and this is my mother.
	My husband lost his mother to breast cancer.
Carolyn Breshears Susan's Mom	And there's a history of breast cancer in our family.
Susan	Today there is no reason why any woman should die from breast cancer.
B-roll of exam	A mammogram x-ray can detect breast cancer 2 years before you can feel it through self-exam.
	Almost all breast cancers can be successfully treated if caught early.
Susan & Mom	So this year, give your Mom something really special. . . give her a mammogram.
Squeeze box with font	We'll give you this special card to go along with it.
For information call Indiana's American Cancer Society 1-800-ACS-2345	

Total Tape Time :30   Begin airdates 4/18/91   End 5/9/91

Source: Indiana State Department of Health, Indianapolis. Reprinted by permission of the Indiana State Department of Health.

Ryan White "For Teens Only" PSA #1
Choices

Produced by the Indiana State Department of Health :30
For air 10/2/90 – 9/31/91

Video	Audio
Ryan up full on camera	You know there's 3 ways to get AIDS.
	Sex, needles, and ignorance.
	It's the last one that gets most people today.
	I didn't have a choice. You do. Don't be afraid to ask questions.
	You can get confidential answers by calling the AIDS Hotline.
Lower third key over Elton:	(Elton John singing to end)
Indiana AIDS Hotline 1-800-848-AIDS	"Skyline Pigeon fly, to all the dreams he left so very far behind."
	(piano under to end)

TTT – :30

Please note we put :04 pad at the end for those who need a little extra time. You can cut out at your discretion. It won't affect the PSA.

Source: Indiana State Department of Health, Indianapolis. Reprinted by permission of the Indiana State Department of Health.

Baby Bottle Tooth Decay
Indiana State Department of Health
Childhood Dental Health PSA Feb. 1990 :30

Video	Audio
Mom puts child down	Bedtime bottles could be dangerous to your child's health. If your child has a bedtime bottle habit—break that habit now.
Closeup pouring milk into bottle	When sweetened liquids, juices, or milk stay on their teeth all night long, or naptime, your child's teeth can go from
Good teeth wipe to bad teeth	this—to this—before you know it.
Cee'Ann in dental chair	Find out how you can prevent this painful tooth decay and break the
Get kid to throw down his bottle	bottle habit.
Squeeze box and font Phone #	Call the Indiana State Department of Health Dental Division at (317) 383-6418.

Source: Indiana State Department of Health, Indianapolis. Reprinted by permission of the Indiana State Department of Health.

APPENDIX E ☐ Code of Practice for Smoking Cessation Programs

PREAMBLE

The national organizations listed below have developed and subscribe to the following Code of Practice for group programs of smoking cessation. They, thereby, have agreed that all such programs conducted under their aegis will comply with this code of self-regulation. The Code of Practice is intended to provide assurance and protection to individuals seeking assistance in smoking cessation. It is not intended either to endorse or to interfere with the methodology or content of any program or eliminate its unique features. The Code will be reviewed annually by the subscribing organizations.

I. Criteria of Success

Complete cessation, and continued abstinence from smoking for one year, should be the primary criteria of success. A uniform approach to the determination of rates of success is set forth in *Standards for the Evaluation of Group Smoking Cessation Programs.*

II. Disclosure

Program participants should be given an accurate description of the services rendered including a general explanation of the treatment approach, time and costs involved, and qualifications of leaders or facilitators.

Introductory sessions or some other method of informing participants of the major facts about the program, including any possible physiological risks involved, should be provided. Participants with relevant medical problems should be referred to their family physicians.

III. Continuity/Availability

Maintenance programs or other services should be available to participants (or past participants who require continued help).

Each program should have some provision for furnishing information, counseling, or referral to the participants who do not respond to its approach.

IV. Training of Leaders

Only adequately trained and experienced individuals should be allowed to lead groups.

A written protocol for training and written criteria for evaluation of leaders should be on file in each organization.

V. Program Uniformity

Programs identified with a particular organization should be similar, unless otherwise noted.

Each organization should plan for quality control and standardization of its approved program models.

VI. Record Keeping

Adequate records of all participants should be maintained in accordance with the standards set forth in *Standards for the Evaluation of Group Smoking Cessation Programs.*

VII. Evaluation

All national organizations should carry out evaluation of their own programs on at least an annual basis in accordance with *Standards for the Evaluation of Group Smoking Cessation Programs.*

Reports of these annual evaluations should be made to the Peer Review Committee on National Smoking Cessation Programs. In addition, organizations should participate in peer-reviewed evaluation as requested by this body.

VIII. Advertising, Promotion, and Public Relations

No quantitative claims of success should be made in advertising.

No guarantees of success should be made.

Statistics cited to the press should be referenced to peer-reviewed evaluation conducted in accordance with *Standards for the Evaluation of Group Smoking Cessation Programs* and must include results both at the end of treatment and after one year.

IX. Human Dignity

All programs should respect the human dignity of their participants.

There should be no discrimination in admission to or treatment in programs on the basis of race, religion, color, or sex.

All records should be confidential and lists of names should not be sold to outside groups without the approval of the participants.

American Cancer Society
American Health Foundation
American Heart Association
American Lung Association
Five-Day Plan to Stop Smoking
SmokEnders

Source: American Cancer Society, Atlanta, GA. Reprinted by permission of the American Cancer Society.

APPENDIX F ☐ How to Select the Right Vendor for Your Company's Health Promotion Program

The development of interest by employers in health promotion programs for their employees has been paralleled by a growth of vendors interested in selling health promotion services to these employers. A checklist indicating the particular services offered and the methods by which they will be provided and at what costs can help the employer make the decision for the most suitable and efficient service.

There has been a tremendous growth during the past 15 years in the number of corporate employers who have begun offering employee health promotion programs (EHPPs) (1). Many of the early programs were begun because of the intuitive projection that improved employee lifestyle would not only improve the health of the individual employees but also have an impact on the health care programs of the company. However, much of the recent growth has come about because of the relatively recent empirical data indicating that EHPPs can be cost-effective and can have a significant effect on employee health, absenteeism, morale, and productivity. Additionally, the data have indicated that EHPPs may help a company increase its own image and its ability to recruit new personnel and decrease employee turnover (2–9).

With the growth of EHPPs in the business community there has come a parallel growth in the number of organizations (vendors) who are interested in selling health promotion services (products) to the companies. It is not uncommon to find hospitals, health clubs, YMCAs/YWCAs, voluntary health agencies (i.e., American Lung Association, American Red Cross, etc.), health departments, other community organizations, and for-profit health promotion companies trying to market their services. Just as with any service, some of what these vendors are marketing is good, while some is not. Unless your company employs trained health promotion professionals who can identify the difference in these services, a good salesperson can make the poor services appear comparable to, if not better than, the good ones. Because of the newness of the EHPPs, there are few guidelines (10) to help companies select appropriate vendors. Thus, in order to help those companies who do not employ trained health promotion professionals and those who have hired one with limited experience, a checklist for evaluating health promotion vendors has been developed.

THE INSTRUMENT

The checklist comprises 50 yes–no type questions. It includes several questions that are "common sense" or basic "good business" questions. However, it has been our experience that unless a company specifically asks the questions of the vendor, the vendor may not provide information, and thus a company must make a decision to buy or not to buy based upon insufficient and/or perhaps inaccurate data.

The checklist is divided into six sections. The first section deals with the initial meeting with the vendor. Basically, this portion of the checklist presents questions which ask: "How well prepared was the vendor for the meeting?"

The second and third portions of the checklist pose questions that ask about the quality of the service being marketed. These include questions such as: "How effective is it?" "How does it compare to services being marketed by other vendors?" and "What are the qualifications of those who will actually provide the service?"

Section four of the checklist presents a series of questions that examine how the vendor will deliver and service the product. You want to work with a vendor who will provide excellent service when the agreement has been signed. The fifth section of the checklist provides questions that can be used in determining an appropriate cost for the product. The last portion of the checklist includes several general questions that deal with image, contracts, and legal concerns.

It should be noted that the checklist has been standardized and there is no set score that will assure that a vendor will be a good supplier of health promotion services. When using the checklist, those responsible for EHPPs should be very skeptical of those vendors who have a large number of checks in the "no" column of the instrument. At the same time, it will probably be difficult to find a vendor that will receive all "yes" responses. Although final decisions are usually made on a subjective basis, one should feel more confident when using the services of a vendor with a large number of "yes" responses. And finally, it should be pointed out that some areas of the country are better supplied with vendors than others, and thus all ratings would be relative to the geographic locations.

REFERENCES

1. Fielding JE, Breslow L. Health promotion programs sponsored by California employees. *Am J Public Health* 73:538–542, 1983.
2. Erfurt JC, Foote A. Cost-effectiveness of worksite blood pressure control programs. *J Occup Med* 26:892–900, 1984.
3. Fielding JE. Effectiveness of employee health improvement programs. *J Occup Med* 24:907–916, 1982.
4. Fielding JE. Health promotion and disease prevention at the worksite. *Annu Rev Public Health* xx:237–265, 1984.
5. Gibbs JO, Mulvaney D, Henes C, Reed RW. Work-site health promotion: five-year trend in employee health care costs. *J Occup Med* 27: 826–830, 1985.
6. Kristein MM. The economics of health promotion at the worksite. *Health Educ Q* 9 (special suppl):27–36, 1982.
7. Rogers PJ, Eaton EK, Bruhn JG. Is health promotion cost effective? *Prev Med* 10:324–339, 1981.
8. Schwartz RM, Rollins PL. Measuring the cost benefit of wellness strategies. *Business Health* 2(10):24–26, 1985.
9. Stason WG. Measuring the "payoff" of worksite health strategies. *Business Health* 1(4):19–22, 1984.
10. Zuti WB. Weighting—and minimizing—the risks of joint venturing. *Promoting Health* January–February, 4–5, 1986.
11. Kelly KE. Building a successful health promotion program. *Business Health* 3(March):44–45, 1986.
12. Opatz JP. *A Primer of Health Promotion: Creating Healthy Organizational Cultures.* Oryn Publications, Inc., Washington, DC, 1985.
13. Kelly KE. Separate yourself from the crowd. *Optimal Health* 2(March/April):30–32, 34, 1986.

Checklist for Selecting Health Promotion Vendors

Code: **Yes**—Yes, the vendor does/did this. **NA**—Not applicable
No —No, the vendor does not/did not do this. **NS**—Not sure

	Yes	No	NA/NS	Comments
1. Initial experience with vendor				
A. Did the vendor present a good professional image?				
B. Did the vendor do his/her homework on your company prior to the initial meeting?				
C. Is the vendor's philosophy of health promtion consistent with your company's philosophy (11)?				
D. Can the vendor explain why his/her product is appropriate for your company?				
E. Did the vendor appear responsive to your company's needs?				
F. Did the vendor explain how his/her product can meet the needs of your company (11)?				
G. Was the vendor willing to listen to you or was he/she too busy trying to sell his/her product?				
H. Is the vendor willing to make a presentation to your company's management?				
I. Did the vendor demonstrate his/her organization's expertise with regard to the product?				
J. Did the vendor provide you with a reference list of other customers (12)?				
K. Did the vendor leave written materials that summarize his/her product?				
2. Product quality				
A. Did the vendor provide an overview of the product content?				
B. Can the vendor provide careful documentation of product effectiveness?				
C. Does the vendor have evaluative data to back up the product?				
D. Does the vendor have data to compare sucess rates of the product to those of his/her competitors?				
E. Can the vendor provide data which show the adequacy of his/her products with a population similar to yours (12)?				
F. Can the vendor provide several different products (health promotion activities), or does he/she just specialize in one area?				

	Yes	No	NA/NS	Comments
2. Product quality, *continued*				
G. Did the vendor explain the types of interventions (behavior modification, aversive techniques, etc.) that are used with the product?				
H. Will the vendor "customize" the product to meet the needs of your company?				
I. Can the vendor offer a variety of interventions (i.e., different approaches to smoking cessation) from which you can choose to best meet the needs of your employees (13)?				
J. Can the vendor offer a product which can meet special needs of your employees (e.g., reading levels, various levels of health status, etc.) (13)?				
K. When appropriate, does the vendor provide written instructional materials to accompany the product?				
L. If written informational materials are provided, are they written clearly and presented in an attractive way?				
3. Individuals who provide the service				
A. What type of education and training do the staff and/or instructors have?				
B. Are the instructors certified by a professional and/ or health organization?				
C. Are the instructors required to update their training periodically?				
D. Are the instructor-to-participant ratios reasonable?				
4. Product delivery and service				
A. Can the vendor put in writing the actual services that will be provided?				
B. If a written presentation of services is made, does it spell out the responsibilities of both parties?				
C. Is the vendor willing to market the product inside your company?				
D. Does purchase of the product include an evaluation?				
E. Can the vendor appropriately serve the size of your company's population?				
F. Can the vendor provide the product at all sites desired?				
G. Can the vendor provide the product at the time desired?				

	Yes	No	NA/NS	Comments
4. Product delivery and service, *continued*				
H. Are the length of the product sessions appropriate for your work day?				
I. Does the vendor provide you with the name of one of their employees who can act as a trouble-shooter?				
J. Can the vendor also provide other products/services to other departments (units) (i.e., the safety division, health policy, etc.) in your company?				
K. Has the vendor been in business for at least five years (10)?				
L. Is the vendor's company well managed and financially sound (10)?				
M. Does the vendor enjoy a good reputation in the community (10)?				
5. Product cost				
A. Is the cost of the product competitive with the cost of other vendors?				
B. Does the vendor provide written bids for the product?				
C. Does the cost per unit go down when the number of participants increases?				
D. Does the cost per unit go down if additional products are purchased from the same vendor?				
E. Does the vendor offer corporate discounts?				
6. General concerns				
A. Does the vendor carry adequate liability insurance?				
B. Does the vendor put in writing a "statement of reasonable expectations" for the product (13)?				
C. Is the vendor willing to sign a contract?				
D. If you buy the product of this vendor, will it improve the image of your company in the community?				
E. If you buy the product of this vendor, will it improve the image of your company with the employees?				

APPENDIX G ☐ Selected Organizations/Agencies Offering Free or Inexpensive Health Promotion Materials

Organization/Agency	Topics Covered	Address
Alzheimer's Association	Alzheimer's disease and aging	919 N. Michigan Ave. Suite 1000 Chicago, IL 60611
American Association of Retired Persons	Aging	601 E St., N.W. Washington, DC 20049
American Cancer Society	Cancer, nutrition, smoking, smokeless tobacco, smoking cessation	Contact local affiliate
American Diabetes Association	Diabetes	Contact local affiliate
American Dietetic Association	Nutrition	ADA Sales Order Department Suite 1100 208 S. LaSalle St. Chicago, IL 60604-1003
American Heart Association	Cardiovascular disease, CPR, nutrition, smoking	Contact local affiliate
American Hospital Association	Variety of areas	AHA Center for Health Promotion 840 N. Lake Shore Drive Chicago, IL 60611
American Lung Association	Lung diseases, smoking, smoking cessation	Contact local affiliate
American Red Cross	CPR, blood pressure, first aid, nutrition, safety, stress management	Contact local affiliate
Consumer Information Center	Variety of topics	Consumer Information Center Pueblo, CO 81009
Health Insurance Association of America	Worksite wellness	HIAA Public Relations Dept. 1001 Pennsylvania Ave., NW Washington, DC 20004
Kidney Foundation	Kidney disease	Contact local affiliate
Local colleges and universities	Variety of areas	Check local telephone book
Local health department	All areas	Contact local department
Local public library	All areas	Contact local library

Organization/Agency	Topics Covered	Address
March of Dimes	Birth defects, pregnancy, and worksite wellness	Contact local affiliate
Mothers Against Drunk Drivers (MADD)	Alcohol and driving	P.O. Box 541688 Dallas, TX 75354
National AIDS Information Clearinghouse	AIDS	P.O. Box 6003 Rockville, MD 20850
National Center for Chronic Disease and Health Promotion	Variety of areas	1600 Clifton Rd., N.E. Atlanta, GA 30333
National Heart, Lung, and Blood Institute	Cholesterol, heart disease, high blood pressure, smoking	NHLBI Bethesda, MD 20892
National Health Information Center	Referral to health information	NHIC P.O. Box 1133 Washington, DC 20013
National Institute for Occupational Safety & Health (NIOSH)	Occupational safety and health	4676 Columbia Parkway Cincinnati, OH 45226
National Kidney Foundation	High blood pressure control	Contact local affiliate
National Rural Health Network	Variety of topics to rural areas	NRHN 1800 Massachusetts Ave., N.W. Washington, DC 20036
National Safety Council	Safety	44 N. Michigan Ave. Chicago, IL 60611
National Wellness Institute, Inc.	Variety of areas	NWI, Inc. 1319 Fremont St. Stevens Point, WI 54481
Office of Cancer Communication NCI/NIH	Cancer	Bldg. 31, Room 10A24 9000 Rockville Pike Bethesda, MD 20892
Planned Parenthood	AIDS, contraception, pregnancy, STDs	Contact local affiliate
Office on Smoking and Health	Smoking cessation	OSH Technical Information Center Park Building, Room 1–10 5600 Fishers Lane Rockville, MD 20857

Organization/Agency	Topics Covered	Address
Society of Nutrition Education	Nutrition	SNE 1736 Franklin St. Suite 900 Oakland, CA 94612
State health department	All areas	Contact state health department
U.S. Department of Agriculture (USDA)	Nutrition	USDA Food and Nutrition Center National Agriculture Library Room 304 Beltsville, MD 20705
U.S. Department of Agriculture Cooperative Extension Service	Nutrition	Contact county extension office or state land-grant university
U.S. Department of Transportation, National Traffic and Highway Safety Administration	Occupant safety, child safety seats, drunken driving, trauma prevention, and injury prevention	USDT National Traffic and Highway Safety Administration 400 7th St., S.W. Washington, DC 20590
Washington Business Group on Health	Worksite wellness	Washington Business Group on Health Institute for Organizational Health 229 ½ Pennsylvania Ave., S.E. Washington, DC 20023
Wellness Councils of America	Worksite wellness	WCA Historic Library Plaza 1823 Harney St. Suite 201 Omaha, NE 68102
YMCAs and YWCAs	Exercise	Contact local YMCA or YWCA

APPENDIX H ☐ Selected List of "Canned" Health Education Programs

Organization/Agency	Type of Program	Title of Program
American Cancer Society	Breast cancer detection	Special Touch
	Cancer prevention	Taking Control
	High school cancer curriculum	Right Choices
	Involuntary tobacco	Where There's Smoke
	Nutrition education	Changing the Course (for youth)
		Eating Smart (for adults)
	Smoking cessation	FreshStart
		Smart Move
	Smoking cessation for pregnant women	Special Delivery
American Heart Association	Cardiovascular risk reduction	Heart at Work
	Cooking course	Culinary Hearts Cooking Course
	Preschool health program	Heart Treasure Chest
American Institute for Preventive Medicine	Weight control and behavior modification for 8–18-year-olds	The Body Shop
	Self-esteem	Self-Esteem and Positive Performance
	Smoking cessation	Smokeless
	Stress management	Systematic Stress Management
	Weight loss	Weight No More and Healthylife Weight
	Weight loss for teens	Weight No More for Teens
	Self-care	Healthylife Self-Care Guide
American Lung Association	Asthma and school children	Open Airways for Schools
	Smoking cessation self-help	Freedom from Smoking in 20 Days—A Self-Help Quit Smoking Program
	Self-help smoking cessation for pregnant women	Freedom from Smoking for You and Your Baby
	Self-help smoking cessation maintenance	A Lifetime of Freedom from Smoking: A Maintenance Program for Ex-smokers
	Smoking cessation	Freedom from Smoking Clinics
	Stop-smoking videos	In Control
	Smoking cessation for worksites	Team Up for Freedom from Smoking (TUFFS)
American Red Cross	Measuring blood pressure	How to Measure Blood Pressure

Organization/Agency	Type of Program	Title of Program
American Red Cross (continued)	Disease prevention	Preventing Disease Transmission
	Prenatal care	Health Pregnancy, Healthy Baby
	Back injury prevention	Protect Your Back
Control Data	General health	The StayWell Program
Johnson & Johnson	General health promotion	Live for Life
March of Dimes	Health promotion	Good Health Is Good Business
National Center for Health Promotion	Weight management and cholesterol reduction	The Leaner Weigh
	Cancer and heart disease risk reduction	The Leaner Weigh to Low-Fat, High-Fiber Fare
	Stress management (group and self-help)	Personal Stress Management
	Smoking cessation (group, one-on-one, self-help)	Smoke Stoppers and Staying Stopped
	Health promotion	Healthy Ways
National Dairy Council	General nutrition	Guide to Good Eating (Daily Food Guide Pyramid Leader Guide)
	General nutrition	Food Models and Comparison Cards (Leader Guide)
	Labeling	Label-Ease Video Program
	Sports nutrition	Food Power
	Weight management	Lifesteps
U.S. Department of Transportation, National Traffic Highway Safety Administration	Safety belts	The Great American Habit Plan (GAHP)
Wellness Councils of America	Traffic safety education	Dare To Be Safe
	Clinical depression	DOWNTIME: A Worksite Guide to Understanding Clinical Depression
	Menopause	Understanding Menopause
	Headache	Managing Headache in the Workplace
	Alcohol abuse education	By the Numbers 0-1-2-4
	Health fairs	Health Fairs for Your Wealthfare
	Diversity	Health Promotion for All
	General health promotion planning	Healthy, Wealthy, & Wise: Fundamentals of Workplace Health Promotion

APPENDIX I ☐ Health Behavior Contract

Being of sound mind and in need of health behavior change, I (insert name of person wanting to make the change) do hereby commit myself to the following health behavior change for the next eight weeks. This contract with (insert the name of the other person who is entering into this contract) shall be in effect from (insert starting date) to (insert ending date). For completing this contract, I will be rewarded/reinforced with (insert reward or reinforcer). This reward/reinforcer will be received when I (insert desired behavior). If I do not successfully fulfill this contract, I will (insert what will happen if person is not successful).

A. The behavior I plan to change is:

____

____

B. The reason I want to change this behavior is because:

____

____

C. I have set the following objectives for myself. (Reminder: objectives must be measurable so that you will know if you have reached them. For example, choose practicing relaxation techniques once a day, 5 times per week as an objective rather than indicating stress reduction as a goal.)

1. ________________________________
2. ________________________________
3. ________________________________

D. To meet these goals, I will (provide a description of your daily/weekly activity):

____

____

E. To carry out my plan, I am going to solicit the help of (names of friends, family, roommate, or significant others and how they will help):

____

____

F. I expect to receive the following benefits from this activity:

____

____

Your signature: ____________________ Date: __________

Facilitator's signature: ____________________ Date: __________

APPENDIX J □ Example of an Informed Consent Form for a Cholesterol Screening Program

I hereby grant permission to the Institute for Health Promotion personnel to perform a cholesterol screening on me. I am engaging in this screening voluntarily. I have been told that this screening is an analysis of total blood cholesterol and that my blood will be taken from a fingerstick blood sample by a trained employee. I understand that the results of this screening are considered to be preliminary in nature and in no way conclusive. Results of a blood cholesterol screening like this can be affected by a number of factors including, but not limited to, smoking, stress level, amount of exercise, hormone levels, foods eaten, heredity, and pregnancy. I also understand that my physician can perform a more complete blood lipid (fat) analysis for me, if I so desire.

Further, I have been told that all information related to this screening is considered confidential.

I have read the above statement and understand what it means. I have also had an opportunity to ask questions about the screening, and all my questions have been answered to my satisfaction.

____________________	______________	____________________
Participant's Signature	Date	Signature of Witness

To ensure it meets with all related local and state laws, this form, or any others like it, should be submitted to legal counsel before use.

APPENDIX K ☐ Sample Medical Clearance Form

I hereby certify that ___(name of participant)___ has been examined and cleared by me to participate, with the noted restrictions, in the programs indicated below. This person should not be placed into any of the other programs until he/she has been cleared by me to do so.

☐ Vigorous exercise programs. This type of program would include all-out effort for the development of cardiovascular endurance, muscular strength, and flexibility.
Physician's comments: ______________________________

____

____

☐ Moderate exercise program. This type of program is for those participants who would be unable to participate in the vigorous exercise program because of physical limitations. These programs should be modified as per my instructions.
Physician's comments: ______________________________

____

____

☐ Mild exercise program. This type of program is for those participants who would be unable to participate in the moderate exercise program because of physical limitations. These programs should be modified as per my instructions.
Physician's comments: ______________________________

____

____

______________________ ______________________
Physician's signature Date

APPENDIX L □ Code of Ethics for Health Educators

PREAMBLE

Health education is a process concerned with designing, implementing, and evaluating educational programs that enable individuals, families, groups, organizations, and communities to play active roles in achieving, protecting, and sustaining health. Its purpose is to contribute to health and well-being by promoting lifestyles, community actions, and conditions that make it possible to live healthful lives. Health educators have professional responsibilities to the community and society in which they work and live. They apply and make public their knowledge of health with integrity and dedication to the truth. Health education is not the answer to every health problem and should not be positioned as a stand-alone, independent strategy. However, carefully planned and implemented programs are an essential component of effective health promotion, disease prevention, treatment, and care.

Health education is based on humanitarian and democratic ideals. Health educators are dedicated to improving the health of individuals and groups through educational interventions and other strategies that are characterized by respect for competing value systems, an overriding commitment to self-determination, justice, and the right of individuals to make informed choices. Health educators employ a recognized body of knowledge about human health and disease in order to promote well-being. They liberate people through the honest exchange of accurate and valid information, with appropriate consideration and respect for human diversity and the right of individuals and communities to determine their own ways of living.

Effective health education is planned with input from representatives of target populations and is influenced by the nature of the health problem and setting (e.g., school, community, workplace, or health care organizations). Health education methodologies and strategies are uniquely tailored to address the circumstances of a given population, person, or situation, and are consistent with empirically supported health education and learning theories.

Health educators have knowledge of scientific, behavioral, cultural, and philosophical foundations of health and health behavior. As a result of their professional preparation, health educators are able to apply this knowledge in planning, implementing, and evaluating health education programs.

This Code of Ethics provides a common set of values designed to guide health educators in resolving many of the ethical dilemmas experienced in professional life. These guidelines regarding professional conduct of health educators require a commitment to behave ethically and to encourage and support the ethical behavior of others.

ARTICLE I Responsibility to the Public

Health educators' ultimate responsibility is to educate people about health in order to promote wellness and quality of life. Health educators recognize that decisions about health are made at individual, family, peer, community, societal, and global levels. When there is a conflict of interest among individuals, groups, agencies, or institutions, health educators consider all issuers and give priority to the principles of responsibility and freedom of choice.

Section 1

Health educators support the right of individuals to make informed decisions regarding their own health.

Section 2

Health educators encourage actions and social policies which support the best balance of benefits over harm for all affected parties.

Section 3

Health educators accurately communicate the potential benefits and consequences of services.

Section 4

Health educators act on conditions that can adversely affect the health of individuals and communities.

Section 5

Health educators are truthful about their qualifications and the limitations of their expertise and provide services consistent with these qualifications and limitations.

Section 6

Health educators are committed to providing professional services equitably to all people.

Section 7

Health educators respect the rights of others to hold diverse values, attitudes, and opinions.

Section 8

Health educators protect individuals' privacy and dignity.

ARTICLE II Responsibility to the Profession

Health educators are responsible for the reputation of their profession. Their professional behavior is consistent with the Code of Ethics. When appropriate, they consult with colleagues in order to promote ethical conduct.

Section 1

Health educators maintain their professional competence through continued study and education.

Section 2

Health educators treat all individuals equitably in professional actions (e.g., hiring, promotion, retention, work assignments, and admission policies) regardless of age, gender, race, ethnicity, national origin, religion, sexual orientation, disability, socioeconomic status, or any basis prescribed by law.

Section 3

Health educators encourage and accept critical discourse in order to improve the profession.

Section 4

Health educators contribute to the development of the profession by sharing program components they have found to be effective.

Section 5

Health educators do not manipulate or violate others' rights in sexual, emotional, financial, or other ways.

Section 6

Health educators are aware of possible conflicts of interest and exercise integrity in these situations.

Section 7

Health educators give appropriate recognition to students and colleagues for their professional contributions.

ARTICLE III Responsibility to Employers

Health educators recognize the boundaries of their professional competence. They provide services and programs for which they are qualified by education and experience and they are accountable for their professional activities.

Section 1

Health educators accurately represent their own qualifications and the qualifications of others they recommend.

Section 2

Health educators use current professional standards, theory, and guidelines as criteria when accepting consultations, when delegating health education activities, and when making referrals.

Section 3

Health educators accurately represent potential program outcomes to employers.

Section 4

Health educators make known competing commitments, conflicts of interest, and endorsement of products when the quality of health education delivered could be adversely affected by these activities.

Section 5

Health educators openly communicate to employers when expectations or job-related assignments conflict with professional ethics.

ARTICLE IV Responsibility in the Delivery of Health Education

Health educators promote integrity in the delivery of health education and respect the fundamental rights, dignity, confidentiality, and worth of all people by adapting strategies and methods to the needs of different populations.

Section 1

Health educators are sensitive to the variety of cultural and social norms.

Section 2

Health educators promote the right of individuals and groups to be actively involved in all aspects of the educational process.

Section 3

Health educators use educational strategies and methods that reflect the Code of Ethics and applicable laws. If neither law nor the Code of Ethics provides guidance in resolving an issue, health educators consider other professional standards as well as their own personal standards of ethical behavior, and consult other health educators.

Section 4

Health educators implement strategies and methods that enable individuals to adopt healthy lifestyles through choice rather than by coercion.

Section 5

Health educators conduct regular evaluations of program effectiveness.

Section 6

Health educators provide educational interventions that are grounded in a theoretical framework and supported by empirical evidence.

ARTICLE V Responsibility in Research and Evaluation

Health educators contribute to the health of the population and to the profession through research and evaluation activities. When planning and conducting research or evaluation, health educators do so in accordance with federal and state laws and regulations, organizational and institutional policies, and professional standards.

Section 1

Health educators conduct research in accordance with recognized scientific and ethical standards.

Section 2

Health educators ensure that the consent of participants in research is voluntary and informed.

Section 3

Health educators implement standards to protect the rights, health, safety, and welfare of human research participants.

Section 4

Health educators maintain confidentiality and protect the privacy of research participants in accordance with law and professional standards.

Section 5

Health educators take credit, including authorship, only for work they have actually performed and give credit to the contributions of others.

Section 6

Health educators who serve as research or evaluation consultants discuss their results only with those to whom they are providing service, unless maintaining such confidentiality would jeopardize the health or safety of others.

Section 7

Health educators honor commitments they have made to research participants.

Section 8

Health educators report the results of their research and evaluation accurately and in a timely fashion.

The AAHE Code of Ethics was developed over a two year period of time by a committee appointed by the AAHE president. Over 500 health educators working in a variety of settings participated in providing opinions on the various drafts of the document. Credit is given to SOPHE's Code of Ethics, which served as a basis for the development of this document. The preface includes information adopted from the report of the 1990 joint committee on health education terminology and a joint document of WHO and IUHE published in 1991, titled "Meeting Global Challenges: A Position Paper on Health Education."

Source: Reprinted by permission of the *Journal of Health Education,* July/August 1994, Vol. 25, No. 4, pp. 197–200 and the Association for the Advancement of Health Education, 1900 Association Drive, Reston, VA 22091.

APPENDIX M ☐ Cost-Benefit and Cost-Effectiveness as a Part of the Evaluation of Health Promotion Programs

ABSTRACT

Economic evaluation should be a component of program evaluation. To encourage and help with this process, definitions of common economic terms, a review of the literature, steps for conducting an economic evaluation, and the use of economic evaluation, with health promotion program is presented.

INTRODUCTION

The idea of promoting good health practices is not new in the United States. However, it is only in recent years that the concept of health promotion has grown in popularity and that the number of health promotion programs has flourished. The growth has occurred because of the ". . . increasing evidence of an association between patterns of lifestyle and health status of individuals and population groups, and associations between environmental and workplace hazards and the health and well-being of communities and workers" (Work Group on Health Promotion/Disease Prevention, 1987).

Though the number of health promotion programs continues to increase, the evaluation of said programs lags behind. There are several reasons for this. First, many of the first generation health promotion programs were developed without regard to an appropriate plan of evaluation. Thus data were not and could not be collected. Second, the very nature of health promotion programs, that of being "in the field" and being geared toward the long-term outcome of "impovered health," makes them difficult to evaluate. Concerns such as evaluation expertise, confidentiality of participants, and resources of time, money, and personnel have proven to be stumbling blocks in collecting the needed data.

If health promotion programs are to prosper and grow, empirical evidence of their worth should be provided. This can be done only through appropriate evaluation of the programs; evaluation that pays considerable attention to problems of design and measurement, and that can be reproducible. Green (1979) stated that "Evaluation of a health promotion plan certifies its appropriateness and its effectiveness and ensures that the practitioner is accountable to the patient (consumer), the community, and the hospital administrator." Though Green's comments were directed toward hospital health promotion programs these same ideas can be transferred to any health promotion setting because all program planners need to be accountable to the consumer (Work Group on Health Promotion/Disease Prevention, 1987).

The question now is not whether or not health promotion programs should be evaluated but how should it be done? Green (1979) has defined three different levels of evaluation—process, impact, and outcome. Process evaluation deals with the professional practice of those presenting the health promotion program. Impact evaluation is concerned with the immediate difference that the health promotion program has on the knowledge, attitude, behavior, and environment. Outcome evaluation focuses on long-term concerns such as morbidity, morality, and years of survival following the health promotion program. There are many strategies for evaluating health promotion programs within each of these levels, and they have been thoroughly covered in the works of Windsor, Baranowski, Clark, and Cutter (1984) and Green and Lewis (1986). However, there is one evaluation strategy that these authors have addressed that merits further discussion because of the importance being placed on it in today's practice: the economic evaluation of health promotion programs. In the business world the economic evaluation of a program is often referred to as the "bottom line."

In writing about corporate health promotion programs, Fielding (1982, p. 85) has stated:

> Although current evidence suggests a very favorable return on investment for disease prevention and health promotion programs, much more information is needed to quantify costs and benefits and to suggest which models work best in different corporate settings. Therefore, it is imperative that all efforts include long-term evaluation of effects of programs on both direct and indirect costs.

The remaining portion of this paper will focus on the economic evaluation of health promotion programs. This refers to the cost-benefit and cost-effectiveness analysis (CBA and CEA, respectively) of the programs.

DEFINITIONS OF CBA AND CEA

Simply stated, CBA and CEA are formal analytical techniques used for comparing the negative and positive consequences of alternative uses of resources. They are not formulas for making decisions, but rather they are tools to help individuals make decisions (Warner & Luce, 1982). More specifically, Green and Lewis (1986, p. 361) have defined cost-benefit as "a measure of the cost of an intervention relative to the benefits it yields, usually expressed as a ratio of dollars saved or gained for every dollar spent on the program," and cost-effectiveness as "a measure of the cost of an intervention relative to its impact, usually expressed in dollars per unit of effect." Common CEA measures may include years of life saved, days of morbidity and disability avoided, number of smokers who quit, and number of pounds lost.

When first reading these definitions, they appear to be very much alike. The basic technical distinction between CBA and CEA lies in the process of valuing the desirable consequences of health promotion programs (Warner & Luce, 1982). CBA requires that all desirable consequences be expressed in monetary (dollar) terms. For many of the consequences this is a manageable task, but there are some desirable consequences that researchers have found most difficult to quantify in dollars—the value of human life may be the most notable. Several researchers (Rice, 1966; Cooper and Rice, 1976; Acton, 1976) have offered means of dealing with the problem.

More recently the difference between CBA and CEA seems to be fading. Warner and Luce have pointed out that as they have reviewed the literature on CBA and CEA, the two techniques are becoming more alike in the way analysts are applying the concepts. They have indicated that "recent sophisticated health care CEAs are incorporating some dollar-valued benefits into the cost side of the equation (as negative costs), and increasing recognition of the meaning of CBA in health care is bringing it closer to CEA. The human capital approach to measuring indirect benefits in CBA values livelihood, not life itself; thus a CBA is really a net dollar benefit for some nonmonetized health outcomes. The newer more sophisticated CEA seems to be a significant step forward in that it combines the best of both CBA and CEA" (Warner & Luce, 1982, p. 213).

THE POPULARITY OF CBA AND CEA

The evaluation techniques of CEA and CBA are by no means new concepts, for they can be traced back hundreds of years. However, there has been a tremendous growth in their use and interest in the health professions in the past fifteen years. Much of this growth has paralleled the increase of health care costs during the same period of time. Many feel that this burgeoning interest of CEA and CBA in the health professions has resulted from health professionals seeking to identify and convey the meaning of cost-beneficial and cost-effective health care interventions. It is now quite common to find CBA and CEA citations on most all health care topics.

REVIEW OF LITERATURE

As Warner and Hutton (1980) have pointed out, the contributions to the health care CBA and CEA literature have grown exponentially in recent years. Over the years the majority of the literature has dealt with medical interventions. Since this paper is focused on nonmedical interventions—health promotion activities—the medical intervention CBA and CEA literature is not reviewed here. However, it is well presented in Warner and Luce (1982).

The references to the nonmedical CBA and CEA literature are much more limited. The nonmedical literature falls into three major areas—public health measures (i.e., water fluoridation, food inspection, etc.), identification of health risks via screenings (for hypertension, cancer and other diseases), and personal health lifestyle (i.e., exercise, smoking, nutrition, stress, etc.). Public health measures have generally not been considered a part of health promotion activities. And even though screenings have been a portion of a number of health promotion programs, it is the category of personal health lifestyle on which most health promotion programs are planned. It is this literature that is reviewed below.

A number of reviews of the CBA and CEA of health promotion type activities have been found in the literature (Fielding, 1982; Rogers, Eaton, & Bruhn, 1981; Scheffler & Paringer, 1980; and

Warner, 1979). These reviews report on basically two types of studies. One group includes studies that have calculated a CBA or CEA on a specific health problem in terms of what the costs and benefits would be for the entire United States if a health promotion program were implemented. One such paper is presented by Kristein (1977). In his paper, Kristein examines several different health concerns such as hypertension, cancer of the colon, heavy cigarette smoking, alcohol abuse, and breast cancer. A summary of his heavy cigarette smoking calculations provides a good example of this approach. He calculated that the costs of heavy cigarette smoking were approximately $20.3 billion (in 1975 dollars). This includes the cost of hospital care, medical care, absenteeism, and premature deaths. If a smoking cessation program were implemented for the 22 million heavy smokers in the United States (a 1975 estimate) at $125 per person and there was a 25% success rate, Kristein estimated a cost-benefit ratio of 1.8 to 1.0. This means that for every dollar put into such a program a $1.80 could be saved. This type of CBA is useful in showing that smoking cessation programs can provide financial benefits, but the exactness of the figures must be put into perspective because of the lack of detail in the analysis.

The other major group of studies that appear in the reviews are those which report on the results of a CBA or CEA calculated on a specific health promotion activity offered by a specific organization. For example, Fielding (1982) has reviewed the results of a number of employee health promotion programs. His findings show that a number of different techniques have been used to calculate CBAs and CEAs, that calculations are based on a number of assumptions and thus the results are difficult to compare. In another paper, Fielding (1984) offers the following example:

> Campbell's analysis of the savings attributable to their colorectal cancer screening programs hinges on assumptions regarding the number of cases of colorectal cancer that would have occurred in the absence of screening, and the direct and indirect costs associated with each case. It also assumes that all cases prevented were due to on-site screening rather than screening that occurred in another setting (e.g., doctor's office or HMO) at the encouragement of an outside health professional. While these estimates of savings due to health promotion measures are useful in showing the value companies themselves have placed in the savings, it is difficult to know if their assertions can be applied to other companies. (p. 259)

Further indication of the inconsistency in the way CBA and CEA for health promotion activities have been calculated was noted by Rogers et al. (1981, p. 333)—" . . . carefully designed cost analyses have not been conducted so that various approaches can be compared as to the expense, as well as to short-term impact and long-term outcome." There is clearly a need for authors to describe in detail all the steps they follow in calculating their CBA or CEA so that other evaluators can use the same steps and thus be able to compare results.

The health promotion literature includes more reports of CBAs and CEAs on identification of health risks than in personal health lifestyle change, with the more reports dealing with hypertension screening programs than any other (Alderman, Madhavan, & Davis, 1983; Erfurt & Foote, 1984; Foote & Erfurt, 1977; Ruchlin & Alderman, 1980; and Ruchlin, Melcher, & Alderman, 1984). Only two recent reports on personal health lifestyle change could be found. One dealt with weight loss (Seidman, Sevelius, & Ewald, 1984) and the other with smoking cessation (Weiss, Jurs, Lesage, & Iverson, 1984). Scheffler and Paringer (1980) have pointed out the need for empirical evidence of the economic soundness of other lifestyle change programs such as physical exercise and dietary changes.

Finally, there are many more reports using CEA than CBA in the health promotion literature. Only two reports of CBA (Alderman et al., 1983; and Weiss et al., 1984) could be found. All others were CEAs. The reasons for this will become clear from subsequent discussion.

CALCULATING CBAs AND CEAs

As suggested in preceding portions of this paper, the calculation of CBAs and CEAs for health promotion activities is no easy task. In most cases they will be difficult and in some cases impossible to calculate. However, if evaluations of health promotion activities are going to be complete, they should be attempted.

Though there are certain processes that must be included in calculating CBAs and CEAs, the exact steps one could use may vary. The important point to remember is that whatever steps are used, they should be reported accurately and in detail so others can replicate and compare results. The steps presented below are a combination of techniques suggested by a governmental agency and several different individuals (OTA, 1978; OTA, 1980; Rogers et al., 1981; Shepard & Thompson, 1979; and Warner & Luce, 1982).

Step 1: Defining the Problem

The initial step in calculating a CBA or CEA is defining the problem to be analyzed. The problem should be stated as clearly and explicitly as possible. Seemingly small differences in the definition of the problem could have a large impact on the calculated costs, benefits and effects. The statement of the problem should also clearly specify for whom the analysis is going to be calculated. For example, a cost-analysis of a health promotion program would differ greatly if it were being calculated from the employer's point of view as opposed to the costs, benefits, and effects experienced by the employee.

Commonly defined problems for which health promotion programs are usually designed deal with either a specific health concern or an economic issue. An example of a problem that deals with a health concern might be to reduce the risk of cardiovascular disease in white collar employees, while a problem revolving around an economic issue may be to reduce the amount of money the company spends on health insurance claims per year. Both of these problems would be appropriate for calculating a CBA or CEA; however, for the purposes of this paper, the cardiovascular disease problem will be used as an example through the remaining steps in the process.

Step 2: Specifying the Objectives

Closely related to defining the problem is setting one or more objectives against which programmatic alternatives are to be evaluated. If the defined problem is not readily measurable, further specification may help qualify it. For example, the problem of reducing cardiovascular disease in white collar employees is too broad to be readily quantified.

A possible specification of an appropriate objective would be to reduce the risk of cardiovascular disease in this employee group by getting 50% of the high-risk employees in an appropriate exercise program. It is known that the high-risk group includes individuals who have hypertension and are overweight. These individuals cost a company more money in medical care, accidents, etc. than individuals without them. Exercise has been shown to help both of these health concerns.

Step 3: Identifying Alternatives

To determine if a specific approach to a problem is cost-effective or cost-beneficial, it needs to be compared to other approaches that could also be used to achieve the stated objectives. Again using the problem of cardiovascular disease as an example, an alternative approach may be to reduce disease via a nutrition and weight control program as opposed to the exercise program.

When identifying alternatives for health promotion programs, it should be noted that the alternatives do not need to attack the problem using similar approaches. For example, if the problem is to reduce health costs due to cigarette smoking within an organization, one cost analysis may be completed on an educational smoking cessation approach. Another analysis of costs could be calculated on the alternative which mandates, via a company policy, that there be no smoking in the workplace.

It is helpful to keep the following concerns in mind when identifying appropriate alternatives: (1) select only alternatives that are believed to be potentially quite cost-effective, (2) select alternatives that offer variety in their approach, and (3) select alternatives that would be appropriate for comparison—do not select an alternative that is obviously an inappropriate approach for solving the problem (i.e., getting *every* employee to adopt a specific exercise program).

Step 4: Describing Production Relationships

The first three steps of this process set the conceptual framework for calculating a CBA or CEA.

When one describes the production relationships, he/she is creating the technical framework for the quantitative assessment and comparison of costs and benefits of the alternatives. This may be the most important step in the CBA and CEA processes. To set up the technical framework, the evaluator must identify the resources necessary to carry out the alternative, explain how the resources are combined, and then predict the outcome(s). As Warner and Luce (1982) have pointed out, this can be completed in several different ways ranging from a simple flow chart to a sophisticated, multi-equation computer simulation.

In the cardiovascular disease problem, the resources would include personnel time—of both the high-risk employees participating in this program and the program leaders, educational materials (i.e., booklets, films, handouts, etc.), supplies (i.e., exercise clothing, laundry expenses, etc.), pre- and post-program exercise testings, pre-program medical examinations, fee for facility use, and any other pre-participant program expenses. The outcomes of the program may include 50% of the participants getting involved in a life-long exercise program, 50% reducing their weight, and 75% getting their blood pressure under control. These in turn may result in fewer health insurance claims because of reduced illness, less absenteeism, and fewer accidents, thus increasing productivity. In the long run it is hoped these programs will decrease both morbidity and premature mortality.

As one can see from this example, this step can become quite involved. One may need to examine previous programs—conducted either in house or in another setting—or obtain the services of a technical consultant to try to adequately identify all resources and outcomes. However, the evaluator of the health promotion programs should be aware that even this additional work may not ensure the identification of all health outcomes. It is because of this inability to identify specific health outcomes that the use of CBA with health promotion programs has been limited. If the health benefits of a program cannot be identified, then one cannot put a dollar value on them and thus the cost of the benefit cannot be analyzed. For example, what are the health benefits of a nutrition education program? Unless these benefits can be identified,* CBA would be an inappropriate cost analysis technique to use with health promotion programs.

On the other hand, CEA can be applied very well to some health promotion programs. For the outcomes of concern are not benefits but effects, and with a CEA the evaluator is not required to put a dollar value on the effects. Thus when analyzing the nutrition education program, one can identify effects such as the reduction of calorie intake or the reduction of serum fat levels without trying to identify the health benefit of such. It should be noted that these effects are immediate (i.e., reduction in calories) or intermediate (i.e., decrease in serum fat levels) outcomes only and not long-term (i.e., decreased premature mortality) like some financiers of health promotion programs want to see.

Whether one is using CBA or CEA, the more completely the production relationships have been described, the easier it will be to complete steps 5 and 6 in the process—analyzing costs, benefits, and effectiveness.

Step 5: Analyzing the Costs

Costs should be defined as those resources that one must give up to gain some benefit or effect (Warner & Luce, 1982). This would include not only those direct controllable costs but also overhead uncontrollable costs.

The cost of some resources may be obvious. Using the cardiovascular disease example, it may be very easy to determine the cost of the educational materials because they can be purchased at a cost of Y per set. The cost of the group leader may be obvious, too, but how about the cost of the four volunteers who are helping conduct the program? Since the program could not be run without the four volunteers, this is a cost to the program. In this situation the economic concept of "opportunity cost" would be used. "The opportunity cost is its value in another use" (Warner & Luce, 1982, p. 77). So if these volunteers were not helping in this program, how much would they be worth in

*See the related literature section of this paper for examples of where evaluators have been able to apply CBA to health promotion programs.

another setting? It may be found that they would be worth $7.50 per hour working in a similar capacity at a local health agency. Therefore, their cost could be determined with this figure.

Since one of the major reasons for calculating CBA and CEA is to be able to compare alternatives, it is important that costs (and for that matter benefits and effects) of the different alternatives are calculated in a similar manner. For example, if one is comparing different cardiovascular exercise programs and both programs include the help of volunteers, the same opportunity costs should be used in determining the total cost of volunteers.

Step 6: Analyzing Benefits and Effectiveness

There are usually numerous desired outcomes (benefits) that result from health promotion programs. Some are obvious while others are much more difficult to identify. For this reason, it may help the evaluator to try to categorize the different outcomes. Warner and Luce (1982) have identified the following classification scheme for outcomes associated with health care activities: (1) Personal health benefits—improvements in health such as increased life expectancy, decreased morbidity, and reduced disability; (2) Health care resource benefits—the saving of unused resources resulting from the implementation of an activity (for example, an exercise program could reduce the resources put into cardiac surgery); (3) Other economic benefits—desired outcomes that are not identified as either health or health care benefits, such as work productivity; (4) Other social benefits—desired outcomes that have positive social effects like increased access to health services or compassion; and (5) Intermediate outcomes—benefits that occur prior to a final outcome. Because it is sometimes difficult to measure final outcomes, one often must use the intermediate outcome. For example, the long-term impact of an exercise program on one's health would be difficult to determine, but one could measure the intermediate outcome of weight loss.

It should be noted that not all outcomes are benefits. The best example of this appears in screening programs when false positive outcomes appear. If such outcomes do exist, they need to be treated as costs.

The measurement of benefits and effectiveness is very much like the measurement of costs in that some aspects are straightforward while others are very difficult. For example, not all social benefits can be quantified, such as compassion. There is no standard unit of compassion on which one could attach a dollar value.

It is at this point in the calculations of CBA and CEA that the differences in the two analyses can be seen. The CEA ends with the measurement of effectiveness. No dollar value is placed on the outcomes. Thus, the number of lives saved, trips to the health clinic, or persons involved in the exercise program are all that are needed. However, in order to calculate a CBA, monetary units must be attached to each outcome. This is not too difficult when market prices are available. But they are not always available, and the one area that has caused considerable discussion is trying to put a monetary label on the "value of life." Techniques that have been used include (1) human capital—value of being productively employed in the labor market plus direct benefit of health care resource savings, (2) willingness to pay—value that individuals place on reducing risks of death and illness, (3) court awards in civil cases—value of productive life and emotional costs, and (4) life insurance holdings—value of one's life insurance.

Step 7: Discounting

A necessary step in calculating an accurate CBA or CEA is that of discounting. Since the costs and benefits of some programs do not occur entirely in the present, for comparison purposes all future costs and monetary values of future benefits should be discounted to their present value. In other words, a dollar today is worth more to an individual than the promise of having the dollar tomorrow and more still than having the dollar the day after tomorrow. "The discount rate attempts to adjust for what a dollar invested today would earn in interest" (Collen & Goodman, 1985). " . . . Discounting is particularly important in the case of preventive activities since so many of the benefits occur well into the future. In addition, discounting helps to explain how 'postponing' illness costs can have the effect of 'containing them'" (Warner, 1979).

To carry out the discounting process, one must first decide on a discount rate. The discount rate expresses the degree to which tomorrow's dollar loses value relative to today's dollar. Since there is little consensus on what discount rate should be used and because the particular discount rate chosen can have a substantial impact on the outcome of the analysis [In relative terms, low discount rates tend to favor projects whose benefits occur in the distant future (OTA, 1980)], CBAs and CEAs are usually calculated using several different rates, usually ranging from 3–10%. This process of using several different rates is called sensitivity analysis.

For example, if one wanted to spend $1,000 today on an exercise program expecting to save $2,000 in medical costs in five years, there would be a need to discount the benefit ($2,000) to its estimated present value. For the sake of the example the discount rate will be set at 5%. The present discounted value today of the net benefit would be $567 ($1,567–1,000) and not $1,000 ($2,000–$1,000).

Both time (in years) and the discount rate have an impact on the discounted value. Tables 1 and 2 are presented to illustrate the effect of each. Table 1 shows how an expected $2,000 benefit decreases in value over time when the discount rate stays constant (5% in this example).

Table 2 illustrates how again a $2,000 benefit decreases in value as the discount rate increases and the time stays constant (5 years in this example).

TABLE 1
Effect of Time on Discounted Value

Discount Rate	Time (in years)	Present Value of Cost	Present Value of Benefit	Present Value of Net Benefit
.05	0	$1,000	$2,000	$1,000
.05	1	1,000	1,905	905
.05	2	1,000	1,814	814
.05	5	1,000	1,567	567
.05	10	1,000	1,228	228
.05	20	1,000	754	–246

TABLE 2
Effect of Discounted Rate on Discounted Value

Discount Rate	Time (in years)	Present Value of Cost	Present Value of Benefit	Present Value of Net Benefit
0	5	$1,000	$2,000	$1,000
3	5	1,000	1,725	725
5	5	1,000	1,567	567
7	5	1,000	1,426	426
10	5	1,000	1,242	242
15	5	1,000	994	- 6

It is obvious from these tables that given a large enough discount rate and/or a substantial number of years, the net benefit could be a negative number. Such a number would indicate that the costs would outweigh the benefits and the cost-benefits ratio would be less than one point zero (1.0) to 1.0. In other words, it would cost more than one dollar to get a dollar worth of benefit.

For those interested in other examples of the discounting process, see Collen and Goodman (1985) and Warner and Luce (1982).

Step 8: Analyzing Uncertainties

As has been demonstrated throughout this discussion of calculating a CBA or CEA, there will be times when the evaluator will be uncertain of some data that need to be included. In such cases there are several alternatives available to the evaluator. As with discounting, the evaluator could use a sensitivity analysis. For example, if the evaluator were figuring a CEA on a smoking cessation program and was not sure of the cost of an instructor for the program, he/she could make several different estimates of the cost. Each of these estimates could then be "plugged into" the analysis to give the evaluator a range for the CEA.

Another approach to dealing with uncertainties would be to elicit the help of a group of experts in the field. Such a technique is called consensus development. With this technique a group of experts is brought together to listen to a presentation of uncertain areas. Following the presentation, the group is then isolated to discuss the presentation and to reach a consensus as to what should be used in place of the uncertain data.

Step 9: Interpreting the Results

Because of all the concerns noted in calculating a CBA or CEA, one needs to be careful in interpreting the results of an analysis. There are many assumptions and uncertainties that both the evaluator and/or the interpreter of the results could overlook. Thus, one needs to proceed with caution when reading the analysis reports.

Assuming all steps have been carried out properly and appropriate CBA and CEA data have been calculated, the decision maker must not forget that the economic evaluation is only one piece of the data needed to make decisions about programs. Most programs have important ethical, legal, and/or societal issues that must be identified and discussed before final program decisions can be made.

Using CBAs and CEAs with Health Promotion Programs

The need for incorporating an economic component in the evaluation of a health promotion program should be obvious. The question that remains is, what specific technique would be most appropriate? In most situations the answer would be CEA. The reasons for using CEA as opposed to CBA with health promotion programs are: (1) the inability to determine and then measure all the effects of a program, and (2) the inability to put a monetary value on the measured effect. These inabilities of not being able to identify the effects and then in turn being able to determine the value (in dollars) of these effects are critical steps in the CBA process. Without them an evaluator could not calculate an accurate CBA. It would probably be a rare situation in which a CBA would be an appropriate technique to use in an evaluation of a health promotion program. Even if an evaluator were able to determine these values, there are some (Fielding, 1979; Kristein, 1983) who believe the cost-benefit ratio would not favor the health promotion programs. These individuals have indicated that there are several cost issues that evaluators to date have not considered when calculating a CBA. One of these issues revolves around the additional costs of human longevity. When an individual lives longer, he/she is more likely to have incurred additional medical costs and an employee will have to pay pensions for a longer period of time.

CONCLUSION

Many of the early health promotion programs planned in this country were implemented on the premise that it was more economically sound to spend health care dollars on prevention activities than on curing disease. At the present time, there is little empirical data to prove such economic evaluation—even though CBA and CEA have been used in many other areas of the health care system. As one looks to the future, it seems reasonable that if health promotion program planners are going to convince policy makers that such programs are an effective means of improving health status, then economic evaluation must be a part of the total evaluation process.

REFERENCES

Acton, J. (1976). Measuring the monetary value of lifesaving programs. *Law and Contemporary Problems, 40,* 46.

Alderman, M.H., Madhavan, S., & Davis, T. (1983). Reduction of cardiovascular disease events by worksite hypertension treatment. *Hypertension, 5* (supplement V). V138–V143.

Collen, M., & Goodman, C. (1985). Cost-effectiveness and cost-benefit analysis. In Institute of Medicine, *Assessing Medical Technologies* (pp. 136–144, 160–164). Washington, D.C.: National Medical Press.

Cooper, B., & Rice, D. (1976). The economic cost of illness revisited. *Social Security Bulletin, 39,* 21.

Erfurt, J.C., & Foote, A. (1984). Cost-effectiveness of work-site blood pressure control programs. *Journal of Occupational Medicine, 26,* 892–900.

Fielding, J.E. (1982). Effectiveness of employee health improvement programs. *Journal of Occupational Medicine, 24,* 907–916.

Fielding, J.E. (1984). Health promotion and disease prevention at the worksite. In L. Breslow (Ed.), *Annual review in public health* (pp. 237–265). Palo Alto, California: Annual Reviews, Inc.

Fielding, J.E. (1979). Preventive medicine and the bottom line. *Journal of Occupational Medicine, 21,* 79–88.

Foote, A., & Erfurt, J.C. (1977). Controlling hypertension: A cost-effective model. *Preventive Medicine, 6,* 319–343.

Green, L.W. (1979). How to evaluate health promotion. *Hospitals, 53,* 106–108.

Green, L.W., & Lewis, F.M. (1986). *Measurement and evaluation in health education and health promotion.* Palo Alto, California: Mayfield Publishing Company.

Kristein, M.M. (1977). Economic issues in prevention. *Preventive Medicine, 6,* 252–264.

Kristein, M.M. (1983). How much can business expect to profit from smoking cessation? *Preventive Medicine, 12,* 358–381.

Office of Technology Assessment, U.S. Congress. (1978). *Assessing the efficacy and safety of medical technologies.* Washington, D.C.: U.S. Government Printing Office.

Office of Technology Assessment, U.S. Congress (1980). *The implications of cost-effectiveness analysis of medical technology/background paper #1: Methodological issues and literature review.* Washington, D.C.: U.S. Government Printing Office.

Rogers, P.J., Eaton, E.K., & Bruhn, J.G. (1981). Is health promotion cost effective? *Preventive Medicine, 10,* 324–339.

Rice, D. (1966). *Estimating the cost of illness.* U.S. Department of Health, Education and Welfare, PHS, Health Economic Series No. 6.

Ruchlin, H.S., & Alderman, M.H. (1980). Cost of hypertension control at the workplace. *Journal of Occupational Medicine, 22,* 795–800.

Ruchlin, H.S., Melcher, L.A., & Alderman, M.H. (1984). A comparative economic analysis of work-related hypertension care programs. *Journal of Occupation Medicine, 26,* 45–49.

Scheffler, R.M., & Paringer, L. (1980). A review of the economic evidence on prevention. *Medical Care, 18,* 473–484.

Schwartz, R.M., & Rollins, P.L. (1985). Measuring the cost benefit of wellness strategies. *Business and Health, 2,* 10, 24–26.

Seidman, L.S., Sevelius, G.G., & Ewald, P. (1984). A cost-effective weight loss program at the worksite. *Journal of Occupational Medicine, 26,* 725–730.

Shepard, D.S., & Thompson, M.S. (1979). First principles of cost-effectiveness analysis in health. *Public Health Reports, 94,* 535–543.

Warner, K.E., & Hutton, R.C. (1980). Cost-benefit and cost-effective analysis in health care. *Medical Care, 18,* 1069–1084.

Warner, K.E., & Luce, B.R. (1982). *Cost-benefit and cost-effectiveness in health care: Principles, practice, and potential.* Ann Arbor, Michigan: Health Administration Press.

Warner, K.E. (1979). The economic implications of preventive health care. *Social Science and Medicine, 13C,* 227–237.

Weiss, S.J., Jurs, S., Lesage, J. P., & Iverson, D.C. (1984). A cost-benefit analysis of a smoking cessation program. *Evaluation and Program Planning, 7,* 337–346.

Windsor, R.A., Baranowski, T., Clark, N., & Cutter, G. (1984). *Evaluation of health promotion and education programs.* Palo Alto, California: Mayfield Publishing Company.

Work Group on Health Promotion Disease Prevention. (1987). Criteria for the development of health promotion and education programs. *American Journal of Public Health, 77,* 89–92.

Source: "Cost-Benefit and Cost-Effectiveness as a Part of the Evaluation of Health Promotion Programs," by J. F. McKenzie, 1986, *The Eta Sigma Gamman, 18*(2), pp. 10–16. Reprinted by permission of *The Health Educator* (formerly *The Eta Sigma Gamman*).

References

Ad Hoc Work Group of the American Public Health Association. (1987). Criteria for the development of health promotion and education programs. *American Journal of Public Health, 77*(1), 89–92.

Airhihenbuwa, C. O. (1994). Health promotion and the discourse on culture: Implications for empowerment. *Health Education Quarterly, 21*(3), 345–353.

Ajzen, I. (1988). *Attitudes, personality, and behavior.* Chicago: Dorsey Press.

Alexy, B. J. (1985). Health risk appraisal: Reliability demonstrated. In *Proceedings of the 20th Meeting of the Society of Prospective Medicine.* Bethesda, MD: Society of Prospective Medicine.

Alinsky, S. D. (1971). *Rules for radicals: A pragmatic primer for realistic radicals.* New York: Random House.

Allensworth, D. D., & Kolbe, L. J. (1987). The comprehensive school health program: Exploring an expanded concept. *Journal of School Health, 57*(10), 409–412.

American Association of School Administrators (AASA). (1990). *Healthy kids for the year 2000: An action plan for schools.* Arlington, VA: Author.

American College Health Association (ACHA). (no date). *Healthy campus 2000: Making it happen.* Rockville, MD: Author.

American College of Sports Medicine. (1980). *Guidelines for graded exercise testing and exercise prescription* (2nd ed.). Philadelphia: Lea & Febiger.

American Indian Health Care Association. (AIHCA). (no date). *Promoting health traditions workbook—A Guide to the healthy people 2000 campaign.* St. Paul, MN: Author.

American Public Health Association (1991). *Healthy communities 2000: Model standards—Guidelines for community attainment of the year 2000 national health objectives* (3rd ed.). Washington, DC: Author.

Anderson, D. M., & Portnoy, B. (1989). Diffusion of cancer education into the schools. *Journal of School Health, 59*(5), 214–217.

Anderson, D. R., & O'Donnell, M. P. (1994). Toward a health promotion research agenda: "State of the science" reviews. *American Journal of Health Promotion, 8*(6), 462–465.

Archer, S. E., & Fleshman, R. P. (1985). *Community health nursing.* Monterey, CA: Wadsworth Health Sciences.

Archer, S. E., Kelly, C. D., & Bisch, S. A. (1984). *Implementing change in communities: A collaborative process.* St. Louis: C.V. Mosby.

Arkin, E. B. (1990). Opportunities for improving the nation's health through collaboration with the mass media. *Public Health Reports, 105*(3), 219–223.

Bandura, A. (1977a). Self-efficacy: Toward a unifying theory of behavioral change. *Psychological Review, 84*(2), 191–215.

Bandura, A. (1977b). *Social learning theory.* Englewood Cliffs, NJ: Prentice-Hall.

Bandura, A. (1986). *Social foundations of thought and action.* Englewood Cliffs, NJ: Prentice-Hall.

Baranowski, T. (1985). Methodologic issues in self-report of health behavior. *Journal of School Health, 55*(5), 179–182.

Bartlett, E. E., Windsor, R. A., Lowe, J. B., & Nelson, G. (1986). Guidelines for conducting smoking cessation programs. *Health Education, 17*(1), 31–37.

Basch, C. (1984). Research on disseminating and implementing health education programs in schools. *Health Education, 15*(4), 57–66; *Journal of School Health, 54*(6), 57–66.

Basch, C. E., & Sliepcevich, E. M. (1983). Innovators, innovations, and implementation: A framework for curricular research in school health education. *Health Education, 14* (2), 20–24.

Bates, I. J., & Winder, A. E. (1984). *Introduction to health education.* Palo Alto, CA: Mayfield.

Baumgartner, T. A., & Strong, C. H. (1994). *Conducting and reading research on health and human performance.* Madison, WI: WCB Brown & Benchmark Publishers.

Baun, W., Bernacki, E., & Tsai, S. (1986). A preliminary investigation: Effect of a corporate fitness program on absenteeism and health care costs. *Journal of Occupational Medicine, 28,* 18–22.

Becker, M. H., Drachman, R. H., & Kirscht, J. P. (1974). A new approach to explaining sick-role behavior in low income populations. *American Journal of Public Health, 64*(March), 205–216.

Becker, M. H., & Green, L. W. (1975). A family approach to compliance with medical treatment, a selective review of the literature. *International Journal of Health Education, 18*(3), 2–11.

Becker, M. H., & Maiman, L. (1983). Models of health-related behavior. In D. Mechanic (Ed.), *Handbook of health, health care and the health professions* (pp. 539–568). New York: Free Press.

Behrens, R. (1983). *Work-site health promotion: Some questions and answers to help you get started.* Washington, DC: Office of Disease Prevention and Health Promotion.

Bellicha, T., & McGrath, J. (1990). Mass media approaches to reducing cardiovascular disease risk. *Public Health Reports, 105*(3), 245–252.

Bensley, L. B. (1989). A review of the use of mass media and marketing in health education: A look at theory and practice. *Eta Sigma Gamman, 21*(1), 18–23.

Bensley, L. B. (1991). Schoolsite health promotion: Ways of sustaining interest. *Journal of Health Education, 22*(2), 86–89.

Berkman, L. F., & Syme, S. L. (1979). Social networks, host resistance and mortality: A nine-year follow-up of Alameda County residents. *American Journal of Epidemiology, 109*(2), 186–204.

Best, J. A., & Milsum, J. H. (1978). HHA and the evaluation of lifestyle change programs: Methodological issues. In *Proceedings of the 13th Meeting of the Society of Prospective Medicine.* Bethesda, MD: Society of Prospective Medicine.

Bettman, J. R. (1979). *An information processing theory of consumer choice.* Reading, MA: Addison-Wesley.

Blackburn, H. (1983). Research and demonstration projects in community cardiovascular disease prevention. *Journal of Public Health Policy, 4*(4), 398–421.

Blair, S. N., Collingwood, T., Reynolds, R., Smith, M., Hagen, R. D., & Sterling, C. L. (1984). Health promotion for educators: Impact on health behaviors, satisfaction, and general well-being. *American Journal of Public Health, 74*(2), 147–149.

Blair, S. N., Smith, M., Collingwood, T., Reynolds, R., Prentice, M. C., & Sterling, C. L. (1986). Health promotion for educators: Impact on absenteeism. *Preventive Medicine, 15,* 166–175.

Blair, S. N., Tritsch, L., & Kutsch, S. (1987). Worksite health promotion for school faculty and staff. *Journal of School Health, 57*(10), 469–473.

Bloomquist, K. (1981). Physical fitness programs in industry: Applications of social learning theory. *Occupational Health Nursing, 29*(7), 30–33.

Bly, L., Jones, R. C., & Richardson, J. E. (1986). Impact of worksite health promotion on health care costs and utilization: Evaluation of Johnson & Johnson's live for life program. *Journal of the American Medical Association, 256*(23), 3235–3240.

Borg, W. R., & Gall, M. D. (1989). *Educational research: An introduction* (5th ed.). New York: Longman.

Bowne, D. W., Russell, M. L., Morgan, J. L., Optenberg, S. A., & Clarke, A. E. (1984). Reduced disability and health care costs in an industrial fitness program. *Journal of Occupational Medicine, 26*(1), 809–816.

Brager, G., Specht, H., & Torczyner, J. L. (1987). *Community organizing.* New York: Columbia University Press.

Braithwaite, R. L., Murphy, F., Lythcott, N., & Blumenthal, D. S. (1989). Community organization and development for health promotion within an urban black community: A conceptual model. *Health Education, 20*(5), 56–60.

Breckon, D. J., Harvey, J. R., & Lancaster, R. B. (1994). *Community health education: Settings, roles, and skills for the 21st Century* (3rd ed.). Gaithersburg, MD: Aspen.

Breslow, L. (1992). Empowerment, not outreach: Serving the health promotion needs of the inner city. *American Journal of Health Promotion, 7*(1), 7–8.

Burdine, J. N., & McLeroy, K. R. (1992). Practitioners' use of theory: Examples from a workgroup. *Health Education Quarterly, 19*(3), 331–340.

Chaplin, J. P., & Krawiec, T. S. (1979). *Systems and theories of psychology* (4th ed.). New York: Holt, Rinehart & Winston.

Checkoway, B. (1989). Community participation for health promotion: Prescription for public policy. *Wellness Perspectives: Research, Theory and Practice, 6*(1), 18–26.

Checkoway, B., & Van Til, J. (1978). What do we know about citizen participation? A selected review of research. In S. Langton (Ed.), *Citizen participation in America* (pp. 25–42). Lexington, MA: Lexington Books.

Chenoweth, D. H. (1987). *Planning health promotion at the worksite.* Indianapolis: Benchmark Press.

Cinelli, B., Rose-Colley, M., & Hayes, D. M. (1988). Health promotion efforts in Pennsylvania schools. *American Journal of Health Promotion, 2*(4), 36–44.

Clapp, J. D., Packard, T. R., & Stanger, L. A. (1993). Community organizing in alcohol and other drug prevention coalition building: The role of strategic decisions. *Journal of Health Education, 24*(3), 157–161.

Clark, N. M., Janz, N. K., Dodge, J. A., & Sharpe, P. A. (1992). Self-regulation of health behavior: The "take PRIDE" program. *Health Education Quarterly, 19*(3), 341–354.

Clift, E., & Freimuth, V. (1995). Health communication: What is it and what can it do for you? *Journal of Health Education, 26*(2), 68–74.

Clinton, J. (Ed.). (1988). *National guide to foundation funding in health.* New York: The Foundation Center.

Cohen, S., & Lichtenstein, E. (1990). Partner behaviors that support quitting smoking. *Journal of Consulting and Clinical Psychology, 58,* 304–309.

Colletti, G., & Brownell, K. (1982). *The physical and emotional benefits of social support: Application to obesity, smoking and alcoholism.* In M. Eisler et al. (Eds.), *Progress in behavior modification* (vol. 13). New York: Academic Press.

Conner, R. F. (1980). Ethical issues in the use of control groups. In R. Perloff & E. Perloff (Eds.), *New Directions for Program Evaluation* (pp. 63–75). San Francisco: Jossey-Bass.

Connor, D. M. (1968). *Strategies for development.* Ottawa: Development Press.

Cook, T. D., & Campbell, D. T. (1979). *Quasi-experimentation: Design and analysis issues for field settings.* Boston: Houghton Mifflin.

Cooper, K. H. (1982). *The aerobics program for total well-being.* Toronto: Bantam Books.

Cowdery, J. E., Wang, M. Q., Eddy, J. M., & Trucks, J. K. (1995). A theory driven health promotion program in a university setting. *Journal of Health Education, 26*(4), 248–250.

Cox, M., Shepard, R. J., & Corey, P. (1981). Influence of an employee fitness programme upon fitness, productivity and absenteeism. *Ergonomics, 24*(10), 795–806.

Cummings, C., Gordon, J. R., & Marlatt, G. A. (1980). Relapse: Prevention and prediction. In W. R. Miller (Ed.), *Addictive behaviors* (pp. 291–322). Oxford, U. K.: Pergamon Press.

Cummings, K., Becker, M. H., & Maile, M. (1980). Bringing the models together in an empirical approach to combining variables used to explain health actions. *Journal of Behavioral Medicine, 3*(2), 123–145.

Davis, J. (1990). Employee health newsletters: Analysis of characteristics. *AAOHN Journal, 38*(8), 360–367.

Deeds, S. G. (1992). *The health education specialist: Self-study for professional competence.* Los Alamitos, CA: Loose Canon.

Dennison, D. (1984). Activated health education: The development and refinement of an intervention model. *Health Values, 8*(2), 18–24.

DiBlase, D. (1985). Small businesses lead into wellness. *Business Insurance,* (December 2), 16.

DiClemente, C. C., & Prochaska, J. O. (1982). Self-change and therapy change of smoking behavior: A comparison of processes of change in cessation and maintenance. *Addictive Behaviors, 7*(2), 133–142.

DiClemente, C. C., Prochaska, J. O., Fairhurst, S. K., Velicer, W. F., Velasquez, M. M., & Rossi, J. S. (1991). The process of smoking cessation: An analysis of precontemplation, contemplation, and preparation stages of change. *Journal of Consulting and Clinical Psychology, 59,* 259–304.

Dignan, M. B. (1986). *Measurement and evaluation of health education.* Springfield, IL: Charles C Thomas.

Dignan, M. B., & Carr, P. A. (1992). *Program planning for health education and health promotion.* Philadelphia: Lea & Febiger.

Directory of research grants 1995 (20th ed.). (1995). Phoenix, AZ: Oryx Press.

Dishman, R. K. (Ed.). (1988). *Exercise adherence: Its impact on public health.* Champaign, IL: Human Kinetics.

Dishman, R. K., Sallis, J. F., & Orenstein, D. R. (1985). The determinants of physical activity and exercise. *Public Health Reports, 100*(2), 158–171.

D'Onofrio, C. N. (1992). Theory and the empowerment of health education practitioners. *Health Education Quarterly, 19*(3), 385–403.

Dunbar, J. M., Marshall, G. D., & Howell, M. F. (1979). Behavioral strategies for improving compliance. In R. B. Haynes, D. W. Taylor, & D. L. Sackett (Eds.), *Compliance in health care* (pp. 174–190). Baltimore: Johns Hopkins University Press.

Edington, D.W., & Yen, L. (1992). Is it possible to simultaneously reduce risk factors and excess health care costs? *American Journal of Health Promotion, 6*(6), 403–406, 409.

Elias, W. S., & Dunton, S. (1981). Effect of reliability on risk factor estimation by a health hazard appraisal. In *Proceedings of the 16th Meeting of the Society of Prospective Medicine.* Bethesda, MD: Society of Prospective Medicine.

Emont, S. L., & Cummings, K. M. (1989). Adoption of smoking policies by automobile dealerships. *Public Health Reports, 104*(5), 509–514.

Erfurt, J. C., Foote, A., Heirich, M. A., & Gregg, W. (1990). Improving participation in worksite wellness: Comparing health education classes, a menu approach, and follow-up counseling. *American Journal of Health Promotion, 4*(4), 270–278.

Erickson, A. C., McKenna, J. W., & Romano, R. M. (1990). Past lessons and new uses of the mass media in reducing tobacco consumption. *Public Health Reports, 105*(3), 239–244.

Feldman, R. H. L. (1983). Strategies for improving compliance with health promotion programs in industry. *Health Education, 14*(4), 21–25.

Fennell, R., & Beyrer, M. K. (1989). AIDS: Some ethical considerations for the health educator. *Journal of American College Health, 38*(November), 145–147.

Fink, A., & Kosecoff, J. (1978). *An evaluation primer.* Washington, DC: Capitol Publications.

Finkler, S. A. (1992). *Budgeting concepts for nurse managers* (2nd ed.). Philadelphia: W. B. Saunders.

Fishbein, M., & Ajzen, I. (1975). *Belief, attitude, intention and behavior: An introduction to theory and research.* Reading, MA: Addison-Wesley.

Forster, J., Jeffery, R., Sullivan, S., & Snell, M. (1985). A worksite weight control program using financial incentives collected through payroll deduction. *Journal of Occupational Medicine, 27*(11), 804–808.

Frederiksen, L. (1984). Using incentives in worksite wellness. *Corporate Commentary, 1*(2), 51–57.

Freimuth, V. S., & Mettger, W. (1990). Is there a hard-to-reach audience? *Public Health Reports, 105*(3), 232–238.

Freire, P. (1973). *Education: The practice of freedom.* London: Writer's and Reader's Publishing.

Freire, P. (1974). *Pedagogy of the oppressed.* New York: Seabury Press.

French, S. A., Jeffery, R. W., & Oliphant, J. A. (1994). Facility access and self-reward as methods to promote physical activity among healthy sedentary adults. *American Journal of Health Promotion, 8*(4), 257–259, 262.

Gilbert, G., & Sawyer, R. (1995). *Health education: Creating strategies for school and community health.* Boston: Jones & Bartlett.

Gilmore, G. D., & Campbell, M. D. (1996). *Needs assessment strategies for health education and health promotion* (2nd ed.). Madison, WI: WCB Brown & Benchmark.

Gilmore, G., Campbell, M. D., & Becker, B. L. (1989). *Needs assessment strategies for health education and health promotion.* Indianapolis: Benchmark Press.

Glanz, K., & Rimer, B. K. (1995). *Theory at a glance: A guide for health promotion practice* [NIH Pub. No. 95-3896]. Washington, DC: National Cancer Institute.

Golaszewski, T. J., Yen, L., Clearie, A., Lynch, W., & Vickery, D. (1989, September). Characteristics of employees reporting medical visits saved from use of the medical self-care text, Take care of yourself: The consumer's guide to medical care (pp. 152–161). In *Proceedings of the 25th Annual Meeting of the Society of Prospective Medicine.* Indianapolis, IN: Society of Prospective Medicine.

Gold, R. S. (1995). Application of technology to disease prevention and health promotion. In G. G. Gilbert & R. G. Sawyer, *Health education: Creating strategies for school and community health* (pp. 79–81). Boston: Jones and Bartlett.

Goodman, R. M., McLeroy, K. R., Steckler, A. B., & Hoyle, R. H. (1993). Development of level of institutionalization scales for health promotion programs. *Health Education Quarterly, 20*(2), 161–178.

Granat, J. P. (1994). *Persuasive advertising for entrepreneurs and small business owners: How to create more effective sales messages.* Binghamton, NY: The Haworth Press.

Green, L. W. (1973). Planning for patient educators: Considerations and implications. *Proceedings of the Maryland Conference on Patient Program* [DHEW Publication No. (HRA) 74-002]. Rockville: Health Care Facilities Service, Health Resources Administration.

Green, L. W. (1974). Toward cost-benefit evaluations of health education: Some concepts, methods, and examples. *Health Education Monographs, 2* (Suppl. 1), 34–64.

Green, L. W. (1975). Evaluation of patient education programs. Criteria and measurement techniques. In *Rx: Education for the patient: Proceedings of the Continuing Education Institution, Southern Illinois University* (pp. 89–98). Carbondale, IL: Southern Illinois University Press.

Green, L. W. (1976). Methods available to evaluate the health education components of preventive health programs. In *Preventive Medicine,* USA (pp. 162–171). New York: Prodist.

Green, L. W. (1979). National policy on the promotion of health. *International Journal of Health Education, 22,* 161–168.

Green, L. W. (1980). Healthy People: The Surgeon General's report and the prospects. In W. J. McNervey (Ed.), *Working for a healthier America* (pp. 95–110). Cambridge, MA: Ballinger.

Green, L. W. (1981a). Emerging federal perspectives on health promotion. In J. P. Allegrante (Ed.), *Health Promotion Monographs* (28 pp.). New York: Teachers College, Columbia University.

Green, L. W. (1981b). The objectives for the nation in disease prevention and health promotion: A challenge to health education training. *Proceedings of the National Conference for Institutions Preparing Health Educators,* (DHHS Publication No. 81-50171) (pp. 61–73). Washington, DC: U.S. Office of Health Information and Health Promotion.

Green, L. W. (1982). Reconciling policy in health education and primary care. *International Journal of Health Education, 24* (Suppl. 3), 1–11.

Green, L. W. (1983a). New policies in education for health. *World Health* (April–May), 13–17.

Green, L. W. (1983b). *New policies for health education in primary health care* (Background document for the technical discussions of the 36th World Health Assembly, May 1983). Geneva: World Health Organization.

Green, L. W. (1984a). A triage and stepped approach to self-care education. *Medical Times, 111,* 75–80.

Green, L. W. (1984b). Health education models. In J. D. Matarazzo, S. M. Weiss, & J. A. Herd (Eds.),

Behavioral health: A handbook of health enhancement and disease prevention (pp. 181–198). New York: Wiley.

Green, L. W. (1984c). La educacion para la salud en el medio urbano. In *Conferencia InterAmericana de Educacion Para La Salud* (pp. 80–82). Mexico City: Sector Salud, SEP, and International Union for Health Education and World Health Organization.

Green, L. W. (1984d). Modifying and developing health behavior. *Annual Review of Public Health, 5,* 215–236.

Green, L. W. (1986a, October). *Applications and trials of the PRECEDE framework for planning and evaluation of health programs.* Paper presented at the meeting of the American Public Health Association, Las Vegas, NV.

Green, L. W. (1986b). Evaluation model: A framework for the design of rigorous evaluation of efforts in health promotion. *American Journal of Health Promotion, 1*(1), 77–79.

Green, L. W. (1986c). *New policies for health education in primary health care.* Geneva: World Health Organization.

Green, L. W. (1986d). Research agenda: Building a consensus on research questions. *American Journal of Health Promotion, 1*(2), 70–72.

Green, L. W. (1986e). The theory of participation: A qualitative analysis of its expression in national and international health policies. In W. B. Ward (Ed.), *Advances in Health Education and Promotion* (pp. 211–236). Greenwich, CT: JAI Press.

Green, L. W. (1987a). How physicians can improve patients' participation and maintenance in self-care. *Western Journal of Medicine, 147,* 346–349.

Green, L. W. (1987b). *Program planning and evaluation guide for Lung Associations.* New York: American Lung Association.

Green, L. W. (1989, March). *The health promotion program of the Henry J. Kaiser Family Foundation.* Paper presented at a public lecture at Mankato State University, Mankato, MN.

Green, L. W. (1990). The revival of community and the public obligation of academic health centers. In R. E. Bulger and S. J. Reiser (Eds.), *Integrity in institutions: Humane environments for teaching* (pp. 163–178). Iowa City: University of Iowa Press.

Green, L. W., & Allen, J. (1980). *Toward a healthy community: Organizing events for community health promotion* (PHS Publication No. 80-50113). Washington, DC: USDHHS, Office of Disease Prevention and Health Promotion.

Green, L. W., Gold, R., Tan, J., & Kreuter, M. (1994). The EMPOWER/Canadian Health Expert System: The application of artificial intelligence and expert system technology to community health program planning and evaluation. *Canadian Medical Infamatics*, Nov./Dec., 20–23.

Green, L. W., & Kreuter, M. W. (1991). *Health promotion planning: An educational and environmental approach* (2nd ed.). Mountain View, CA: Mayfield.

Green, L. W., & Kreuter, M. W. (1992). CDC's planned approach to community health as an application of PRECEDE and an inspiration for PROCEED. *Journal of Health Education, 23*(3), 140–147.

Green, L. W., Kreuter, M. W., Deeds, S. G., & Partridge, K. B. (1980). *Health education planning: A diagnostic approach.* Palo Alto, CA: Mayfield.

Green, L. W., Levine, D. M., & Deeds, S. G. (1975). Clinical trials of health education for hypertensive outpatients: Design and baseline data. *Preventive Medicine, 4,* 417–425.

Green, L. W., & Lewis, F. M. (1986). *Measurement and evaluation in health education and health promotion.* Palo Alto, CA: Mayfield.

Green, L. W., & McAlister, A. L. (1984). Macro-intervention to support health behavior: Some theoretical perspectives and practical reflections. *Health Education Quarterly, 11,* 323–339.

Green, L. W., Mullen, P. D., & Friedman, R. (1986). An epidemiological approach to targeting drug information. *Patient Education and Counseling, 8,* 255–268.

Green, L. W., Wang, V. L., Deeds, S. G., Fisher, A. A., Windsor, R., & Rogers, C. (1978). Guidelines for health education in maternal and child health programs. *International Journal of Health Education, 21* (suppl.), 1–33.

Green, L. W., Wilson, A. L., & Lovato, C. Y. (1986). What changes can health promotion achieve and how long do these changes last? The tradeoffs between expediency and durability. *Preventive Medicine, 15,* 508–521.

Green, L. W., Wilson, R. W., & Bauer, K. G. (1983). Data required to measure progress on the objectives for the nation in disease prevention and health promotion. *American Journal of Public Health, 73,* 18–24.

Greenberg, J. (1978). Health education as freeing. *Health Education, 9*(2), 20–21.

Greer, A. (1977). Advances in the study of diffusion of innovation in health care organizations. *Milbank Memorial Fund Quarterly, 55*(4) 505–532.

Grimley, D. M., Prochaska, J. O., Velicer, W. F., & Prochaska, G. E. (1995). Contraceptive and condom use adoption and maintenance: A stage paradigm approach. *Health Education Quarterly, 22*(1), 20–35.

Grimley, D. M., Riley, G. E., Bellis, J. M., & Prochaska, J. O. (1993). Assessing the stages of change and decision making for contraceptive use for the prevention of pregnancy, sexually transmitted

diseases, and acquired immunodeficiency syndrome. *Health Education Quarterly, 20*(4), 455–470.
Hall, C. L. (1943). *Principles of behavior.* New York: Appleton-Century-Crofts.
Hanlon, J. J. (1974). *Administration of public health.* St. Louis: C. V. Mosby.
Harris, J. H., McKenzie, J. F., & Zuti, W. B. (1986). How to select the right vendor for your company's health promotion program. *Fitness in Business, 1*(October), pp. 53–56.
Health Insurance Association of America. (1983). *Your guide to wellness at the worksite.* Pamphlet issued by the Public Relations Division of the Health Insurance Association of America, Washington, DC.
Healthy people: The Surgeon General's report on health promotion and disease prevention. (1979). (Publication No. 79-55071). Washington, DC: Department of Health, Education, and Welfare (Public Health Service).
Hempel, C. (1977). Formulation and formation of scientific theories. In F. Suppe (Ed.), *The structure of scientific theories* (2nd ed.) (pp. 244–265). Urbana: University of Illinois Press.
Hertoz, J. K., Finnegan, J. R., Rooney, B., Viswanath, K., & Potter, J. (1993). *Health Communication, 5*(1), 21–40.
Hochbaum, G. M., Sorenson, J. R., & Lorig, K. (1992). Theory in health education practice. *Health Education Quarterly, 19*(3), 295–313.
Horman, S. (1989). The role of social support on health throughout the lifestyle. *Health Education, 20*(4), 18–21.
Horne, W. M. (1975). Effects of a physical activity program on middle-aged, sedentary corporation executives. *American Industrial Hygiene Journal,* (March), 241–245.
Hosokawa, M. C. (1984). Insurance incentives for health promotion. *Health Education, 15*(6), 9–12.
House, E. R. (1980). *Evaluating with validity.* Beverly Hills, CA: Sage.
Houston, J. E. (Ed.). (1987). *Thesaurus of ERIC descriptors* (11th ed.). Phoenix, AZ: Oryx Press.
Hunt, W. A., Barnett, L. W., & Branch, L. G. (1971). Relapse rates in addiction programs. *Journal of Clinical Psychology, 27*(4), 455–456.
Indiana State Department of Health (ISDH). (1992). *Healthy Hoosiers 2000: Health promotion and disease prevention objectives.* Indianapolis, IN: Author.
Institute of Medicine (IOM). (1988). *The future of public health.* Washington, DC: National Academy Press.
IOX Assessment Associates. (1988). Program evaluation handbooks for health promotion and health education. Los Angeles: Author.
Israel, B. A., Checkoway, B., Schulz, A., & Zimmerman, M. (1994). Health education and community empowerment: Conceptualizing and measuring perceptions of individual, organizational, and community control. *Health Education Quarterly, 21*(2), 149–170.
Jacobsen, D., Eggen, P., & Kauchak, D. (1989). *Methods for teaching: A skills approach* (3rd ed.). Columbus, OH: Merrill, an imprint of Macmillan Publishing Company.
Janz, N. K., & Becker, M. H. (1984). The health belief model: A decade later. *Health Education Quarterly, 11*(1), 1–47.
Jason, L. A., Jayaraj, S., Blitz, C. C., Michaels, M. H., & Klett, L. E. (1990). Incentives and competition in a worksite smoking cessation intervention. *American Journal of Public Health, 80*(2), 205–206.
Jeffery, R. W., Forster, J. L., Baxter, J. E., French, S. A., & Kelder, S. H. (1993). An empirical evaluation of the effectiveness of tangible incentives in increasing participation and behavior change in a worksite health promotion program. *American Journal of Health Promotion, 8*(2), 98–100.
Jessor, R., Graves, T. D., Hanson, R. C., & Jessor, S. L. (1968). *Society, personality, and deviant behavior: A study of tri ethnic community.* New York: Holt, Rinehart & Winston.
Jessor, R., & Jessor, S. L. (1977). *Problem behavior and psychosocial development: A longitudinal study of youth.* New York: Academic Press.
Joint Committee on Health Education Terminology. (1991). Report of the 1990 joint committee on health education terminology. *Journal of Health Education, 22*(2), 97–108.
Jones, R., Bly, J., & Richardson, J. (1990). A study of worksite health promotion programs and absenteeism. *Journal of Occupational Medicine, 32,* 95–99.
Kaplan, B., & Cassel, J. (1977). Social support and health. *Medical Care, 15*(5), 47–58.
Kendall, R. (1984). Rewarding safety excellence. *Occupational Hazards,* (March), 45–50.
Kickbusch, I. (1989). Healthy cities: A working project and a growing movement. *Health Promotion, 4*(2), 77–82.
Kolbe, L. J., & Iverson, D. C. (1981). Implementing comprehensive health education: Educational innovations and social change. *Health Education Quarterly, 8*(1), 57–80.
Kotler, P., & Andreasen, A. R. (1987). *Strategic marketing for nonprofit organizations* (3rd ed.). Englewood Cliffs, NJ: Prentice-Hall.
Kotler, P., & Andreasen, A. R. (1991). *Strategic marketing for nonprofit organizations* (4th ed.). Englewood Cliffs, NJ: Prentice-Hall.
Kotler, P., & Clarke, R. N. (1987). *Marketing for health care organizations.* Englewood Cliffs, NJ: Prentice-Hall.
Kreuter, M. W. (1992). PATCH: Its origin, basic concepts, and links to contemporary public health policy. *Journal of Health Education, 23*(3), 135–139.
Kreuter, M. W., Nelson, C. F., Stoddard, R. P., & Watkins, N. B. (1985). *Planned approach to com-*

munity health. Atlanta, GA: Centers for Disease Control.

Kumpfer, K., Turner, C., & Alvarado, R. (1991). A community change model for school health promotion. *Journal of Health Education, 22*(2), 94–96, 109–110.

Kviz, F. J., Crittenden, K. S., Madura, K. J., & Warnecke, R. B. (1994). Use and effectiveness of buddy support in a self-help smoking cessation program. *American Journal of Health Promotion, 8*(3), 191–201.

Labonte, R. (1994). Health promotion and empowerment: Reflections on professional practice. *Health Education Quarterly, 21*(2), 253–268.

Lefebvre, R. C., & Flora, J. A. (1988). Social marketing and public health intervention. *Health Education Quarterly, 15*(3), 299–315.

LeMaster, P. L., & Connell, C. M. (1994). Health education interventions among native Americans: A review and analysis. *Health Education Quarterly, 21*(4), 521–538.

Leventhal, H., & Cleary, P. D. (1980). The smoking problem: A review of the research and theory in behavioral risk modification. *Psychological Bulletin, 88*(2), 370–405.

Lewin, K. (1935). *A dynamic theory of personality.* New York: McGraw-Hill.

Lewin, K. (1936). *Principles of topological psychology.* New York: McGraw-Hill.

Lewin, K., Dembo, T., Festinger, L., & Sears, P. S. (1944). Level of aspiration. In J. Hunt (Ed.), *Personality and the behavior disorders* (pp. 333–378). New York: Ronald Press.

Lindberg, D. A. B. (Ed.). (1995). *Index Medicus* (NIH Publication No. 95-252). Washington, DC: U.S. Government Printing Office.

Lindsay, G. B., & Edwards, G. (1988). Creating effective health coalitions. *Health Education, 19*(4), 35–36.

Maccoby, N., & Solomon, D. S. (1981). Heart disease prevention: Community studies. In R. E. Rice, et al. (Eds.), *Public communication campaigns* (pp. 105–125). Beverly Hills, CA: Sage.

Marcarin, S. (Ed.). (1995). *Cumulative index to nursing & allied health literature: CINAHL.* Volume 40, Part A. Glendale, CA.

Marlatt, G. A. (1982). Relapse prevention: A self-control program for treatment of addictive behaviors. In R. B. Sturat (Ed.), *Adherence, compliance, and generalization in behavioral medicine* (pp. 329–377). New York: Brunner/Mazel.

Marlatt, G. A. (1985). Relapse prevention: Theoretical rationale and overview of the model. In G. A. Marlatt & J. R. Gordon (Eds.), *Relapse prevention* (pp. 3–70). New York: Guilford Press.

Marlatt, G. A., & Gordon, J. R. (1980). Determinants of relapse: Implications for maintenance of behavior change. In P. O. Davidson & S. M. Davidson (Eds.), *Behavioral medicine: Changing health lifestyles* (pp. 410–452). New York: Brunner/Mazel.

Mason, J. O., & McGinnis, J. M. (1990). "Healthy people 2000": An overview of the national health promotion and disease prevention objectives. *Public Health Reports, 105*(5), 441–446.

Matson, D. M., Lee, J. W., & Hopp, J. W. (1993). The impact of incentives and competitions on participation and quit rates in worksite smoking cessation programs. *American Journal of Health Promotion, 7*(4), 270–280, 295.

McAlister, A. L., Puska, P., Salonen, J. T., Tuomilehot, J., & Koskelia, A. (1982). Theory and action for health promotion: Illustrations from the North Karelia project. *American Journal of Public Health, 72*(1), 43–50.

McCarthy, E. J. (1978). *Basic marketing: A managerial approach* (6th ed.). Homewood, IL: Richard D. Irwin.

McConnaughy, E. A., Prochaska, J. O., & Velicer, W. F. (1983). Stages of change in psychotherapy: Measurement and sample profiles. *Psychotherapy: Theory, Research, and Practice, 20*(3), 368–375.

McDonald, T. L., Treser, C. D., & Hatlan, J. B. (1994). Development of an environmental health addendum to the assessment protocol for excellence in public health. *Journal of Public Health Policy, 15*(2), 203–217.

McGuire, W. J. (1981). Behavioral medicine, public health and communication theories. *Health Education, 12*(3), 8–13.

McKenzie, J. F. (1986). Cost-benefit and cost-effectiveness as a part of the evaluation of health promotion programs. *The Eta Sigma Gamman, 18*(2), 10–16.

McKenzie, J. F. (1988). Twelve steps in developing a schoolsite health education/promotion program for faculty and staff. *The Journal of School Health, 58*(4), 149–153.

McKenzie, J. F., Luebke, J., & Romas, J. A. (1992). Incentives: A means of getting and keeping workers involved in health promotion programs. *Journal of Health Education, 23*(2), 70–73.

McKenzie, J. F., & Pinger, R. R. (1995). *An introduction to community health.* New York: Harper Collins College Publishers.

McLeroy, K. R. (1993). Theory and practice in health education: Which practice, which theory? *American Public Health Association, Public Health Education and Health Promotion Section Newsletter,* Summer, 7–8.

McLeroy, K. R., Bibeau, D., Steckler, A., & Glanz, K. (1988). An ecological perspective on health promotion programs. *Health Education Quarterly, 15,* 351–377.

Meyer, J., & Rainey, J. (1994). Writing health education material for low-literacy populations. *Journal of Health Education, 25*(6), 372–374.
Mikanowicz, C. K., & Altman, N. H. (1995). Developing policies on smoking in the workplace. *Journal of Health Education, 26*(3), 183–185.
Miller, R. E. (1992). Health communication through workplace smoking discourage-ment posters. *Journal of Health Education, 23*(4), 250–252.
Miller, R. E., & Golaszewski, T. J. (1992). Analysis of commercial health newsletters by worksite decision makers. *American Journal of Health Promotion, 7*(1), 11–12, 75.
Mills, C. R. (Ed.). (1993). *Foundation grants to individuals* (8th ed). New York: Foundation Center NW.
Miner, K. J., & Ward, S. E. (1992). Ecological health promotion: The promise of empowerment education. *Journal of Health Education, 23*(7), 429–432.
Minkler, M. (1994). Challenges for health promotion in the 1990s. Social inequities, empowerment, negative consequences and the common good. *American Journal of Health Promotion, 8*(6), 403–413.
Minter, S. G. (1986). Occupational health professionals control health care costs. *Occupational Hazards,* (April), 63–66.
Monahan, J. L., & Scheirer, M. A. (1988). The role of linking agents in the diffusion of health promotion programs. *Health Education Quarterly, 15*(4), 417–433.
Morris, L. L., Fitz-Gibbon, C. T., & Freeman, M. E. (1987). *How to communicate evaluation findings.* Newbury Park, CA: Sage.
Moskowitz, J. M. (1989). Preliminary guidelines for reporting outcome evaluation studies of health promotion and disease prevention programs. In M. Braverman (Ed.), *New directions for program evaluation* (pp. 59–74). San Francisco: Jossey-Bass.
Murphy, W. G., & Brubaker, R. G. (1990). Effects of a theory-based intervention on the practice of testicular self-examination by high school males. *Journal of School Health, 60*(9), 459–462.
National Association of County Health Officials (NACHO). (1991). *APEX/PH, Assessment protocol for excellence in public health.* Washington, DC: Author.
National Dairy Council. (1992). *2000 and counting.* Rosemont, IL: Author.
National Task Force on the Preparation and Practice of Health Educators, Inc. (1985). *A framework for the development of competency-based curricula for entry-level health educators.* New York: Author.
Newcomer, K. E. (1994). Using statistics appropriately. In J. S. Wholey, H. P. Hatry, & K. E. Newcomer (Eds.), *Handbook of practical program evaluation* (pp. 389–416). San Francisco: Jossey-Bass.
Norcross, J. C., Prochaska, J. O., & Hambrecht, M. (1991). Treating ourselves vs. treating our clients: A replication with alcohol abuse. *Journal of Substance Abuse, 3,* 123–129.
Novelli, W. D. (1988). Marketing health and social issues: What works? In R. Dunmire (Ed.), *Social marketing: Accepting the challenge in public health.* Atlanta, GA: Centers for Disease Control.
Novelli, W. D., & Ziska, D. (1982). Health promotion in the workplace: An overview. *Health Education Quarterly, 9*(suppl.), 20–26.
Nye, R. D. (1979). *What is B. F. Skinner really saying?* Englewood Cliffs, NJ: Prentice-Hall.
Nye, R. D. (1992). *The legacy of B. F. Skinner: Concepts and perspectives, controversies, and misunderstandings.* Pacific Grove, CA: Brooks/Cole.
O'Donnell, M. (1992). Design of workplace health promotion programs (2nd ed.). Rochester Hills, MI: *American Journal of Health Promotion.*
O'Donnell, M., & Ainsworth, T. (Eds.). (1984). *Health promotion in the workplace.* New York: John Wiley and Sons.
Orlaldi, M. A. (1986). The diffusion and adoption of worksite health promotion innovations: An analysis of barriers. *Preventive Medicine, 15*(5), 522–536.
O'Rourke, T. W., & Macrina, D. M. (1989). Beyond victim blaming: Examining the micro-macro issues in health promotion. *Wellness Perspectives: Research, Theory and Practice, 6*(1), 7–17.
Pahnos, M. L. (1992). The continuing challenge of multicultural health education. *Journal of School Health, 62*(1), 24–26.
Parcel, G. S. (1983). Theoretical models for application in school health education research. *Health Education, 15*(4), 39–49.
Parcel, G. S., & Baranowski, T. (1981). Social learning theory and health education. *Health Education, 12*(3), 14–18.
Parcel, G. S., Ericksen, M. P., Lovato, C. Y., Gottlieb, N. H., Brink, S. G., & Green, L. W. (1989). The diffusion of school-based tobacco-use prevention programs: Project description and baseline data. *Health Education Research, 4*(1), 111–124.
Parkinson, R. S., & Associates. (1982). *Managing health promotion in the workplace: Guidelines for implementation and evaluation.* Palo Alto. CA: Mayfield.
Patton, M. Q. (1986). *Utilization-focused evaluation.* Beverly Hills, CA: Sage.
Patton, M. Q. (1988). *How to use qualitative methods in evaluation.* Newbury Park, CA: Sage.
Patton, R. P., Corry, J. M., Gettman, L. R., & Graff, J. S. (1986). *Implementing health/fitness programs.* Champaign, IL: Human Kinetics.
Pavlov, I. (1927). *Conditional reflexes.* Oxford: Oxford University Press.
Penner, M. (1989). Economic incentives to reduce employee smoking: A health insurance surcharge

for tobacco using state of Kansas employees. *American Journal of Health Promotion, 4*(1), 5–11.

Pentz, M. A., Johnson, C. A., Dwyer, J. H., MacKinnon, D. M., Hansen, W. B., & Flay, B. R. (1989). A comprehensive community approach to adolescent drug abuse prevention: Effects on cardiovascular disease risk behaviors. *Annals of Medicine, 21*(3), 382–388.

Perlman, J. (1978). Grassroots participation from neighborhood to nation. In S. Langton (Ed.), *Citizen participation in America* (pp. 65–79). Lexington, MA: Lexington Books.

Perlman, R., & Gurin, A. (1972). *Community organization and social planning.* New York: John Wiley & Sons.

Pickett, G. E., & Hanlon, J. J. (1990). *Public health: Administration and practice.* St. Louis: Mosby-Year Book, Inc.

Piniat, A. J. (1984). How to put spirit in an incentive program. *National Safety News,* (January), 46–49.

Pollock, M. L., Foster, C., Salisburg, R., & Smith, R. (1982). Effects of a YMCA starter fitness program. *The Physician and Sportsmedicine, 10*(1), 89–91, 95–99, 120.

Popham, W. J. (1988). *Educational evaluation.* Englewood Cliffs, NJ: Prentice-Hall.

Price, J. H., Telljohann, S. K., Roberts, S. M., & Smit, D. (1992). Effects of incentives in an inner city junior high school smoking prevention program. *Journal of Health Education, 23*(7), 388–396.

Prochaska, J. O. (1979). *Systems of psychotherapy: A transtheoretical analysis.* Homewood, IL: Dorsey Press.

Prochaska, J. O. (1989, August). *What causes people to change from unhealthy to health-enhancing behavior?* Paper presented at the American Cancer Society's Human Behavior and Cancer Risk Reduction Conference, Bloomington, IN.

Prochaska, J. O., & DiClemente, C. C. (1982). Transtheoretical therapy: Toward a more integrative model of change. *Psychotherapy: Theory, Research, and Practice, 19*(3), 276–288.

Prochaska, J. O., & DiClemente, C. C. (1983). Stages and processes of self-change of smoking: Toward an integrative model of change. *Journal of Consulting and Clinical Psychology, 51*(3), 390–395.

Prochaska, J. O., & DiClemente, C. C. (1985). Common processes of change for smoking, weight control, and psychological distress. In S. Shiffman & T. Wills (Eds.), *Coping and Substance Abuse* (pp. 345–363). New York: Academic Press.

Prochaska, J. O., DiClemente, C. C., & Norcross, J. C. (1992). In search of how people change: Applications to addictive behaviors. *American Psychologist, 47*(9), 1102–1114.

Prochaska, J. O., DiClemente, C. C., Velicer, W. F., Ginpil, S., & Norcross, J. C. (1985). Predicting change in smoking status for self-changers. *Addictive Behaviors, 10*(4), 395–406.

Prochaska, J. O., Harlow, L. L., Redding, C. A., Snow, M. G., Rossi, J. S., & Velicer, W. F. (1990). *Stages of charge, self-efficacy, and decisional balance of condom use in a high HIV risk sample.* Atlanta, GA: Technical Report for Centers for Disease Control Contract Grant 0-4115-002.

Prochaska, J. O., Norcross, J. C., Fowler, J. L., Follick, M. J., & Abrams, D. B. (1992). Attendance and outcome in a worksite weight control program: Processes and stages of change as process and predictor variables. *Addictive Behaviors, 17,* 35–45.

Prochaska, J. O., Redding, C. A., Harlow, L. L., Rossi, J. S., & Velicer, W. F. (1994). The transtheoretical model of change and HIV prevention: A review. *Health Education Quarterly, 21*(4), 471–486.

Rakich, J. S., Longest, B. B., & O'Donovan, T. R. (1977). *Managing health care organizations.* Philadelphia: W. B. Saunders.

Rich, R. F., & Sugrue, N. M. (1989). Health promotion, disease prevention, and public policy. *Wellness Perspectives: Research, Theory and Practice, 6*(1), 27–35.

Rifkin, S. B. (1986). Lessons from community participation in health programmes. *Health Policy and Planning, 1*(3), 240–249.

Robertson, A., & Minkler, M. (1994). New health promotion movement: A critical examination. *Health Education Quarterly, 21*(3), 295–312.

Rogers, E. M. (1962). *Diffusion of innovations.* New York: Free Press of Glencoe.

Rogers, E. M. (1983). *Diffusion of innovations* (3rd ed.). New York: Free Press.

Rokeach, M. (1969). *Beliefs, attitudes and values: A theory of organization and change.* San Francisco: Jossey-Bass.

Romer, D., & Kim, S. (1995). Health interventions for African American and Latino youth: The potential role of mass media. *Health Education Quarterly, 22*(2), 172–189.

Rosenstock, I. M. (1966). Why people use health services. *Milbank Memorial Fund Quarterly, 44,* 94–124.

Rosenstock, I. M., Strecher, V. J., & Becker, M. H. (1988). Social learning theory and the health belief model. *Health Education Quarterly, 15*(2), 175–183.

Ross, H. S., & Mico, P. R. (1980). *Theory and practice in health education.* Palo Alto, CA: Mayfield.

Ross, M. G. (1967). *Community organization: Theory, principles, and practice.* New York: Harper & Row.

Rothman, J., & Tropman, J. E. (1987). Models of community organization and macro practice perspectives: Their mixing and phasing. In F. M. Cox, J. L. Erlich, J. Rothman, & J. E. Tropman (Eds.), *Strategies of community organization: Macro practice* (pp. 3–26). Itasca, IL: F. E. Peacock.

Rotter, J. B. (1954). *Social learning and clinical psychology.* New York: Prentice-Hall.

Rotter, J. B. (1966). Generalized expectancies for internal versus external control of reinforcement. *Psychological Monographs, 80*(1).

Sachs, J. J., Krushat, W. M., & Newman, J. (1980). Reliability of the health hazard appraisal. *American Journal of Public Health, 70,* 730–732.

Sarvela, P. D., & McDermott, R. J. (1993). *Health education evaluation and measurement: A practitioner's perspective.* Madison, WI: WCB Brown & Benchmark Publishers.

Scandrett, A. (1994). The black church as a participant in community interventions. *Journal of Health Education, 25*(3), 183–185.

Schechter, C., Vanchieri, C., & Crofton, C. (1990). Evaluating women's attitudes and perceptions in developing mammography promotion messages. *Public Health Reports, 105*(3), 253–257.

Sciacca, J., Seehafer, R., Reed, R., & Mulvaney, D. (1993). The impact of participation in health promotion on medical costs: A reconsideration of the Blue Cross and Blue Shield of Indiana study. *American Journal of Health Promotion, 7*(5), 374–383, 395.

Scriven, M. (1973). Goal-free evaluation. In E. House (Ed.), *School evaluation: The politics and procedures* (pp. 319–328). Berkeley, CA: McCutchan.

Seffrin, J. R. (1994). America's interest in comprehensive school health education. *Journal of School Health, 64,* 397–399.

Shea, S., & Basch, C. E. (1990). A review of five major community-based cardiovascular disease prevention programs: Part I, rationale, design and theoretical framework. *American Journal of Health Promotion, 4*(3), 203–213.

Shepard, M. (1985). Motivation: The key to fitness compliance. *The Physician and Sportsmedicine, 13*(7), 88–101.

Shepard, R. (1992). Twelve years experience of a fitness program for salaried employees of a Toronto life assurance company. *American Journal of Health Promotion, 6*(4), 292–301.

Shepard, R. J., Corey, P., Renzland, P., & Cox, M. (1982). The influence of an employee fitness and lifestyle modification program upon medical care costs. *Canadian Journal of Public Health, 73*(4), 259–263.

Sherwood, S. (Ed.). (1987). *Alcohol programs and policies on campus* (NASPA Monograph No. 7). Washington, DC: National Association of Student Personnel Administrators.

Shim, J. K., & Siegel, J. G. (1994). *Complete budgeting workbook and guide.* New York: New York Institute of Finance.

Shirreffs, J., Odom, J., McLeroy, K., Cryer, D., & Fors, S. (1990, April). *Incorporating ethics in the health education curriculum.* Papers presented at the meeting of the Association for the Advancement of Health Education, New Orleans, LA.

SilverPlatter. (1992, April). PsycLIT on SilverPlatter.

Skinner, B. F. (1953). *Science and human behavior.* New York: Free Press.

Sloan, R., Gruman, J., & Allegrante, J. (1987). *Investing in employee health.* San Francisco: Jossey-Bass.

Smith, K. W., McKinlay, S. M., & McKinlay, J. B. (1989). The reliability of health risk appraisals: A field trial of four instruments. *American Journal of Public Health, 79*(12), 1603–1606.

Solomon, D. D. (1987). Evaluating community programs. In F. M. Cox, J. L. Erlich, J. Rolhman, & J. E. Tropman (Eds.), *Strategies of community organization: Macro practices* (pp. 366–368). Itasca, IL: F. E. Peacock.

Sorensen, G., Rigotti, N., Rosen, A., Pinney, J., and Prible, R. (1991). Effects of a worksite nonsmoking policy: Evidence for increased cessation. *American Journal of Public Health, 81*(2), 202–204.

Speers, M. (1992). Preface. *Journal of Health Education, 23*(3), 132–133.

Spilman, M. A., Goetz, A., Schultz, J., Bellingham, R., & Johnson, D. (1986). Effects of a corporate health promotion program. *Journal of Occupational Medicine, 28*(4), 285–289.

Stacy, R. D. (1987). Instrument evaluation guides for survey research in health education and health promotion. *Health Education, 18*(5), 65–67.

Stake, R. E. (1983). Program evaluation, particularly responsive evaluation. In G. F. Madaus, M. Scriven, & D. L. Stufflebeam (Eds.), *Evaluation models* (pp. 287–310). Boston: Kluwer-Nijhoff.

Steckler, A., Goodman, R. M., McLeroy, K. R., Davis, S., & Koch, G. (1992). Measuring the diffusion of innovative health promotion programs. *American Journal of Health Promotion, 6*(3), 214–224.

Strecher, V. J., DeVellis, B. M., Becker, M. H., & Rosenstock, I. M. (1986). The role of self-efficacy in achieving health behavior change. *Health Education Quarterly, 13*(1), 73–91.

Stufflebeam, D. L., & Members of the National Study Committee on Evaluation of Phi Delta Kappa (1971). *Educational evaluation and decision making.* Itasca, IL: F. E. Peacock.

Stunkard, A. J., & Braunwell, K. D. (1980). Worksite treatment for obesity. *American Journal of Psychiatry, 137,* 252–253.

Suchman, E. A. (1967). *Evaluative Research.* New York: Russell Sage Foundation.

Sullivan, D. (1973). Model for comprehensive, systematic program development in health education. *Health Education Report, 1*(1) (November-December), 4–5.

Sutherland, M. S., Harris, G. J., Kissinger, M., Barber, M., & Lewis, J. L. (1994). Creating awareness of drug prevention: Using beauty shops as information outlets. *Journal of Health Education, 25*(3), 186–187.

Syre, T. R., & Wilson, R. W. (1990). Health care marketing: Role evolution of the community health educator. *Health Education, 21*(1), 6–8.

Task Force of the Society of Prospective Medicine. (1981). *Guidelines for health risk appraisal/reduction systems.* (Available from Society of Prospective Medicine, 4405 East-West Hwy., Bethesda, MD, 20814.)

Thorndike, E. L. (1898). Animal intelligence: An experimental study of the associative processes in animals. *Psychological Monographs, 2*(8).

Toufexis, A. (1985). Giving goodies to the good. *Time* (November 18), 98.

Tsai, S., Baun, W., & Bernacki, E. (1987). Relationship of employee turnover to exercise adherence in a corporate fitness program. *Journal of Occupational Medicine, 29,* 572–575.

Udinsky, B. F., Osterlind, S. J., & Lynch, S. W. (1981). *Evaluation resource handbook: Gathering, analyzing, reporting data.* San Diego: EdITS.

United Nations. (1955). *Social progress through community development.* New York: United Nations.

U.S. Bureau of Census. (1994). *Statistical abstract of the United States: 1994* (114th ed). Washington, DC: U.S. Government Printing Office.

U.S. Department of Commerce (USDC), Bureau of the Census. (1989). *Statistical brief: Single parents and their children* (SB-3-89). Washington, DC: U.S. Government Printing Office.

U.S. Department of Commerce (USDC), Bureau of the Census. (1992). *Statistical brief: Family life today . . . and how it has changed* (SB-92-13). Washington, DC: U.S. Government Printing Office.

U.S. Department of Health and Human Services (USDHHS). (1980). *Promoting health/preventing disease: Objectives for the nation.* Washington, DC: U.S. Government Printing Office.

U.S. Department of Health and Human Services (USDHHS). (1985). *No smoking: A decision maker's guide to reducing smoking at the worksite.* Washington, DC: U.S. Government Printing Office.

U.S. Department of Health and Human Services (USDHHS). (1986a). *Integration of risk factor interventions.* Washington, DC: U.S. Government Printing Office.

U.S. Department of Health and Human Services (USDHHS). (1986b). *The 1990 health objectives for the nation: A midcourse review.* Washington, DC: U.S. Government Printing Office.

U.S. Department of Health and Human Services (USDHHS). (1987). *Strategies for diffusing health information to minority populations: Executive summary.* Washington, DC: U.S. Government Printing Office.

U.S. Department of Health and Human Services (USDHHS). (1989). *Making health communication programs work: A planner's guide* (NIH Publication No. 89-1493). Washington, DC: U.S. Government Printing Office.

U.S. Department of Health and Human Services (USDHHS). (1990a). *Healthy people 2000: National health promotion disease prevention objectives* (DHHS Publication No. [PHS] 90-50212). Washington, DC: U.S. Government Printing Office.

U.S. Department of Health and Human Services (USDHHS). (1990b). *Prevention '89/'90.* Washington, DC: U.S. Government Printing Office.

U.S. Department of Health and Human Services (USDHHS). (1994). *Healthy People 2000 Review, 1993* (DHHS Publication No. [PHS] 94-1232-1). Washington, DC: U.S. Government Printing Office.

U.S. Department of Health and Human Services (USDHHS), Office of Substance Abuse Prevention (1991). *The fact is . . . you can prepare easy-to-read materials.* Rockville, MD: Author.

van Ryn, M., & Heaney, C. A. (1992). What's the use of theory? *Health Education Quarterly, 19*(3), 315–330.

Wagner, E. H., & Guild, P. A. (1989). Choosing an evaluation strategy. *American Journal of Health Promotion, 4*(2), 134–139.

Walker, R. A., & Bibeau, D. (1985/1986). Health education as freeing—Part II. *Health Education, 16*(6), (December/January), 4–8.

Wallerstein, N. (1992). Powerlessness, empowerment, and health: Implications for health promotion programs. *American Journal of Health Promotion, 6*(3), 197–205.

Wallerstein, N. (1994). Empowerment education applied to youth. In A. C. Matiella (Ed.). *The multicultural challenge in health education* (pp. 153–176). Santa Cruz, CA: ETR Associates.

Wallerstein, N., & Bernstein, E. (1988). Empowerment education: Freier's ideas adapted to health education. *Health Education Quarterly, 15*(4), 379–394.

Wallston, K. A. (1992). Hocus-pocus, the focus isn't strictly on locus: Rotter's social learning theory modified for health. *Cognitive Therapy and Research, 16,* 183–199.

Wallston, K. A. (1994). Theoretically based strategies for health behavior change. In M. P. O'Donnell, & J. S. Harris (Eds.). *Health promotion in the workplace* (2nd ed.). (pp.185–203). Albany, NY: Delmar.

Wallston, K. A., Wallston, B. S., & DeVellis, R. (1978). Development of the multidimensional health locus of control (MHLC) scales. *Health Education Monographs, 6,* 160–170.

Ward, W. B. (1981). Determining health education impact through proxy measures of behavior change. *Health Education, 12*(3), 19–23.

Warner, K. E. (1987). Selling health promotion to corporate America: Uses and abuses of the economic argument. *Health Education Quarterly, 14*(1), 39–55.

Warner, K. E., Wickizer, T., Wolfe, R., Schildroth, J., & Samuelson, M. (1988). Economic implications of workplace health promotion programs: Review of literature. *Journal of Occupational Medicine, 30*(2), 106–112.

Washington, R. (1987). Alternative frameworks for program evaluation. In F. M. Cox, J. L. Erlich, J. Rolhman, & J. E. Tropman (Eds.), *Strategies of community organization: Macro practices* (pp. 373–374). Itasca, IL: F. E. Peacock.

Watson, J. B. (1925). *Behaviorism.* New York: W. W. Norton.

Weiss, C. H. (1984). Increasing the likelihood of influencing decisions. In L. Rutman (Ed.), *Evaluation research methods: A basic guide* (2nd ed.) (pp. 159–190). Beverly Hills, CA: Sage.

Wilbur, C. (1983). Live for life—The Johnson & Johnson program. *Preventive Medicine, 12*(5), 672–681.

Williams, J. E., & Flora, J. A. (1995). Health behavior segmentation and campaign planning to reduce cardiovascular disease risk among Hispanics. *Health Education Quarterly, 22*(1), 36–38.

Wilson, M. G. (1990). Factors associated with, issues related to, and suggestions for increasing participation in workplace health promotion programs. *Health Values, 14*(4), 29–36.

Wilson, M. G., and Olds, S. (1991). Application of the marketing mix to health promotion marketing. *Journal of Health Education, 22*(4), 254–259.

Windsor, R. A., Baranowski, T., Clark, N., & Cutter, G. (1984). *Evaluation of health promotion and education programs.* Palo Alto, CA: Mayfield.

Windsor, R., Baranowski, T., Clark, N., & Cutter, G. (1994). *Evaluation of health promotion, health education, and disease prevention programs* (2nd ed.). Mountain View, CA: Mayfield.

Wolfe, R., Slack, T., & Rose-Hearn, T. (1993). Factors influencing the adoption and maintenance of Canadian, facility-based worksite health promotion programs. *American Journal of Health Promotion, 7*(3), 189–198.

Woolf, H. B. (Ed.). (1979). *Webster's new collegiate dictionary.* Springfield, MA: G. & C. Merriam.

Author Index

Subject Index